PostgreSQL Reference Manual

Volume 2: Programming Guide
for version 8.2.4.
June 2007

The PostgreSQL Global Development Group

Published by Network Theory Ltd.

A catalogue record for this book is available from the British Library.

First Printing, June 2007 (7/6/2007)

Published by Network Theory Limited.

15 Royal Park
Bristol
BS8 3AL
United Kingdom

Email: info@network-theory.co.uk

ISBN 0-9546120-3-5

Further information about this book is available from
http://www.network-theory.co.uk/postgresql/

This book has an unconditional guarantee. If you are not fully satisfied with
your purchase for any reason, please contact the publisher at the address above.

Table of Contents

Publisher's Preface 1

Client Interfaces 3

1   libpq - C Library 5
    1.1   Database Connection Control Functions 5
    1.2   Connection Status Functions 12
    1.3   Command Execution Functions 15
         1.3.1   Main Functions 15
         1.3.2   Retrieving Query Result Information 23
         1.3.3   Retrieving Result Information for Other Commands
                   27
         1.3.4   Escaping Strings for Inclusion in SQL Commands
                   28
         1.3.5   Escaping Binary Strings for Inclusion in SQL
                Commands 29
    1.4   Asynchronous Command Processing 31
    1.5   Cancelling Queries in Progress 35
    1.6   The Fast-Path Interface 36
    1.7   Asynchronous Notification 37
    1.8   Functions Associated with the COPY Command 38
         1.8.1   Functions for Sending COPY Data 39
         1.8.2   Functions for Receiving COPY Data 40
         1.8.3   Obsolete Functions for COPY 40
    1.9   Control Functions 43
    1.10 Miscellaneous Functions 44
    1.11 Notice Processing 44
    1.12 Environment Variables 45
    1.13 The Password File 47
    1.14 The Connection Service File 48
    1.15 LDAP Lookup of Connection Parameters 48
    1.16 SSL Support 49
    1.17 Behavior in Threaded Programs 49
    1.18 Building libpq Programs 50
    1.19 Example Programs 51

2 Large Objects 63

2.1 Introduction 63
2.2 Implementation Features 63
2.3 Client Interfaces 63
    2.3.1 Creating a Large Object 64
    2.3.2 Importing a Large Object 64
    2.3.3 Exporting a Large Object 64
    2.3.4 Opening an Existing Large Object 65
    2.3.5 Writing Data to a Large Object 65
    2.3.6 Reading Data from a Large Object 65
    2.3.7 Seeking in a Large Object 66
    2.3.8 Obtaining the Seek Position of a Large Object 66
    2.3.9 Closing a Large Object Descriptor 66
    2.3.10 Removing a Large Object 66
2.4 Server-Side Functions 66
2.5 Example Program 67

3 ECPG - Embedded SQL in C 73

3.1 The Concept 73
3.2 Connecting to the Database Server 74
3.3 Closing a Connection 75
3.4 Running SQL Commands 75
3.5 Choosing a Connection 76
3.6 Using Host Variables 77
    3.6.1 Overview 77
    3.6.2 Declare Sections 77
    3.6.3 Different types of host variables 78
    3.6.4 SELECT INTO and FETCH INTO 79
    3.6.5 Indicators 80
3.7 Dynamic SQL 81
3.8 pgtypes library 82
    3.8.1 The numeric type 82
    3.8.2 The date type 85
    3.8.3 The timestamp type 89
    3.8.4 The interval type 93
    3.8.5 The decimal type 94
    3.8.6 errno values of pgtypeslib 94
    3.8.7 Special constants of pgtypeslib 95
3.9 Informix compatibility mode 95
    3.9.1 Additional embedded SQL statements 95
    3.9.2 Additional functions 96
    3.9.3 Additional constants 105
3.10 Using SQL Descriptor Areas 107
3.11 Error Handling 108
    3.11.1 Setting Callbacks 108
    3.11.2 sqlca 110
    3.11.3 SQLSTATE vs SQLCODE 111

3.12   Preprocessor directives 114
        3.12.1   Including files 114
        3.12.2   The #define and #undef directives 114
        3.12.3   ifdef, ifndef, else, elif and endif directives 115
3.13   Processing Embedded SQL Programs 115
3.14   Library Functions 116
3.15   Internals 117

4   The Information Schema 119

4.1   The Schema 119
4.2   Data Types 119
4.3   information_schema_catalog_name 120
4.4   administrable_role_authorizations 120
4.5   applicable_roles 120
4.6   attributes 121
4.7   check_constraint_routine_usage 124
4.8   check_constraints 124
4.9   column_domain_usage 125
4.10   column_privileges 125
4.11   column_udt_usage 126
4.12   columns 127
4.13   constraint_column_usage 131
4.14   constraint_table_usage 132
4.15   data_type_privileges 132
4.16   domain_constraints 133
4.17   domain_udt_usage 134
4.18   domains 134
4.19   element_types 137
4.20   enabled_roles 140
4.21   key_column_usage 141
4.22   parameters 142
4.23   referential_constraints 145
4.24   role_column_grants 146
4.25   role_routine_grants 147
4.26   role_table_grants 147
4.27   role_usage_grants 148
4.28   routine_privileges 149
4.29   routines 149
4.30   schemata 157
4.31   sequences 158
4.32   sql_features 159
4.33   sql_implementation_info 159
4.34   sql_languages 160
4.35   sql_packages 161
4.36   sql_parts 162
4.37   sql_sizing 162
4.38   sql_sizing_profiles 163

4.39   table_constraints 164
4.40   table_privileges 164
4.41   tables 165
4.42   triggers 167
4.43   usage_privileges 169
4.44   view_column_usage 170
4.45   view_routine_usage 170
4.46   view_table_usage 171
4.47   views 172

Server Programming **173**

5   Extending SQL **175**
5.1   How Extensibility Works 175
5.2   The PostgreSQL Type System 175
       5.2.1   Base Types 176
       5.2.2   Composite Types 176
       5.2.3   Domains 176
       5.2.4   Pseudo-Types 176
       5.2.5   Polymorphic Types 176
5.3   User-Defined Functions 177
5.4   Query Language (SQL) Functions 178
       5.4.1   SQL Functions on Base Types 179
       5.4.2   SQL Functions on Composite Types 180
       5.4.3   Functions with Output Parameters 183
       5.4.4   SQL Functions as Table Sources 184
       5.4.5   SQL Functions Returning Sets 185
       5.4.6   Polymorphic SQL Functions 186
5.5   Function Overloading 187
5.6   Function Volatility Categories 188
5.7   Procedural Language Functions 189
5.8   Internal Functions 190
5.9   C-Language Functions 190
       5.9.1   Dynamic Loading 190
       5.9.2   Base Types in C-Language Functions 192
       5.9.3   Version 0 Calling Conventions 194
       5.9.4   Version 1 Calling Conventions 197
       5.9.5   Writing Code 200
       5.9.6   Compiling and Linking Dynamically-Loaded
                Functions 201
       5.9.7   Extension Building Infrastructure 203
       5.9.8   Composite-Type Arguments 205
       5.9.9   Returning Rows (Composite Types) 207
       5.9.10   Returning Sets 208
       5.9.11   Polymorphic Arguments and Return Types 213
       5.9.12   Shared Memory and LWLocks 215
5.10   User-Defined Aggregates 216

5.11 User-Defined Types.. 218
5.12 User-Defined Operators.................................... 221
5.13 Operator Optimization Information...................... 222
    5.13.1 COMMUTATOR 223
    5.13.2 NEGATOR................................... 224
    5.13.3 RESTRICT.................................. 224
    5.13.4 JOIN...................................... 225
    5.13.5 HASHES 226
    5.13.6 MERGES (SORT1, SORT2, LTCMP, GTCMP)
          226
5.14 Interfacing Extensions To Indexes 228
    5.14.1 Index Methods and Operator Classes........... 228
    5.14.2 Index Method Strategies...................... 229
    5.14.3 Index Method Support Routines 230
    5.14.4 An Example.................................. 232
    5.14.5 Cross-Data-Type Operator Classes............. 234
    5.14.6 System Dependencies on Operator Classes...... 235
    5.14.7 Special Features of Operator Classes 236

6 Triggers...................................... 237
6.1 Overview of Trigger Behavior............................. 237
6.2 Visibility of Data Changes................................ 239
6.3 Writing Trigger Functions in C 240
6.4 A Complete Example...................................... 242

7 The Rule System 247
7.1 The Query Tree... 247
7.2 Views and the Rule System............................... 249
    7.2.1 How SELECT Rules Work 250
    7.2.2 View Rules in Non-SELECT Statements......... 255
    7.2.3 The Power of Views in PostgreSQL.............. 256
    7.2.4 Updating a View.............................. 257
7.3 Rules on INSERT, UPDATE, and DELETE 257
    7.3.1 How Update Rules Work....................... 257
        7.3.1.1 A First Rule Step by Step............ 259
    7.3.2 Cooperation with Views....................... 262
7.4 Rules and Privileges...................................... 268
7.5 Rules and Command Status 269
7.6 Rules versus Triggers..................................... 270

8 Procedural Languages 273
8.1 Installing Procedural Languages 273

9   PL/pgSQL - SQL Procedural Language....... 277

9.1   Overview.. 277
    9.1.1   Advantages of Using PL/pgSQL................. 278
    9.1.2   Supported Argument and Result Data Types.... 279
9.2   Tips for Developing in PL/pgSQL 279
    9.2.1   Handling of Quotation Marks 280
9.3   Structure of PL/pgSQL.................................. 282
9.4   Declarations... 283
    9.4.1   Aliases for Function Parameters................. 284
    9.4.2   Copying Types................................. 286
    9.4.3   Row Types 286
    9.4.4   Record Types................................. 287
    9.4.5   RENAME 287
9.5   Expressions 288
9.6   Basic Statements....................................... 289
    9.6.1   Assignment 289
    9.6.2   Executing a Query With No Result.............. 289
    9.6.3   Executing a Query with a Single-Row Result 290
    9.6.4   Doing Nothing At All.......................... 292
    9.6.5   Executing Dynamic Commands 292
    9.6.6   Obtaining the Result Status.................... 294
9.7   Control Structures....................................... 294
    9.7.1   Returning From a Function 294
        9.7.1.1   RETURN 295
        9.7.1.2   RETURN NEXT..................... 295
    9.7.2   Conditionals 296
        9.7.2.1   IF-THEN 296
        9.7.2.2   IF-THEN-ELSE..................... 296
        9.7.2.3   IF-THEN-ELSE IF 297
        9.7.2.4   IF-THEN-ELSIF-ELSE.............. 297
        9.7.2.5   IF-THEN-ELSEIF-ELSE 298
    9.7.3   Simple Loops 298
        9.7.3.1   LOOP.............................. 298
        9.7.3.2   EXIT 298
        9.7.3.3   CONTINUE.......................... 299
        9.7.3.4   WHILE 299
        9.7.3.5   FOR (integer variant) 300
    9.7.4   Looping Through Query Results................. 300
    9.7.5   Trapping Errors............................... 302
9.8   Cursors 304
    9.8.1   Declaring Cursor Variables..................... 304
    9.8.2   Opening Cursors.............................. 304
        9.8.2.1   OPEN FOR query................... 305
        9.8.2.2   OPEN FOR EXECUTE.............. 305
        9.8.2.3   Opening a Bound Cursor 305
    9.8.3   Using Cursors................................. 305
        9.8.3.1   FETCH 306
        9.8.3.2   CLOSE 306

        9.8.3.3 Returning Cursors.................... 306
9.9   Errors and Messages...................................... 308
9.10 Trigger Procedures....................................... 308
9.11 Porting from Oracle PL/SQL............................. 315
      9.11.1 Porting Examples.............................. 315
      9.11.2 Other Things to Watch For 322
              9.11.2.1 Implicit Rollback after Exceptions ... 322
              9.11.2.2 EXECUTE......................... 322
              9.11.2.3 Optimizing PL/pgSQL Functions.... 322
      9.11.3 Appendix..................................... 323

10 PL/Tcl - Tcl Procedural Language 327

10.1 Overview... 327
10.2 PL/Tcl Functions and Arguments 328
10.3 Data Values in PL/Tcl.................................. 329
10.4 Global Data in PL/Tcl.................................. 329
10.5 Database Access from PL/Tcl........................... 330
10.6 Trigger Procedures in PL/Tcl........................... 332
10.7 Modules and the unknown command 334
10.8 Tcl Procedure Names.................................... 335

11 PL/Perl - Perl Procedural Language 337

11.1 PL/Perl Functions and Arguments....................... 337
11.2 Database Access from PL/Perl 340
11.3 Data Values in PL/Perl 343
11.4 Global Values in PL/Perl............................... 344
11.5 Trusted and Untrusted PL/Perl 345
11.6 PL/Perl Triggers 346
11.7 Limitations and Missing Features....................... 347

12 PL/Python - Python Procedural Language .. 349

12.1 PL/Python Functions 349
12.2 Trigger Functions....................................... 353
12.3 Database Access.. 354

13 Server Programming Interface 357

13.1 Interface Functions 357
    13.1.1   SPI_connect 357
    13.1.2   SPI_finish................................... 358
    13.1.3   SPI_push 358
    13.1.4   SPI_pop 359
    13.1.5   SPI_execute 359
    13.1.6   SPI_exec..................................... 362
    13.1.7   SPI_prepare 363
    13.1.8   SPI_getargcount 364
    13.1.9   SPI_getargtypeid 364
    13.1.10 SPI_is_cursor_plan 365
    13.1.11 SPI_execute_plan 365
    13.1.12 SPI_execp 366
    13.1.13 SPI_cursor_open 367
    13.1.14 SPI_cursor_find 368
    13.1.15 SPI_cursor_fetch 369
    13.1.16 SPI_cursor_move 369
    13.1.17 SPI_cursor_close 370
    13.1.18 SPI_saveplan 370
13.2 Interface Support Functions 371
    13.2.1   SPI_fname.................................... 371
    13.2.2   SPI_fnumber................................. 372
    13.2.3   SPI_getvalue................................. 372
    13.2.4   SPI_getbinval................................ 373
    13.2.5   SPI_gettype 374
    13.2.6   SPI_gettypeid................................ 374
    13.2.7   SPI_getrelname 375
    13.2.8   SPI_getnspname 375
13.3 Memory Management 376
    13.3.1   SPI_palloc................................... 376
    13.3.2   SPI_repalloc................................. 377
    13.3.3   SPI_pfree.................................... 377
    13.3.4   SPI_copytuple 378
    13.3.5   SPI_returntuple.............................. 378
    13.3.6   SPI_modifytuple 379
    13.3.7   SPI_freetuple 380
    13.3.8   SPI_freetuptable............................. 380
    13.3.9   SPI_freeplan 381
13.4 Visibility of Data Changes............................. 381
13.5 Examples 382

Books from the publisher 387

Index... 391

Publisher's Preface

This volume is part of the official reference documentation for the PostgreSQL database management system.

PostgreSQL (pronounced "Postgres-Q-L") is a powerful database system with a long history, going back over 20 years to the POSTGRES project at the University of California at Berkeley. Today it provides a high level of conformance with the ANSI-SQL 92/99 standards and is fully ACID compliant.

In addition to its technical strengths, PostgreSQL offers a fundamental advantage over proprietary database software: the complete source code to PostgreSQL is available to everyone under a free software license, so users are not reliant on a single company to fix problems with it. Free software removes the single point of failure that exists when one company owns and controls a program.

To support the ongoing development of PostgreSQL, we will donate $1 to the PostgreSQL project for each copy of this book sold.

Brian Gough
Publisher
June 2007

Client Interfaces

This part describes the client programming interfaces distributed with Post-greSQL. Each of these chapters can be read independently. Note that there are many other programming interfaces for client programs that are distributed separately and contain their own documentation. Readers of this part should be familiar with using SQL commands to manipulate and query the database (see Volume 1, *The SQL Language*) and of course with the programming language that the interface uses.

1 libpq - C Library

libpq is the C application programmer's interface to PostgreSQL. libpq is a set of library functions that allow client programs to pass queries to the PostgreSQL backend server and to receive the results of these queries.

libpq is also the underlying engine for several other PostgreSQL application interfaces, including those written for C++, Perl, Python, Tcl and ECPG. So some aspects of libpq's behavior will be important to you if you use one of those packages. In particular, Section 1.12 *Environment Variables*, page 45, Section 1.13 *The Password File*, page 47 and Section 1.16 *SSL Support*, page 49 describe behavior that is visible to the user of any application that uses libpq.

Some short programs are included at the end of this chapter (Section 1.19 *Example Programs*, page 51) to show how to write programs that use libpq. There are also several complete examples of libpq applications in the directory 'src/test/examples' in the source code distribution.

Client programs that use libpq must include the header file 'libpq-fe.h' and must link with the libpq library.

1.1 Database Connection Control Functions

The following functions deal with making a connection to a PostgreSQL backend server. An application program can have several backend connections open at one time. (One reason to do that is to access more than one database.) Each connection is represented by a PGconn object, which is obtained from the function PQconnectdb or PQsetdbLogin. Note that these functions will always return a non-null object pointer, unless perhaps there is too little memory even to allocate the PGconn object. The PQstatus function should be called to check whether a connection was successfully made before queries are sent via the connection object.

PQconnectdb

Makes a new connection to the database server.

> PGconn *PQconnectdb(const char *conninfo);

This function opens a new database connection using the parameters taken from the string conninfo. Unlike PQsetdbLogin below, the parameter set can be extended without changing the function signature, so use of this function (or its nonblocking analogues PQconnectStart and PQconnectPoll) is preferred for new application programming.

The passed string can be empty to use all default parameters, or it can contain one or more parameter settings separated by whitespace. Each parameter setting is in the form keyword = value. Spaces around the equal sign are optional. To write an empty value or a value containing spaces, surround it with single quotes, e.g., keyword = 'a value'. Single quotes and backslashes within the value must be escaped with a backslash, i.e., \' and \\.

The currently recognized parameter key words are:

host

> Name of host to connect to. If this begins with a slash, it spec-
> ifies Unix-domain communication rather than TCP/IP communica-
> tion; the value is the name of the directory in which the socket file is
> stored. The default behavior when host is not specified is to connect
> to a Unix-domain socket in '/tmp' (or whatever socket directory was
> specified when PostgreSQL was built). On machines without Unix-
> domain sockets, the default is to connect to localhost.

hostaddr

> Numeric IP address of host to connect to. This should be in the
> standard IPv4 address format, e.g., 172.28.40.9. If your machine
> supports IPv6, you can also use those addresses. TCP/IP commu-
> nication is always used when a nonempty string is specified for this
> parameter.

> Using hostaddr instead of host allows the application to avoid a host
> name look-up, which may be important in applications with time con-
> straints. However, Kerberos authentication requires the host name.
> The following therefore applies: If host is specified without hostaddr,
> a host name lookup occurs. If hostaddr is specified without host, the
> value for hostaddr gives the remote address. When Kerberos is used,
> a reverse name query occurs to obtain the host name for Kerberos. If
> both host and hostaddr are specified, the value for hostaddr gives
> the remote address; the value for host is ignored, unless Kerberos
> is used, in which case that value is used for Kerberos authentication.
> (Note that authentication is likely to fail if libpq is passed a host name
> that is not the name of the machine at hostaddr.) Also, host rather
> than hostaddr is used to identify the connection in '~/.pgpass' (see
> Section 1.13 *The Password File*, page 47).

> Without either a host name or host address, libpq will connect using
> a local Unix-domain socket; or on machines without Unix-domain
> sockets, it will attempt to connect to localhost.

port

> Port number to connect to at the server host, or socket file name
> extension for Unix-domain connections.

dbname

> The database name. Defaults to be the same as the user name.

user

> PostgreSQL user name to connect as. Defaults to be the same as the
> operating system name of the user running the application.

password

> Password to be used if the server demands password authentication.

connect_timeout

> Maximum wait for connection, in seconds (write as a decimal inte-
> ger string). Zero or not specified means wait indefinitely. It is not
> recommended to use a timeout of less than 2 seconds.

options
> Command-line options to be sent to the server.

tty
> Ignored (formerly, this specified where to send server debug output).

sslmode
> This option determines whether or with what priority an SSL connection will be negotiated with the server. There are four modes: disable will attempt only an unencrypted SSL connection; allow will negotiate, trying first a non-SSL connection, then if that fails, trying an SSL connection; prefer (the default) will negotiate, trying first an SSL connection, then if that fails, trying a regular non-SSL connection; require will try only an SSL connection.
>
> If PostgreSQL is compiled without SSL support, using option require will cause an error, while options allow and prefer will be accepted but libpq will not in fact attempt an SSL connection.

requiressl
> This option is deprecated in favor of the sslmode setting.
>
> If set to 1, an SSL connection to the server is required (this is equivalent to sslmode require). libpq will then refuse to connect if the server does not accept an SSL connection. If set to 0 (default), libpq will negotiate the connection type with the server (equivalent to sslmode prefer). This option is only available if PostgreSQL is compiled with SSL support.

krbsrvname
> Kerberos service name to use when authenticating with Kerberos 5. This must match the service name specified in the server configuration for Kerberos authentication to succeed. (See also Volume 3, Section 7.2.3 *Kerberos authentication*.)

service
> Service name to use for additional parameters. It specifies a service name in 'pg_service.conf' that holds additional connection parameters. This allows applications to specify only a service name so connection parameters can be centrally maintained. See Section 1.14 *The Connection Service File*, page 48.

If any parameter is unspecified, then the corresponding environment variable (see Section 1.12 *Environment Variables*, page 45) is checked. If the environment variable is not set either, then the indicated built-in defaults are used.

PQsetdbLogin
> Makes a new connection to the database server.

```
PGconn *PQsetdbLogin(const char *pghost,
                     const char *pgport,
                     const char *pgoptions,
                     const char *pgtty,
                     const char *dbName,
                     const char *login,
                     const char *pwd);
```

This is the predecessor of PQconnectdb with a fixed set of parameters. It has the same functionality except that the missing parameters will always take on default values. Write NULL or an empty string for any one of the fixed parameters that is to be defaulted.

PQsetdb

Makes a new connection to the database server.

```
PGconn *PQsetdb(char *pghost,
                char *pgport,
                char *pgoptions,
                char *pgtty,
                char *dbName);
```

This is a macro that calls PQsetdbLogin with null pointers for the login and pwd parameters. It is provided for backward compatibility with very old programs.

PQconnectStart
PQconnectPoll

Make a connection to the database server in a nonblocking manner.

```
PGconn *PQconnectStart(const char *conninfo);

PostgresPollingStatusType PQconnectPoll(PGconn *conn);
```

These two functions are used to open a connection to a database server such that your application's thread of execution is not blocked on remote I/O whilst doing so. The point of this approach is that the waits for I/O to complete can occur in the application's main loop, rather than down inside PQconnectdb, and so the application can manage this operation in parallel with other activities.

The database connection is made using the parameters taken from the string conninfo, passed to PQconnectStart. This string is in the same format as described above for PQconnectdb.

Neither PQconnectStart nor PQconnectPoll will block, so long as a number of restrictions are met:

- The hostaddr and host parameters are used appropriately to ensure that name and reverse name queries are not made. See the documentation of these parameters under PQconnectdb above for details.

- If you call PQtrace, ensure that the stream object into which you trace will not block.

- You ensure that the socket is in the appropriate state before calling PQconnectPoll, as described below.

To begin a nonblocking connection request, call the connect function as conn = PQconnectStart("*connection_info_string*"). If conn is null, then libpq has been unable to allocate a new PGconn structure. Otherwise, a valid PGconn pointer is returned (though not yet representing a valid connection to the database). On return from PQconnectStart, call status = PQstatus(conn). If status equals CONNECTION_BAD, PQconnectStart has failed.

If PQconnectStart succeeds, the next stage is to poll libpq so that it may proceed with the connection sequence. Use PQsocket(conn) to obtain the descriptor of the socket underlying the database connection. Loop thus: If PQconnectPoll(conn) last returned PGRES_POLLING_READING, wait until the socket is ready to read (as indicated by select(), poll(), or similar system function). Then call PQconnectPoll(conn) again. Conversely, if PQconnectPoll(conn) last returned PGRES_POLLING_WRITING, wait until the socket is ready to write, then call PQconnectPoll(conn) again. If you have yet to call PQconnectPoll, i.e., just after the call to PQconnectStart, behave as if it last returned PGRES_POLLING_WRITING. Continue this loop until PQconnectPoll(conn) returns PGRES_POLLING_FAILED, indicating the connection procedure has failed, or PGRES_POLLING_OK, indicating the connection has been successfully made.

At any time during connection, the status of the connection may be checked by calling PQstatus. If this gives CONNECTION_BAD, then the connection procedure has failed; if it gives CONNECTION_OK, then the connection is ready. Both of these states are equally detectable from the return value of PQconnectPoll, described above. Other states may also occur during (and only during) an asynchronous connection procedure. These indicate the current stage of the connection procedure and may be useful to provide feedback to the user for example. These statuses are:

CONNECTION_STARTED
    Waiting for connection to be made.

CONNECTION_MADE
    Connection OK; waiting to send.

CONNECTION_AWAITING_RESPONSE
    Waiting for a response from the server.

CONNECTION_AUTH_OK
    Received authentication; waiting for backend start-up to finish.

CONNECTION_SSL_STARTUP
    Negotiating SSL encryption.

CONNECTION_SETENV
    Negotiating environment-driven parameter settings.

Note that, although these constants will remain (in order to maintain compatibility), an application should never rely upon these occurring in a particular order, or at all, or on the status always being one of these documented values. An application might do something like this:

```
switch(PQstatus(conn))
{
    case CONNECTION_STARTED:
        feedback = "Connecting...";
        break;

    case CONNECTION_MADE:
        feedback = "Connected to server...";
        break;
    .
    .
    .

    default:
        feedback = "Connecting...";
}
```

The connect_timeout connection parameter is ignored when using PQconnectPoll; it is the application's responsibility to decide whether an excessive amount of time has elapsed. Otherwise, PQconnectStart followed by a PQconnectPoll loop is equivalent to PQconnectdb.

Note that if PQconnectStart returns a non-null pointer, you must call PQfinish when you are finished with it, in order to dispose of the structure and any associated memory blocks. This must be done even if the connection attempt fails or is abandoned.

PQconndefaults

Returns the default connection options.

```
PQconninfoOption *PQconndefaults(void);

typedef struct {
    char *keyword;          /* The keyword of the option */
    char *envvar;           /* Fallback environment variable
                               name */
    char *compiled;         /* Fallback compiled in default
                               value */
    char *val;              /* Option's current value, or NULL
                               */
    char *label;            /* Label for field in connect
                               dialog */
    char *dispchar;         /* Character to display for this
                               field in a connect dialog.
                               Values are: "" Display entered
                               value as is "*" Password field
                               - hide value "D" Debug option -
                               don't show by default */
    int dispsize;           /* Field size in characters for
                               dialog */
} PQconninfoOption;
```

Returns a connection options array. This may be used to determine all possible PQconnectdb options and their current default values. The return value points to an array of PQconninfoOption structures, which ends with an entry having a null keyword pointer. The null pointer is returned if memory could not be allocated. Note that the current default values (val fields) will depend on environment variables and other context. Callers must treat the connection options data as read-only.

After processing the options array, free it by passing it to PQconninfoFree. If this is not done, a small amount of memory is leaked for each call to PQconndefaults.

PQfinish

Closes the connection to the server. Also frees memory used by the PGconn object.

```
void PQfinish(PGconn *conn);
```

Note that even if the server connection attempt fails (as indicated by PQstatus), the application should call PQfinish to free the memory used by the PGconn object. The PGconn pointer must not be used again after PQfinish has been called.

PQreset

Resets the communication channel to the server.

```
void PQreset(PGconn *conn);
```

This function will close the connection to the server and attempt to reestablish a new connection to the same server, using all the same parameters previously used. This may be useful for error recovery if a working connection is lost.

PQresetStart
PQresetPoll

Reset the communication channel to the server, in a nonblocking manner.

```
int PQresetStart(PGconn *conn);
```

```
PostgresPollingStatusType PQresetPoll(PGconn *conn);
```

These functions will close the connection to the server and attempt to reestablish a new connection to the same server, using all the same parameters previously used. This may be useful for error recovery if a working connection is lost. They differ from PQreset (above) in that they act in a nonblocking manner. These functions suffer from the same restrictions as PQconnectStart and PQconnectPoll.

To initiate a connection reset, call PQresetStart. If it returns 0, the reset has failed. If it returns 1, poll the reset using PQresetPoll in exactly the same way as you would create the connection using PQconnectPoll.

1.2 Connection Status Functions

These functions may be used to interrogate the status of an existing database connection object.

> **Tip:** libpq application programmers should be careful to maintain the PGconn abstraction. Use the accessor functions described below to get at the contents of PGconn. Reference to internal PGconn fields using 'libpq-int.h' is not recommended because they are subject to change in the future.

The following functions return parameter values established at connection. These values are fixed for the life of the PGconn object.

PQdb
> Returns the database name of the connection.
>
>   char *PQdb(const PGconn *conn);

PQuser
> Returns the user name of the connection.
>
>   char *PQuser(const PGconn *conn);

PQpass
> Returns the password of the connection.
>
>   char *PQpass(const PGconn *conn);

PQhost
> Returns the server host name of the connection.
>
>   char *PQhost(const PGconn *conn);

PQport
> Returns the port of the connection.
>
>   char *PQport(const PGconn *conn);

PQtty
> Returns the debug TTY of the connection. (This is obsolete, since the server no longer pays attention to the TTY setting, but the function remains for backwards compatibility.)
>
>   char *PQtty(const PGconn *conn);

PQoptions
> Returns the command-line options passed in the connection request.
>
>   char *PQoptions(const PGconn *conn);

The following functions return status data that can change as operations are executed on the PGconn object.

PQstatus
> Returns the status of the connection.

        `ConnStatusType PQstatus(const PGconn *conn);`

The status can be one of a number of values. However, only two of these are seen outside of an asynchronous connection procedure: `CONNECTION_OK` and `CONNECTION_BAD`. A good connection to the database has the status `CONNECTION_OK`. A failed connection attempt is signaled by status `CONNECTION_BAD`. Ordinarily, an OK status will remain so until `PQfinish`, but a communications failure might result in the status changing to `CONNECTION_BAD` prematurely. In that case the application could try to recover by calling `PQreset`.

See the entry for `PQconnectStart` and `PQconnectPoll` with regards to other status codes that might be seen.

PQtransactionStatus

    Returns the current in-transaction status of the server.

        `PGTransactionStatusType PQtransactionStatus(const PGconn`
        `*conn);`

The status can be `PQTRANS_IDLE` (currently idle), `PQTRANS_ACTIVE` (a command is in progress), `PQTRANS_INTRANS` (idle, in a valid transaction block), or `PQTRANS_INERROR` (idle, in a failed transaction block). `PQTRANS_UNKNOWN` is reported if the connection is bad. `PQTRANS_ACTIVE` is reported only when a query has been sent to the server and not yet completed.

> **Caution:** PQtransactionStatus will give incorrect results when using a PostgreSQL 7.3 server that has the parameter autocommit set to off. The server-side autocommit feature has been deprecated and does not exist in later server versions.

PQparameterStatus

    Looks up a current parameter setting of the server.

        `const char *PQparameterStatus(const PGconn *conn, const`
        `char *paramName);`

Certain parameter values are reported by the server automatically at connection startup or whenever their values change. `PQparameterStatus` can be used to interrogate these settings. It returns the current value of a parameter if known, or `NULL` if the parameter is not known.

Parameters reported as of the current release include `server_version`, `server_encoding`, `client_encoding`, `is_superuser`, `session_authorization`, `DateStyle`, `TimeZone`, `integer_datetimes`, and `standard_conforming_strings`. (`server_encoding`, `TimeZone`, and `integer_datetimes` were not reported by releases before 8.0; `standard_conforming_strings` was not reported by releases before 8.1.) Note that `server_version`, `server_encoding` and `integer_datetimes` cannot change after startup.

Pre-3.0-protocol servers do not report parameter settings, but libpq includes logic to obtain values for `server_version` and `client_encoding` anyway. Applications are encouraged to use `PQparameterStatus` rather than *ad hoc* code to determine these values. (Beware however that on a pre-3.0 connection, changing `client_encoding` via SET after connection startup will not be reflected by PQparameterStatus.) For server_version, see also PQserverVersion, which returns the information in a numeric form that is much easier to compare against.

If no value for standard_conforming_strings is reported, applications may assume it is off, that is, backslashes are treated as escapes in string literals. Also, the presence of this parameter may be taken as an indication that the escape string syntax (E'...') is accepted.

Although the returned pointer is declared const, it in fact points to mutable storage associated with the PGconn structure. It is unwise to assume the pointer will remain valid across queries.

PQprotocolVersion
Interrogates the frontend/backend protocol being used.

        int PQprotocolVersion(const PGconn *conn);

Applications may wish to use this to determine whether certain features are supported. Currently, the possible values are 2 (2.0 protocol), 3 (3.0 protocol), or zero (connection bad). This will not change after connection startup is complete, but it could theoretically change during a connection reset. The 3.0 protocol will normally be used when communicating with PostgreSQL 7.4 or later servers; pre-7.4 servers support only protocol 2.0. (Protocol 1.0 is obsolete and not supported by libpq.)

PQserverVersion
Returns an integer representing the backend version.

        int PQserverVersion(const PGconn *conn);

Applications may use this to determine the version of the database server they are connected to. The number is formed by converting the major, minor, and revision numbers into two-decimal-digit numbers and appending them together. For example, version 8.1.5 will be returned as 80105, and version 8.2 will be returned as 80200 (leading zeroes are not shown). Zero is returned if the connection is bad.

PQerrorMessage
Returns the error message most recently generated by an operation on the connection.

        char *PQerrorMessage(const PGconn *conn);

Nearly all libpq functions will set a message for PQerrorMessage if they fail. Note that by libpq convention, a nonempty PQerrorMessage result will include a trailing newline. The caller should not free the result directly. It will be freed when the associated PGconn handle is passed to PQfinish. The result string should not be expected to remain the same across operations on the PGconn structure.

PQsocket
Obtains the file descriptor number of the connection socket to the server. A valid descriptor will be greater than or equal to 0; a result of -1 indicates that no server connection is currently open. (This will not change during normal operation, but could change during connection setup or reset.)

```
    int PQsocket(const PGconn *conn);
```

PQbackendPID

> Returns the process ID (PID) of the backend server process handling this connection.

```
    int PQbackendPID(const PGconn *conn);
```

> The backend PID is useful for debugging purposes and for comparison to NOTIFY messages (which include the PID of the notifying backend process). Note that the PID belongs to a process executing on the database server host, not the local host!

PQgetssl

> Returns the SSL structure used in the connection, or null if SSL is not in use.

```
    SSL *PQgetssl(const PGconn *conn);
```

> This structure can be used to verify encryption levels, check server certificates, and more. Refer to the OpenSSL documentation for information about this structure.

> You must define USE_SSL in order to get the correct prototype for this function. Doing this will also automatically include 'ssl.h' from OpenSSL.

1.3 Command Execution Functions

Once a connection to a database server has been successfully established, the functions described here are used to perform SQL queries and commands.

1.3.1 Main Functions

PQexec

> Submits a command to the server and waits for the result.

```
    PGresult *PQexec(PGconn *conn, const char *command);
```

> Returns a PGresult pointer or possibly a null pointer. A non-null pointer will generally be returned except in out-of-memory conditions or serious errors such as inability to send the command to the server. If a null pointer is returned, it should be treated like a PGRES_FATAL_ERROR result. Use PQerrorMessage to get more information about such errors.

It is allowed to include multiple SQL commands (separated by semicolons) in the command string. Multiple queries sent in a single PQexec call are processed in a single transaction, unless there are explicit BEGIN/COMMIT commands included in the query string to divide it into multiple transactions. Note however that the returned PGresult structure describes only the result of the last command executed from the string. Should one of the commands fail, processing of the string stops with it and the returned PGresult describes the error condition.

PQexecParams

> Submits a command to the server and waits for the result, with the ability to pass parameters separately from the SQL command text.

```
PGresult *PQexecParams(PGconn *conn,
                       const char *command,
                       int nParams,
                       const Oid *paramTypes,
                       const char * const *paramValues,
                       const int *paramLengths,
                       const int *paramFormats,
                       int resultFormat);
```

PQexecParams is like PQexec, but offers additional functionality: parameter values can be specified separately from the command string proper, and query results can be requested in either text or binary format. PQexecParams is supported only in protocol 3.0 and later connections; it will fail when using protocol 2.0.

The function arguments are:

conn

> The connection object to send the command through.

command

> The SQL command string to be executed. If parameters are used, they are referred to in the command string as $1, $2, etc.

nParams

> The number of parameters supplied; it is the length of the arrays paramTypes[], paramValues[], paramLengths[], and paramFormats[]. (The array pointers may be NULL when nParams is zero.)

paramTypes[]

> Specifies, by OID, the data types to be assigned to the parameter symbols. If paramTypes is NULL, or any particular element in the array is zero, the server infers a data type for the parameter symbol in the same way it would do for an untyped literal string.

paramValues[]

> Specifies the actual values of the parameters. A null pointer in this array means the corresponding parameter is null; otherwise the pointer points to a zero-terminated text string (for text format) or binary data in the format expected by the server (for binary format).

paramLengths[]

> Specifies the actual data lengths of binary-format parameters. It is ignored for null parameters and text-format parameters. The array pointer may be null when there are no binary parameters.

paramFormats[]

> Specifies whether parameters are text (put a zero in the array entry for the corresponding parameter) or binary (put a one in the array entry for the corresponding parameter). If the array pointer is null then all parameters are presumed to be text strings.

resultFormat

Specify zero to obtain results in text format, or one to obtain results in binary format. (There is not currently a provision to obtain different result columns in different formats, although that is possible in the underlying protocol.)

The primary advantage of PQexecParams over PQexec is that parameter values may be separated from the command string, thus avoiding the need for tedious and error-prone quoting and escaping.

Unlike PQexec, PQexecParams allows at most one SQL command in the given string. (There can be semicolons in it, but not more than one nonempty command.) This is a limitation of the underlying protocol, but has some usefulness as an extra defense against SQL-injection attacks.

Tip: Specifying parameter types via OIDs is tedious, particularly if you prefer not to hard-wire particular OID values into your program. However, you can avoid doing so even in cases where the server by itself cannot determine the type of the parameter, or chooses a different type than you want. In the SQL command text, attach an explicit cast to the parameter symbol to show what data type you will send. For example,

```
select * from mytable where x = $1::bigint;
```

This forces parameter $1 to be treated as bigint, whereas by default it would be assigned the same type as x. Forcing the parameter type decision, either this way or by specifying a numeric type OID, is strongly recommended when sending parameter values in binary format, because binary format has less redundancy than text format and so there is less chance that the server will detect a type mismatch mistake for you.

PQprepare

Submits a request to create a prepared statement with the given parameters, and waits for completion.

```
PGresult *PQprepare(PGconn *conn,
                    const char *stmtName,
                    const char *query,
                    int nParams,
                    const Oid *paramTypes);
```

PQprepare creates a prepared statement for later execution with PQexecPrepared. This feature allows commands that will be used repeatedly to be parsed and planned just once, rather than each time they are executed. PQprepare is supported only in protocol 3.0 and later connections; it will fail when using protocol 2.0.

The function creates a prepared statement named stmtName from the query string, which must contain a single SQL command. stmtName may be "" to create an unnamed statement, in which case any pre-existing unnamed statement is automatically replaced; otherwise it is an error if the statement name is already defined in the current session. If any parameters are used, they are referred to in the query as $1, $2, etc. nParams is the number of parameters for which types are pre-specified in the array paramTypes[]. (The array pointer may be NULL when nParams is zero.) paramTypes[] specifies, by OID, the data types to be assigned to the parameter symbols. If paramTypes is NULL, or any particular element in the array is zero, the server assigns a data type to the parameter symbol in the same way it would do for an untyped literal string. Also, the query may use parameter symbols with numbers higher than nParams; data types will be inferred for these symbols as well. (See PQdescribePrepared for a means to find out what data types were inferred.)

As with PQexec, the result is normally a PGresult object whose contents indicate server-side success or failure. A null result indicates out-of-memory or inability to send the command at all. Use PQerrorMessage to get more information about such errors.

Prepared statements for use with PQexecPrepared can also be created by executing SQL PREPARE statements. (But PQprepare is more flexible since it does not require parameter types to be pre-specified.) Also, although there is no libpq function for deleting a prepared statement, the SQL DEALLOCATE statement can be used for that purpose.

PQexecPrepared

Sends a request to execute a prepared statement with given parameters, and waits for the result.

```
PGresult *PQexecPrepared(PGconn *conn,
                         const char *stmtName,
                         int nParams,
                         const char * const *paramValues,
                         const int *paramLengths,
                         const int *paramFormats,
                         int resultFormat);
```

PQexecPrepared is like PQexecParams, but the command to be executed is specified by naming a previously-prepared statement, instead of giving a query string. This feature allows commands that will be used repeatedly to be parsed and planned just once, rather than each time they are executed. The statement must have been prepared previously in the current session. PQexecPrepared is supported only in protocol 3.0 and later connections; it will fail when using protocol 2.0.

The parameters are identical to PQexecParams, except that the name of a prepared statement is given instead of a query string, and the paramTypes[] parameter is not present (it is not needed since the prepared statement's parameter types were determined when it was created).

PQdescribePrepared

Submits a request to obtain information about the specified prepared statement, and waits for completion.

> PGresult *PQdescribePrepared(PGconn *conn, const char
> *stmtName);

PQdescribePrepared allows an application to obtain information about a previously prepared statement. PQdescribePrepared is supported only in protocol 3.0 and later connections; it will fail when using protocol 2.0.

stmtName may be "" or NULL to reference the unnamed statement, otherwise it must be the name of an existing prepared statement. On success, a PGresult with status PGRES_COMMAND_OK is returned. The functions PQnparams and PQparamtype may be applied to this PGresult to obtain information about the parameters of the prepared statement, and the functions PQnfields, PQfname, PQftype, etc provide information about the result columns (if any) of the statement.

PQdescribePortal

Submits a request to obtain information about the specified portal, and waits for completion.

> PGresult *PQdescribePortal(PGconn *conn, const char
> *portalName);

PQdescribePortal allows an application to obtain information about a previously created portal. (libpq does not provide any direct access to portals, but you can use this function to inspect the properties of a cursor created with a DECLARE CURSOR SQL command.) PQdescribePortal is supported only in protocol 3.0 and later connections; it will fail when using protocol 2.0.

portalName may be "" or NULL to reference the unnamed portal, otherwise it must be the name of an existing portal. On success, a PGresult with status PGRES_COMMAND_OK is returned. The functions PQnfields, PQfname, PQftype, etc may be applied to the PGresult to obtain information about the result columns (if any) of the portal.

The PGresult structure encapsulates the result returned by the server. libpq application programmers should be careful to maintain the PGresult abstraction. Use the accessor functions below to get at the contents of PGresult. Avoid directly referencing the fields of the PGresult structure because they are subject to change in the future.

PQresultStatus

Returns the result status of the command.

> ExecStatusType PQresultStatus(const PGresult *res);

PQresultStatus can return one of the following values:

PGRES_EMPTY_QUERY

The string sent to the server was empty.

PGRES_COMMAND_OK

Successful completion of a command returning no data.

PGRES_TUPLES_OK

Successful completion of a command returning data (such as a SELECT or SHOW).

PGRES_COPY_OUT
> Copy Out (from server) data transfer started.

PGRES_COPY_IN
> Copy In (to server) data transfer started.

PGRES_BAD_RESPONSE
> The server's response was not understood.

PGRES_NONFATAL_ERROR
> A nonfatal error (a notice or warning) occurred.

PGRES_FATAL_ERROR
> A fatal error occurred.

If the result status is PGRES_TUPLES_OK, then the functions described below can be used to retrieve the rows returned by the query. Note that a SELECT command that happens to retrieve zero rows still shows PGRES_TUPLES_OK. PGRES_COMMAND_OK is for commands that can never return rows (INSERT, UPDATE, etc.). A response of PGRES_EMPTY_QUERY may indicate a bug in the client software.

A result of status PGRES_NONFATAL_ERROR will never be returned directly by PQexec or other query execution functions; results of this kind are instead passed to the notice processor (see Section 1.11 *Notice Processing*, page 44).

PQresStatus
> Converts the enumerated type returned by PQresultStatus into a string constant describing the status code. The caller should not free the result.
>
>   char *PQresStatus(ExecStatusType status);

PQresultErrorMessage
> Returns the error message associated with the command, or an empty string if there was no error.
>
>   char *PQresultErrorMessage(const PGresult *res);
>
> If there was an error, the returned string will include a trailing newline. The caller should not free the result directly. It will be freed when the associated PGresult handle is passed to PQclear.
>
> Immediately following a PQexec or PQgetResult call, PQerrorMessage (on the connection) will return the same string as PQresultErrorMessage (on the result). However, a PGresult will retain its error message until destroyed, whereas the connection's error message will change when subsequent operations are done. Use PQresultErrorMessage when you want to know the status associated with a particular PGresult; use PQerrorMessage when you want to know the status from the latest operation on the connection.

PQresultErrorField
> Returns an individual field of an error report.

```
char *PQresultErrorField(const PGresult *res, int fieldcode);
```

fieldcode is an error field identifier; see the symbols listed below. NULL is returned if the PGresult is not an error or warning result, or does not include the specified field. Field values will normally not include a trailing newline. The caller should not free the result directly. It will be freed when the associated PGresult handle is passed to PQclear.

The following field codes are available:

PG_DIAG_SEVERITY
> The severity; the field contents are ERROR, FATAL, or PANIC (in an error message), or WARNING, NOTICE, DEBUG, INFO, or LOG (in a notice message), or a localized translation of one of these. Always present.

PG_DIAG_SQLSTATE
> The SQLSTATE code for the error. The SQLSTATE code identifies the type of error that has occurred; it can be used by front-end applications to perform specific operations (such as error handling) in response to a particular database error. For a list of the possible SQL-STATE codes, see Volume 1, Appendix A *PostgreSQL Error Codes*. This field is not localizable, and is always present.

PG_DIAG_MESSAGE_PRIMARY
> The primary human-readable error message (typically one line). Always present.

PG_DIAG_MESSAGE_DETAIL
> Detail: an optional secondary error message carrying more detail about the problem. May run to multiple lines.

PG_DIAG_MESSAGE_HINT
> Hint: an optional suggestion what to do about the problem. This is intended to differ from detail in that it offers advice (potentially inappropriate) rather than hard facts. May run to multiple lines.

PG_DIAG_STATEMENT_POSITION
> A string containing a decimal integer indicating an error cursor position as an index into the original statement string. The first character has index 1, and positions are measured in characters not bytes.

PG_DIAG_INTERNAL_POSITION
> This is defined the same as the PG_DIAG_STATEMENT_POSITION field, but it is used when the cursor position refers to an internally generated command rather than the one submitted by the client. The PG_DIAG_INTERNAL_QUERY field will always appear when this field appears.

PG_DIAG_INTERNAL_QUERY
> The text of a failed internally-generated command. This could be, for example, a SQL query issued by a PL/pgSQL function.

PG_DIAG_CONTEXT
> An indication of the context in which the error occurred. Presently this includes a call stack traceback of active procedural language functions and internally-generated queries. The trace is one entry per line, most recent first.

PG_DIAG_SOURCE_FILE
> The file name of the source-code location where the error was reported.

PG_DIAG_SOURCE_LINE
> The line number of the source-code location where the error was reported.

PG_DIAG_SOURCE_FUNCTION
> The name of the source-code function reporting the error.

The client is responsible for formatting displayed information to meet its needs; in particular it should break long lines as needed. Newline characters appearing in the error message fields should be treated as paragraph breaks, not line breaks.

Errors generated internally by libpq will have severity and primary message, but typically no other fields. Errors returned by a pre-3.0-protocol server will include severity and primary message, and sometimes a detail message, but no other fields.

Note that error fields are only available from PGresult objects, not PGconn objects; there is no PQerrorField function.

PQclear
> Frees the storage associated with a PGresult. Every command result should be freed via PQclear when it is no longer needed.
>
>   void PQclear(PGresult *res);
>
> You can keep a PGresult object around for as long as you need it; it does not go away when you issue a new command, nor even if you close the connection. To get rid of it, you must call PQclear. Failure to do this will result in memory leaks in your application.

PQmakeEmptyPGresult
> Constructs an empty PGresult object with the given status.
>
>   PGresult *PQmakeEmptyPGresult(PGconn *conn,
>   ExecStatusType status);
>
> This is libpq's internal function to allocate and initialize an empty PGresult object. This function returns NULL if memory could not be allocated. It is exported because some applications find it useful to generate result objects (particularly objects with error status) themselves. If conn is not null and status indicates an error, the current error message of the specified connection is copied into the PGresult. Note that PQclear should eventually be called on the object, just as with a PGresult returned by libpq itself.

1.3.2 Retrieving Query Result Information

These functions are used to extract information from a PGresult object that represents a successful query result (that is, one that has status PGRES_TUPLES_OK). They can also be used to extract information from a successful Describe operation: a Describe's result has all the same column information that actual execution of the query would provide, but it has zero rows. For objects with other status values, these functions will act as though the result has zero rows and zero columns.

PQntuples

> Returns the number of rows (tuples) in the query result.
>
>   int PQntuples(const PGresult *res);

PQnfields

> Returns the number of columns (fields) in each row of the query result.
>
>   int PQnfields(const PGresult *res);

PQfname

> Returns the column name associated with the given column number. Column numbers start at 0. The caller should not free the result directly. It will be freed when the associated PGresult handle is passed to PQclear.
>
>   char *PQfname(const PGresult *res,
>   int column_number);
>
> NULL is returned if the column number is out of range.

PQfnumber

> Returns the column number associated with the given column name.
>
>   int PQfnumber(const PGresult *res,
>   const char *column_name);
>
> -1 is returned if the given name does not match any column.
>
> The given name is treated like an identifier in an SQL command, that is, it is downcased unless double-quoted. For example, given a query result generated from the SQL command
>
>   select 1 as FOO, 2 as "BAR";
>
> we would have the results:
>
>   PQfname(res, 0)   foo
>   PQfname(res, 1)   BAR
>   PQfnumber(res, "FOO")   0
>   PQfnumber(res, "foo")   0
>   PQfnumber(res, "BAR")   -1
>   PQfnumber(res, "\"BAR\"")   1

PQftable

> Returns the OID of the table from which the given column was fetched. Column numbers start at 0.

```
Oid PQftable(const PGresult *res,
             int column_number);
```

InvalidOid is returned if the column number is out of range, or if the
specified column is not a simple reference to a table column, or when using
pre-3.0 protocol. You can query the system table pg_class to determine
exactly which table is referenced.

The type Oid and the constant InvalidOid will be defined when you include
the libpq header file. They will both be some integer type.

PQftablecol

Returns the column number (within its table) of the column making up
the specified query result column. Query-result column numbers start at
0, but table columns have nonzero numbers.

```
int PQftablecol(const PGresult *res,
                int column_number);
```

Zero is returned if the column number is out of range, or if the specified
column is not a simple reference to a table column, or when using pre-3.0
protocol.

PQfformat

Returns the format code indicating the format of the given column. Column numbers start at 0.

```
int PQfformat(const PGresult *res,
              int column_number);
```

Format code zero indicates textual data representation, while format code
one indicates binary representation. (Other codes are reserved for future
definition.)

PQftype

Returns the data type associated with the given column number. The
integer returned is the internal OID number of the type. Column numbers
start at 0.

```
Oid PQftype(const PGresult *res,
            int column_number);
```

You can query the system table pg_type to obtain the names and properties
of the various data types. The OIDs of the built-in data types are defined
in the file 'src/include/catalog/pg_type.h' in the source tree.

PQfmod

Returns the type modifier of the column associated with the given column
number. Column numbers start at 0.

```
int PQfmod(const PGresult *res,
           int column_number);
```

The interpretation of modifier values is type-specific; they typically indicate
precision or size limits. The value -1 is used to indicate "no information
available". Most data types do not use modifiers, in which case the value
is always -1.

PQfsize

Returns the size in bytes of the column associated with the given column number. Column numbers start at 0.

```
int PQfsize(const PGresult *res,
            int column_number);
```

PQfsize returns the space allocated for this column in a database row, in other words the size of the server's internal representation of the data type. (Accordingly, it is not really very useful to clients.) A negative value indicates the data type is variable-length.

PQbinaryTuples

Returns 1 if the PGresult contains binary data and 0 if it contains text data.

```
int PQbinaryTuples(const PGresult *res);
```

This function is deprecated (except for its use in connection with COPY), because it is possible for a single PGresult to contain text data in some columns and binary data in others. PQfformat is preferred. PQbinaryTuples returns 1 only if all columns of the result are binary (format 1).

PQgetvalue

Returns a single field value of one row of a PGresult. Row and column numbers start at 0. The caller should not free the result directly. It will be freed when the associated PGresult handle is passed to PQclear.

```
char *PQgetvalue(const PGresult *res,
                 int row_number,
                 int column_number);
```

For data in text format, the value returned by PQgetvalue is a null-terminated character string representation of the field value. For data in binary format, the value is in the binary representation determined by the data type's typsend and typreceive functions. (The value is actually followed by a zero byte in this case too, but that is not ordinarily useful, since the value is likely to contain embedded nulls.)

An empty string is returned if the field value is null. See PQgetisnull to distinguish null values from empty-string values.

The pointer returned by PQgetvalue points to storage that is part of the PGresult structure. One should not modify the data it points to, and one must explicitly copy the data into other storage if it is to be used past the lifetime of the PGresult structure itself.

PQgetisnull

Tests a field for a null value. Row and column numbers start at 0.

```
int PQgetisnull(const PGresult *res,
                int row_number,
                int column_number);
```

This function returns 1 if the field is null and 0 if it contains a non-null value. (Note that PQgetvalue will return an empty string, not a null pointer, for a null field.)

PQgetlength

> Returns the actual length of a field value in bytes. Row and column numbers start at 0.

```
int PQgetlength(const PGresult *res,
                int row_number,
                int column_number);
```

> This is the actual data length for the particular data value, that is, the size of the object pointed to by PQgetvalue. For text data format this is the same as strlen(). For binary format this is essential information. Note that one should *not* rely on PQfsize to obtain the actual data length.

PQnparams

> Returns the number of parameters of a prepared statement.

```
int PQnparams(const PGresult *res);
```

> This function is only useful when inspecting the result of PQdescribePrepared. For other types of queries the return value is zero.

PQparamtype

> Returns the data type of the indicated statement parameter. Parameter numbers start at 0.

```
Oid PQparamtype(const PGresult *res, int param_number);
```

> This function is only useful when inspecting the result of PQdescribePrepared. For other types of queries the return value is zero.

PQprint

> Prints out all the rows and, optionally, the column names to the specified output stream.

```
void PQprint(FILE * fout, /* output stream */
             const PGresult * res, const PQprintOpt * po);

typedef struct {
  pqbool header;          /* print output field headings and
                             row count */
  pqbool align;           /* fill align the fields */
  pqbool standard;        /* old brain dead format */
  pqbool html3;           /* output HTML tables */
  pqbool expanded;        /* expand tables */
  pqbool pager;           /* use pager for output if needed */
  char *fieldSep;         /* field separator */
  char *tableOpt;         /* attributes for HTML table
                             element */
  char *caption;          /* HTML table caption */
  char **fieldName;       /* null-terminated array of
                             replacement field names */
} PQprintOpt;
```

This function was formerly used by psql to print query results, but this is no longer the case. Note that it assumes all the data is in text format.

1.3.3 Retrieving Result Information for Other Commands

These functions are used to extract information from PGresult objects that are not SELECT results.

PQcmdStatus

Returns the command status tag from the SQL command that generated the PGresult.

    char *PQcmdStatus(PGresult *res);

Commonly this is just the name of the command, but it may include additional data such as the number of rows processed. The caller should not free the result directly. It will be freed when the associated PGresult handle is passed to PQclear.

PQcmdTuples

Returns the number of rows affected by the SQL command.

    char *PQcmdTuples(PGresult *res);

This function returns a string containing the number of rows affected by the SQL statement that generated the PGresult. This function can only be used following the execution of an INSERT, UPDATE, DELETE, MOVE, FETCH, or COPY statement, or an EXECUTE of a prepared query that contains an INSERT, UPDATE, or DELETE statement. If the command that generated the PGresult was anything else, PQcmdTuples returns an empty string. The caller should not free the return value directly. It will be freed when the associated PGresult handle is passed to PQclear.

PQoidValue

Returns the OID of the inserted row, if the SQL command was an INSERT that inserted exactly one row into a table that has OIDs, or a EXECUTE of a prepared query containing a suitable INSERT statement. Otherwise, this function returns InvalidOid. This function will also return InvalidOid if the table affected by the INSERT statement does not contain OIDs.

    Oid PQoidValue(const PGresult *res);

PQoidStatus

Returns a string with the OID of the inserted row, if the SQL command was an INSERT that inserted exactly one row, or a EXECUTE of a prepared statement consisting of a suitable INSERT. (The string will be 0 if the INSERT did not insert exactly one row, or if the target table does not have OIDs.) If the command was not an INSERT, returns an empty string.

    char *PQoidStatus(const PGresult *res);

This function is deprecated in favor of PQoidValue. It is not thread-safe.

1.3.4 Escaping Strings for Inclusion in SQL Commands

PQescapeStringConn escapes a string for use within an SQL command. This is useful when inserting data values as literal constants in SQL commands. Certain characters (such as quotes and backslashes) must be escaped to prevent them from being interpreted specially by the SQL parser. PQescapeStringConn performs this operation.

> **Tip:** It is especially important to do proper escaping when handling strings that were received from an untrustworthy source. Otherwise there is a security risk: you are vulnerable to "SQL injection" attacks wherein unwanted SQL commands are fed to your database.

Note that it is not necessary nor correct to do escaping when a data value is passed as a separate parameter in PQexecParams or its sibling routines.

```
size_t PQescapeStringConn (PGconn *conn,
                           char *to, const char *from,
                           size_t length,
                           int *error);
```

PQescapeStringConn writes an escaped version of the from string to the to buffer, escaping special characters so that they cannot cause any harm, and adding a terminating zero byte. The single quotes that must surround Post-greSQL string literals are not included in the result string; they should be provided in the SQL command that the result is inserted into. The parameter from points to the first character of the string that is to be escaped, and the length parameter gives the number of bytes in this string. A terminating zero byte is not required, and should not be counted in length. (If a terminating zero byte is found before length bytes are processed, PQescapeStringConn stops at the zero; the behavior is thus rather like strncpy.) to shall point to a buffer that is able to hold at least one more byte than twice the value of length, otherwise the behavior is undefined. Behavior is likewise undefined if the to and from strings overlap.

If the error parameter is not NULL, then *error is set to zero on success, nonzero on error. Presently the only possible error conditions involve invalid multibyte encoding in the source string. The output string is still generated on error, but it can be expected that the server will reject it as malformed. On error, a suitable message is stored in the conn object, whether or not error is NULL.

PQescapeStringConn returns the number of bytes written to to, not including the terminating zero byte.

```
size_t PQescapeString (char *to, const char *from, size_t
          length);
```

PQescapeString is an older, deprecated version of PQescapeStringConn; the difference is that it does not take conn or error parameters. Because of this, it cannot adjust its behavior depending on the connection properties (such as character encoding) and therefore *it may give the wrong results*. Also, it has no way to report error conditions.

PQescapeString can be used safely in single-threaded client programs that work with only one PostgreSQL connection at a time (in this case it can find out what it needs to know "behind the scenes"). In other contexts it is a security hazard and should be avoided in favor of PQescapeStringConn.

1.3.5 Escaping Binary Strings for Inclusion in SQL Commands

PQescapeByteaConn

Escapes binary data for use within an SQL command with the type bytea. As with PQescapeStringConn, this is only used when inserting data directly into an SQL command string.

```
unsigned char *PQescapeByteaConn(PGconn *conn,
                                 const unsigned char *from,
                                 size_t from_length,
                                 size_t *to_length);
```

Certain byte values *must* be escaped (but all byte values *can* be escaped) when used as part of a bytea literal in an SQL statement. In general, to escape a byte, it is converted into the three digit octal number equal to the octet value, and preceded by usually two backslashes. The single quote (') and backslash (\) characters have special alternative escape sequences. See Volume 1, Section 6.4 *Binary Data Types* for more information. PQescapeByteaConn performs this operation, escaping only the minimally required bytes.

The from parameter points to the first byte of the string that is to be escaped, and the from_length parameter gives the number of bytes in this binary string. (A terminating zero byte is neither necessary nor counted.) The to_length parameter points to a variable that will hold the resultant escaped string length. This result string length includes the terminating zero byte of the result.

PQescapeByteaConn returns an escaped version of the from parameter binary string in memory allocated with malloc(). This memory must be freed using PQfreemem() when the result is no longer needed. The return string has all special characters replaced so that they can be properly processed by the PostgreSQL string literal parser, and the bytea input function. A terminating zero byte is also added. The single quotes that must surround PostgreSQL string literals are not part of the result string.

On error, a NULL pointer is returned, and a suitable error message is stored in the conn object. Currently, the only possible error is insufficient memory for the result string.

PQescapeBytea

PQescapeBytea is an older, deprecated version of PQescapeByteaConn.

```
unsigned char *PQescapeBytea(const unsigned char *from,
                             size_t from_length,
                             size_t *to_length);
```

The only difference from PQescapeByteaConn is that PQescapeBytea does not take a PGconn parameter. Because of this, it cannot adjust its behavior depending on the connection properties (in particular, whether standard-conforming strings are enabled) and therefore *it may give the wrong results.* Also, it has no way to return an error message on failure.

PQescapeBytea can be used safely in single-threaded client programs that work with only one PostgreSQL connection at a time (in this case it can find out what it needs to know "behind the scenes"). In other contexts it is a security hazard and should be avoided in favor of PQescapeByteaConn.

PQunescapeBytea

Converts a string representation of binary data into binary data—the reverse of PQescapeBytea. This is needed when retrieving bytea data in text format, but not when retrieving it in binary format.

```
unsigned char *PQunescapeBytea(const unsigned char *from,
size_t *to_length);
```

The from parameter points to a string such as might be returned by PQgetvalue when applied to a bytea column. PQunescapeBytea converts this string representation into its binary representation. It returns a pointer to a buffer allocated with malloc(), or null on error, and puts the size of the buffer in to_length. The result must be freed using PQfreemem when it is no longer needed.

This conversion is not exactly the inverse of PQescapeBytea, because the string is not expected to be "escaped" when received from PQgetvalue. In particular this means there is no need for string quoting considerations, and so no need for a PGconn parameter.

PQfreemem

Frees memory allocated by libpq.

```
void PQfreemem(void *ptr);
```

Frees memory allocated by libpq, particularly PQescapeByteaConn, PQescapeBytea, PQunescapeBytea, and PQnotifies. It is particularly important that this function, rather than free(), be used on Microsoft Windows. This is because allocating memory in a DLL and releasing it in the application works only if multithreaded/single-threaded, release/debug, and static/dynamic flags are the same for the DLL and the application. On non-Microsoft Windows platforms, this function is the same as the standard library function free().

1.4 Asynchronous Command Processing

The PQexec function is adequate for submitting commands in normal, synchronous applications. It has a couple of deficiencies, however, that can be of importance to some users:

- PQexec waits for the command to be completed. The application may have other work to do (such as maintaining a user interface), in which case it won't want to block waiting for the response.

- Since the execution of the client application is suspended while it waits for the result, it is hard for the application to decide that it would like to try to cancel the ongoing command. (It can be done from a signal handler, but not otherwise.)

- PQexec can return only one PGresult structure. If the submitted command string contains multiple SQL commands, all but the last PGresult are discarded by PQexec.

Applications that do not like these limitations can instead use the underlying functions that PQexec is built from: PQsendQuery and PQgetResult. There are also PQsendQueryParams, PQsendPrepare, PQsendQueryPrepared, PQsendDescribePrepared, and PQsendDescribePortal, which can be used with PQgetResult to duplicate the functionality of PQexecParams, PQprepare, PQexecPrepared, PQdescribePrepared, and PQdescribePortal respectively.

PQsendQuery

Submits a command to the server without waiting for the result(s). 1 is returned if the command was successfully dispatched and 0 if not (in which case, use PQerrorMessage to get more information about the failure).

```
int PQsendQuery(PGconn *conn, const char *command);
```

After successfully calling PQsendQuery, call PQgetResult one or more times to obtain the results. PQsendQuery may not be called again (on the same connection) until PQgetResult has returned a null pointer, indicating that the command is done.

PQsendQueryParams

Submits a command and separate parameters to the server without waiting for the result(s).

```
int PQsendQueryParams(PGconn *conn,
                      const char *command,
                      int nParams,
                      const Oid *paramTypes,
                      const char * const *paramValues,
                      const int *paramLengths,
                      const int *paramFormats,
                      int resultFormat);
```

This is equivalent to PQsendQuery except that query parameters can be specified separately from the query string. The function's parameters are handled identically to PQexecParams. Like PQexecParams, it will not work on 2.0-protocol connections, and it allows only one command in the query string.

PQsendPrepare

Sends a request to create a prepared statement with the given parameters, without waiting for completion.

```
int PQsendPrepare(PGconn *conn,
                  const char *stmtName,
                  const char *query,
                  int nParams,
                  const Oid *paramTypes);
```

This is an asynchronous version of PQprepare: it returns 1 if it was able to dispatch the request, and 0 if not. After a successful call, call PQgetResult to determine whether the server successfully created the prepared statement. The function's parameters are handled identically to PQprepare. Like PQprepare, it will not work on 2.0-protocol connections.

PQsendQueryPrepared

Sends a request to execute a prepared statement with given parameters, without waiting for the result(s).

```
int PQsendQueryPrepared(PGconn *conn,
                        const char *stmtName,
                        int nParams,
                        const char * const *paramValues,
                        const int *paramLengths,
                        const int *paramFormats,
                        int resultFormat);
```

This is similar to PQsendQueryParams, but the command to be executed is specified by naming a previously-prepared statement, instead of giving a query string. The function's parameters are handled identically to PQexecPrepared. Like PQexecPrepared, it will not work on 2.0-protocol connections.

PQsendDescribePrepared

Submits a request to obtain information about the specified prepared statement, without waiting for completion.

```
int PQsendDescribePrepared(PGconn *conn, const char
*stmtName);
```

This is an asynchronous version of PQdescribePrepared: it returns 1 if it was able to dispatch the request, and 0 if not. After a successful call, call PQgetResult to obtain the results. The function's parameters are handled identically to PQdescribePrepared. Like PQdescribePrepared, it will not work on 2.0-protocol connections.

PQsendDescribePortal

Submits a request to obtain information about the specified portal, without waiting for completion.

```
int PQsendDescribePortal(PGconn *conn, const char
*portalName);
```

This is an asynchronous version of PQdescribePortal: it returns 1 if it
was able to dispatch the request, and 0 if not. After a successful call, call
PQgetResult to obtain the results. The function's parameters are handled
identically to PQdescribePortal. Like PQdescribePortal, it will not work
on 2.0-protocol connections.

PQgetResult

Waits for the next result from a prior PQsendQuery, PQsendQueryParams,
PQsendPrepare, or PQsendQueryPrepared call, and returns it. A null
pointer is returned when the command is complete and there will be no
more results.

```
PGresult *PQgetResult(PGconn *conn);
```

PQgetResult must be called repeatedly until it returns a null pointer, indicating that the command is done. (If called when no command is active,
PQgetResult will just return a null pointer at once.) Each non-null result
from PQgetResult should be processed using the same PGresult accessor
functions previously described. Don't forget to free each result object with
PQclear when done with it. Note that PQgetResult will block only if a
command is active and the necessary response data has not yet been read
by PQconsumeInput.

Using PQsendQuery and PQgetResult solves one of PQexec's problems: If a
command string contains multiple SQL commands, the results of those commands can be obtained individually. (This allows a simple form of overlapped
processing, by the way: the client can be handling the results of one command
while the server is still working on later queries in the same command string.)
However, calling PQgetResult will still cause the client to block until the server
completes the next SQL command. This can be avoided by proper use of two
more functions:

PQconsumeInput

If input is available from the server, consume it.

```
int PQconsumeInput(PGconn *conn);
```

PQconsumeInput normally returns 1 indicating "no error", but returns 0
if there was some kind of trouble (in which case PQerrorMessage can be
consulted). Note that the result does not say whether any input data
was actually collected. After calling PQconsumeInput, the application may
check PQisBusy and/or PQnotifies to see if their state has changed.

PQconsumeInput may be called even if the application is not prepared to
deal with a result or notification just yet. The function will read available
data and save it in a buffer, thereby causing a select() read-ready indication to go away. The application can thus use PQconsumeInput to clear the
select() condition immediately, and then examine the results at leisure.

PQisBusy

> Returns 1 if a command is busy, that is, PQgetResult would block wait-
> ing for input. A 0 return indicates that PQgetResult can be called with
> assurance of not blocking.
>
>   int PQisBusy(PGconn *conn);
>
> PQisBusy will not itself attempt to read data from the server; therefore
> PQconsumeInput must be invoked first, or the busy state will never end.

A typical application using these functions will have a main loop that uses
select() or poll() to wait for all the conditions that it must respond to. One
of the conditions will be input available from the server, which in terms of
select() means readable data on the file descriptor identified by PQsocket.
When the main loop detects input ready, it should call PQconsumeInput to read
the input. It can then call PQisBusy, followed by PQgetResult if PQisBusy
returns false (0). It can also call PQnotifies to detect NOTIFY messages (see
Section 1.7 *Asynchronous Notification*, page 37).

A client that uses PQsendQuery/PQgetResult can also attempt to cancel a
command that is still being processed by the server; see Section 1.5 *Cancelling
Queries in Progress*, page 35. But regardless of the return value of PQcancel,
the application must continue with the normal result-reading sequence using
PQgetResult. A successful cancellation will simply cause the command to ter-
minate sooner than it would have otherwise.

By using the functions described above, it is possible to avoid blocking while
waiting for input from the database server. However, it is still possible that the
application will block waiting to send output to the server. This is relatively un-
common but can happen if very long SQL commands or data values are sent. (It
is much more probable if the application sends data via COPY IN, however.) To
prevent this possibility and achieve completely nonblocking database operation,
the following additional functions may be used.

PQsetnonblocking

> Sets the nonblocking status of the connection.
>
>   int PQsetnonblocking(PGconn *conn, int arg);
>
> Sets the state of the connection to nonblocking if arg is 1, or blocking if
> arg is 0. Returns 0 if OK, -1 if error.
>
> In the nonblocking state, calls to PQsendQuery, PQputline, PQputnbytes,
> and PQendcopy will not block but instead return an error if they need to
> be called again.
>
> Note that PQexec does not honor nonblocking mode; if it is called, it will
> act in blocking fashion anyway.

PQisnonblocking

> Returns the blocking status of the database connection.
>
>   int PQisnonblocking(const PGconn *conn);
>
> Returns 1 if the connection is set to nonblocking mode and 0 if blocking.

PQflush

>   Attempts to flush any queued output data to the server. Returns 0 if
>   successful (or if the send queue is empty), -1 if it failed for some reason, or
>   1 if it was unable to send all the data in the send queue yet (this case can
>   only occur if the connection is nonblocking).

>   ```
>   int PQflush(PGconn *conn);
>   ```

After sending any command or data on a nonblocking connection, call
PQflush. If it returns 1, wait for the socket to be write-ready and call it again;
repeat until it returns 0. Once PQflush returns 0, wait for the socket to be
read-ready and then read the response as described above.

1.5 Cancelling Queries in Progress

A client application can request cancellation of a command that is still being
processed by the server, using the functions described in this section.

PQgetCancel

>   Creates a data structure containing the information needed to cancel a
>   command issued through a particular database connection.

>   ```
>   PGcancel *PQgetCancel(PGconn *conn);
>   ```

>   PQgetCancel creates a PGcancel object given a PGconn connection object.
>   It will return NULL if the given conn is NULL or an invalid connection.
>   The PGcancel object is an opaque structure that is not meant to be ac-
>   cessed directly by the application; it can only be passed to PQcancel or
>   PQfreeCancel.

PQfreeCancel

>   Frees a data structure created by PQgetCancel.

>   ```
>   void PQfreeCancel(PGcancel *cancel);
>   ```

>   PQfreeCancel frees a data object previously created by PQgetCancel.

PQcancel

>   Requests that the server abandon processing of the current command.

>   ```
>   int PQcancel(PGcancel *cancel, char *errbuf, int errbufsize);
>   ```

>   The return value is 1 if the cancel request was successfully dispatched and
>   0 if not. If not, errbuf is filled with an error message explaining why not.
>   errbuf must be a char array of size errbufsize (the recommended size is
>   256 bytes).

>   Successful dispatch is no guarantee that the request will have any effect,
>   however. If the cancellation is effective, the current command will termi-
>   nate early and return an error result. If the cancellation fails (say, because
>   the server was already done processing the command), then there will be
>   no visible result at all.

>   PQcancel can safely be invoked from a signal handler, if the errbuf is a
>   local variable in the signal handler. The PGcancel object is read-only as
>   far as PQcancel is concerned, so it can also be invoked from a thread that
>   is separate from the one manipulating the PGconn object.

PQrequestCancel

> Requests that the server abandon processing of the current command.

>> `int PQrequestCancel(PGconn *conn);`

> PQrequestCancel is a deprecated variant of PQcancel. It operates directly on the PGconn object, and in case of failure stores the error message in the PGconn object (whence it can be retrieved by PQerrorMessage). Although the functionality is the same, this approach creates hazards for multiple-thread programs and signal handlers, since it is possible that overwriting the PGconn's error message will mess up the operation currently in progress on the connection.

1.6 The Fast-Path Interface

PostgreSQL provides a fast-path interface to send simple function calls to the server.

> **Tip:** This interface is somewhat obsolete, as one may achieve similar performance and greater functionality by setting up a prepared statement to define the function call. Then, executing the statement with binary transmission of parameters and results substitutes for a fast-path function call.

The function PQfn requests execution of a server function via the fast-path interface:

```
PGresult *PQfn(PGconn *conn,
               int fnid,
               int *result_buf,
               int *result_len,
               int result_is_int,
               const PQArgBlock *args,
               int nargs);

typedef struct {
    int len;
    int isint;
    union {
        int *ptr;
        int integer;
    } u;
} PQArgBlock;
```

The fnid argument is the OID of the function to be executed. args and nargs define the parameters to be passed to the function; they must match the declared function argument list. When the isint field of a parameter structure is true, the u.integer value is sent to the server as an integer of the indicated length (this must be 1, 2, or 4 bytes); proper byte-swapping occurs. When isint is false, the indicated number of bytes at *u.ptr are sent with no processing; the data must be in the format expected by the server for binary transmission of the function's argument data type. result_buf is the buffer in which to place the return value. The caller must have allocated sufficient space to store the return value. (There is no check!) The actual result length will be returned in the integer pointed to by `result_len`. If a 1, 2, or 4-byte integer result is expected, set `result_is_int` to 1, otherwise set it to 0. Setting `result_is_int` to 1 causes libpq to byte-swap the value if necessary, so that it is delivered as a proper `int` value for the client machine. When `result_is_int` is 0, the binary-format byte string sent by the server is returned unmodified.

PQfn always returns a valid `PGresult` pointer. The result status should be checked before the result is used. The caller is responsible for freeing the `PGresult` with `PQclear` when it is no longer needed.

Note that it is not possible to handle null arguments, null results, nor set-valued results when using this interface.

1.7 Asynchronous Notification

PostgreSQL offers asynchronous notification via the `LISTEN` and `NOTIFY` commands. A client session registers its interest in a particular notification condition with the `LISTEN` command (and can stop listening with the `UNLISTEN` command). All sessions listening on a particular condition will be notified asynchronously when a `NOTIFY` command with that condition name is executed by any session. No additional information is passed from the notifier to the listener. Thus, typically, any actual data that needs to be communicated is transferred through a database table. Commonly, the condition name is the same as the associated table, but it is not necessary for there to be any associated table.

libpq applications submit `LISTEN` and `UNLISTEN` commands as ordinary SQL commands. The arrival of `NOTIFY` messages can subsequently be detected by calling `PQnotifies`.

The function `PQnotifies` returns the next notification from a list of unhandled notification messages received from the server. It returns a null pointer if there are no pending notifications. Once a notification is returned from `PQnotifies`, it is considered handled and will be removed from the list of notifications.

```
PGnotify *PQnotifies(PGconn * conn);
```

```
typedef struct pgNotify {
  char *relname;          /* notification condition name */
  int be_pid;             /* process ID of notifying server
                             process */
  char *extra;            /* notification parameter */
} PGnotify;
```

After processing a PGnotify object returned by PQnotifies, be sure to free it with PQfreemem. It is sufficient to free the PGnotify pointer; the `relname` and `extra` fields do not represent separate allocations. (At present, the `extra` field is unused and will always point to an empty string.)

libpq Example Program 2, page 55 gives a sample program that illustrates the use of asynchronous notification.

PQnotifies does not actually read data from the server; it just returns messages previously absorbed by another libpq function. In prior releases of libpq, the only way to ensure timely receipt of NOTIFY messages was to constantly submit commands, even empty ones, and then check PQnotifies after each PQexec. While this still works, it is deprecated as a waste of processing power.

A better way to check for NOTIFY messages when you have no useful commands to execute is to call PQconsumeInput, then check PQnotifies. You can use select() to wait for data to arrive from the server, thereby using no CPU power unless there is something to do. (See PQsocket to obtain the file descriptor number to use with select().) Note that this will work OK whether you submit commands with PQsendQuery/PQgetResult or simply use PQexec. You should, however, remember to check PQnotifies after each PQgetResult or PQexec, to see if any notifications came in during the processing of the command.

1.8 Functions Associated with the COPY Command

The COPY command in PostgreSQL has options to read from or write to the network connection used by libpq. The functions described in this section allow applications to take advantage of this capability by supplying or consuming copied data.

The overall process is that the application first issues the SQL COPY command via PQexec or one of the equivalent functions. The response to this (if there is no error in the command) will be a PGresult object bearing a status code of PGRES_COPY_OUT or PGRES_COPY_IN (depending on the specified copy direction). The application should then use the functions of this section to receive or transmit data rows. When the data transfer is complete, another PGresult object is returned to indicate success or failure of the transfer. Its status will be PGRES_COMMAND_OK for success or PGRES_FATAL_ERROR if some problem was encountered. At this point further SQL commands may be issued via PQexec. (It is not possible to execute other SQL commands using the same connection while the COPY operation is in progress.)

If a COPY command is issued via PQexec in a string that could contain additional commands, the application must continue fetching results via PQgetResult after completing the COPY sequence. Only when PQgetResult returns NULL is it certain that the PQexec command string is done and it is safe to issue more commands.

The functions of this section should be executed only after obtaining a result status of PGRES_COPY_OUT or PGRES_COPY_IN from PQexec or PQgetResult.

A PGresult object bearing one of these status values carries some additional data about the COPY operation that is starting. This additional data is available using functions that are also used in connection with query results:

PQnfields
    Returns the number of columns (fields) to be copied.

PQbinaryTuples
    0 indicates the overall copy format is textual (rows separated by newlines, columns separated by separator characters, etc). 1 indicates the overall copy format is binary. See COPY (Volume 1) for more information.

PQfformat

> Returns the format code (0 for text, 1 for binary) associated with each
> column of the copy operation. The per-column format codes will always
> be zero when the overall copy format is textual, but the binary format
> can support both text and binary columns. (However, as of the current
> implementation of COPY, only binary columns appear in a binary copy; so
> the per-column formats always match the overall format at present.)
>
> Note: These additional data values are only available when using
> protocol 3.0. When using protocol 2.0, all these functions will return
> 0.

1.8.1 Functions for Sending COPY Data

These functions are used to send data during COPY FROM STDIN. They will fail
if called when the connection is not in COPY_IN state.

PQputCopyData

> Sends data to the server during COPY_IN state.
>
>   int PQputCopyData(PGconn *conn,
>   const char *buffer,
>   int nbytes);
>
> Transmits the COPY data in the specified buffer, of length nbytes, to the
> server. The result is 1 if the data was sent, zero if it was not sent because
> the attempt would block (this case is only possible if the connection is
> in nonblocking mode), or -1 if an error occurred. (Use PQerrorMessage
> to retrieve details if the return value is -1. If the value is zero, wait for
> write-ready and try again.)
>
> The application may divide the COPY data stream into buffer loads of any
> convenient size. Buffer-load boundaries have no semantic significance when
> sending. The contents of the data stream must match the data format
> expected by the COPY command; see COPY (Volume 1) for details.

PQputCopyEnd

> Sends end-of-data indication to the server during COPY_IN state.
>
>   int PQputCopyEnd(PGconn *conn,
>   const char *errormsg);
>
> Ends the COPY_IN operation successfully if errormsg is NULL. If errormsg
> is not NULL then the COPY is forced to fail, with the string pointed to
> by errormsg used as the error message. (One should not assume that
> this exact error message will come back from the server, however, as the
> server might have already failed the COPY for its own reasons. Also note
> that the option to force failure does not work when using pre-3.0-protocol
> connections.)
>
> The result is 1 if the termination data was sent, zero if it was not sent
> because the attempt would block (this case is only possible if the connection
> is in nonblocking mode), or -1 if an error occurred. (Use PQerrorMessage
> to retrieve details if the return value is -1. If the value is zero, wait for
> write-ready and try again.)

After successfully calling PQputCopyEnd, call PQgetResult to obtain the final result status of the COPY command. One may wait for this result to be available in the usual way. Then return to normal operation.

1.8.2 Functions for Receiving COPY Data

These functions are used to receive data during COPY TO STDOUT. They will fail if called when the connection is not in COPY_OUT state.

PQgetCopyData

Receives data from the server during COPY_OUT state.

```
int PQgetCopyData(PGconn *conn,
                  char **buffer,
                  int async);
```

Attempts to obtain another row of data from the server during a COPY. Data is always returned one data row at a time; if only a partial row is available, it is not returned. Successful return of a data row involves allocating a chunk of memory to hold the data. The buffer parameter must be non-NULL. *buffer is set to point to the allocated memory, or to NULL in cases where no buffer is returned. A non-NULL result buffer must be freed using PQfreemem when no longer needed.

When a row is successfully returned, the return value is the number of data bytes in the row (this will always be greater than zero). The returned string is always null-terminated, though this is probably only useful for textual COPY. A result of zero indicates that the COPY is still in progress, but no row is yet available (this is only possible when async is true). A result of -1 indicates that the COPY is done. A result of -2 indicates that an error occurred (consult PQerrorMessage for the reason).

When async is true (not zero), PQgetCopyData will not block waiting for input; it will return zero if the COPY is still in progress but no complete row is available. (In this case wait for read-ready and then call PQconsumeInput before calling PQgetCopyData again.) When async is false (zero), PQgetCopyData will block until data is available or the operation completes.

After PQgetCopyData returns -1, call PQgetResult to obtain the final result status of the COPY command. One may wait for this result to be available in the usual way. Then return to normal operation.

1.8.3 Obsolete Functions for COPY

These functions represent older methods of handling COPY. Although they still work, they are deprecated due to poor error handling, inconvenient methods of detecting end-of-data, and lack of support for binary or nonblocking transfers.

PQgetline

Reads a newline-terminated line of characters (transmitted by the server) into a buffer string of size length.

```
int PQgetline(PGconn *conn,
              char *buffer,
              int length);
```

This function copies up to length-1 characters into the buffer and converts the terminating newline into a zero byte. PQgetline returns EOF at the end of input, 0 if the entire line has been read, and 1 if the buffer is full but the terminating newline has not yet been read.

Note that the application must check to see if a new line consists of the two characters \., which indicates that the server has finished sending the results of the COPY command. If the application might receive lines that are more than length-1 characters long, care is needed to be sure it recognizes the \. line correctly (and does not, for example, mistake the end of a long data line for a terminator line).

PQgetlineAsync

Reads a row of COPY data (transmitted by the server) into a buffer without blocking.

```
int PQgetlineAsync(PGconn *conn,
                   char *buffer,
                   int bufsize);
```

This function is similar to PQgetline, but it can be used by applications that must read COPY data asynchronously, that is, without blocking. Having issued the COPY command and gotten a PGRES_COPY_OUT response, the application should call PQconsumeInput and PQgetlineAsync until the end-of-data signal is detected.

Unlike PQgetline, this function takes responsibility for detecting end-of-data.

On each call, PQgetlineAsync will return data if a complete data row is available in libpq's input buffer. Otherwise, no data is returned until the rest of the row arrives. The function returns -1 if the end-of-copy-data marker has been recognized, or 0 if no data is available, or a positive number giving the number of bytes of data returned. If -1 is returned, the caller must next call PQendcopy, and then return to normal processing.

The data returned will not extend beyond a data-row boundary. If possible a whole row will be returned at one time. But if the buffer offered by the caller is too small to hold a row sent by the server, then a partial data row will be returned. With textual data this can be detected by testing whether the last returned byte is \n or not. (In a binary COPY, actual parsing of the COPY data format will be needed to make the equivalent determination.) The returned string is not null-terminated. (If you want to add a terminating null, be sure to pass a bufsize one smaller than the room actually available.)

PQputline

Sends a null-terminated string to the server. Returns 0 if OK and EOF if unable to send the string.

```
int PQputline(PGconn *conn,
              const char *string);
```

The COPY data stream sent by a series of calls to PQputline has the same format as that returned by PQgetlineAsync, except that applications are not obliged to send exactly one data row per PQputline call; it is okay to send a partial line or multiple lines per call.

> **Note:** Before PostgreSQL protocol 3.0, it was necessary for the application to explicitly send the two characters \. as a final line to indicate to the server that it had finished sending COPY data. While this still works, it is deprecated and the special meaning of \. can be expected to be removed in a future release. It is sufficient to call PQendcopy after having sent the actual data.

PQputnbytes

Sends a non-null-terminated string to the server. Returns 0 if OK and EOF if unable to send the string.

```
int PQputnbytes(PGconn *conn,
                const char *buffer,
                int nbytes);
```

This is exactly like PQputline, except that the data buffer need not be null-terminated since the number of bytes to send is specified directly. Use this procedure when sending binary data.

PQendcopy

Synchronizes with the server.

```
int PQendcopy(PGconn *conn);
```

This function waits until the server has finished the copying. It should either be issued when the last string has been sent to the server using PQputline or when the last string has been received from the server using PGgetline. It must be issued or the server will get "out of sync" with the client. Upon return from this function, the server is ready to receive the next SQL command. The return value is 0 on successful completion, nonzero otherwise. (Use PQerrorMessage to retrieve details if the return value is nonzero.)

When using PQgetResult, the application should respond to a PGRES_COPY_OUT result by executing PQgetline repeatedly, followed by PQendcopy after the terminator line is seen. It should then return to the PQgetResult loop until PQgetResult returns a null pointer. Similarly a PGRES_COPY_IN result is processed by a series of PQputline calls followed by PQendcopy, then return to the PQgetResult loop. This arrangement will ensure that a COPY command embedded in a series of SQL commands will be executed correctly.

Older applications are likely to submit a COPY via PQexec and assume that the transaction is done after PQendcopy. This will work correctly only if the COPY is the only SQL command in the command string.

1.9 Control Functions

These functions control miscellaneous details of libpq's behavior.

PQsetErrorVerbosity

Determines the verbosity of messages returned by PQerrorMessage and PQresultErrorMessage.

```
typedef enum {
    PQERRORS_TERSE,
    PQERRORS_DEFAULT,
    PQERRORS_VERBOSE
} PGVerbosity;


PGVerbosity PQsetErrorVerbosity(PGconn *conn, PGVerbosity
    verbosity);
```

PQsetErrorVerbosity sets the verbosity mode, returning the connection's previous setting. In *TERSE* mode, returned messages include severity, primary text, and position only; this will normally fit on a single line. The default mode produces messages that include the above plus any detail, hint, or context fields (these may span multiple lines). The *VERBOSE* mode includes all available fields. Changing the verbosity does not affect the messages available from already-existing PGresult objects, only subsequently-created ones.

PQtrace

Enables tracing of the client/server communication to a debugging file stream.

```
void PQtrace(PGconn *conn, FILE *stream);
```

Note: On Windows, if the libpq library and an application are compiled with different flags, this function call will crash the application because the internal representation of the FILE pointers differ. Specifically, multithreaded/single-threaded, release/debug, and static/dynamic flags should be the same for the library and all applications using that library.

PQuntrace

Disables tracing started by PQtrace.

```
void PQuntrace(PGconn *conn);
```

1.10 Miscellaneous Functions

As always, there are some functions that just don't fit anywhere.

PQencryptPassword
>   Prepares the encrypted form of a PostgreSQL password.
>
>   ```
>   char * PQencryptPassword(const char *passwd, const char
>   *user);
>   ```
>
>   This function is intended to be used by client applications that wish to
>   send commands like ALTER USER joe PASSWORD 'pwd'. It is good practice
>   not to send the original cleartext password in such a command, because it
>   might be exposed in command logs, activity displays, and so on. Instead,
>   use this function to convert the password to encrypted form before it is
>   sent. The arguments are the cleartext password, and the SQL name of the
>   user it is for. The return value is a string allocated by malloc, or NULL
>   if out of memory. The caller may assume the string doesn't contain any
>   special characters that would require escaping. Use PQfreemem to free the
>   result when done with it.

1.11 Notice Processing

Notice and warning messages generated by the server are not returned by
the query execution functions, since they do not imply failure of the query.
Instead they are passed to a notice handling function, and execution continues
normally after the handler returns. The default notice handling function prints
the message on 'stderr', but the application can override this behavior by
supplying its own handling function.

For historical reasons, there are two levels of notice handling, called the notice
receiver and notice processor. The default behavior is for the notice receiver
to format the notice and pass a string to the notice processor for printing.
However, an application that chooses to provide its own notice receiver will
typically ignore the notice processor layer and just do all the work in the notice
receiver.

The function PQsetNoticeReceiver sets or examines the current notice receiver for a connection object. Similarly, PQsetNoticeProcessor sets or examines the current notice processor.

```
typedef void (*PQnoticeReceiver) (void *arg, const PGresult
*res);

PQnoticeReceiver
PQsetNoticeReceiver(PGconn *conn,
                    PQnoticeReceiver proc,
                    void *arg);

typedef void (*PQnoticeProcessor) (void *arg, const char
*message);

PQnoticeProcessor
```

```
PQsetNoticeProcessor(PGconn *conn,
                     PQnoticeProcessor proc,
                     void *arg);
```

Each of these functions returns the previous notice receiver or processor function pointer, and sets the new value. If you supply a null function pointer, no action is taken, but the current pointer is returned.

When a notice or warning message is received from the server, or generated internally by libpq, the notice receiver function is called. It is passed the message in the form of a PGRES_NONFATAL_ERROR PGresult. (This allows the receiver to extract individual fields using PQresultErrorField, or the complete preformatted message using PQresultErrorMessage.) The same void pointer passed to PQsetNoticeReceiver is also passed. (This pointer can be used to access application-specific state if needed.)

The default notice receiver simply extracts the message (using PQresultErrorMessage) and passes it to the notice processor.

The notice processor is responsible for handling a notice or warning message given in text form. It is passed the string text of the message (including a trailing newline), plus a void pointer that is the same one passed to PQsetNoticeProcessor. (This pointer can be used to access application-specific state if needed.)

The default notice processor is simply

```
static void
defaultNoticeProcessor(void *arg, const char *message)
{
    fprintf(stderr, "%s", message);
}
```

Once you have set a notice receiver or processor, you should expect that that function could be called as long as either the PGconn object or PGresult objects made from it exist. At creation of a PGresult, the PGconn's current notice handling pointers are copied into the PGresult for possible use by functions like PQgetvalue.

1.12 Environment Variables

The following environment variables can be used to select default connection parameter values, which will be used by PQconnectdb, PQsetdbLogin and PQsetdb if no value is directly specified by the calling code. These are useful to avoid hard-coding database connection information into simple client applications, for example.

- PGHOST sets the database server name. If this begins with a slash, it specifies Unix-domain communication rather than TCP/IP communication; the value is then the name of the directory in which the socket file is stored (in a default installation setup this would be '/tmp').

- PGHOSTADDR specifies the numeric IP address of the database server. This can be set instead of or in addition to PGHOST to avoid DNS lookup overhead. See the documentation of these parameters, under PQconnectdb above, for details on their interaction.

  When neither PGHOST nor PGHOSTADDR is set, the default behavior is to connect using a local Unix-domain socket; or on machines without Unix-domain sockets, libpq will attempt to connect to localhost.

- PGPORT sets the TCP port number or Unix-domain socket file extension for communicating with the PostgreSQL server.

- PGDATABASE sets the PostgreSQL database name.

- PGUSER sets the user name used to connect to the database.

- PGPASSWORD sets the password used if the server demands password authentication. Use of this environment variable is not recommended for security reasons (some operating systems allow non-root users to see process environment variables via ps); instead consider using the '~/.pgpass' file (see Section 1.13 *The Password File*, page 47).

- PGPASSFILE specifies the name of the password file to use for lookups. If not set, it defaults to '~/.pgpass' (see Section 1.13 *The Password File*, page 47).

- PGSERVICE sets the service name to be looked up in 'pg_service.conf'. This offers a shorthand way of setting all the parameters.

- PGREALM sets the Kerberos realm to use with PostgreSQL, if it is different from the local realm. If PGREALM is set, libpq applications will attempt authentication with servers for this realm and use separate ticket files to avoid conflicts with local ticket files. This environment variable is only used if Kerberos authentication is selected by the server.

- PGOPTIONS sets additional run-time options for the PostgreSQL server.

- PGSSLMODE determines whether and with what priority an SSL connection will be negotiated with the server. There are four modes: disable will attempt only an unencrypted SSL connection; allow will negotiate, trying first a non-SSL connection, then if that fails, trying an SSL connection; prefer (the default) will negotiate, trying first an SSL connection, then if that fails, trying a regular non-SSL connection; require will try only an SSL connection. If PostgreSQL is compiled without SSL support, using option require will cause an error, while options allow and prefer will be accepted but libpq will not in fact attempt an SSL connection.

- PGREQUIRESSL sets whether or not the connection must be made over SSL. If set to "1", libpq will refuse to connect if the server does not accept an SSL connection (equivalent to sslmode prefer). This option is deprecated in favor of the sslmode setting, and is only available if PostgreSQL is compiled with SSL support.

- PGKRBSRVNAME sets the Kerberos service name to use when authenticating with Kerberos 5.

- PGCONNECT_TIMEOUT sets the maximum number of seconds that libpq will wait when attempting to connect to the PostgreSQL server. If unset or set to zero, libpq will wait indefinitely. It is not recommended to set the timeout to less than 2 seconds.

The following environment variables can be used to specify default behavior for each PostgreSQL session. (See also the ALTER USER and ALTER DATABASE commands for ways to set default behavior on a per-user or per-database basis.)

- PGDATESTYLE sets the default style of date/time representation. (Equivalent to SET datestyle TO ....)

- PGTZ sets the default time zone. (Equivalent to SET timezone TO ....)

- PGCLIENTENCODING sets the default client character set encoding. (Equivalent to SET client_encoding TO ....)

- PGGEQO sets the default mode for the genetic query optimizer. (Equivalent to SET geqo TO ....)

Refer to the SQL command SET for information on correct values for these environment variables.

The following environment variables determine internal behavior of libpq; they override compiled-in defaults.

- PGSYSCONFDIR sets the directory containing the 'pg_service.conf' file.

- PGLOCALEDIR sets the directory containing the locale files for message internationalization.

1.13 The Password File

The file '.pgpass' in a user's home directory or the file referenced by PGPASSFILE can contain passwords to be used if the connection requires a password (and no password has been specified otherwise). On Microsoft Windows the file is named '%APPDATA%\postgresql\pgpass.conf' (where '%APPDATA%' refers to the Application Data subdirectory in the user's profile).

This file should contain lines of the following format:

hostname : *port* : *database* : *username* : *password*

Each of the first four fields may be a literal value, or *, which matches anything. The password field from the first line that matches the current connection parameters will be used. (Therefore, put more-specific entries first when you are using wildcards.) If an entry needs to contain : or \, escape this character with \. A host name of localhost matches both TCP (hostname localhost) and Unix domain socket (pghost empty or the default socket directory) connections coming from the local machine.

The permissions on '.pgpass' must disallow any access to world or group; achieve this by the command chmod 0600 ~/.pgpass. If the permissions are less strict than this, the file will be ignored. (The file permissions are not currently checked on Microsoft Windows, however.)

1.14 The Connection Service File

The connection service file allows libpq connection parameters to be associated with a single service name. That service name can then be specified by a libpq connection, and the associated settings will be used. This allows connection parameters to be modified without requiring a recompile of the libpq application. The service name can also be specified using the PGSERVICE environment variable.

To use this feature, copy the file 'share/pg_service.conf.sample' to 'etc/pg_service.conf' and edit it to add service names and parameters. This file can be used for client-only installs too. The file's location can also be specified by the PGSYSCONFDIR environment variable.

1.15 LDAP Lookup of Connection Parameters

If libpq has been compiled with LDAP support (option --with-ldap for configure) it is possible to retrieve connection options like host or dbname via LDAP from a central server. The advantage is that if the connection parameters for a database change, the connection information doesn't have to be updated on all client machines.

LDAP connection parameter lookup uses the connection service file 'pg_service.conf' (see Section 1.14 *The Connection Service File*). A line in a 'pg_service.conf' stanza that starts with ldap:// will be recognized as an LDAP URL and an LDAP query will be performed. The result must be a list of keyword = value pairs which will be used to set connection options. The URL must conform to RFC 1959 and be of the form

    ldap://[hostname[:port]]/search_base?attribute?search_scope?
    filter

where *hostname* defaults to localhost and *port* defaults to 389.

Processing of 'pg_service.conf' is terminated after a successful LDAP lookup, but is continued if the LDAP server cannot be contacted. This is to provide a fallback with further LDAP URL lines that point to different LDAP servers, classical keyword = value pairs, or default connection options. If you would rather get an error message in this case, add a syntactically incorrect line after the LDAP URL.

A sample LDAP entry that has been created with the LDIF file

    version:1
    dn:cn=mydatabase,dc=mycompany,dc=com
    changetype:add
    objectclass:top
    objectclass:groupOfUniqueNames
    cn:mydatabase
    uniqueMember:host=dbserver.mycompany.com
    uniqueMember:port=5439
    uniqueMember:dbname=mydb
    uniqueMember:user=mydb_user
    uniqueMember:sslmode=require

might be queried with the following LDAP URL:

```
ldap://ldap.mycompany.com/dc=mycompany,dc=com?uniqueMember?
one?(cn=mydatabase)
```

1.16 SSL Support

PostgreSQL has native support for using SSL connections to encrypt client/server communications for increased security. See Volume 3, Section 3.7 *Secure TCP/IP Connections with SSL* for details about the server-side SSL functionality.

If the server demands a client certificate, libpq will send the certificate stored in the file '~/.postgresql/postgresql.crt' within the user's home directory. A matching private key file '~/.postgresql/postgresql.key' must also be present, and must not be world-readable. (On Microsoft Windows these files are named '%APPDATA%\postgresql\postgresql.crt' and '%APPDATA%\postgresql\postgresql.key'.)

If the file '~/.postgresql/root.crt' is present in the user's home directory, libpq will use the certificate list stored therein to verify the server's certificate. (On Microsoft Windows the file is named '%APPDATA%\postgresql\root.crt'.) The SSL connection will fail if the server does not present a certificate; therefore, to use this feature the server must have a 'server.crt' file. Certificate Revocation List (CRL) entries are also checked if the file '~/.postgresql/root.crl' exists ('%APPDATA%\postgresql\root.crl' on Microsoft Windows).

If you are using SSL inside your application (in addition to inside libpq), you can use PQinitSSL(int) to tell libpq that the SSL library has already been initialized by your application.

1.17 Behavior in Threaded Programs

libpq is reentrant and thread-safe if the 'configure' command-line option --enable-thread-safety was used when the PostgreSQL distribution was built. In addition, you might need to use additional compiler command-line options when you compile your application code. Refer to your system's documentation for information about how to build thread-enabled applications, or look in 'src/Makefile.global' for PTHREAD_CFLAGS and PTHREAD_LIBS. This function allows the querying of libpq's thread-safe status:

PQisthreadsafe
   Returns the thread safety status of the libpq library.

```
      int PQisthreadsafe();
```

   Returns 1 if the libpq is thread-safe and 0 if it is not.

One thread restriction is that no two threads attempt to manipulate the same PGconn object at the same time. In particular, you cannot issue concurrent commands from different threads through the same connection object. (If you need to run concurrent commands, use multiple connections.)

PGresult objects are read-only after creation, and so can be passed around freely between threads.

The deprecated functions `PQrequestCancel` and `PQoidStatus` are not thread-safe and should not be used in multithread programs. `PQrequestCancel` can be replaced by `PQcancel`. `PQoidStatus` can be replaced by `PQoidValue`.

If you are using Kerberos inside your application (in addition to inside libpq), you will need to do locking around Kerberos calls because Kerberos functions are not thread-safe. See function `PQregisterThreadLock` in the libpq source code for a way to do cooperative locking between libpq and your application.

If you experience problems with threaded applications, run the program in 'src/tools/thread' to see if your platform has thread-unsafe functions. This program is run by 'configure', but for binary distributions your library might not match the library used to build the binaries.

1.18 Building libpq Programs

To build (i.e., compile and link) a program using libpq you need to do all of the following things:

- Include the 'libpq-fe.h' header file:

  ```
  #include <libpq-fe.h>
  ```

  If you failed to do that then you will normally get error messages from your compiler similar to

  ```
  foo.c: In function 'main':
  foo.c:34: 'PGconn' undeclared (first use in this function)
  foo.c:35: 'PGresult' undeclared (first use in this function)
  foo.c:54: 'CONNECTION_BAD' undeclared (first use in this
   function)
  foo.c:68: 'PGRES_COMMAND_OK' undeclared (first use in
   this function)
  foo.c:95: 'PGRES_TUPLES_OK' undeclared (first use in this
   function)
  ```

- Point your compiler to the directory where the PostgreSQL header files were installed, by supplying the -I*directory* option to your compiler. (In some cases the compiler will look into the directory in question by default, so you can omit this option.) For instance, your compile command line could look like:

  ```
  cc -c -I/usr/local/pgsql/include testprog.c
  ```

  If you are using makefiles then add the option to the `CPPFLAGS` variable:

  ```
  CPPFLAGS += -I/usr/local/pgsql/include
  ```

  If there is any chance that your program might be compiled by other users then you should not hardcode the directory location like that. Instead, you can run the utility `pg_config` to find out where the header files are on the local system:

  ```
  $ pg_config --includedir
  /usr/local/include
  ```

  Failure to specify the correct option to the compiler will result in an error message such as

```
testlibpq.c:8:22: libpq-fe.h: No such file or directory
```

- When linking the final program, specify the option -lpq so that the libpq library gets pulled in, as well as the option -L*directory* to point the compiler to the directory where the libpq library resides. (Again, the compiler will search some directories by default.) For maximum portability, put the -L option before the -lpq option. For example:

```
cc -o testprog testprog1.o testprog2.o -L/usr/local/pgsql/
lib -lpq
```

You can find out the library directory using pg_config as well:

```
$ pg_config --libdir
/usr/local/pgsql/lib
```

Error messages that point to problems in this area could look like the following.

```
testlibpq.o: In function 'main':
testlibpq.o(.text+0x60): undefined reference to
 'PQsetdbLogin'
testlibpq.o(.text+0x71): undefined reference to 'PQstatus'
testlibpq.o(.text+0xa4): undefined reference to
 'PQerrorMessage'
```

This means you forgot -lpq.

```
/usr/bin/ld: cannot find -lpq
```

This means you forgot the -L option or did not specify the right directory.

1.19 Example Programs

These examples and others can be found in the directory 'src/test/examples' in the source code distribution.

libpq Example Program 1:

```
/* testlibpq.c Test the C version of libpq, the PostgreSQL
   frontend library. */
#include <stdio.h>
#include <stdlib.h>
#include "libpq-fe.h"

static void
exit_nicely(PGconn * conn)
{
  PQfinish(conn);
  exit(1);
}

int
main(int argc, char **argv)
{
  const char *conninfo;
  PGconn *conn;
  PGresult *res;
  int nFields;
  int i, j;

  /* If the user supplies a parameter on the command line,
     use it as the conninfo string; otherwise default to
     setting dbname=postgres and using environment
     variables or defaults for all other connection
     parameters. */
  if (argc > 1)
    conninfo = argv[1];
  else
    conninfo = "dbname = postgres";

  /* Make a connection to the database */
  conn = PQconnectdb(conninfo);

  /* Check to see that the backend connection was
     successfully made */
  if (PQstatus(conn) != CONNECTION_OK) {
    fprintf(stderr, "Connection to database failed: %s",
            PQerrorMessage(conn));
    exit_nicely(conn);
  }

  /* Our test case here involves using a cursor, for which
     we must be inside a transaction block. We could do
     the whole thing with a single PQexec() of "select *
     from pg_database", but that's too trivial to make a
```

```
    good example. */

/* Start a transaction block */
res = PQexec(conn, "BEGIN");
if (PQresultStatus(res) != PGRES_COMMAND_OK) {
  fprintf(stderr, "BEGIN command failed: %s",
          PQerrorMessage(conn));
  PQclear(res);
  exit_nicely(conn);
}

/* Should PQclear PGresult whenever it is no longer
   needed to avoid memory leaks */
PQclear(res);

/* Fetch rows from pg_database, the system catalog of
   databases */
res =
    PQexec(conn,
            "DECLARE myportal CURSOR FOR select * from
             pg_database");
if (PQresultStatus(res) != PGRES_COMMAND_OK) {
  fprintf(stderr, "DECLARE CURSOR failed: %s",
          PQerrorMessage(conn));
  PQclear(res);
  exit_nicely(conn);
}
PQclear(res);

res = PQexec(conn, "FETCH ALL in myportal");
if (PQresultStatus(res) != PGRES_TUPLES_OK) {
  fprintf(stderr, "FETCH ALL failed: %s",
          PQerrorMessage(conn));
  PQclear(res);
  exit_nicely(conn);
}

/* first, print out the attribute names */
nFields = PQnfields(res);
for (i = 0; i < nFields; i++)
  printf("%-15s", PQfname(res, i));
printf("\n\n");

/* next, print out the rows */
for (i = 0; i < PQntuples(res); i++) {
  for (j = 0; j < nFields; j++)
    printf("%-15s", PQgetvalue(res, i, j));
  printf("\n");
```

```
        }

        PQclear(res);

        /* close the portal ... we don't bother to check for
            errors ... */
        res = PQexec(conn, "CLOSE myportal");
        PQclear(res);

        /* end the transaction */
        res = PQexec(conn, "END");
        PQclear(res);

        /* close the connection to the database and cleanup */
        PQfinish(conn);

        return 0;
}
```

libpq Example Program 2:

```
/*testlibpq2.c
 *      Test of the asynchronous notification interface
 *
 * Start this program, then from psql in another window do
 *   NOTIFY TBL2;
 * Repeat four times to get this program to exit.
 *
 * Or, if you want to get fancy, try this:
 * populate a database with the following commands
 * (provided in src/test/examples/testlibpq2.sql):
 *
 *   CREATE TABLE TBL1 (i int4);
 *
 *   CREATE TABLE TBL2 (i int4);
 *
 *   CREATE RULE r1 AS ON INSERT TO TBL1 DO
 *     (INSERT INTO TBL2 VALUES (new.i); NOTIFY TBL2);
 *
 * and do this four times:
 *
 *   INSERT INTO TBL1 VALUES (10);
 */

#include <stdio.h>
#include <stdlib.h>
#include <string.h>
#include <errno.h>
#include <sys/time.h>
#include "libpq-fe.h"

static void
exit_nicely(PGconn * conn)
{
  PQfinish(conn);
  exit(1);
}

int
main(int argc, char **argv)
{
  const char *conninfo;
  PGconn *conn;
  PGresult *res;
  PGnotify *notify;
  int nnotifies;

    /* If the user supplies a parameter on the command line,
```

```
   use it as the conninfo string; otherwise default to
   setting dbname=postgres and using environment
   variables or defaults for all other connection
   parameters. */
if (argc > 1)
  conninfo = argv[1];
else
  conninfo = "dbname = postgres";

/* Make a connection to the database */
conn = PQconnectdb(conninfo);

/* Check to see that the backend connection was
   successfully made */
if (PQstatus(conn) != CONNECTION_OK) {
  fprintf(stderr, "Connection to database failed: %s",
          PQerrorMessage(conn));
  exit_nicely(conn);
}

/* Issue LISTEN command to enable notifications from the
   rule's NOTIFY. */
res = PQexec(conn, "LISTEN TBL2");
if (PQresultStatus(res) != PGRES_COMMAND_OK) {
  fprintf(stderr, "LISTEN command failed: %s",
          PQerrorMessage(conn));
  PQclear(res);
  exit_nicely(conn);
}

/* should PQclear PGresult whenever it is no longer
   needed to avoid memory leaks */
PQclear(res);

/* Quit after four notifies are received. */
nnotifies = 0;
while (nnotifies < 4) {
  /* Sleep until something happens on the connection.  We
     use select(2) to wait for input, but you could also
     use poll() or similar facilities. */
  int sock;
  fd_set input_mask;

  sock = PQsocket(conn);

  if (sock < 0)
    break;  /* shouldn't happen */
```

```
        FD_ZERO(&input_mask);
        FD_SET(sock, &input_mask);

        if (select(sock + 1, &input_mask, NULL, NULL, NULL) < 0) {
          fprintf(stderr, "select() failed: %s\n",
                  strerror(errno));
          exit_nicely(conn);
        }

        /* Now check for input */
        PQconsumeInput(conn);
        while ((notify = PQnotifies(conn)) != NULL) {
          fprintf(stderr,
                  "ASYNC NOTIFY of '%s' received from
                   backend pid %d\n",
                  notify->relname, notify->be_pid);
          PQfreemem(notify);
          nnotifies++;
        }
      }

    fprintf(stderr, "Done.\n");

    /* close the connection to the database and cleanup */
    PQfinish(conn);

    return 0;
}
```

libpq Example Program 3:

```
/*testlibpq3.c
 *       Test out-of-line parameters and binary I/O.
 *
 * Before running this, populate a database with the
 following commands
 * (provided in src/test/examples/testlibpq3.sql):
 *
 * CREATE TABLE test1 (i int4, t text, b bytea);
 *
 * INSERT INTO test1 values (1, 'joe''s place',
 '\\000\\001\\002\\003\\004');
 * INSERT INTO test1 values (2, 'ho there',
 '\\004\\003\\002\\001\\000');
 *
 * The expected output is:
 *
 * tuple 0: got
 *   i = (4 bytes) 1
 *   t = (11 bytes) 'joe's place'
 *   b = (5 bytes) \000\001\002\003\004
 *
 * tuple 0: got
 *   i = (4 bytes) 2
 *   t = (8 bytes) 'ho there'
 *   b = (5 bytes) \004\003\002\001\000
 */

#include <stdio.h>
#include <stdlib.h>
#include <string.h>
#include <sys/types.h>
#include "libpq-fe.h"

/* for ntohl/htonl */
#include <netinet/in.h>
#include <arpa/inet.h>


static void
exit_nicely(PGconn * conn)
{
  PQfinish(conn);
  exit(1);
}

/* This function prints a query result that is a
   binary-format fetch from a table defined as in the
```

```
     comment above.  We split it out because the main()
     function uses it twice. */
static void
show_binary_results(PGresult * res)
{
  int i, j;
  int i_fnum, t_fnum, b_fnum;

  /* Use PQfnumber to avoid assumptions about field order
     in result */
  i_fnum = PQfnumber(res, "i");
  t_fnum = PQfnumber(res, "t");
  b_fnum = PQfnumber(res, "b");

  for (i = 0; i < PQntuples(res); i++) {
    char *iptr;
    char *tptr;
    char *bptr;
    int blen;
    int ival;

    /* Get the field values (we ignore possibility they are
       null!) */
    iptr = PQgetvalue(res, i, i_fnum);
    tptr = PQgetvalue(res, i, t_fnum);
    bptr = PQgetvalue(res, i, b_fnum);

    /* The binary representation of INT4 is in network byte
       order, which we'd better coerce to the local byte
       order. */
    ival = ntohl(*((uint32_t *) iptr));

    /* The binary representation of TEXT is, well, text,
       and since libpq was nice enough to append a zero
       byte to it, it'll work just fine as a C string. The
       binary representation of BYTEA is a bunch of bytes,
       which could include embedded nulls so we have to pay
       attention to field length. */
    blen = PQgetlength(res, i, b_fnum);

    printf("tuple %d: got\n", i);
    printf(" i = (%d bytes) %d\n",
           PQgetlength(res, i, i_fnum), ival);
    printf(" t = (%d bytes) '%s'\n",
           PQgetlength(res, i, t_fnum), tptr);
    printf(" b = (%d bytes) ", blen);
    for (j = 0; j < blen; j++)
      printf("\\%03o", bptr[j]);
```

```
      printf("\n\n");
  }
}

int
main(int argc, char **argv)
{
  const char *conninfo;
  PGconn *conn;
  PGresult *res;
  const char *paramValues[1];
  int paramLengths[1];
  int paramFormats[1];
  uint32_t binaryIntVal;

  /* If the user supplies a parameter on the command line,
     use it as the conninfo string; otherwise default to
     setting dbname=postgres and using environment
     variables or defaults for all other connection
     parameters. */
  if (argc > 1)
    conninfo = argv[1];
  else
    conninfo = "dbname = postgres";

  /* Make a connection to the database */
  conn = PQconnectdb(conninfo);

  /* Check to see that the backend connection was
     successfully made */
  if (PQstatus(conn) != CONNECTION_OK) {
    fprintf(stderr, "Connection to database failed: %s",
            PQerrorMessage(conn));
    exit_nicely(conn);
  }

  /* The point of this program is to illustrate use of
     PQexecParams() with out-of-line parameters, as well as
     binary transmission of data. This first example
     transmits the parameters as text, but receives the
     results in binary format.  By using out-of-line
     parameters we can avoid a lot of tedious mucking about
     with quoting and escaping, even though the data is
     text.  Notice how we don't have to do anything special
     with the quote mark in the parameter value. */

  /* Here is our out-of-line parameter value */
  paramValues[0] = "joe's place";
```

```
res =
    PQexecParams(conn, "SELECT * FROM test1 WHERE t = $1",
                /* one param */
                1,
                /* let the backend deduce param type */
                NULL, paramValues, NULL, /* don't need
                                            param
                                            lengths
                                            since text */
                NULL,  /* default to all text params */
                /* ask for binary results */
                1);

if (PQresultStatus(res) != PGRES_TUPLES_OK) {
  fprintf(stderr, "SELECT failed: %s",
          PQerrorMessage(conn));
  PQclear(res);
  exit_nicely(conn);
}

show_binary_results(res);

PQclear(res);

/* In this second example we transmit an integer
   parameter in binary form, and again retrieve the
   results in binary form. Although we tell PQexecParams
   we are letting the backend deduce parameter type, we
   really force the decision by casting the parameter
   symbol in the query text.  This is a good safety
   measure when sending binary parameters. */

/* Convert integer value "2" to network byte order */
binaryIntVal = htonl((uint32_t) 2);

/* Set up parameter arrays for PQexecParams */
paramValues[0] = (char *) &binaryIntVal;
paramLengths[0] = sizeof(binaryIntVal);
paramFormats[0] = 1;   /* binary */

res =
    PQexecParams(conn,
                "SELECT * FROM test1 WHERE i =
                 $1::int4",
                /* one param */
                1,
                /* let the backend deduce param type */
```

```
                        NULL, paramValues, paramLengths,
                        paramFormats,
                        /* ask for binary results */
                        1);

  if (PQresultStatus(res) != PGRES_TUPLES_OK) {
    fprintf(stderr, "SELECT failed: %s",
            PQerrorMessage(conn));
    PQclear(res);
    exit_nicely(conn);
  }

  show_binary_results(res);

  PQclear(res);

  /* close the connection to the database and cleanup */
  PQfinish(conn);

  return 0;
}
```

2 Large Objects

PostgreSQL has a *large object* facility, which provides stream-style access
to user data that is stored in a special large-object structure. Streaming access is useful when working with data values that are too large to manipulate
conveniently as a whole.

This chapter describes the implementation and the programming and query
language interfaces to PostgreSQL large object data. We use the libpq C library
for the examples in this chapter, but most programming interfaces native to
PostgreSQL support equivalent functionality. Other interfaces may use the large
object interface internally to provide generic support for large values. This is
not described here.

2.1 Introduction

All large objects are placed in a single system table called pg_largeobject.
PostgreSQL also supports a storage system called "TOAST" that automatically
stores values larger than a single database page into a secondary storage area per
table. This makes the large object facility partially obsolete. One remaining
advantage of the large object facility is that it allows values up to 2 GB in
size, whereas TOASTed fields can be at most 1 GB. Also, large objects can be
randomly modified using a read/write API that is more efficient than performing
such operations using TOAST.

2.2 Implementation Features

The large object implementation breaks large objects up into "chunks" and
stores the chunks in rows in the database. A B-tree index guarantees fast
searches for the correct chunk number when doing random access reads and
writes.

2.3 Client Interfaces

This section describes the facilities that PostgreSQL client interface libraries
provide for accessing large objects. All large object manipulation using these
functions *must* take place within an SQL transaction block. The PostgreSQL
large object interface is modeled after the Unix file-system interface, with analogues of open, read, write, lseek, etc.

Client applications which use the large object interface in libpq should include
the header file 'libpq/libpq-fs.h' and link with the libpq library.

2.3.1 Creating a Large Object

The function

```
Oid lo_creat(PGconn *conn, int mode);
```

creates a new large object. The return value is the OID that was assigned to the new large object, or InvalidOid (zero) on failure. *mode* is unused and ignored as of PostgreSQL 8.1; however, for backwards compatibility with earlier releases it is best to set it to INV_READ, INV_WRITE, or INV_READ | INV_WRITE. (These symbolic constants are defined in the header file 'libpq/libpq-fs.h'.)

An example:

```
inv_oid = lo_creat(conn, INV_READ|INV_WRITE);
```

The function

```
Oid lo_create(PGconn *conn, Oid lobjId);
```

also creates a new large object. The OID to be assigned can be specified by *lobjId*; if so, failure occurs if that OID is already in use for some large object. If *lobjId* is InvalidOid (zero) then lo_create assigns an unused OID (this is the same behavior as lo_creat). The return value is the OID that was assigned to the new large object, or InvalidOid (zero) on failure.

lo_create is new as of PostgreSQL 8.1; if this function is run against an older server version, it will fail and return InvalidOid.

An example:

```
inv_oid = lo_create(conn, desired_oid);
```

2.3.2 Importing a Large Object

To import an operating system file as a large object, call

```
Oid lo_import(PGconn *conn, const char *filename);
```

filename specifies the operating system name of the file to be imported as a large object. The return value is the OID that was assigned to the new large object, or InvalidOid (zero) on failure. Note that the file is read by the client interface library, not by the server; so it must exist in the client file system and be readable by the client application.

2.3.3 Exporting a Large Object

To export a large object into an operating system file, call

```
int lo_export(PGconn *conn, Oid lobjId, const char *filename);
```

The lobjId argument specifies the OID of the large object to export and the filename argument specifies the operating system name of the file. Note that the file is written by the client interface library, not by the server. Returns 1 on success, -1 on failure.

2.3.4 Opening an Existing Large Object

To open an existing large object for reading or writing, call

```
int lo_open(PGconn *conn, Oid lobjId, int mode);
```

The `lobjId` argument specifies the OID of the large object to open. The mode bits control whether the object is opened for reading (`INV_READ`), writing (`INV_WRITE`), or both. (These symbolic constants are defined in the header file 'libpq/libpq-fs.h'.) A large object cannot be opened before it is created. `lo_open` returns a (non-negative) large object descriptor for later use in `lo_read`, `lo_write`, `lo_lseek`, `lo_tell`, and `lo_close`. The descriptor is only valid for the duration of the current transaction. On failure, -1 is returned.

The server currently does not distinguish between modes `INV_WRITE` and `INV_READ | INV_WRITE`: you are allowed to read from the descriptor in either case. However there is a significant difference between these modes and `INV_READ` alone: with `INV_READ` you cannot write on the descriptor, and the data read from it will reflect the contents of the large object at the time of the transaction snapshot that was active when `lo_open` was executed, regardless of later writes by this or other transactions. Reading from a descriptor opened with `INV_WRITE` returns data that reflects all writes of other committed transactions as well as writes of the current transaction. This is similar to the behavior of `SERIALIZABLE` versus `READ COMMITTED` transaction modes for ordinary SQL `SELECT` commands.

An example:

```
inv_fd = lo_open(conn, inv_oid, INV_READ|INV_WRITE);
```

2.3.5 Writing Data to a Large Object

The function

```
int lo_write(PGconn *conn, int fd, const char *buf, size_t len);
```

writes `len` bytes from `buf` to large object descriptor `fd`. The `fd` argument must have been returned by a previous `lo_open`. The number of bytes actually written is returned. In the event of an error, the return value is negative.

2.3.6 Reading Data from a Large Object

The function

```
int lo_read(PGconn *conn, int fd, char *buf, size_t len);
```

reads `len` bytes from large object descriptor `fd` into `buf`. The `fd` argument must have been returned by a previous `lo_open`. The number of bytes actually read is returned. In the event of an error, the return value is negative.

2.3.7 Seeking in a Large Object

To change the current read or write location associated with a large object descriptor, call

```
int lo_lseek(PGconn *conn, int fd, int offset, int whence);
```

This function moves the current location pointer for the large object descriptor identified by fd to the new location specified by offset. The valid values for whence are SEEK_SET (seek from object start), SEEK_CUR (seek from current position), and SEEK_END (seek from object end). The return value is the new location pointer, or -1 on error.

2.3.8 Obtaining the Seek Position of a Large Object

To obtain the current read or write location of a large object descriptor, call

```
int lo_tell(PGconn *conn, int fd);
```

If there is an error, the return value is negative.

2.3.9 Closing a Large Object Descriptor

A large object descriptor may be closed by calling

```
int lo_close(PGconn *conn, int fd);
```

where fd is a large object descriptor returned by lo_open. On success, lo_close returns zero. On error, the return value is negative.

Any large object descriptors that remain open at the end of a transaction will be closed automatically.

2.3.10 Removing a Large Object

To remove a large object from the database, call

```
int lo_unlink(PGconn *conn, Oid lobjId);
```

The lobjId argument specifies the OID of the large object to remove. Returns 1 if successful, -1 on failure.

2.4 Server-Side Functions

There are server-side functions callable from SQL that correspond to each of the client-side functions described above; indeed, for the most part the client-side functions are simply interfaces to the equivalent server-side functions. The ones that are actually useful to call via SQL commands are lo_creat, lo_create, lo_unlink, lo_import, and lo_export. Here are examples of their use:

```
CREATE TABLE image (
    name        text,
    raster      oid
);

SELECT lo_creat(-1);       -- returns OID of new, empty large
    object
```

```
SELECT lo_create(43213);    -- attempts to create large object
  with OID 43213

SELECT lo_unlink(173454);  -- deletes large object with OID
  173454

INSERT INTO image (name, raster)
    VALUES ('beautiful image', lo_import('/etc/motd'));

SELECT lo_export(image.raster, '/tmp/motd') FROM image
    WHERE name = 'beautiful image';
```

The server-side lo_import and lo_export functions behave considerably differently from their client-side analogs. These two functions read and write files in the server's file system, using the permissions of the database's owning user. Therefore, their use is restricted to superusers. In contrast, the client-side import and export functions read and write files in the client's file system, using the permissions of the client program. The client-side functions can be used by any PostgreSQL user.

2.5 Example Program

Large Objects with libpq Example Program is a sample program which shows how the large object interface in libpq can be used. Parts of the program are commented out but are left in the source for the reader's benefit. This program can also be found in 'src/test/examples/testlo.c' in the source distribution.

Large Objects with libpq Example Program:

```
/*-------------------------------------------------------------------
 *
 * testlo.c--
 *    test using large objects with libpq
 *
 * Copyright (c) 1994, Regents of the University of California
 *
 *-------------------------------------------------------------------
 */
#include <stdio.h>
#include "libpq-fe.h"
#include "libpq/libpq-fs.h"

#define BUFSIZE         1024

/* importFile import file "in_filename" into database as
   large object "lobjOid" */
Oid
importFile(PGconn * conn, char *filename)
{
  Oid lobjId;
  int lobj_fd;
```

```
  char buf[BUFSIZE];
  int nbytes, tmp;
  int fd;

  /* open the file to be read in */
  fd = open(filename, O_RDONLY, 0666);
  if (fd < 0) { /* error */
    fprintf(stderr, "can't open unix file %s\n", filename);
  }

  /* create the large object */
  lobjId = lo_creat(conn, INV_READ | INV_WRITE);
  if (lobjId == 0)
    fprintf(stderr, "can't create large object\n");

  lobj_fd = lo_open(conn, lobjId, INV_WRITE);

  /* read in from the Unix file and write to the inversion
     file */
  while ((nbytes = read(fd, buf, BUFSIZE)) > 0) {
    tmp = lo_write(conn, lobj_fd, buf, nbytes);
    if (tmp < nbytes)
      fprintf(stderr, "error while reading large object\n");
  }

  (void) close(fd);
  (void) lo_close(conn, lobj_fd);

  return lobjId;
}

void
pickout(PGconn * conn, Oid lobjId, int start, int len)
{
  int lobj_fd;
  char *buf;
  int nbytes;
  int nread;

  lobj_fd = lo_open(conn, lobjId, INV_READ);
  if (lobj_fd < 0) {
    fprintf(stderr, "can't open large object %d\n", lobjId);
  }

  lo_lseek(conn, lobj_fd, start, SEEK_SET);
  buf = malloc(len + 1);

  nread = 0;
```

```
      while (len - nread > 0) {
        nbytes = lo_read(conn, lobj_fd, buf, len - nread);
        buf[nbytes] = ' ';
        fprintf(stderr, ">>> %s", buf);
        nread += nbytes;
      }
      free(buf);
      fprintf(stderr, "\n");
      lo_close(conn, lobj_fd);
    }

    void
    overwrite(PGconn * conn, Oid lobjId, int start, int len)
    {
      int lobj_fd;
      char *buf;
      int nbytes;
      int nwritten;
      int i;

      lobj_fd = lo_open(conn, lobjId, INV_WRITE);
      if (lobj_fd < 0) {
        fprintf(stderr, "can't open large object %d\n", lobjId);
      }

      lo_lseek(conn, lobj_fd, start, SEEK_SET);
      buf = malloc(len + 1);

      for (i = 0; i < len; i++)
        buf[i] = 'X';
      buf[i] = ' ';

      nwritten = 0;
      while (len - nwritten > 0) {
        nbytes =
            lo_write(conn, lobj_fd, buf + nwritten,
                    len - nwritten);
        nwritten += nbytes;
      }
      free(buf);
      fprintf(stderr, "\n");
      lo_close(conn, lobj_fd);
    }

    /* exportFile export large object "lobjOid" to file
       "out_filename" */
    void
    exportFile(PGconn * conn, Oid lobjId, char *filename)
```

```
{
  int lobj_fd;
  char buf[BUFSIZE];
  int nbytes, tmp;
  int fd;

  /* open the large object */
  lobj_fd = lo_open(conn, lobjId, INV_READ);
  if (lobj_fd < 0) {
    fprintf(stderr, "can't open large object %d\n", lobjId);
  }

  /* open the file to be written to */
  fd = open(filename, O_CREAT | O_WRONLY, 0666);
  if (fd < 0) { /* error */
    fprintf(stderr, "can't open unix file %s\n", filename);
  }

  /* read in from the inversion file and write to the Unix
     file */
  while ((nbytes =
          lo_read(conn, lobj_fd, buf, BUFSIZE)) > 0) {
    tmp = write(fd, buf, nbytes);
    if (tmp < nbytes) {
      fprintf(stderr, "error while writing %s\n", filename);
    }
  }

  (void) lo_close(conn, lobj_fd);
  (void) close(fd);

  return;
}

void
exit_nicely(PGconn * conn)
{
  PQfinish(conn);
  exit(1);
}

int
main(int argc, char **argv)
{
  char *in_filename, *out_filename;
  char *database;
  Oid lobjOid;
  PGconn *conn;
```

```
PGresult *res;

if (argc != 4) {
  fprintf(stderr,
          "Usage: %s database_name in_filename
           out_filename\n",
          argv[0]);
  exit(1);
}

database = argv[1];
in_filename = argv[2];
out_filename = argv[3];

/* set up the connection */
conn = PQsetdb(NULL, NULL, NULL, NULL, database);

/* check to see that the backend connection was
   successfully made */
if (PQstatus(conn) == CONNECTION_BAD) {
  fprintf(stderr, "Connection to database '%s' failed.\n",
          database);
  fprintf(stderr, "%s", PQerrorMessage(conn));
  exit_nicely(conn);
}

res = PQexec(conn, "begin");
PQclear(res);

printf("importing file %s\n", in_filename);
/* lobjOid = importFile(conn, in_filename); */
lobjOid = lo_import(conn, in_filename);
/*
   printf("as large object %d.\n", lobjOid);

   printf("picking out bytes 1000-2000 of the large
   object\n"); pickout(conn, lobjOid, 1000, 1000);

   printf("overwriting bytes 1000-2000 of the large
   object with X's\n"); overwrite(conn, lobjOid, 1000,
   1000); */

printf("exporting large object to file %s\n",
       out_filename);
/* exportFile(conn, lobjOid, out_filename); */
lo_export(conn, lobjOid, out_filename);

res = PQexec(conn, "end");
```

```
        PQclear(res);
        PQfinish(conn);
        exit(0);
}
```

3 ECPG - Embedded SQL in C

This chapter describes the embedded SQL package for PostgreSQL. It was written by Linus Tolke[1] and Michael Meskes[2]. Originally it was written to work with C. It also works with C++, but it does not recognize all C++ constructs yet.

This chapter describes ECPG but does not provide a complete reference for embedded SQL in general. Additional information about embedded SQL can be found in Part 5 of the SQL standard, and many other resources about SQL.

3.1 The Concept

An embedded SQL program consists of code written in an ordinary programming language, in this case C, mixed with SQL commands in specially marked sections. To build the program, the source code is first passed through the embedded SQL preprocessor, which converts it to an ordinary C program, and afterwards it can be processed by a C compiler.

Embedded SQL has advantages over other methods for handling SQL commands from C code. First, it takes care of the tedious passing of information to and from variables in your C program. Second, the SQL code in the program is checked at build time for syntactical correctness. Third, embedded SQL in C is specified in the SQL standard and supported by many other SQL database systems. The PostgreSQL implementation is designed to match this standard as much as possible, and it is usually possible to port embedded SQL programs written for other SQL databases to PostgreSQL with relative ease.

As already stated, programs written for the embedded SQL interface are normal C programs with special code inserted to perform database-related actions. This special code always has the form

        EXEC SQL ...;

These statements syntactically take the place of a C statement. Depending on the particular statement, they may appear at the global level or within a function. Embedded SQL statements follow the case-sensitivity rules of normal SQL code, and not those of C.

The following sections explain all the embedded SQL statements.

---

[1] linus@epact.se

[2] meskes@postgresql.org

3.2 Connecting to the Database Server

A connection to a database can be made using the following statement:

```
EXEC SQL CONNECT TO target AS connection-name USER user-name;
```

The *target* can be specified in the following ways:

- *dbname* [*@hostname*] [*:port*]
- tcp:postgresql://*hostname* [*:port*] [*/dbname*] [*?options*]
- unix:postgresql://*hostname* [*:port*] [*/dbname*] [*?options*]
- an SQL string literal containing one of the above forms
- a reference to a character variable containing one of the above forms (see examples)
- DEFAULT

If you specify the connection target literally (that is, not through a variable reference) and you don't quote the value, then the case-insensitivity rules of normal SQL are applied. In that case you can also double-quote the individual parameters separately as needed. In practice, it is probably less error-prone to use a (single-quoted) string literal or a variable reference. The connection target DEFAULT initiates a connection to the default database under the default user name. No separate user name or connection name may be specified in that case.

There are also different ways to specify the user name:

- *username*
- *username*/*password*
- *username* IDENTIFIED BY *password*
- *username* USING *password*

As above, the parameters *username* and *password* may be an SQL identifier, an SQL string literal, or a reference to a character variable.

The *connection-name* is used to handle multiple connections in one program. It can be omitted if a program uses only one connection. The most recently opened connection becomes the current connection, which is used by default when an SQL statement is to be executed (see later in this chapter).

Here are some examples of CONNECT statements:

```
EXEC SQL CONNECT TO mydb@sql.mydomain.com;

EXEC SQL CONNECT TO unix:postgresql://sql.mydomain.com/mydb
 AS myconnection USER john;

EXEC SQL BEGIN DECLARE SECTION;
const char *target = "mydb@sql.mydomain.com";
const char *user = "john";
EXEC SQL END DECLARE SECTION;
 ...
EXEC SQL CONNECT TO :target USER :user;
```

The last form makes use of the variant referred to above as character variable reference. You will see in later sections how C variables can be used in SQL statements when you prefix them with a colon.

Be advised that the format of the connection target is not specified in the SQL standard. So if you want to develop portable applications, you might want to use something based on the last example above to encapsulate the connection target string somewhere.

3.3 Closing a Connection

To close a connection, use the following statement:

```
EXEC SQL DISCONNECT connection;
```

The *connection* can be specified in the following ways:

* *connection-name*
* DEFAULT
* CURRENT
* ALL

If no connection name is specified, the current connection is closed.

It is good style that an application always explicitly disconnect from every connection it opened.

3.4 Running SQL Commands

Any SQL command can be run from within an embedded SQL application. Below are some examples of how to do that.

Creating a table:

```
EXEC SQL CREATE TABLE foo (number integer, ascii char(16));
EXEC SQL CREATE UNIQUE INDEX num1 ON foo(number);
EXEC SQL COMMIT;
```

Inserting rows:

```
EXEC SQL INSERT INTO foo (number, ascii) VALUES (9999, 'doodad');
EXEC SQL COMMIT;
```

Deleting rows:

```
EXEC SQL DELETE FROM foo WHERE number = 9999;
EXEC SQL COMMIT;
```

Single-row select:

```
EXEC SQL SELECT foo INTO :FooBar FROM table1 WHERE ascii =
'doodad';
```

Select using cursors:

```
EXEC SQL DECLARE foo_bar CURSOR FOR
    SELECT number, ascii FROM foo
    ORDER BY ascii;
EXEC SQL OPEN foo_bar;
EXEC SQL FETCH foo_bar INTO :FooBar, DooDad;
```

```
...
EXEC SQL CLOSE foo_bar;
EXEC SQL COMMIT;
```

Updates:

```
EXEC SQL UPDATE foo
    SET ascii = 'foobar'
    WHERE number = 9999;
EXEC SQL COMMIT;
```

The tokens of the form :*something* are *host variables*, that is, they refer to variables in the C program. They are explained in Section 3.6 *Using Host Variables*, page 77.

In the default mode, statements are committed only when EXEC SQL COMMIT is issued. The embedded SQL interface also supports autocommit of transactions (similar to libpq behavior) via the -t command-line option to ecpg (see below) or via the EXEC SQL SET AUTOCOMMIT TO ON statement. In autocommit mode, each command is automatically committed unless it is inside an explicit transaction block. This mode can be explicitly turned off using EXEC SQL SET AUTOCOMMIT TO OFF.

3.5 Choosing a Connection

The SQL statements shown in the previous section are executed on the current connection, that is, the most recently opened one. If an application needs to manage multiple connections, then there are two ways to handle this.

The first option is to explicitly choose a connection for each SQL statement, for example

```
EXEC SQL AT connection-name SELECT ...;
```

This option is particularly suitable if the application needs to use several connections in mixed order.

If your application uses multiple threads of execution, they cannot share a connection concurrently. You must either explicitly control access to the connection (using mutexes) or use a connection for each thread. If each thread uses its own connection, you will need to use the AT clause to specify which connection the thread will use.

The second option is to execute a statement to switch the current connection. That statement is:

```
EXEC SQL SET CONNECTION connection-name;
```

This option is particularly convenient if many statements are to be executed on the same connection. It is not thread-aware.

3.6 Using Host Variables

In Section 3.4 *Running SQL Commands*, page 75 you saw how you can execute SQL statements from an embedded SQL program. Some of those statements only used fixed values and did not provide a way to insert user-supplied values into statements or have the program process the values returned by the query. Those kinds of statements are not really useful in real applications. This section explains in detail how you can pass data between your C program and the embedded SQL statements using a simple mechanism called *host variables*. In an embedded SQL program we consider the SQL statements to be *guests* in the C program code which is the *host language*. Therefore the variables of the C program are called *host variables*.

3.6.1 Overview

Passing data between the C program and the SQL statements is particularly simple in embedded SQL. Instead of having the program paste the data into the statement, which entails various complications, such as properly quoting the value, you can simply write the name of a C variable into the SQL statement, prefixed by a colon. For example:

```
EXEC SQL INSERT INTO sometable VALUES (:v1, 'foo', :v2);
```

This statements refers to two C variables named v1 and v2 and also uses a regular SQL string literal, to illustrate that you are not restricted to use one kind of data or the other.

This style of inserting C variables in SQL statements works anywhere a value expression is expected in an SQL statement.

3.6.2 Declare Sections

To pass data from the program to the database, for example as parameters in a query, or to pass data from the database back to the program, the C variables that are intended to contain this data need to be declared in specially marked sections, so the embedded SQL preprocessor is made aware of them.

This section starts with

```
EXEC SQL BEGIN DECLARE SECTION;
```

and ends with

```
EXEC SQL END DECLARE SECTION;
```

Between those lines, there must be normal C variable declarations, such as

```
int    x = 4;
char   foo[16], bar[16];
```

As you can see, you can optionally assign an initial value to the variable. The variable's scope is determined by the location of its declaring section within the program. You can also declare variables with the following syntax which implicitly creates a declare section:

```
EXEC SQL int i = 4;
```
You can have as many declare sections in a program as you like.

The declarations are also echoed to the output file as normal C variables, so there's no need to declare them again. Variables that are not intended to be used in SQL commands can be declared normally outside these special sections.

The definition of a structure or union also must be listed inside a DECLARE section. Otherwise the preprocessor cannot handle these types since it does not know the definition.

3.6.3 Different types of host variables

As a host variable you can also use arrays, typedefs, structs and pointers. Moreover there are special types of host variables that exist only in ECPG.

Here are a few examples of host variables:

Arrays
> One of the most common uses of an array declaration is probably the allocation of a char array as in
>
> ```
> EXEC SQL BEGIN DECLARE SECTION;
>     char str[50];
> EXEC SQL END DECLARE SECTION;
> ```
>
> Note that you have to take care of the length for yourself. If you use this host variable as the target variable of a query which returns a string with more than 49 characters, a buffer overflow occurs.

Typedefs
> Use the typedef keyword to map new types to already existing types.
>
> ```
> EXEC SQL BEGIN DECLARE SECTION;
>     typedef char mychartype[40];
>     typedef long serial_t;
> EXEC SQL END DECLARE SECTION;
> ```
>
> Note that you could also use
>
> ```
> EXEC SQL TYPE serial_t IS long;
> ```
>
> This declaration does not need to be part of a declare section.

Pointers
> You can declare pointers to the most common types. Note however that you cannot use pointers as target variables of queries without auto-allocation. See Section 3.10 *Using SQL Descriptor Areas*, page 107 for more information on auto-allocation.
>
> ```
> EXEC SQL BEGIN DECLARE SECTION;
>     int   *intp;
>     char **charp;
> EXEC SQL END DECLARE SECTION;
> ```

Special types of variables

ECPG contains some special types that help you to interact easily with data from the SQL server. For example it has implemented support for the varchar, numeric, date, timestamp, and interval types. Section 3.8 *pgtypes library*, page 82 contains basic functions to deal with those types, such that you do not need to send a query to the SQL server just for adding an interval to a timestamp for example.

The special type VARCHAR is converted into a named struct for every variable. A declaration like

```
VARCHAR var[180];
```

is converted into

```
struct varchar_var { int len; char arr[180]; } var;
```

This structure is suitable for interfacing with SQL datums of type varchar.

3.6.4 SELECT INTO and FETCH INTO

Now you should be able to pass data generated by your program into an SQL command. But how do you retrieve the results of a query? For that purpose, embedded SQL provides special variants of the usual commands SELECT and FETCH. These commands have a special INTO clause that specifies which host variables the retrieved values are to be stored in.

Here is an example:

```
/*assume this table:
 * CREATE TABLE test1 (a int, b varchar(50));
 */

EXEC SQL BEGIN DECLARE SECTION;
int v1;
VARCHAR v2;
EXEC SQL END DECLARE SECTION;


    ...


EXEC SQL SELECT a, b INTO :v1, :v2 FROM test;
```

So the INTO clause appears between the select list and the FROM clause. The number of elements in the select list and the list after INTO (also called the target list) must be equal.

Here is an example using the command FETCH:

```
EXEC SQL BEGIN DECLARE SECTION;
int v1;
VARCHAR v2;
EXEC SQL END DECLARE SECTION;


    ...


EXEC SQL DECLARE foo CURSOR FOR SELECT a, b FROM test;
```

```
    ...
do {
    ...
    EXEC SQL FETCH NEXT FROM foo INTO :v1, :v2;
    ...
} while (...);
```
Here the INTO clause appears after all the normal clauses.

Both of these methods only allow retrieving one row at a time. If you need to process result sets that potentially contain more than one row, you need to use a cursor, as shown in the second example.

3.6.5 Indicators

The examples above do not handle null values. In fact, the retrieval examples will raise an error if they fetch a null value from the database. To be able to pass null values to the database or retrieve null values from the database, you need to append a second host variable specification to each host variable that contains data. This second host variable is called the *indicator* and contains a flag that tells whether the datum is null, in which case the value of the real host variable is ignored. Here is an example that handles the retrieval of null values correctly:

```
EXEC SQL BEGIN DECLARE SECTION;
VARCHAR val;
int val_ind;
EXEC SQL END DECLARE SECTION:

    ...

EXEC SQL SELECT b INTO :val :val_ind FROM test1;
```
The indicator variable val_ind will be zero if the value was not null, and it will be negative if the value was null.

The indicator has another function: if the indicator value is positive, it means that the value is not null, but it was truncated when it was stored in the host variable.

3.7 Dynamic SQL

In many cases, the particular SQL statements that an application has to execute are known at the time the application is written. In some cases, however, the SQL statements are composed at run time or provided by an external source. In these cases you cannot embed the SQL statements directly into the C source code, but there is a facility that allows you to call arbitrary SQL statements that you provide in a string variable.

The simplest way to execute an arbitrary SQL statement is to use the command EXECUTE IMMEDIATE. For example:

```
EXEC SQL BEGIN DECLARE SECTION;
const char *stmt = "CREATE TABLE test1 (...);";
EXEC SQL END DECLARE SECTION;

EXEC SQL EXECUTE IMMEDIATE :stmt;
```

You may not execute statements that retrieve data (e.g., SELECT) this way.

A more powerful way to execute arbitrary SQL statements is to prepare them once and execute the prepared statement as often as you like. It is also possible to prepare a generalized version of a statement and then execute specific versions of it by substituting parameters. When preparing the statement, write question marks where you want to substitute parameters later. For example:

```
EXEC SQL BEGIN DECLARE SECTION;
const char *stmt = "INSERT INTO test1 VALUES(?, ?);";
EXEC SQL END DECLARE SECTION;

EXEC SQL PREPARE mystmt FROM :stmt;
 ...
EXEC SQL EXECUTE mystmt USING 42, 'foobar';
```

If the statement you are executing returns values, then add an INTO clause:

```
EXEC SQL BEGIN DECLARE SECTION;
const char *stmt = "SELECT a, b, c FROM test1 WHERE a > ?";
int v1, v2;
VARCHAR v3;
EXEC SQL END DECLARE SECTION;

EXEC SQL PREPARE mystmt FROM :stmt;
 ...
EXEC SQL EXECUTE mystmt INTO v1, v2, v3 USING 37;
```

An EXECUTE command may have an INTO clause, a USING clause, both, or neither.

When you don't need the prepared statement anymore, you should deallocate it:

```
EXEC SQL DEALLOCATE PREPARE name;
```

3.8 pgtypes library

The pgtypes library maps PostgreSQL database types to C equivalents that can be used in C programs. It also offers functions to do basic calculations with those types within C, i.e. without the help of the PostgreSQL server. See the following example:

```
EXEC SQL BEGIN DECLARE SECTION;
    date date1;
    timestamp ts1, tsout;
    interval iv1;
    char *out;
EXEC SQL END DECLARE SECTION;

PGTYPESdate_today(&date1);
EXEC SQL SELECT started, duration INTO :ts1, :iv1 FROM
 datetbl WHERE d=:date1;
PGTYPEStimestamp_add_interval(&ts1, &iv1, &tsout);
out = PGTYPEStimestamp_to_asc(&tsout);
printf("Started + duration: %s\n", out);
free(out);
```

3.8.1 The numeric type

The numeric type allows calculations with arbitrary precision. See Volume 1, Section 6.1 *Numeric Types* for the equivalent type in the PostgreSQL server. Because of the arbitrary precision this variable needs to be able to expand and shrink dynamically. That's why you can only create variables on the heap by means of the PGTYPESnumeric_new and PGTYPESnumeric_free functions. The decimal type, which is similar but limited in the precision, can be created on the stack as well as on the heap.

The following functions can be used to work with the numeric type:

PGTYPESnumeric_new
> Request a pointer to a newly allocated numeric variable.

> > `numeric *PGTYPESnumeric_new(void);`

PGTYPESnumeric_free
> Free a numeric type, release all of its memory.

> > `void PGTYPESnumeric_free(numeric *var);`

PGTYPESnumeric_from_asc
> Parse a numeric type from its string notation.

> > `numeric *PGTYPESnumeric_from_asc(char *str, char **endptr);`

> Valid formats are for example: -2, .794, +3.44, 592.49E07 or -32.84e-4. If the value could be parsed successfully, a valid pointer is returned, else the NULL pointer. At the moment ecpg always parses the complete string and so it currently does not support storing the address of the first invalid character in *endptr. You can safely set endptr to NULL.

PGTYPESnumeric_to_asc

> Returns a pointer to a string allocated by malloc that contains the string representation of the numeric type num.
>
>> `char *PGTYPESnumeric_to_asc(numeric *num, int dscale);`
>
> The numeric value will be printed with dscale decimal digits, with rounding applied if necessary.

PGTYPESnumeric_add

> Add two numeric variables into a third one.
>
>> `int PGTYPESnumeric_add(numeric *var1, numeric *var2,`
>> `numeric *result);`
>
> The function adds the variables var1 and var2 into the result variable result. The function returns 0 on success and -1 in case of error.

PGTYPESnumeric_sub

> Subtract two numeric variables and return the result in a third one.
>
>> `int PGTYPESnumeric_sub(numeric *var1, numeric *var2,`
>> `numeric *result);`
>
> The function subtracts the variable var2 from the variable var1. The result of the operation is stored in the variable result. The function returns 0 on success and -1 in case of error.

PGTYPESnumeric_mul

> Multiply two numeric variables and return the result in a third one.
>
>> `int PGTYPESnumeric_mul(numeric *var1, numeric *var2,`
>> `numeric *result);`
>
> The function multiplies the variables var1 and var2. The result of the operation is stored in the variable result. The function returns 0 on success and -1 in case of error.

PGTYPESnumeric_div

> Divide two numeric variables and return the result in a third one.
>
>> `int PGTYPESnumeric_div(numeric *var1, numeric *var2,`
>> `numeric *result);`
>
> The function divides the variables var1 by var2. The result of the operation is stored in the variable result. The function returns 0 on success and -1 in case of error.

PGTYPESnumeric_cmp

> Compare two numeric variables.
>
>> `int PGTYPESnumeric_cmp(numeric *var1, numeric *var2)`
>
> This function compares two numeric variables. In case of error, INT_MAX is returned. On success, the function returns one of three possible results:
>
> - 1, if var1 is bigger than var2
> - -1, if var1 is smaller than var2
> - 0, if var1 and var2 are equal

PGTYPESnumeric_from_int

> Convert an int variable to a numeric variable.

>> int PGTYPESnumeric_from_int(signed int int_val, numeric
>> *var);

> This function accepts a variable of type signed int and stores it in the numeric variable var. Upon success, 0 is returned and -1 in case of a failure.

PGTYPESnumeric_from_long

> Convert a long int variable to a numeric variable.

>> int PGTYPESnumeric_from_long(signed long int long_val,
>> numeric *var);

> This function accepts a variable of type signed long int and stores it in the numeric variable var. Upon success, 0 is returned and -1 in case of a failure.

PGTYPESnumeric_copy

> Copy over one numeric variable into another one.

>> int PGTYPESnumeric_copy(numeric *src, numeric *dst);

> This function copies over the value of the variable that src points to into the variable that dst points to. It returns 0 on success and -1 if an error occurs.

PGTYPESnumeric_from_double

> Convert a variable of type double to a numeric.

>> int PGTYPESnumeric_from_double(double d, numeric *dst);

> This function accepts a variable of type double and stores the result in the variable that dst points to. It returns 0 on success and -1 if an error occurs.

PGTYPESnumeric_to_double

> Convert a variable of type numeric to double.

>> int PGTYPESnumeric_to_double(numeric *nv, double *dp)

> The function converts the numeric value from the variable that nv points to into the double variable that dp points to. It returns 0 on success and -1 if an error occurs, including overflow. On overflow, the global variable errno will also be set to PGTYPES_NUM_OVERFLOW.

PGTYPESnumeric_to_int

> Convert a variable of type numeric to int.

>> int PGTYPESnumeric_to_int(numeric *nv, int *ip);

> The function converts the numeric value from the variable that nv points to into the integer variable that ip points to. It returns 0 on success and -1 if an error occurs, including overflow. On overflow, the global variable errno will also be set to PGTYPES_NUM_OVERFLOW.

PGTYPESnumeric_to_long

> Convert a variable of type numeric to long.

```
int PGTYPESnumeric_to_long(numeric *nv, long *lp);
```

The function converts the numeric value from the variable that nv points to into the long integer variable that lp points to. It returns 0 on success and -1 if an error occurs, including overflow. On overflow, the global variable errno will also be set to PGTYPES_NUM_OVERFLOW.

PGTYPESnumeric_to_decimal
Convert a variable of type numeric to decimal.

```
int PGTYPESnumeric_to_decimal(numeric *src, decimal *dst);
```

The function converts the numeric value from the variable that src points to into the decimal variable that dst points to. It returns 0 on success and -1 if an error occurs, including overflow. On overflow, the global variable errno will also be set to PGTYPES_NUM_OVERFLOW.

PGTYPESnumeric_from_decimal
Convert a variable of type decimal to numeric.

```
int PGTYPESnumeric_from_decimal(decimal *src, numeric *dst);
```

The function converts the decimal value from the variable that src points to into the numeric variable that dst points to. It returns 0 on success and -1 if an error occurs. Since the decimal type is implemented as a limited version of the numeric type, overflow cannot occur with this conversion.

3.8.2 The date type

The date type in C enables your programs to deal with data of the SQL type date. See Volume 1, Section 6.5 *Date/Time Types* for the equivalent type in the PostgreSQL server.

The following functions can be used to work with the date type:

PGTYPESdate_from_timestamp
Extract the date part from a timestamp.

```
date PGTYPESdate_from_timestamp(timestamp dt);
```

The function receives a timestamp as its only argument and returns the extracted date part from this timestamp.

PGTYPESdate_from_asc
Parse a date from its textual representation.

```
date PGTYPESdate_from_asc(char *str, char **endptr);
```

The function receives a C char* string str and a pointer to a C char* string endptr. At the moment ecpg always parses the complete string and so it currently does not support storing the address of the first invalid character in *endptr. You can safely set endptr to NULL.

Note that the function always assumes MDY-formatted dates and there is currently no variable to change that within ecpg.

The following input formats are allowed:

INPUT	RESULT
January 8, 1999	January 8, 1999
1999-01-08	January 8, 1999
1/8/1999	January 8, 1999
1/18/1999	January 18, 1999
01/02/03	February 1, 2003
1999-Jan-08	January 8, 1999
Jan-08-1999	January 8, 1999
08-Jan-1999	January 8, 1999
99-Jan-08	January 8, 1999
08-Jan-99	January 8, 1999
08-Jan-06	January 8, 2006
Jan-08-99	January 8, 1999
19990108	ISO 8601; January 8, 1999
990108	ISO 8601; January 8, 1999
1999.008	year and day of year
J2451187	Julian day
January 8, 99 BC	year 99 before the Common Era

Table 3.1: Valid input formats for PGTYPESdate_from_asc

PGTYPESdate_to_asc

Return the textual representation of a date variable.

    char *PGTYPESdate_to_asc(date dDate);

The function receives the date dDate as its only parameter. It will output the date in the form 1999-01-18, i.e. in the YYYY-MM-DD format.

PGTYPESdate_julmdy

Extract the values for the day, the month and the year from a variable of type date.

    void PGTYPESdate_julmdy(date d, int *mdy);

The function receives the date d and a pointer to an array of 3 integer values mdy. The variable name indicates the sequential order: mdy[0] will be set to contain the number of the month, mdy[1] will be set to the value of the day and mdy[2] will contain the year.

PGTYPESdate_mdyjul

Create a date value from an array of 3 integers that specify the day, the month and the year of the date.

    void PGTYPESdate_mdyjul(int *mdy, date *jdate);

The function receives the array of the 3 integers (mdy) as its first argument and as its second argument a pointer to a variable of type date that should hold the result of the operation.

PGTYPESdate_dayofweek

Return a number representing the day of the week for a date value.

```
int PGTYPESdate_dayofweek(date d);
```

The function receives the date variable d as its only argument and returns an integer that indicates the day of the week for this date.

- 0 - Sunday
- 1 - Monday
- 2 - Tuesday
- 3 - Wednesday
- 4 - Thursday
- 5 - Friday
- 6 - Saturday

PGTYPESdate_today

Get the current date.

```
void PGTYPESdate_today(date *d);
```

The function receives a pointer to a date variable (d) that it sets to the current date.

PGTYPESdate_fmt_asc

Convert a variable of type date to its textual representation using a format mask.

```
int PGTYPESdate_fmt_asc(date dDate, char *fmtstring, char
    *outbuf);
```

The function receives the date to convert (dDate), the format mask (fmtstring) and the string that will hold the textual representation of the date (outbuf).

On success, 0 is returned and a negative value if an error occurred.

The following literals are the field specifiers you can use:

- dd - The number of the day of the month.
- mm - The number of the month of the year.
- yy - The number of the year as a two digit number.
- yyyy - The number of the year as a four digit number.
- ddd - The name of the day (abbreviated).
- mmm - The name of the month (abbreviated).

All other characters are copied 1:1 to the output string.

The following table indicates a few possible formats. This will give you an idea of how to use this function. All output lines are based on the same date: November, 23rd, 1959.

FMT	RESULT
mmddyy	112359
ddmmyy	231159
yymmdd	591123
yy/mm/dd	59/11/23
yy mm dd	59 11 23
yy.mm.dd	59.11.23
.mm.yyyy.dd.	.11.1959.23.
mmm. dd, yyyy	Nov. 23, 1959
mmm dd yyyy	Nov 23 1959
yyyy dd mm	1959 23 11
ddd, mmm. dd, yyyy	Mon, Nov. 23, 1959
(ddd) mmm. dd, yyyy	(Mon) Nov. 23, 1959

Table 3.2: Valid input formats for PGTYPESdate_fmt_asc

PGTYPESdate_defmt_asc

Use a format mask to convert a C char* string to a value of type date.

```
int PGTYPESdate_defmt_asc(date *d, char *fmt, char *str);
```

The function receives a pointer to the date value that should hold the result of the operation (d), the format mask to use for parsing the date (fmt) and the C char* string containing the textual representation of the date (str). The textual representation is expected to match the format mask. However you do not need to have a 1:1 mapping of the string to the format mask. The function only analyzes the sequential order and looks for the literals yy or yyyy that indicate the position of the year, mm to indicate the position of the month and dd to indicate the position of the day.

The following table indicates a few possible formats. This will give you an idea of how to use this function.

FMT	STR	RESULT
ddmmyy	21-2-54	1954-02-21
ddmmyy	2-12-54	1954-12-02
ddmmyy	20111954	1954-11-20
ddmmyy	130464	1964-04-13
mmm.dd.yyyy	MAR-12-1967	1967-03-12
yy/mm/dd	1954, February 3rd	1954-02-03
mmm.dd.yyyy	041269	1969-04-12
yy/mm/dd	In the year 2525, in the month of July, mankind will be alive on the 28th day	2525-07-28
dd-mm-yy	I said on the 28th of July in the year 2525	2525-07-28
mmm.dd.yyyy	9/14/58	1958-09-14
yy/mm/dd	47/03/29	1947-03-29
mmm.dd.yyyy	oct 28 1975	1975-10-28
mmddyy	Nov 14th, 1985	1985-11-14

Table 3.3: Valid input formats for rdefmtdate

3.8.3 The timestamp type

The timestamp type in C enables your programs to deal with data of the SQL type timestamp. See Volume 1, Section 6.5 *Date/Time Types* for the equivalent type in the PostgreSQL server.

The following functions can be used to work with the timestamp type:

PGTYPEStimestamp_from_asc

Parse a timestamp from its textual representation into a timestamp variable.

```
timestamp PGTYPEStimestamp_from_asc(char *str, char
    **endptr);
```

The function receives the string to parse (str) and a pointer to a C char* (endptr). At the moment ecpg always parses the complete string and so it currently does not support storing the address of the first invalid character in *endptr. You can safely set endptr to NULL.

The function returns the parsed timestamp on success. On error, PGTYPESInvalidTimestamp is returned and errno is set to PGTYPES_TS_ BAD_TIMESTAMP. See *PGTYPESInvalidTimestamp*, page 95 for important notes on this value.

In general, the input string can contain any combination of an allowed date specification, a whitespace character and an allowed time specification. Note that timezones are not supported by ecpg. It can parse them but does not apply any calculation as the PostgreSQL server does for example. Timezone specifiers are silently discarded.

The following table contains a few examples for input strings:

INPUT	RESULT
1999-01-08 04:05:06	1999-01-08 04:05:06
January 8 04:05:06 1999 PST	1999-01-08 04:05:06
1999-Jan-08 04:05:06.789-8	1999-01-08 04:05:06.789 (time zone specifier ignored)
J2451187 04:05-08:00	1999-01-08 04:05:00 (time zone specifier ignored)

Table 3.4: Valid input formats for PGTYPEStimestamp_from_asc

PGTYPEStimestamp_to_asc

Converts a date to a C char* string.

```
char *PGTYPEStimestamp_to_asc(timestamp tstamp);
```

The function receives the timestamp tstamp as its only argument and returns an allocated string that contains the textual representation of the timestamp.

PGTYPEStimestamp_current

Retrieve the current timestamp.

```
void PGTYPEStimestamp_current(timestamp *ts);
```

The function retrieves the current timestamp and saves it into the timestamp variable that ts points to.

PGTYPEStimestamp_fmt_asc

Convert a timestamp variable to a C char* using a format mask.

```
int PGTYPEStimestamp_fmt_asc(timestamp *ts, char *output,
int str_len, char *fmtstr);
```

The function receives a pointer to the timestamp to convert as its first argument (ts), a pointer to the output buffer (output), the maximal length that has been allocated for the output buffer (str_len) and the format mask to use for the conversion (fmtstr).

Upon success, the function returns 0 and a negative value if an error occurred.

You can use the following format specifiers for the format mask. The format specifiers are the same ones that are used in the strftime function in libc. Any non-format specifier will be copied into the output buffer.

- %A - is replaced by national representation of the full weekday name.
- %a - is replaced by national representation of the abbreviated weekday name.
- %B - is replaced by national representation of the full month name.
- %b - is replaced by national representation of the abbreviated month name.
- %C - is replaced by (year / 100) as decimal number; single digits are preceded by a zero.
- %c - is replaced by national representation of time and date.
- %D - is equivalent to %m/%d/%y.
- %d - is replaced by the day of the month as a decimal number (01-31).
- %E* %O* - POSIX locale extensions. The sequences %Ec %EC %Ex %EX %Ey %EY %Od %Oe %OH %OI %Om %OM %OS %Ou %OU %OV %Ow %OW %Oy are supposed to provide alternate representations.

  Additionally %OB implemented to represent alternative months names (used standalone, without day mentioned).
- %e - is replaced by the day of month as a decimal number (1-31); single digits are preceded by a blank.
- %F - is equivalent to %Y-%m-%d.
- %G - is replaced by a year as a decimal number with century. This year is the one that contains the greater part of the week (Monday as the first day of the week).
- %g - is replaced by the same year as in %G, but as a decimal number without century (00-99).
- %H - is replaced by the hour (24-hour clock) as a decimal number (00-23).
- %h - the same as %b.
- %I - is replaced by the hour (12-hour clock) as a decimal number (01-12).

- %j - is replaced by the day of the year as a decimal number (001-366).
- %k - is replaced by the hour (24-hour clock) as a decimal number (0-23); single digits are preceded by a blank.
- %l - is replaced by the hour (12-hour clock) as a decimal number (1-12); single digits are preceded by a blank.
- %M - is replaced by the minute as a decimal number (00-59).
- %m - is replaced by the month as a decimal number (01-12).
- %n - is replaced by a newline.
- %O* - the same as %E*.
- %p - is replaced by national representation of either "ante meridiem" or "post meridiem" as appropriate.
- %R - is equivalent to %H:%M.
- %r - is equivalent to %I:%M:%S %p.
- %S - is replaced by the second as a decimal number (00-60).
- %s - is replaced by the number of seconds since the Epoch, UTC.
- %T - is equivalent to %H:%M:%S
- %t - is replaced by a tab.
- %U - is replaced by the week number of the year (Sunday as the first day of the week) as a decimal number (00-53).
- %u - is replaced by the weekday (Monday as the first day of the week) as a decimal number (1-7).
- %V - is replaced by the week number of the year (Monday as the first day of the week) as a decimal number (01-53). If the week containing January 1 has four or more days in the new year, then it is week 1; otherwise it is the last week of the previous year, and the next week is week 1.
- %v - is equivalent to %e-%b-%Y.
- %W - is replaced by the week number of the year (Monday as the first day of the week) as a decimal number (00-53).
- %w - is replaced by the weekday (Sunday as the first day of the week) as a decimal number (0-6).
- %X - is replaced by national representation of the time.
- %x - is replaced by national representation of the date.
- %Y - is replaced by the year with century as a decimal number.
- %y - is replaced by the year without century as a decimal number (00-99).
- %Z - is replaced by the time zone name.
- %z - is replaced by the time zone offset from UTC; a leading plus sign stands for east of UTC, a minus sign for west of UTC, hours and minutes follow with two digits each and no delimiter between them (common form for RFC 822 date headers).

- %+ - is replaced by national representation of the date and time.
- %-* - GNU libc extension. Do not do any padding when performing numerical outputs.
- $_* - GNU libc extension. Explicitly specify space for padding.
- %0* - GNU libc extension. Explicitly specify zero for padding.
- %% - is replaced by %.

PGTYPEStimestamp_sub

Subtract one timestamp from another one and save the result in a variable of type interval.

```
int PGTYPEStimestamp_sub(timestamp *ts1, timestamp *ts2,
interval *iv);
```

The function will subtract the timestamp variable that ts2 points to from the timestamp variable that ts1 points to and will store the result in the interval variable that iv points to.

Upon success, the function returns 0 and a negative value if an error occurred.

PGTYPEStimestamp_defmt_asc

Parse a timestamp value from its textual representation using a formatting mask.

```
int PGTYPEStimestamp_defmt_asc(char *str, char *fmt,
timestamp *d);
```

The function receives the textual representation of a timestamp in the variable str as well as the formatting mask to use in the variable fmt. The result will be stored in the variable that d points to.

If the formatting mask fmt is NULL, the function will fall back to the default formatting mask which is %Y-%m-%d %H:%M:%S.

This is the reverse function to *PGTYPEStimestamp_fmt_asc*, page 89. See the documentation there in order to find out about the possible formatting mask entries.

PGTYPEStimestamp_add_interval

Add an interval variable to a timestamp variable.

```
int PGTYPEStimestamp_add_interval(timestamp *tin,
interval *span, timestamp *tout);
```

The function receives a pointer to a timestamp variable tin and a pointer to an interval variable span. It adds the interval to the timestamp and saves the resulting timestamp in the variable that tout points to.

Upon success, the function returns 0 and a negative value if an error occurred.

PGTYPEStimestamp_sub_interval

Subtract an interval variable from a timestamp variable.

```
int PGTYPEStimestamp_sub_interval(timestamp *tin,
    interval *span, timestamp *tout);
```

The function subtracts the interval variable that span points to from the timestamp variable that tin points to and saves the result into the variable that tout points to.

Upon success, the function returns 0 and a negative value if an error occurred.

3.8.4 The interval type

The interval type in C enables your programs to deal with data of the SQL type interval. See Volume 1, Section 6.5 *Date/Time Types* for the equivalent type in the PostgreSQL server.

The following functions can be used to work with the interval type:

PGTYPESinterval_new
> Return a pointer to a newly allocated interval variable.
>
> ```
> interval *PGTYPESinterval_new(void);
> ```

PGTYPESinterval_free
> Release the memory of a previously allocated interval variable.
>
> ```
> void PGTYPESinterval_new(interval *intvl);
> ```

PGTYPESinterval_from_asc
> Parse an interval from its textual representation.
>
> ```
> interval *PGTYPESinterval_from_asc(char *str, char **endptr);
> ```
>
> The function parses the input string str and returns a pointer to an allocated interval variable. At the moment ecpg always parses the complete string and so it currently does not support storing the address of the first invalid character in *endptr. You can safely set endptr to NULL.

PGTYPESinterval_to_asc
> Convert a variable of type interval to its textual representation.
>
> ```
> char *PGTYPESinterval_to_asc(interval *span);
> ```
>
> The function converts the interval variable that span points to into a C char*. The output looks like this example: @ 1 day 12 hours 59 mins 10 secs.

PGTYPESinterval_copy
> Copy a variable of type interval.
>
> ```
> int PGTYPESinterval_copy(interval *intvlsrc, interval *intvldest);
> ```
>
> The function copies the interval variable that intvlsrc points to into the variable that intvldest points to. Note that you need to allocate the memory for the destination variable before.

3.8.5 The decimal type

The decimal type is similar to the numeric type. However it is limited to
a maximal precision of 30 significant digits. In contrast to the numeric type
which can be created on the heap only, the decimal type can be created either
on the stack or on the heap (by means of the functions `PGTYPESdecimal_new`
and `PGTYPESdecimal_free`). There are a lot of other functions that deal with
the decimal type in the Informix compatibility mode described in Section 3.9
Informix compatibility mode, page 95.

The following functions can be used to work with the decimal type and are
not only contained in the `libcompat` library.

PGTYPESdecimal_new
> Request a pointer to a newly allocated decimal variable.
>
> > `decimal *PGTYPESdecimal_new(void);`

PGTYPESdecimal_free
> Free a decimal type, release all of its memory.
>
> > `void PGTYPESdecimal_free(decimal *var);`

3.8.6 errno values of pgtypeslib

PGTYPES_NUM_BAD_NUMERIC
> An argument should contain a numeric variable (or point to a numeric
> variable) but in fact its in-memory representation was invalid.

PGTYPES_NUM_OVERFLOW
> An overflow occurred. Since the numeric type can deal with almost arbi-
> trary precision, converting a numeric variable into other types might cause
> overflow.

PGTYPES_NUM_OVERFLOW
> An underflow occurred. Since the numeric type can deal with almost arbi-
> trary precision, converting a numeric variable into other types might cause
> underflow.

PGTYPES_NUM_DIVIDE_ZERO
> A division by zero has been attempted.

PGTYPES_DATE_BAD_DATE
PGTYPES_DATE_ERR_EARGS
PGTYPES_DATE_ERR_ENOSHORTDATE
PGTYPES_INTVL_BAD_INTERVAL
PGTYPES_DATE_ERR_ENOTDMY
PGTYPES_DATE_BAD_DAY
PGTYPES_DATE_BAD_MONTH
PGTYPES_TS_BAD_TIMESTAMP

3.8.7 Special constants of pgtypeslib

PGTYPESInvalidTimestamp

A value of type timestamp representing an invalid time stamp. This is returned by the function PGTYPEStimestamp_from_asc on parse error. Note that due to the internal representation of the timestamp datatype, PGTYPESInvalidTimestamp is also a valid timestamp at the same time. It is set to 1899-12-31 23:59:59. In order to detect errors, make sure that your application does not only test for PGTYPESInvalidTimestamp but also for errno != 0 after each call to PGTYPEStimestamp_from_asc.

3.9 Informix compatibility mode

ecpg can be run in a so-called *Informix compatibility mode*. If this mode is active, it tries to behave as if it were the Informix precompiler for Informix E/SQL. This allows you to use the dollar sign instead of the EXEC SQL primitive to introduce embedded SQL commands.

```
$int j = 3;
$CONNECT TO :dbname;
$CREATE TABLE test(i INT PRIMARY KEY, j INT);
$INSERT INTO test(i, j) VALUES (7, :j);
$COMMIT;
```

There are two compatiblity modes: INFORMIX, INFORMIX_SE

When linking programs that use this compatibility mode, remember to link against libcompat that is shipped with ecpg.

Besides the previously explained syntactic sugar, the Informix compatibility mode ports some functions for input, output and transformation of data as well as embedded SQL statements known from E/SQL to ecpg.

Informix compatibility mode is closely connected to the pgtypeslib library of ecpg. pgtypeslib maps SQL data types to data types within the C host program and most of the additional functions of the Informix compatibility mode allow you to operate on those C host program types. Note however that the extent of the compatibility is limited. It does not try to copy Informix behaviour; it allows you to do more or less the same operations and gives you functions that have the same name and the same basic behavior but it is not a drop-in replacement if you are using Informix at the moment. Moreover, some of the data types are different. For example, PostgreSQL's datetime and interval types do not know about ranges like YEAR TO MINUTE so you won't find support in ecpg for that either.

3.9.1 Additional embedded SQL statements

CLOSE DATABASE

This statement closes the current connection. In fact, this is a synonym for ecpg's DISCONNECT CURRENT.

```
$CLOSE DATABASE;          /* close the current connection */
EXEC SQL CLOSE DATABASE;
```

3.9.2 Additional functions

decadd

Add two decimal type values.

        int decadd(decimal *arg1, decimal *arg2, decimal *sum);

The function receives a pointer to the first operand of type decimal (arg1), a pointer to the second operand of type decimal (arg2) and a pointer to a value of type decimal that will contain the sum (sum). On success, the function returns 0. ECPG_INFORMIX_NUM_OVERFLOW is returned in case of overflow and ECPG_INFORMIX_NUM_UNDERFLOW in case of underflow. -1 is returned for other failures and errno is set to the respective errno number of the pgtypeslib.

deccmp

Compare two variables of type decimal.

        int deccmp(decimal *arg1, decimal *arg2);

The function receives a pointer to the first decimal value (arg1), a pointer to the second decimal value (arg2) and returns an integer value that indicates which is the bigger value.

- 1, if the value that arg1 points to is bigger than the value that var2 points to
- -1, if the value that arg1 points to is smaller than the value that arg2 points to
- 0, if the value that arg1 points to and the value that arg2 points to are equal

deccopy

Copy a decimal value.

        void deccopy(decimal *src, decimal *target);

The function receives a pointer to the decimal value that should be copied as the first argument (src) and a pointer to the target structure of type decimal (target) as the second argument.

deccvasc

Convert a value from its ASCII representation into a decimal type.

        int deccvasc(char *cp, int len, decimal *np);

The function receives a pointer to string that contains the string representation of the number to be converted (cp) as well as its length len. np is a pointer to the decimal value that saves the result of the operation.

Valid formats are for example: -2, .794, +3.44, 592.49E07 or -32.84e-4.

The function returns 0 on success. If overflow or underflow occurred, ECPG_INFORMIX_NUM_OVERFLOW or ECPG_INFORMIX_NUM_UNDERFLOW is returned. If the ASCII representation could not be parsed, ECPG_INFORMIX_BAD_NUMERIC is returned or ECPG_INFORMIX_BAD_EXPONENT if this problem occurred while parsing the exponent.

deccvdbl

Convert a value of type double to a value of type decimal.

```
int deccvdbl(double dbl, decimal *np);
```

The function receives the variable of type double that should be converted as its first argument (dbl). As the second argument (np), the function receives a pointer to the decimal variable that should hold the result of the operation.

The function returns 0 on success and a negative value if the conversion failed.

deccvint

Convert a value of type int to a value of type decimal.

```
int deccvint(int in, decimal *np);
```

The function receives the variable of type int that should be converted as its first argument (in). As the second argument (np), the function receives a pointer to the decimal variable that should hold the result of the operation.

The function returns 0 on success and a negative value if the conversion failed.

deccvlong

Convert a value of type long to a value of type decimal.

```
int deccvlong(long lng, decimal *np);
```

The function receives the variable of type long that should be converted as its first argument (lng). As the second argument (np), the function receives a pointer to the decimal variable that should hold the result of the operation.

The function returns 0 on success and a negative value if the conversion failed.

decdiv

Divide two variables of type decimal.

```
int decdiv(decimal *n1, decimal *n2, decimal *result);
```

The function receives pointers to the variables that are the first (n1) and the second (n2) operands and calculates n1/n2. result is a pointer to the variable that should hold the result of the operation.

On success, 0 is returned and a negative value if the division fails. If overflow or underflow occurred, the function returns ECPG_INFORMIX_NUM_OVERFLOW or ECPG_INFORMIX_NUM_UNDERFLOW respectively. If an attempt to divide by zero is observed, the function returns ECPG_INFORMIX_DIVIDE_ZERO.

decmul

Multiply two decimal values.

```
int decmul(decimal *n1, decimal *n2, decimal *result);
```

The function receives pointers to the variables that are the first (n1) and the second (n2) operands and calculates n1*n2. result is a pointer to the variable that should hold the result of the operation.

On success, 0 is returned and a negative value if the multiplication fails. If overflow or underflow occurred, the function returns ECPG_INFORMIX_NUM_ OVERFLOW or ECPG_INFORMIX_NUM_UNDERFLOW respectively.

decsub

Subtract one decimal value from another.

```
int decsub(decimal *n1, decimal *n2, decimal *result);
```

The function receives pointers to the variables that are the first (n1) and the second (n2) operands and calculates n1-n2. result is a pointer to the variable that should hold the result of the operation.

On success, 0 is returned and a negative value if the subtraction fails. If overflow or underflow occurred, the function returns ECPG_INFORMIX_NUM_ OVERFLOW or ECPG_INFORMIX_NUM_UNDERFLOW respectively.

dectoasc

Convert a variable of type decimal to its ASCII representation in a C char* string.

```
int dectoasc(decimal *np, char *cp, int len, int right)
```

The function receives a pointer to a variable of type decimal (np) that it converts to its textual representation. cp is the buffer that should hold the result of the operation. The parameter right specifies, how many digits right of the decimal point should be included in the output. The result will be rounded to this number of decimal digits. Setting right to -1 indicates that all available decimal digits should be included in the output. If the length of the output buffer, which is indicated by len is not sufficient to hold the textual representation including the trailing NUL character, only a single * character is stored in the result and -1 is returned.

The function returns either -1 if the buffer cp was too small or ECPG_ INFORMIX_OUT_OF_MEMORY if memory was exhausted.

dectodbl

Convert a variable of type decimal to a double.

```
int dectodbl(decimal *np, double *dblp);
```

The function receives a pointer to the decimal value to convert (np) and a pointer to the double variable that should hold the result of the operation (dblp).

On success, 0 is returned and a negative value if the conversion failed.

dectoint

Convert a variable to type decimal to an integer.

```
int dectoint(decimal *np, int *ip);
```

The function receives a pointer to the decimal value to convert (np) and a pointer to the integer variable that should hold the result of the operation (ip).

On success, 0 is returned and a negative value if the conversion failed. If an overflow occurred, `ECPG_INFORMIX_NUM_OVERFLOW` is returned.

Note that the ecpg implementation differs from the Informix implementation. Informix limits an integer to the range from -32767 to 32767, while the limits in the ecpg implementation depend on the architecture (`-INT_MAX .. INT_MAX`).

dectolong
Convert a variable to type decimal to a long integer.

```
int dectolong(decimal *np, long *lngp);
```

The function receives a pointer to the decimal value to convert (np) and a pointer to the long variable that should hold the result of the operation (lngp).

On success, 0 is returned and a negative value if the conversion failed. If an overflow occurred, `ECPG_INFORMIX_NUM_OVERFLOW` is returned.

Note that the ecpg implementation differs from the Informix implementation. Informix limits a long integer to the range from -2,147,483,647 to 2,147,483,647, while the limits in the ecpg implementation depend on the architecture (`-LONG_MAX .. LONG_MAX`).

rdatestr
Converts a date to a C char* string.

```
int rdatestr(date d, char *str);
```

The function receives two arguments, the first one is the date to convert (d) and the second one is a pointer to the target string. The output format is always yyyy-mm-dd, so you need to allocate at least 11 bytes (including the NUL-terminator) for the string.

The function returns 0 on success and a negative value in case of error.

Note that ecpg's implementation differs from the Informix implementation. In Informix the format can be influenced by setting environment variables. In ecpg however, you cannot change the output format.

rstrdate
Parse the textual representation of a date.

```
int rstrdate(char *str, date *d);
```

The function receives the textual representation of the date to convert (str) and a pointer to a variable of type date (d). This function does not allow you to specify a format mask. It uses the default format mask of Informix which is mm/dd/yyyy. Internally, this function is implemented by means of rdefmtdate. Therefore, rstrdate is not faster and if you have the choice you should opt for rdefmtdate which allows you to specify the format mask explicitly.

The function returns the same values as rdefmtdate.

rtoday

> Get the current date.
>
>   void rtoday(date *d);
>
> The function receives a pointer to a date variable (d) that it sets to the current date.
>
> Internally this function uses the *PGTYPESdate_today*, page 87 function.

rjulmdy

> Extract the values for the day, the month and the year from a variable of type date.
>
>   int rjulmdy(date d, short mdy[3]);
>
> The function receives the date d and a pointer to an array of 3 short integer values mdy. The variable name indicates the sequential order: mdy[0] will be set to contain the number of the month, mdy[1] will be set to the value of the day and mdy[2] will contain the year.
>
> The function always returns 0 at the moment.
>
> Internally the function uses the *PGTYPESdate_julmdy*, page 86 function.

rdefmtdate

> Use a format mask to convert a character string to a value of type date.
>
>   int rdefmtdate(date *d, char *fmt, char *str);
>
> The function receives a pointer to the date value that should hold the result of the operation (d), the format mask to use for parsing the date (fmt) and the C char* string containing the textual representation of the date (str). The textual representation is expected to match the format mask. However you do not need to have a 1:1 mapping of the string to the format mask. The function only analyzes the sequential order and looks for the literals yy or yyyy that indicate the position of the year, mm to indicate the position of the month and dd to indicate the position of the day.
>
> The function returns the following values:
>
> - 0 - The function terminated successfully.
> - ECPG_INFORMIX_ENOSHORTDATE - The date does not contain delimiters between day, month and year. In this case the input string must be exactly 6 or 8 bytes long but isn't.
> - ECPG_INFORMIX_ENOTDMY - The format string did not correctly indicate the sequential order of year, month and day.
> - ECPG_INFORMIX_BAD_DAY - The input string does not contain a valid day.
> - ECPG_INFORMIX_BAD_MONTH - The input string does not contain a valid month.
> - ECPG_INFORMIX_BAD_YEAR - The input string does not contain a valid year.
>
> Internally this function is implemented to use the *PGTYPESdate_defmt_asc*, page 88 function. See the reference there for a table of example input.

`rfmtdate`

> Convert a variable of type date to its textual representation using a format mask.
>
> ```
> int rfmtdate(date d, char *fmt, char *str);
> ```
>
> The function receives the date to convert (d), the format mask (fmt) and the string that will hold the textual representation of the date (str).
>
> On success, 0 is returned and a negative value if an error occurred.
>
> Internally this function uses the *PGTYPESdate_fmt_asc*, page 87 function, see the reference there for examples.

`rmdyjul`

> Create a date value from an array of 3 short integers that specify the day, the month and the year of the date.
>
> ```
> int rmdyjul(short mdy[3], date *d);
> ```
>
> The function receives the array of the 3 short integers (mdy) and a pointer to a variable of type date that should hold the result of the operation.
>
> Currently the function returns always 0.
>
> Internally the function is implemented to use the function *PGTYPES-date_mdyjul*, page 86.

`rdayofweek`

> Return a number representing the day of the week for a date value.
>
> ```
> int rdayofweek(date d);
> ```
>
> The function receives the date variable d as its only argument and returns an integer that indicates the day of the week for this date.
>
> - 0 - Sunday
> - 1 - Monday
> - 2 - Tuesday
> - 3 - Wednesday
> - 4 - Thursday
> - 5 - Friday
> - 6 - Saturday
>
> Internally the function is implemented to use the function *PGTYPES-date_dayofweek*, page 86.

`dtcurrent`

> Retrieve the current timestamp.
>
> ```
> void dtcurrent(timestamp *ts);
> ```
>
> The function retrieves the current timestamp and saves it into the timestamp variable that ts points to.

`dtcvasc`

> Parses a timestamp from its textual representation in ANSI standard into a timestamp variable.

```
int dtcvasc(char *str, timestamp *ts);
```

The function receives the string to parse (str) and a pointer to the time-stamp variable that should hold the result of the operation (ts).

The function returns 0 on success and a negative value in case of error.

Internally this function uses the *PGTYPEStimestamp_from_asc*, page 89 function. See the reference there for a table with example inputs.

dtcvfmtasc

Parses a timestamp from its textual representation in ANSI standard using a format mask into a timestamp variable.

```
dtcvfmtasc(char *inbuf, char *fmtstr, timestamp *dtvalue)
```

The function receives the string to parse (inbuf), the format mask to use (fmtstr) and a pointer to the timestamp variable that should hold the result of the operation (ts).

This functions is implemented by means of the *PGTYPEStimestamp_defmt_asc*, page 92. See the documentation there for a list of format specifiers that can be used.

The function returns 0 on success and a negative value in case of error.

dtsub

Subtract one timestamp from another and return a variable of type interval.

```
int dtsub(timestamp *ts1, timestamp *ts2, interval *iv);
```

The function will subtract the timestamp variable that ts2 points to from the timestamp variable that ts1 points to and will store the result in the interval variable that iv points to.

Upon success, the function returns 0 and a negative value if an error occurred.

dttoasc

Convert a timestamp variable to a C char* string.

```
int dttoasc(timestamp *ts, char *output);
```

The function receives a pointer to the timestamp variable to convert (ts) and the string that should hold the result of the operation (output). It converts ts to its textual representation in the ANSI SQL standard which is defined to be YYYY-MM-DD HH:MM:SS.

Upon success, the function returns 0 and a negative value if an error occurred.

dttofmtasc

Convert a timestamp variable to a C char* using a format mask.

```
int dttofmtasc(timestamp *ts, char *output, int str_len,
char *fmtstr);
```

The function receives a pointer to the timestamp to convert as its first argument (ts), a pointer to the output buffer (output), the maximal length that has been allocated for the output buffer (str_len) and the format mask to use for the conversion (fmtstr).

Upon success, the function returns 0 and a negative value if an error occurred.

Internally, this function uses the *PGTYPEStimestamp_fmt_asc*, page 89 function. See the reference there for information on what format mask specifiers can be used.

intoasc

Convert an interval variable to a C char* string.

```
int intoasc(interval *i, char *str);
```

The function receives a pointer to the interval variable to convert (i) and the string that should hold the result of the operation (str). It converts i to its textual representation in the ANSI SQL standard which is defined to be YYYY-MM-DD HH:MM:SS.

Upon success, the function returns 0 and a negative value if an error occurred.

rfmtlong

Convert a long integer value to its textual representation using a format mask.

```
int rfmtlong(long lng_val, char *fmt, char *outbuf);
```

The function receives the long value lng_val, the format mask fmt and a pointer to the output buffer outbuf. It converts the long value according to the format mask to its textual representation.

The format mask can be composed of the following format specifying characters:

- * (asterisk) - if this position would be blank otherwise, fill it with an asterisk.
- & (ampersand) - if this position would be blank otherwise, fill it with a zero.
- # - turn leading zeroes into blanks.
- < - left-justify the number in the string.
- , (comma) - group numbers of four or more digits into groups of three digits separated by a comma.
- . (period) - this character separates the whole-number part of the number from the fractional part.
- - (minus) - the minus sign appears if the number is a negative value.
- + (plus) - the plus sign appears if the number is a positive value.
- (- this replaces the minus sign in front of the negative number. The minus sign will not appear.
-) - this character replaces the minus and is printed behind the negative value.
- $ - the currency symbol.

rupshift

Convert a string to upper case.

```
void rupshift(char *str);
```

The function receives a pointer to the string and transforms every lower case character to upper case.

byleng

Return the number of characters in a string without counting trailing blanks.

```
int byleng(char *str, int len);
```

The function expects a fixed-length string as its first argument (str) and its length as its second argument (len). It returns the number of significant characters, that is the length of the string without trailing blanks.

ldchar

Copy a fixed-length string into a null-terminated string.

```
void ldchar(char *src, int len, char *dest);
```

The function receives the fixed-length string to copy (src), its length (len) and a pointer to the destination memory (dest). Note that you need to reserve at least len+1 bytes for the string that dest points to. The function copies at most len bytes to the new location (less if the source string has trailing blanks) and adds the null-terminator.

rgetmsg

```
int rgetmsg(int msgnum, char *s, int maxsize);
```

Not implemented.

rtypalign

```
int rtypalign(int offset, int type);
```

Not implemented.

rtypmsize

```
int rtypmsize(int type, int len);
```

Not implemented.

rtypwidth

```
int rtypwidth(int sqltype, int sqllen);
```

Not implemented.

rsetnull

Set a variable to NULL.

```
int rsetnull(int t, char *ptr);
```

The function receives an integer that indicates the type of the variable and a pointer to the variable itself that is casted to a C char* pointer.

The following types exist:

- CCHARTYPE - For a variable of type char or char*
- CSHORTTYPE - For a variable of type short int
- CINTTYPE - For a variable of type int
- CBOOLTYPE - For a variable of type boolean

- CFLOATTYPE - For a variable of type float
- CLONGTYPE - For a variable of type long
- CDOUBLETYPE - For a variable of type double
- CDECIMALTYPE - For a variable of type decimal
- CDATETYPE - For a variable of type date
- CDTIMETYPE - For a variable of type timestamp

Here is an example of a call to this function:

```
$char c[] = "abc       ";
$short s = 17;
$int i = -74874;

rsetnull(CCHARTYPE, (char *) c);
rsetnull(CSHORTTYPE, (char *) &s);
rsetnull(CINTTYPE, (char *) &i);
```

risnull

Test if a variable is NULL.

```
int risnull(int t, char *ptr);
```

The function receives the type of the variable to test (t) as well a pointer to this variable (ptr). Note that the latter needs to be casted to a char*. See the function *rsetnull*, page 104 for a list of possible variable types.

Here is an example of how to use this function:

```
$char c[] = "abc       ";
$short s = 17;
$int i = -74874;

risnull(CCHARTYPE, (char *) c);
risnull(CSHORTTYPE, (char *) &s);
risnull(CINTTYPE, (char *) &i);
```

3.9.3 Additional constants

Note that all constants here describe errors and all of them are defined to represent negative values. In the descriptions of the different constants you can also find the value that the constants represent in the current implementation. However you should not rely on this number. You can however rely on the fact all of them are defined to represent negative values.

ECPG_INFORMIX_NUM_OVERFLOW

Functions return this value if an overflow occurred in a calculation. Internally it is defined to -1200 (the Informix definition).

ECPG_INFORMIX_NUM_UNDERFLOW

Functions return this value if an underflow occurred in a calculation. Internally it is defined to -1201 (the Informix definition).

`ECPG_INFORMIX_DIVIDE_ZERO`
> Functions return this value if an attempt to divide by zero is observed. Internally it is defined to -1202 (the Informix definition).

`ECPG_INFORMIX_BAD_YEAR`
> Functions return this value if a bad value for a year was found while parsing a date. Internally it is defined to -1204 (the Informix definition).

`ECPG_INFORMIX_BAD_MONTH`
> Functions return this value if a bad value for a month was found while parsing a date. Internally it is defined to -1205 (the Informix definition).

`ECPG_INFORMIX_BAD_DAY`
> Functions return this value if a bad value for a day was found while parsing a date. Internally it is defined to -1206 (the Informix definition).

`ECPG_INFORMIX_ENOSHORTDATE`
> Functions return this value if a parsing routine needs a short date representation but did not get the date string in the right length. Internally it is defined to -1209 (the Informix definition).

`ECPG_INFORMIX_DATE_CONVERT`
> Functions return this value if Internally it is defined to -1210 (the Informix definition).

`ECPG_INFORMIX_OUT_OF_MEMORY`
> Functions return this value if Internally it is defined to -1211 (the Informix definition).

`ECPG_INFORMIX_ENOTDMY`
> Functions return this value if a parsing routine was supposed to get a format mask (like mmddyy) but not all fields were listed correctly. Internally it is defined to -1212 (the Informix definition).

`ECPG_INFORMIX_BAD_NUMERIC`
> Functions return this value either if a parsing routine cannot parse the textual representation for a numeric value because it contains errors or if a routine cannot complete a calculation involving numeric variables because at least one of the numeric variables is invalid. Internally it is defined to -1213 (the Informix definition).

`ECPG_INFORMIX_BAD_EXPONENT`
> Functions return this value if Internally it is defined to -1216 (the Informix definition).

`ECPG_INFORMIX_BAD_DATE`
> Functions return this value if Internally it is defined to -1218 (the Informix definition).

`ECPG_INFORMIX_EXTRA_CHARS`
> Functions return this value if Internally it is defined to -1264 (the Informix definition).

3.10 Using SQL Descriptor Areas

An SQL descriptor area is a more sophisticated method for processing the result of a SELECT or FETCH statement. An SQL descriptor area groups the data of one row of data together with metadata items into one data structure. The metadata is particularly useful when executing dynamic SQL statements, where the nature of the result columns may not be known ahead of time.

An SQL descriptor area consists of a header, which contains information concerning the entire descriptor, and one or more item descriptor areas, which basically each describe one column in the result row.

Before you can use an SQL descriptor area, you need to allocate one:

    EXEC SQL ALLOCATE DESCRIPTOR identifier;

The identifier serves as the "variable name" of the descriptor area. When you don't need the descriptor anymore, you should deallocate it:

    EXEC SQL DEALLOCATE DESCRIPTOR identifier;

To use a descriptor area, specify it as the storage target in an INTO clause, instead of listing host variables:

    EXEC SQL FETCH NEXT FROM mycursor INTO DESCRIPTOR mydesc;

Now how do you get the data out of the descriptor area? You can think of the descriptor area as a structure with named fields. To retrieve the value of a field from the header and store it into a host variable, use the following command:

    EXEC SQL GET DESCRIPTOR name :hostvar = field;

Currently, there is only one header field defined: *COUNT*, which tells how many item descriptor areas exist (that is, how many columns are contained in the result). The host variable needs to be of an integer type. To get a field from the item descriptor area, use the following command:

    EXEC SQL GET DESCRIPTOR name VALUE num :hostvar = field;

num can be a literal integer or a host variable containing an integer. Possible fields are:

CARDINALITY (integer)
    number of rows in the result set

DATA
    actual data item (therefore, the data type of this field depends on the query)

DATETIME_INTERVAL_CODE (integer)
    —

DATETIME_INTERVAL_PRECISION (integer)
    not implemented

INDICATOR (integer)
    the indicator (indicating a null value or a value truncation)

KEY_MEMBER (integer)
    not implemented

LENGTH (integer)
> length of the datum in characters

NAME (string)
> name of the column

NULLABLE (integer)
> not implemented

OCTET_LENGTH (integer)
> length of the character representation of the datum in bytes

PRECISION (integer)
> precision (for type numeric)

RETURNED_LENGTH (integer)
> length of the datum in characters

RETURNED_OCTET_LENGTH (integer)
> length of the character representation of the datum in bytes

SCALE (integer)
> scale (for type numeric)

TYPE (integer)
> numeric code of the data type of the column

3.11 Error Handling

This section describes how you can handle exceptional conditions and warnings in an embedded SQL program. There are several nonexclusive facilities for this.

3.11.1 Setting Callbacks

One simple method to catch errors and warnings is to set a specific action to be executed whenever a particular condition occurs. In general:

```
EXEC SQL WHENEVER condition action;
```

condition can be one of the following:

SQLERROR
> The specified action is called whenever an error occurs during the execution of an SQL statement.

SQLWARNING
> The specified action is called whenever a warning occurs during the execution of an SQL statement.

NOT FOUND
> The specified action is called whenever an SQL statement retrieves or affects zero rows. (This condition is not an error, but you might be interested in handling it specially.)

action can be one of the following:

CONTINUE
> This effectively means that the condition is ignored. This is the default.

GOTO *label*
GO TO *label*
> Jump to the specified label (using a C goto statement).

SQLPRINT
> Print a message to standard error. This is useful for simple programs or during prototyping. The details of the message cannot be configured.

STOP
> Call exit(1), which will terminate the program.

DO BREAK
> Execute the C statement break. This should only be used in loops or switch statements.

CALL *name* (*args*)
DO *name* (*args*)
> Call the specified C functions with the specified arguments.

The SQL standard only provides for the actions CONTINUE and GOTO (and GO TO).

Here is an example that you might want to use in a simple program. It prints a simple message when a warning occurs and aborts the program when an error happens.

```
EXEC SQL WHENEVER SQLWARNING SQLPRINT;
EXEC SQL WHENEVER SQLERROR STOP;
```

The statement EXEC SQL WHENEVER is a directive of the SQL preprocessor, not a C statement. The error or warning actions that it sets apply to all embedded SQL statements that appear below the point where the handler is set, unless a different action was set for the same condition between the first EXEC SQL WHENEVER and the SQL statement causing the condition, regardless of the flow of control in the C program. So neither of the two following C program excerpts will have the desired effect.

```
/* WRONG */
int main(int argc, char *argv[])
{
    ...
    if (verbose) {
        EXEC SQL WHENEVER SQLWARNING SQLPRINT;
    }
    ...
    EXEC SQL SELECT ...;
    ...
}
```

```
/* WRONG */
int main(int argc, char *argv[])
{
    ...
    set_error_handler();
    ...
    EXEC SQL SELECT ...;
    ...
}

static void set_error_handler(void)
{
    EXEC SQL WHENEVER SQLERROR STOP;
}
```

3.11.2 sqlca

For more powerful error handling, the embedded SQL interface provides a
global variable with the name sqlca that has the following structure:

```
struct
{
    char sqlcaid[8];
    long sqlabc;
    long sqlcode;
    struct
    {
        int sqlerrml;
        char sqlerrmc[70];
    } sqlerrm;
    char sqlerrp[8];
    long sqlerrd[6];
    char sqlwarn[8];
    char sqlstate[5];
} sqlca;
```

(In a multithreaded program, every thread automatically gets its own copy of
sqlca. This works similarly to the handling of the standard C global variable
errno.)

sqlca covers both warnings and errors. If multiple warnings or errors occur
during the execution of a statement, then sqlca will only contain information
about the last one.

If no error occurred in the last SQL statement, sqlca.sqlcode will be 0
and sqlca.sqlstate will be "00000". If a warning or error occurred, then
sqlca.sqlcode will be negative and sqlca.sqlstate will be different from
"00000". A positive sqlca.sqlcode indicates a harmless condition, such as
that the last query returned zero rows. sqlcode and sqlstate are two different
error code schemes; details appear below.

If the last SQL statement was successful, then `sqlca.sqlerrd[1]` contains the OID of the processed row, if applicable, and `sqlca.sqlerrd[2]` contains the number of processed or returned rows, if applicable to the command.

In case of an error or warning, `sqlca.sqlerrm.sqlerrmc` will contain a string that describes the error. The field `sqlca.sqlerrm.sqlerrml` contains the length of the error message that is stored in `sqlca.sqlerrm.sqlerrmc` (the result of `strlen()`, not really interesting for a C programmer). Note that some messages are too long to fit in the fixed-size `sqlerrmc` array; they will be truncated.

In case of a warning, `sqlca.sqlwarn[2]` is set to W. (In all other cases, it is set to something different from W.) If `sqlca.sqlwarn[1]` is set to W, then a value was truncated when it was stored in a host variable. `sqlca.sqlwarn[0]` is set to W if any of the other elements are set to indicate a warning.

The fields `sqlcaid`, `sqlcabc`, `sqlerrp`, and the remaining elements of `sqlerrd` and `sqlwarn` currently contain no useful information.

The structure `sqlca` is not defined in the SQL standard, but is implemented in several other SQL database systems. The definitions are similar at the core, but if you want to write portable applications, then you should investigate the different implementations carefully.

3.11.3 SQLSTATE vs SQLCODE

The fields `sqlca.sqlstate` and `sqlca.sqlcode` are two different schemes that provide error codes. Both are derived from the SQL standard, but SQLCODE has been marked deprecated in the SQL-92 edition of the standard and has been dropped in later editions. Therefore, new applications are strongly encouraged to use SQLSTATE.

SQLSTATE is a five-character array. The five characters contain digits or upper-case letters that represent codes of various error and warning conditions. SQLSTATE has a hierarchical scheme: the first two characters indicate the general class of the condition, the last three characters indicate a subclass of the general condition. A successful state is indicated by the code 00000. The SQLSTATE codes are for the most part defined in the SQL standard. The PostgreSQL server natively supports SQLSTATE error codes; therefore a high degree of consistency can be achieved by using this error code scheme throughout all applications. For further information see Volume 1, Appendix A *PostgreSQL Error Codes*.

SQLCODE, the deprecated error code scheme, is a simple integer. A value of 0 indicates success, a positive value indicates success with additional information, a negative value indicates an error. The SQL standard only defines the positive value +100, which indicates that the last command returned or affected zero rows, and no specific negative values. Therefore, this scheme can only achieve poor portability and does not have a hierarchical code assignment. Historically, the embedded SQL processor for PostgreSQL has assigned some specific SQLCODE values for its use, which are listed below with their numeric value and their symbolic name. Remember that these are not portable to other SQL implementations. To simplify the porting of applications to the SQLSTATE scheme, the corresponding SQLSTATE is also listed. There is, however, no one-to-one or one-to-many mapping between the two schemes (indeed it is many-to-many),

so you should consult the global SQLSTATE listing in Volume 1, Appendix A
PostgreSQL Error Codes in each case.

These are the assigned SQLCODE values:

-12 (ECPG_OUT_OF_MEMORY)
 Indicates that your virtual memory is exhausted. (SQLSTATE YE001)

-200 (ECPG_UNSUPPORTED)
 Indicates the preprocessor has generated something that the library does
 not know about. Perhaps you are running incompatible versions of the
 preprocessor and the library. (SQLSTATE YE002)

-201 (ECPG_TOO_MANY_ARGUMENTS)
 This means that the command specified more host variables than the command expected. (SQLSTATE 07001 or 07002)

-202 (ECPG_TOO_FEW_ARGUMENTS)
 This means that the command specified fewer host variables than the command expected. (SQLSTATE 07001 or 07002)

-203 (ECPG_TOO_MANY_MATCHES)
 This means a query has returned multiple rows but the statement was
 only prepared to store one result row (for example, because the specified
 variables are not arrays). (SQLSTATE 21000)

-204 (ECPG_INT_FORMAT)
 The host variable is of type int and the datum in the database is of a
 different type and contains a value that cannot be interpreted as an int.
 The library uses strtol() for this conversion. (SQLSTATE 42804)

-205 (ECPG_UINT_FORMAT)
 The host variable is of type unsigned int and the datum in the database
 is of a different type and contains a value that cannot be interpreted as
 an unsigned int. The library uses strtoul() for this conversion. (SQL-
 STATE 42804)

-206 (ECPG_FLOAT_FORMAT)
 The host variable is of type float and the datum in the database is of
 another type and contains a value that cannot be interpreted as a float.
 The library uses strtod() for this conversion. (SQLSTATE 42804)

-207 (ECPG_CONVERT_BOOL)
 This means the host variable is of type bool and the datum in the database
 is neither 't' nor 'f'. (SQLSTATE 42804)

-208 (ECPG_EMPTY)
 The statement sent to the PostgreSQL server was empty. (This cannot
 normally happen in an embedded SQL program, so it may point to an
 internal error.) (SQLSTATE YE002)

-209 (ECPG_MISSING_INDICATOR)
 A null value was returned and no null indicator variable was supplied.
 (SQLSTATE 22002)

-210 (ECPG_NO_ARRAY)

An ordinary variable was used in a place that requires an array. (SQL-STATE 42804)

-211 (ECPG_DATA_NOT_ARRAY)

The database returned an ordinary variable in a place that requires array value. (SQLSTATE 42804)

-220 (ECPG_NO_CONN)

The program tried to access a connection that does not exist. (SQLSTATE 08003)

-221 (ECPG_NOT_CONN)

The program tried to access a connection that does exist but is not open. (This is an internal error.) (SQLSTATE YE002)

-230 (ECPG_INVALID_STMT)

The statement you are trying to use has not been prepared. (SQLSTATE 26000)

-240 (ECPG_UNKNOWN_DESCRIPTOR)

The descriptor specified was not found. The statement you are trying to use has not been prepared. (SQLSTATE 33000)

-241 (ECPG_INVALID_DESCRIPTOR_INDEX)

The descriptor index specified was out of range. (SQLSTATE 07009)

-242 (ECPG_UNKNOWN_DESCRIPTOR_ITEM)

An invalid descriptor item was requested. (This is an internal error.) (SQL-STATE YE002)

-243 (ECPG_VAR_NOT_NUMERIC)

During the execution of a dynamic statement, the database returned a numeric value and the host variable was not numeric. (SQLSTATE 07006)

-244 (ECPG_VAR_NOT_CHAR)

During the execution of a dynamic statement, the database returned a non-numeric value and the host variable was numeric. (SQLSTATE 07006)

-400 (ECPG_PGSQL)

Some error caused by the PostgreSQL server. The message contains the error message from the PostgreSQL server.

-401 (ECPG_TRANS)

The PostgreSQL server signaled that we cannot start, commit, or rollback the transaction. (SQLSTATE 08007)

-402 (ECPG_CONNECT)

The connection attempt to the database did not succeed. (SQLSTATE 08001)

100 (ECPG_NOT_FOUND)

This is a harmless condition indicating that the last command retrieved or processed zero rows, or that you are at the end of the cursor. (SQLSTATE 02000)

3.12 Preprocessor directives

3.12.1 Including files

To include an external file into your embedded SQL program, use:

```
EXEC SQL INCLUDE filename;
```

The embedded SQL preprocessor will look for a file named *filename*.h, pre-process it, and include it in the resulting C output. Thus, embedded SQL statements in the included file are handled correctly.

Note that this is *not* the same as

```
#include <filename.h>
```

because this file would not be subject to SQL command preprocessing. Natu-rally, you can continue to use the C #include directive to include other header files.

> **Note:** The include file name is case-sensitive, even though the rest of the EXEC SQL INCLUDE command follows the normal SQL case-sensitivity rules.

3.12.2 The #define and #undef directives

Similar to the directive #define that is known from C, embedded SQL has a similar concept:

```
EXEC SQL DEFINE name;
EXEC SQL DEFINE name value;
```

So you can define a name:

```
EXEC SQL DEFINE HAVE_FEATURE;
```

And you can also define constants:

```
EXEC SQL DEFINE MYNUMBER 12;
EXEC SQL DEFINE MYSTRING 'abc';
```

Use undef to remove a previous definition:

```
EXEC SQL UNDEF MYNUMBER;
```

Of course you can continue to use the C versions #define and #undef in your embedded SQL program. The difference is where your defined values get evaluated. If you use EXEC SQL DEFINE then the ecpg preprocessor evaluates the defines and substitutes the values. For example if you write:

```
EXEC SQL DEFINE MYNUMBER 12;
    ...
EXEC SQL UPDATE Tbl SET col = MYNUMBER;
```

then ecpg will already do the substitution and your C compiler will never see any name or identifier MYNUMBER. Note that you cannot use #define for a constant that you are going to use in an embedded SQL query because in this case the embedded SQL precompiler is not able to see this declaration.

3.12.3 ifdef, ifndef, else, elif and endif directives

You can use the following directives to compile code sections conditionally:

EXEC SQL ifdef *name* ;

> Checks a *name* and processes subsequent lines if *name* has been created
> with EXEC SQL define *name*.

EXEC SQL ifndef *name* ;

> Checks a *name* and processes subsequent lines if *name* has *not* been created
> with EXEC SQL define *name*.

EXEC SQL else;

> Starts processing an alternative section to a section introduced by either
> EXEC SQL ifdef *name* or EXEC SQL ifndef *name*.

EXEC SQL elif *name* ;

> Checks *name* and starts an alternative section if *name* has been created
> with EXEC SQL define *name*.

EXEC SQL endif;

> Ends an alternative section.

Example:

```
exec sql ifndef TZVAR;
exec sql SET TIMEZONE TO 'GMT';
exec sql elif TZNAME;
exec sql SET TIMEZONE TO TZNAME;
exec sql else;
exec sql SET TIMEZONE TO TZVAR;
exec sql endif;
```

3.13 Processing Embedded SQL Programs

Now that you have an idea how to form embedded SQL C programs, you
probably want to know how to compile them. Before compiling you run the file
through the embedded SQL C preprocessor, which converts the SQL statements
you used to special function calls. After compiling, you must link with a special
library that contains the needed functions. These functions fetch information
from the arguments, perform the SQL command using the libpq interface, and
put the result in the arguments specified for output.

The preprocessor program is called 'ecpg' and is included in a normal PostgreSQL installation. Embedded SQL programs are typically named with an
extension '.pgc'. If you have a program file called 'prog1.pgc', you can prepro-
cess it by simply calling

    ecpg prog1.pgc

This will create a file called 'prog1.c'. If your input files do not follow the
suggested naming pattern, you can specify the output file explicitly using the
-o option.

The preprocessed file can be compiled normally, for example:

```
cc -c prog1.c
```

The generated C source files include header files from the PostgreSQL installation, so if you installed PostgreSQL in a location that is not searched by default, you have to add an option such as -I/usr/local/pgsql/include to the compilation command line.

To link an embedded SQL program, you need to include the 'libecpg' library, like so:

```
cc -o myprog prog1.o prog2.o ... -lecpg
```

Again, you might have to add an option like -L/usr/local/pgsql/lib to that command line.

If you manage the build process of a larger project using make, it may be convenient to include the following implicit rule to your makefiles:

```
ECPG = ecpg

%.c: %.pgc
        $(ECPG) $<
```

The complete syntax of the ecpg command is detailed in ecpg.

The ecpg library is thread-safe if it is built using the --enable-thread-safety command-line option to 'configure'. (You might need to use other threading command-line options to compile your client code.)

3.14 Library Functions

The 'libecpg' library primarily contains "hidden" functions that are used to implement the functionality expressed by the embedded SQL commands. But there are some functions that can usefully be called directly. Note that this makes your code unportable.

- ECPGdebug(int on, FILE *stream) turns on debug logging if called with the first argument non-zero. Debug logging is done on *stream*. The log contains all SQL statements with all the input variables inserted, and the results from the PostgreSQL server. This can be very useful when searching for errors in your SQL statements.

    Note: On Windows, if the ecpg libraries and an application are compiled with different flags, this function call will crash the application because the internal representation of the FILE pointers differ. Specifically, multithreaded/single-threaded, release/debug, and static/dynamic flags should be the same for the library and all applications using that library.

- ECPGstatus(int *lineno*, const char* *connection_name*) returns true if you are connected to a database and false if not. *connection_name* can be NULL if a single connection is being used.

3.15 Internals

This section explains how ECPG works internally. This information can occasionally be useful to help users understand how to use ECPG.

The first four lines written by ecpg to the output are fixed lines. Two are comments and two are include lines necessary to interface to the library. Then the preprocessor reads through the file and writes output. Normally it just echoes everything to the output.

When it sees an EXEC SQL statement, it intervenes and changes it. The command starts with EXEC SQL and ends with ;. Everything in between is treated as an SQL statement and parsed for variable substitution.

Variable substitution occurs when a symbol starts with a colon (:). The variable with that name is looked up among the variables that were previously declared within a EXEC SQL DECLARE section.

The most important function in the library is ECPGdo, which takes care of executing most commands. It takes a variable number of arguments. This can easily add up to 50 or so arguments, and we hope this will not be a problem on any platform.

The arguments are:

A line number

This is the line number of the original line; used in error messages only.

A string

This is the SQL command that is to be issued. It is modified by the input variables, i.e., the variables that where not known at compile time but are to be entered in the command. Where the variables should go the string contains ?.

Input variables

Every input variable causes ten arguments to be created. (See below.)

ECPGt_EOIT

An enum telling that there are no more input variables.

Output variables

Every output variable causes ten arguments to be created. (See below.) These variables are filled by the function.

ECPGt_EORT

An enum telling that there are no more variables.

For every variable that is part of the SQL command, the function gets ten arguments:

1. The type as a special symbol.
2. A pointer to the value or a pointer to the pointer.
3. The size of the variable if it is a char or varchar.
4. The number of elements in the array (for array fetches).
5. The offset to the next element in the array (for array fetches).
6. The type of the indicator variable as a special symbol.

7. A pointer to the indicator variable.

8. 0

9. The number of elements in the indicator array (for array fetches).

10. The offset to the next element in the indicator array (for array fetches).

Note that not all SQL commands are treated in this way. For instance, an open cursor statement like

```
EXEC SQL OPEN cursor;
```

is not copied to the output. Instead, the cursor's DECLARE command is used at the position of the OPEN command because it indeed opens the cursor.

Here is a complete example describing the output of the preprocessor of a file 'foo.pgc' (details may change with each particular version of the preprocessor):

```
EXEC SQL BEGIN DECLARE SECTION;
int index;
int result;
EXEC SQL END DECLARE SECTION;
...
EXEC SQL SELECT res INTO :result FROM mytable WHERE index =
  :index;
```

is translated into:

```
/* Processed by ecpg (2.6.0) */
/* These two include files are added by the preprocessor */
#include <ecpgtype.h>;
#include <ecpglib.h>;

/* exec sql begin declare section */

#line 1 "foo.pgc"

 int index;
 int result;
/* exec sql end declare section */
...
ECPGdo(__LINE__, NULL, "SELECT res FROM mytable WHERE index =
?      ",
        ECPGt_int,&(index),1L,1L,sizeof(int),
        ECPGt_NO_INDICATOR, NULL , 0L, 0L, 0L, ECPGt_EOIT,
        ECPGt_int,&(result),1L,1L,sizeof(int),
        ECPGt_NO_INDICATOR, NULL , 0L, 0L, 0L, ECPGt_EORT);
#line 147 "foo.pgc"
```

(The indentation here is added for readability and not something the preprocessor does.)

4 The Information Schema

The information schema consists of a set of views that contain information about the objects defined in the current database. The information schema is defined in the SQL standard and can therefore be expected to be portable and remain stable—unlike the system catalogs, which are specific to PostgreSQL and are modelled after implementation concerns. The information schema views do not, however, contain information about PostgreSQL-specific features; to inquire about those you need to query the system catalogs or other PostgreSQL-specific views.

4.1 The Schema

The information schema itself is a schema named `information_schema`. This schema automatically exists in all databases. The owner of this schema is the initial database user in the cluster, and that user naturally has all the privileges on this schema, including the ability to drop it (but the space savings achieved by that are minuscule).

By default, the information schema is not in the schema search path, so you need to access all objects in it through qualified names. Since the names of some of the objects in the information schema are generic names that might occur in user applications, you should be careful if you want to put the information schema in the path.

4.2 Data Types

The columns of the information schema views use special data types that are defined in the information schema. These are defined as simple domains over ordinary built-in types. You should not use these types for work outside the information schema, but your applications must be prepared for them if they select from the information schema.

These types are:

`cardinal_number`
  A nonnegative integer.

`character_data`
  A character string (without specific maximum length).

`sql_identifier`
  A character string. This type is used for SQL identifiers, the type `character_data` is used for any other kind of text data.

`time_stamp`
  A domain over the type `timestamp with time zone`

Every column in the information schema has one of these four types.

Boolean (true/false) data is represented in the information schema by a column of type character_data that contains either YES or NO. (The information schema was invented before the type boolean was added to the SQL standard, so this convention is necessary to keep the information schema backward compatible.)

4.3 information_schema_catalog_name

information_schema_catalog_name is a table that always contains one row and one column containing the name of the current database (current catalog, in SQL terminology).

Name	Data Type	Description
catalog_name	sql_identifier	Name of the database that contains this information schema

Table 4.1: information_schema_catalog_name Columns

4.4 administrable_role_authorizations

The view administrable_role_authorizations identifies all roles that the current user has the admin option for.

Name	Data Type	Description
grantee	sql_identifier	Name of the role to which this role membership was granted (may be the current user, or a different role in case of nested role memberships)
role_name	sql_identifier	Name of a role
is_grantable	character_data	Always YES

Table 4.2: administrable_role_authorizations Columns

4.5 applicable_roles

The view applicable_roles identifies all roles whose privileges the current user can use. This means there is some chain of role grants from the current user to the role in question. The current user itself is also an applicable role. The set of applicable roles is generally used for permission checking.

Name	Data Type	Description
grantee	sql_identifier	Name of the role to which this role membership was granted (may be the current user, or a different role in case of nested role memberships)
role_name	sql_identifier	Name of a role
is_grantable	character_data	YES if the grantee has the admin option on the role, NO if not

Table 4.3: applicable_roles Columns

4.6 attributes

The view attributes contains information about the attributes of composite data types defined in the database. (Note that the view does not give information about table columns, which are sometimes called attributes in PostgreSQL contexts.)

NAME	DATA TYPE	DESCRIPTION
udt_catalog	sql_identifier	Name of the database containing the data type (always the current database)
udt_schema	sql_identifier	Name of the schema containing the data type
udt_name	sql_identifier	Name of the data type
attribute_name	sql_identifier	Name of the attribute
ordinal_position	cardinal_number	Ordinal position of the attribute within the data type (count starts at 1)
attribute_default	character_data	Default expression of the attribute
is_nullable	character_data	YES if the attribute is possibly nullable, NO if it is known not nullable.
data_type	character_data	Data type of the attribute, if it is a built-in type, or ARRAY if it is some array (in that case, see the view element_types), else USER-DEFINED (in that case, the type is identified in attribute_udt_name and associated columns).
character_maximum_length	cardinal_number	If data_type identifies a character or bit string type, the declared maximum length; null for all other data types or if no maximum length was declared.
character_octet_length	cardinal_number	If data_type identifies a character type, the maximum possible length in octets (bytes) of a datum (this should not be of concern to PostgreSQL users); null for all other data types.

numeric_precision	cardinal_number	If data_type identifies a numeric type, this column contains the (declared or implicit) precision of the type for this attribute. The precision indicates the number of significant digits. It may be expressed in decimal (base 10) or binary (base 2) terms, as specified in the column numeric_precision_radix. For all other data types, this column is null.
numeric_precision_radix	cardinal_number	If data_type identifies a numeric type, this column indicates in which base the values in the columns numeric_precision and numeric_scale are expressed. The value is either 2 or 10. For all other data types, this column is null.
numeric_scale	cardinal_number	If data_type identifies an exact numeric type, this column contains the (declared or implicit) scale of the type for this attribute. The scale indicates the number of significant digits to the right of the decimal point. It may be expressed in decimal (base 10) or binary (base 2) terms, as specified in the column numeric_precision_radix. For all other data types, this column is null.
datetime_precision	cardinal_number	If data_type identifies a date, time, or interval type, the declared precision; null for all other data types or if no precision was declared.
interval_type	character_data	Not yet implemented
interval_precision	character_data	Not yet implemented

`attribute_udt_catalog`	`sql_identifier`	Name of the database that the attribute data type is defined in (always the current database)
`attribute_udt_schema`	`sql_identifier`	Name of the schema that the attribute data type is defined in
`attribute_udt_name`	`sql_identifier`	Name of the attribute data type
`scope_catalog`	`sql_identifier`	Applies to a feature not available in PostgreSQL
`scope_schema`	`sql_identifier`	Applies to a feature not available in PostgreSQL
`scope_name`	`sql_identifier`	Applies to a feature not available in PostgreSQL
`maximum_cardinality`	`cardinal_number`	Always null, because arrays always have unlimited maximum cardinality in PostgreSQL
`dtd_identifier`	`sql_identifier`	An identifier of the data type descriptor of the column, unique among the data type descriptors pertaining to the table. This is mainly useful for joining with other instances of such identifiers. (The specific format of the identifier is not defined and not guaranteed to remain the same in future versions.)
`is_derived_reference_attribute`	`character_data`	Applies to a feature not available in PostgreSQL

Table 4.4: `attributes` Columns

See also under `columns`, a similarly structured view, for further information on some of the columns.

4.7 check_constraint_routine_usage

The view check_constraint_routine_usage identifies routines (functions and procedures) that are used by a check constraint. Only those routines are shown that are owned by a currently enabled role.

NAME	DATA TYPE	DESCRIPTION
constraint_catalog	sql_identifier	Name of the database containing the constraint (always the current database)
constraint_schema	sql_identifier	Name of the schema containing the constraint
constraint_name	sql_identifier	Name of the constraint
specific_catalog	sql_identifier	Name of the database containing the function (always the current database)
specific_schema	sql_identifier	Name of the schema containing the function
specific_name	sql_identifier	The "specific name" of the function. See routines (page 149) for more information.

Table 4.5: check_constraint_routine_usage Columns

4.8 check_constraints

The view check_constraints contains all check constraints, either defined on a table or on a domain, that are owned by a currently enabled role. (The owner of the table or domain is the owner of the constraint.)

NAME	DATA TYPE	DESCRIPTION
constraint_catalog	sql_identifier	Name of the database containing the constraint (always the current database)
constraint_schema	sql_identifier	Name of the schema containing the constraint
constraint_name	sql_identifier	Name of the constraint
check_clause	character_data	The check expression of the check constraint

Table 4.6: check_constraints Columns

4.9 column_domain_usage

The view `column_domain_usage` identifies all columns (of a table or a view) that make use of some domain defined in the current database and owned by a currently enabled role.

NAME	DATA TYPE	DESCRIPTION
domain_catalog	sql_identifier	Name of the database containing the domain (always the current database)
domain_schema	sql_identifier	Name of the schema containing the domain
domain_name	sql_identifier	Name of the domain
table_catalog	sql_identifier	Name of the database containing the table (always the current database)
table_schema	sql_identifier	Name of the schema containing the table
table_name	sql_identifier	Name of the table
column_name	sql_identifier	Name of the column

Table 4.7: `column_domain_usage` Columns

4.10 column_privileges

The view `column_privileges` identifies all privileges granted on columns to a currently enabled role or by a currently enabled role. There is one row for each combination of column, grantor, and grantee.

In PostgreSQL, you can only grant privileges on entire tables, not individual columns. Therefore, this view contains the same information as `table_privileges`, just represented through one row for each column in each appropriate table, but it only covers privilege types where column granularity is possible: SELECT, INSERT, UPDATE, REFERENCES. If you want to make your applications fit for possible future developments, it is generally the right choice to use this view instead of `table_privileges` if one of those privilege types is concerned.

NAME	DATA TYPE	DESCRIPTION
grantor	sql_identifier	Name of the role that granted the privilege
grantee	sql_identifier	Name of the role that the privilege was granted to
table_catalog	sql_identifier	Name of the database that contains the table that contains the column (always the current database)
table_schema	sql_identifier	Name of the schema that contains the table that contains the column
table_name	sql_identifier	Name of the table that contains the column
column_name	sql_identifier	Name of the column
privilege_type	character_data	Type of the privilege: SELECT, INSERT, UPDATE, or REFERENCES
is_grantable	character_data	YES if the privilege is grantable, NO if not

Table 4.8: column_privileges Columns

4.11 column_udt_usage

The view column_udt_usage identifies all columns that use data types owned by a currently enabled role. Note that in PostgreSQL, built-in data types behave like user-defined types, so they are included here as well. See also columns for details.

NAME	DATA TYPE	DESCRIPTION
udt_catalog	sql_identifier	Name of the database that the column data type (the underlying type of the domain, if applicable) is defined in (always the current database)
udt_schema	sql_identifier	Name of the schema that the column data type (the underlying type of the domain, if applicable) is defined in
udt_name	sql_identifier	Name of the column data type (the underlying type of the domain, if applicable)
table_catalog	sql_identifier	Name of the database containing the table (always the current database)
table_schema	sql_identifier	Name of the schema containing the table
table_name	sql_identifier	Name of the table
column_name	sql_identifier	Name of the column

Table 4.9: column_udt_usage Columns

4.12 columns

The view columns contains information about all table columns (or view columns) in the database. System columns (oid, etc.) are not included. Only those columns are shown that the current user has access to (by way of being the owner or having some privilege).

NAME	DATA TYPE	DESCRIPTION
table_catalog	sql_identifier	Name of the database containing the table (always the current database)
table_schema	sql_identifier	Name of the schema containing the table
table_name	sql_identifier	Name of the table
column_name	sql_identifier	Name of the column
ordinal_position	cardinal_number	Ordinal position of the column within the table (count starts at 1)
column_default	character_data	Default expression of the column
is_nullable	character_data	YES if the column is possibly nullable, NO if it is known not nullable. A not-null constraint is one way a column can be known not nullable, but there may be others.
data_type	character_data	Data type of the column, if it is a built-in type, or ARRAY if it is some array (in that case, see the view element_types), else USER-DEFINED (in that case, the type is identified in udt_name and associated columns). If the column is based on a domain, this column refers to the type underlying the domain (and the domain is identified in domain_name and associated columns).
character_maximum_length	cardinal_number	If data_type identifies a character or bit string type, the declared maximum length; null for all other data types or if no maximum length was declared.

character_octet_length	cardinal_number	If data_type identifies a character type, the maximum possible length in octets (bytes) of a datum (this should not be of concern to PostgreSQL users); null for all other data types.
numeric_precision	cardinal_number	If data_type identifies a numeric type, this column contains the (declared or implicit) precision of the type for this column. The precision indicates the number of significant digits. It may be expressed in decimal (base 10) or binary (base 2) terms, as specified in the column numeric_precision_radix. For all other data types, this column is null.
numeric_precision_radix	cardinal_number	If data_type identifies a numeric type, this column indicates in which base the values in the columns numeric_precision and numeric_scale are expressed. The value is either 2 or 10. For all other data types, this column is null.
numeric_scale	cardinal_number	If data_type identifies an exact numeric type, this column contains the (declared or implicit) scale of the type for this column. The scale indicates the number of significant digits to the right of the decimal point. It may be expressed in decimal (base 10) or binary (base 2) terms, as specified in the column numeric_precision_radix. For all other data types, this column is null.
datetime_precision	cardinal_number	If data_type identifies a date, time, or interval type, the declared precision; null for all other data types or if no precision was declared.
interval_type	character_data	Not yet implemented

interval_precision	character_data	Not yet implemented
character_set_catalog	sql_identifier	Applies to a feature not available in PostgreSQL
character_set_schema	sql_identifier	Applies to a feature not available in PostgreSQL
character_set_name	sql_identifier	Applies to a feature not available in PostgreSQL
collation_catalog	sql_identifier	Applies to a feature not available in PostgreSQL
collation_schema	sql_identifier	Applies to a feature not available in PostgreSQL
collation_name	sql_identifier	Applies to a feature not available in PostgreSQL
domain_catalog	sql_identifier	If the column has a domain type, the name of the database that the domain is defined in (always the current database), else null.
domain_schema	sql_identifier	If the column has a domain type, the name of the schema that the domain is defined in, else null.
domain_name	sql_identifier	If the column has a domain type, the name of the domain, else null.
udt_catalog	sql_identifier	Name of the database that the column data type (the underlying type of the domain, if applicable) is defined in (always the current database)
udt_schema	sql_identifier	Name of the schema that the column data type (the underlying type of the domain, if applicable) is defined in
udt_name	sql_identifier	Name of the column data type (the underlying type of the domain, if applicable)
scope_catalog	sql_identifier	Applies to a feature not available in PostgreSQL
scope_schema	sql_identifier	Applies to a feature not available in PostgreSQL
scope_name	sql_identifier	Applies to a feature not available in PostgreSQL
maximum_cardinality	cardinal_number	Always null, because arrays always have unlimited maximum cardinality in PostgreSQL

dtd_identifier	sql_identifier	An identifier of the data type descriptor of the column, unique among the data type descriptors pertaining to the table. This is mainly useful for joining with other instances of such identifiers. (The specific format of the identifier is not defined and not guaranteed to remain the same in future versions.)
is_self_referencing	character_data	Applies to a feature not available in PostgreSQL
is_identity	character_data	Applies to a feature not available in PostgreSQL
identity_generation	character_data	Applies to a feature not available in PostgreSQL
identity_start	character_data	Applies to a feature not available in PostgreSQL
identity_increment	character_data	Applies to a feature not available in PostgreSQL
identity_maximum	character_data	Applies to a feature not available in PostgreSQL
identity_minimum	character_data	Applies to a feature not available in PostgreSQL
identity_cycle	character_data	Applies to a feature not available in PostgreSQL
is_generated	character_data	Applies to a feature not available in PostgreSQL
generation_expression	character_data	Applies to a feature not available in PostgreSQL
is_updatable	character_data	YES if the column is updatable, NO if not (Columns in base tables are always updatable, columns in views not necessarily)

Table 4.10: columns Columns

Since data types can be defined in a variety of ways in SQL, and PostgreSQL contains additional ways to define data types, their representation in the information schema can be somewhat difficult. The column data_type is supposed to identify the underlying built-in type of the column. In PostgreSQL, this means that the type is defined in the system catalog schema pg_catalog. This column may be useful if the application can handle the well-known built-in types specially (for example, format the numeric types differently or use the data in the precision columns). The columns udt_name, udt_schema, and udt_catalog always identify the underlying data type of the column, even if the column is based on a domain. (Since PostgreSQL treats built-in types like user-defined types, built-in types appear here as well. This is an extension of the SQL standard.) These columns should be used if an application wants to process data differently according to the type, because in that case it wouldn't matter if the column is really based on a domain. If the column is based on a domain, the identity of the domain is stored in the columns domain_name, domain_schema, and domain_catalog. If you want to pair up columns with their associated data types and treat domains as separate types, you could write coalesce(domain_name, udt_name), etc.

4.13 constraint_column_usage

The view constraint_column_usage identifies all columns in the current database that are used by some constraint. Only those columns are shown that are contained in a table owned by a currently enabled role. For a check constraint, this view identifies the columns that are used in the check expression. For a foreign key constraint, this view identifies the columns that the foreign key references. For a unique or primary key constraint, this view identifies the constrained columns.

NAME	DATA TYPE	DESCRIPTION
table_catalog	sql_identifier	Name of the database that contains the table that contains the column that is used by some constraint (always the current database)
table_schema	sql_identifier	Name of the schema that contains the table that contains the column that is used by some constraint
table_name	sql_identifier	Name of the table that contains the column that is used by some constraint
column_name	sql_identifier	Name of the column that is used by some constraint
constraint_catalog	sql_identifier	Name of the database that contains the constraint (always the current database)
constraint_schema	sql_identifier	Name of the schema that contains the constraint
constraint_name	sql_identifier	Name of the constraint

Table 4.11: constraint_column_usage Columns

4.14 constraint_table_usage

The view `constraint_table_usage` identifies all tables in the current database that are used by some constraint and are owned by a currently enabled role. (This is different from the view `table_constraints`, which identifies all table constraints along with the table they are defined on.) For a foreign key constraint, this view identifies the table that the foreign key references. For a unique or primary key constraint, this view simply identifies the table the constraint belongs to. Check constraints and not-null constraints are not included in this view.

NAME	DATA TYPE	DESCRIPTION
table_catalog	sql_identifier	Name of the database that contains the table that is used by some constraint (always the current database)
table_schema	sql_identifier	Name of the schema that contains the table that is used by some constraint
table_name	sql_identifier	Name of the table that is used by some constraint
constraint_catalog	sql_identifier	Name of the database that contains the constraint (always the current database)
constraint_schema	sql_identifier	Name of the schema that contains the constraint
constraint_name	sql_identifier	Name of the constraint

Table 4.12: `constraint_table_usage` Columns

4.15 data_type_privileges

The view `data_type_privileges` identifies all data type descriptors that the current user has access to, by way of being the owner of the described object or having some privilege for it. A data type descriptor is generated whenever a data type is used in the definition of a table column, a domain, or a function (as parameter or return type) and stores some information about how the data type is used in that instance (for example, the declared maximum length, if applicable). Each data type descriptor is assigned an arbitrary identifier that is unique among the data type descriptor identifiers assigned for one object (table, domain, function). This view is probably not useful for applications, but it is used to define some other views in the information schema.

NAME	DATA TYPE	DESCRIPTION
object_catalog	sql_identifier	Name of the database that contains the described object (always the current database)
object_schema	sql_identifier	Name of the schema that contains the described object
object_name	sql_identifier	Name of the described object
object_type	character_data	The type of the described object: one of TABLE (the data type descriptor pertains to a column of that table), DOMAIN (the data type descriptors pertains to that domain), ROUTINE (the data type descriptor pertains to a parameter or the return data type of that function).
dtd_identifier	sql_identifier	The identifier of the data type descriptor, which is unique among the data type descriptors for that same object.

Table 4.13: data_type_privileges Columns

4.16 domain_constraints

The view domain_constraints contains all constraints belonging to domains defined in the current database.

NAME	DATA TYPE	DESCRIPTION
constraint_catalog	sql_identifier	Name of the database that contains the constraint (always the current database)
constraint_schema	sql_identifier	Name of the schema that contains the constraint
constraint_name	sql_identifier	Name of the constraint
domain_catalog	sql_identifier	Name of the database that contains the domain (always the current database)
domain_schema	sql_identifier	Name of the schema that contains the domain
domain_name	sql_identifier	Name of the domain
is_deferrable	character_data	YES if the constraint is deferrable, NO if not
initially_deferred	character_data	YES if the constraint is deferrable and initially deferred, NO if not

Table 4.14: domain_constraints Columns

4.17 domain_udt_usage

The view domain_udt_usage identifies all domains that are based on data types owned by a currently enabled role. Note that in PostgreSQL, built-in data types behave like user-defined types, so they are included here as well.

NAME	DATA TYPE	DESCRIPTION
udt_catalog	sql_identifier	Name of the database that the domain data type is defined in (always the current database)
udt_schema	sql_identifier	Name of the schema that the domain data type is defined in
udt_name	sql_identifier	Name of the domain data type
domain_catalog	sql_identifier	Name of the database that contains the domain (always the current database)
domain_schema	sql_identifier	Name of the schema that contains the domain
domain_name	sql_identifier	Name of the domain

Table 4.15: domain_udt_usage Columns

4.18 domains

The view domains contains all domains defined in the current database.

NAME	DATA TYPE	DESCRIPTION
domain_catalog	sql_identifier	Name of the database that contains the domain (always the current database)
domain_schema	sql_identifier	Name of the schema that contains the domain
domain_name	sql_identifier	Name of the domain
data_type	character_data	Data type of the domain, if it is a built-in type, or ARRAY if it is some array (in that case, see the view element_types), else USER-DEFINED (in that case, the type is identified in udt_name and associated columns).
character_maximum_length	cardinal_number	If the domain has a character or bit string type, the declared maximum length; null for all other data types or if no maximum length was declared.

character_octet_length	cardinal_number	If the domain has a character type, the maximum possible length in octets (bytes) of a datum (this should not be of concern to PostgreSQL users); null for all other data types.
character_set_catalog	sql_identifier	Applies to a feature not available in PostgreSQL
character_set_schema	sql_identifier	Applies to a feature not available in PostgreSQL
character_set_name	sql_identifier	Applies to a feature not available in PostgreSQL
collation_catalog	sql_identifier	Applies to a feature not available in PostgreSQL
collation_schema	sql_identifier	Applies to a feature not available in PostgreSQL
collation_name	sql_identifier	Applies to a feature not available in PostgreSQL
numeric_precision	cardinal_number	If the domain has a numeric type, this column contains the (declared or implicit) precision of the type for this column. The precision indicates the number of significant digits. It may be expressed in decimal (base 10) or binary (base 2) terms, as specified in the column numeric_precision_radix. For all other data types, this column is null.
numeric_precision_radix	cardinal_number	If the domain has a numeric type, this column indicates in which base the values in the columns numeric_precision and numeric_scale are expressed. The value is either 2 or 10. For all other data types, this column is null.

numeric_scale	cardinal_number	If the domain has an exact numeric type, this column contains the (declared or implicit) scale of the type for this column. The scale indicates the number of significant digits to the right of the decimal point. It may be expressed in decimal (base 10) or binary (base 2) terms, as specified in the column numeric_precision_radix. For all other data types, this column is null.
datetime_precision	cardinal_number	If the domain has a date, time, or interval type, the declared precision; null for all other data types or if no precision was declared.
interval_type	character_data	Not yet implemented
interval_precision	character_data	Not yet implemented
domain_default	character_data	Default expression of the domain
udt_catalog	sql_identifier	Name of the database that the domain data type is defined in (always the current database)
udt_schema	sql_identifier	Name of the schema that the domain data type is defined in
udt_name	sql_identifier	Name of the domain data type
scope_catalog	sql_identifier	Applies to a feature not available in PostgreSQL
scope_schema	sql_identifier	Applies to a feature not available in PostgreSQL
scope_name	sql_identifier	Applies to a feature not available in PostgreSQL
maximum_cardinality	cardinal_number	Always null, because arrays always have unlimited maximum cardinality in PostgreSQL

dtd_identifier	sql_identifier	An identifier of the data type descriptor of the domain, unique among the data type descriptors pertaining to the domain (which is trivial, because a domain only contains one data type descriptor). This is mainly useful for joining with other instances of such identifiers. (The specific format of the identifier is not defined and not guaranteed to remain the same in future versions.)

Table 4.16: domains Columns

4.19 element_types

The view element_types contains the data type descriptors of the elements of arrays. When a table column, domain, function parameter, or function return value is defined to be of an array type, the respective information schema view only contains ARRAY in the column data_type. To obtain information on the element type of the array, you can join the respective view with this view. For example, to show the columns of a table with data types and array element types, if applicable, you could do

```
SELECT c.column_name, c.data_type, e.data_type AS element_type
FROM information_schema.columns c LEFT JOIN
  information_schema.element_types e
    ON ((c.table_catalog, c.table_schema, c.table_name,
'TABLE', c.dtd_identifier)
       = (e.object_catalog, e.object_schema, e.object_name,
e.object_type, e.dtd_identifier))
WHERE c.table_schema = '...' AND c.table_name = '...'
ORDER BY c.ordinal_position;
```

This view only includes objects that the current user has access to, by way of being the owner or having some privilege.

NAME	DATA TYPE	DESCRIPTION
object_catalog	sql_identifier	Name of the database that contains the object that uses the array being described (always the current database)
object_schema	sql_identifier	Name of the schema that contains the object that uses the array being described
object_name	sql_identifier	Name of the object that uses the array being described
object_type	character_data	The type of the object that uses the array being described: one of TABLE (the array is used by a column of that table), DOMAIN (the array is used by that domain), ROUTINE (the array is used by a parameter or the return data type of that function).
dtd_identifier	sql_identifier	The identifier of the data type descriptor of the array being described
data_type	character_data	Data type of the array elements, if it is a built-in type, else USER-DEFINED (in that case, the type is identified in udt_name and associated columns).
character_maximum_length	cardinal_number	Always null, since this information is not applied to array element data types in PostgreSQL

character_octet_length	cardinal_number	Always null, since this information is not applied to array element data types in PostgreSQL
character_set_catalog	sql_identifier	Applies to a feature not available in PostgreSQL
character_set_schema	sql_identifier	Applies to a feature not available in PostgreSQL
character_set_name	sql_identifier	Applies to a feature not available in PostgreSQL
collation_catalog	sql_identifier	Applies to a feature not available in PostgreSQL
collation_schema	sql_identifier	Applies to a feature not available in PostgreSQL
collation_name	sql_identifier	Applies to a feature not available in PostgreSQL
numeric_precision	cardinal_number	Always null, since this information is not applied to array element data types in PostgreSQL
numeric_precision_radix	cardinal_number	Always null, since this information is not applied to array element data types in PostgreSQL
numeric_scale	cardinal_number	Always null, since this information is not applied to array element data types in PostgreSQL
datetime_precision	cardinal_number	Always null, since this information is not applied to array element data types in PostgreSQL
interval_type	character_data	Always null, since this information is not applied to array element data types in PostgreSQL

interval_precision	character_data	Always null, since this information is not applied to array element data types in PostgreSQL
domain_default	character_data	Not yet implemented
udt_catalog	sql_identifier	Name of the database that the data type of the elements is defined in (always the current database)
udt_schema	sql_identifier	Name of the schema that the data type of the elements is defined in
udt_name	sql_identifier	Name of the data type of the elements
scope_catalog	sql_identifier	Applies to a feature not available in PostgreSQL
scope_schema	sql_identifier	Applies to a feature not available in PostgreSQL
scope_name	sql_identifier	Applies to a feature not available in PostgreSQL
maximum_cardinality	cardinal_number	Always null, because arrays always have unlimited maximum cardinality in PostgreSQL

Table 4.17: element_types Columns

4.20 enabled_roles

The view enabled_roles identifies the currently "enabled roles". The enabled roles are recursively defined as the current user together with all roles that have been granted to the enabled roles with automatic inheritance. In other words, these are all roles that the current user has direct or indirect, automatically inheriting membership in.

For permission checking, the set of "applicable roles" is applied, which may be broader than the set of enabled roles. So generally, it is better to use the view applicable_roles instead of this one; see also there.

NAME	DATA TYPE	DESCRIPTION
role_name	sql_identifier	Name of a role

Table 4.18: enabled_roles Columns

4.21 key_column_usage

The view key_column_usage identifies all columns in the current database that are restricted by some unique, primary key, or foreign key constraint. Check constraints are not included in this view. Only those columns are shown that the current user has access to, by way of being the owner or having some privilege.

NAME	DATA TYPE	DESCRIPTION
constraint_catalog	sql_identifier	Name of the database that contains the constraint (always the current database)
constraint_schema	sql_identifier	Name of the schema that contains the constraint
constraint_name	sql_identifier	Name of the constraint
table_catalog	sql_identifier	Name of the database that contains the table that contains the column that is restricted by some constraint (always the current database)
table_schema	sql_identifier	Name of the schema that contains the table that contains the column that is restricted by some constraint
table_name	sql_identifier	Name of the table that contains the column that is restricted by some constraint
column_name	sql_identifier	Name of the column that is restricted by some constraint
ordinal_position	cardinal_number	Ordinal position of the column within the constraint key (count starts at 1)

position_in_unique_constraint	cardinal_number	Not yet implemented

Table 4.19: key_column_usage Columns

4.22 parameters

The view parameters contains information about the parameters (arguments) of all functions in the current database. Only those functions are shown that the current user has access to (by way of being the owner or having some privilege).

NAME	DATA TYPE	DESCRIPTION
specific_catalog	sql_identifier	Name of the database containing the function (always the current database)
specific_schema	sql_identifier	Name of the schema containing the function
specific_name	sql_identifier	The "specific name" of the function. See routines (page 149) for more information.
ordinal_position	cardinal_number	Ordinal position of the parameter in the argument list of the function (count starts at 1)
parameter_mode	character_data	IN for input parameter, OUT for output parameter, and INOUT for input/output parameter.
is_result	character_data	Applies to a feature not available in PostgreSQL
as_locator	character_data	Applies to a feature not available in PostgreSQL
parameter_name	sql_identifier	Name of the parameter, or null if the parameter has no name

data_type	character_data	Data type of the parameter, if it is a built-in type, or ARRAY if it is some array (in that case, see the view element_types), else USER-DEFINED (in that case, the type is identified in udt_name and associated columns).
character_maximum_length	cardinal_number	Always null, since this information is not applied to parameter data types in PostgreSQL
character_octet_length	cardinal_number	Always null, since this information is not applied to parameter data types in PostgreSQL
character_set_catalog	sql_identifier	Applies to a feature not available in PostgreSQL
character_set_schema	sql_identifier	Applies to a feature not available in PostgreSQL
character_set_name	sql_identifier	Applies to a feature not available in PostgreSQL
collation_catalog	sql_identifier	Applies to a feature not available in PostgreSQL
collation_schema	sql_identifier	Applies to a feature not available in PostgreSQL
collation_name	sql_identifier	Applies to a feature not available in PostgreSQL
numeric_precision	cardinal_number	Always null, since this information is not applied to parameter data types in PostgreSQL
numeric_precision_radix	cardinal_number	Always null, since this information is not applied to parameter data types in PostgreSQL
numeric_scale	cardinal_number	Always null, since this information is not applied to parameter data types in PostgreSQL

`datetime_precision`	`cardinal_number`	Always null, since this information is not applied to parameter data types in PostgreSQL
`interval_type`	`character_data`	Always null, since this information is not applied to parameter data types in PostgreSQL
`interval_precision`	`character_data`	Always null, since this information is not applied to parameter data types in PostgreSQL
`udt_catalog`	`sql_identifier`	Name of the database that the data type of the parameter is defined in (always the current database)
`udt_schema`	`sql_identifier`	Name of the schema that the data type of the parameter is defined in
`udt_name`	`sql_identifier`	Name of the data type of the parameter
`scope_catalog`	`sql_identifier`	Applies to a feature not available in PostgreSQL
`scope_schema`	`sql_identifier`	Applies to a feature not available in PostgreSQL
`scope_name`	`sql_identifier`	Applies to a feature not available in PostgreSQL
`maximum_cardinality`	`cardinal_number`	Always null, because arrays always have unlimited maximum cardinality in PostgreSQL

dtd_identifier	sql_identifier	An identifier of the data type descriptor of the parameter, unique among the data type descriptors pertaining to the function. This is mainly useful for joining with other instances of such identifiers. (The specific format of the identifier is not defined and not guaranteed to remain the same in future versions.)

Table 4.20: parameters Columns

4.23 referential_constraints

The view referential_constraints contains all referential (foreign key) constraints in the current database that belong to a table owned by a currently enabled role.

NAME	DATA TYPE	DESCRIPTION
constraint_catalog	sql_identifier	Name of the database containing the constraint (always the current database)
constraint_schema	sql_identifier	Name of the schema containing the constraint
constraint_name	sql_identifier	Name of the constraint
unique_constraint_catalog	sql_identifier	Name of the database that contains the unique or primary key constraint that the foreign key constraint references (always the current database)
unique_constraint_schema	sql_identifier	Name of the schema that contains the unique or primary key constraint that the foreign key constraint references

unique_constraint_name	sql_identifier	Name of the unique or primary key constraint that the foreign key constraint references
match_option	character_data	Match option of the foreign key constraint: FULL, PARTIAL, or NONE.
update_rule	character_data	Update rule of the foreign key constraint: CASCADE, SET NULL, SET DEFAULT, RESTRICT, or NO ACTION.
delete_rule	character_data	Delete rule of the foreign key constraint: CASCADE, SET NULL, SET DEFAULT, RESTRICT, or NO ACTION.

Table 4.21: referential_constraints Columns

4.24 role_column_grants

The view role_column_grants identifies all privileges granted on columns where the grantor or grantee is a currently enabled role. Further information can be found under column_privileges.

NAME	DATA TYPE	DESCRIPTION
grantor	sql_identifier	Name of the role that granted the privilege
grantee	sql_identifier	Name of the role that the privilege was granted to
table_catalog	sql_identifier	Name of the database that contains the table that contains the column (always the current database)
table_schema	sql_identifier	Name of the schema that contains the table that contains the column
table_name	sql_identifier	Name of the table that contains the column
column_name	sql_identifier	Name of the column
privilege_type	character_data	Type of the privilege: SELECT, INSERT, UPDATE, or REFERENCES
is_grantable	character_data	YES if the privilege is grantable, NO if not

Table 4.22: role_column_grants Columns

4.25 role_routine_grants

The view `role_routine_grants` identifies all privileges granted on functions where the grantor or grantee is a currently enabled role. Further information can be found under `routine_privileges`.

NAME	DATA TYPE	DESCRIPTION
grantor	sql_identifier	Name of the role that granted the privilege
grantee	sql_identifier	Name of the role that the privilege was granted to
specific_catalog	sql_identifier	Name of the database containing the function (always the current database)
specific_schema	sql_identifier	Name of the schema containing the function
specific_name	sql_identifier	The "specific name" of the function. See routines (page 149) for more information.
routine_catalog	sql_identifier	Name of the database containing the function (always the current database)
routine_schema	sql_identifier	Name of the schema containing the function
routine_name	sql_identifier	Name of the function (may be duplicated in case of overloading)
privilege_type	character_data	Always EXECUTE (the only privilege type for functions)
is_grantable	character_data	YES if the privilege is grantable, NO if not

Table 4.23: `role_routine_grants` Columns

4.26 role_table_grants

The view `role_table_grants` identifies all privileges granted on tables or views where the grantor or grantee is a currently enabled role. Further information can be found under `table_privileges`.

NAME	DATA TYPE	DESCRIPTION
grantor	sql_identifier	Name of the role that granted the privilege
grantee	sql_identifier	Name of the role that the privilege was granted to
table_catalog	sql_identifier	Name of the database that contains the table (always the current database)
table_schema	sql_identifier	Name of the schema that contains the table
table_name	sql_identifier	Name of the table
privilege_type	character_data	Type of the privilege: SELECT, DELETE, INSERT, UPDATE, REFERENCES, or TRIGGER
is_grantable	character_data	YES if the privilege is grantable, NO if not
with_hierarchy	character_data	Applies to a feature not available in PostgreSQL

Table 4.24: role_table_grants Columns

4.27 role_usage_grants

The view role_usage_grants is meant to identify USAGE privileges granted on various kinds of objects to a currently enabled role or by a currently enabled role. In PostgreSQL, this currently only applies to domains, and since domains do not have real privileges in PostgreSQL, this view is empty. Further information can be found under usage_privileges. In the future, this view may contain more useful information.

NAME	DATA TYPE	DESCRIPTION
grantor	sql_identifier	In the future, the name of the role that granted the privilege
grantee	sql_identifier	In the future, the name of the role that the privilege was granted to
object_catalog	sql_identifier	Name of the database containing the object (always the current database)
object_schema	sql_identifier	Name of the schema containing the object
object_name	sql_identifier	Name of the object
object_type	character_data	In the future, the type of the object
privilege_type	character_data	Always USAGE
is_grantable	character_data	YES if the privilege is grantable, NO if not

Table 4.25: role_usage_grants Columns

4.28 routine_privileges

The view routine_privileges identifies all privileges granted to a currently enabled role or by a currently enabled role. There is one row for each combination of function, grantor, and grantee.

NAME	DATA TYPE	DESCRIPTION
grantor	sql_identifier	Name of the role that granted the privilege
grantee	sql_identifier	Name of the role that the privilege was granted to
specific_catalog	sql_identifier	Name of the database containing the function (always the current database)
specific_schema	sql_identifier	Name of the schema containing the function
specific_name	sql_identifier	The "specific name" of the function. See routines () for more information.
routine_catalog	sql_identifier	Name of the database containing the function (always the current database)
routine_schema	sql_identifier	Name of the schema containing the function
routine_name	sql_identifier	Name of the function (may be duplicated in case of overloading)
privilege_type	character_data	Always EXECUTE (the only privilege type for functions)
is_grantable	character_data	YES if the privilege is grantable, NO if not

Table 4.26: routine_privileges Columns

4.29 routines

The view routines contains all functions in the current database. Only those functions are shown that the current user has access to (by way of being the owner or having some privilege).

NAME	DATA TYPE	DESCRIPTION
specific_catalog	sql_identifier	Name of the database containing the function (always the current database)
specific_schema	sql_identifier	Name of the schema containing the function
specific_name	sql_identifier	The "specific name" of the function. This is a name that uniquely identifies the function in the schema, even if the real name of the function is overloaded. The format of the specific name is not defined, it should only be used to compare it to other instances of specific routine names.
routine_catalog	sql_identifier	Name of the database containing the function (always the current database)
routine_schema	sql_identifier	Name of the schema containing the function
routine_name	sql_identifier	Name of the function (may be duplicated in case of overloading)
routine_type	character_data	Always FUNCTION (In the future there might be other types of routines.)
module_catalog	sql_identifier	Applies to a feature not available in PostgreSQL
module_schema	sql_identifier	Applies to a feature not available in PostgreSQL
module_name	sql_identifier	Applies to a feature not available in PostgreSQL
udt_catalog	sql_identifier	Applies to a feature not available in PostgreSQL

udt_schema	sql_identifier	Applies to a feature not available in PostgreSQL
udt_name	sql_identifier	Applies to a feature not available in PostgreSQL
data_type	character_data	Return data type of the function, if it is a built-in type, or ARRAY if it is some array (in that case, see the view element_types), else USER-DEFINED (in that case, the type is identified in type_udt_name and associated columns).
character_maximum_length	cardinal_number	Always null, since this information is not applied to return data types in PostgreSQL
character_octet_length	cardinal_number	Always null, since this information is not applied to return data types in PostgreSQL
character_set_catalog	sql_identifier	Applies to a feature not available in PostgreSQL
character_set_schema	sql_identifier	Applies to a feature not available in PostgreSQL
character_set_name	sql_identifier	Applies to a feature not available in PostgreSQL
collation_catalog	sql_identifier	Applies to a feature not available in PostgreSQL
collation_schema	sql_identifier	Applies to a feature not available in PostgreSQL
collation_name	sql_identifier	Applies to a feature not available in PostgreSQL
numeric_precision	cardinal_number	Always null, since this information is not applied to return data types in PostgreSQL

numeric_precision_radix	cardinal_number	Always null, since this information is not applied to return data types in PostgreSQL
numeric_scale	cardinal_number	Always null, since this information is not applied to return data types in PostgreSQL
datetime_precision	cardinal_number	Always null, since this information is not applied to return data types in PostgreSQL
interval_type	character_data	Always null, since this information is not applied to return data types in PostgreSQL
interval_precision	character_data	Always null, since this information is not applied to return data types in PostgreSQL
type_udt_catalog	sql_identifier	Name of the database that the return data type of the function is defined in (always the current database)
type_udt_schema	sql_identifier	Name of the schema that the return data type of the function is defined in
type_udt_name	sql_identifier	Name of the return data type of the function
scope_catalog	sql_identifier	Applies to a feature not available in PostgreSQL
scope_schema	sql_identifier	Applies to a feature not available in PostgreSQL
scope_name	sql_identifier	Applies to a feature not available in PostgreSQL
maximum_cardinality	cardinal_number	Always null, because arrays always have unlimited maximum cardinality in PostgreSQL

dtd_identifier	sql_identifier	An identifier of the data type descriptor of the return data type of this function, unique among the data type descriptors pertaining to the function. This is mainly useful for joining with other instances of such identifiers. (The specific format of the identifier is not defined and not guaranteed to remain the same in future versions.)
routine_body	character_data	If the function is an SQL function, then SQL, else EXTERNAL.
routine_definition	character_data	The source text of the function (null if the function is not owned by a currently enabled role). (According to the SQL standard, this column is only applicable if routine_body is SQL, but in PostgreSQL it will contain whatever source text was specified when the function was created.)
external_name	character_data	If this function is a C function, then the external name (link symbol) of the function; else null. (This works out to be the same value that is shown in routine_definition.)
external_language	character_data	The language the function is written in
parameter_style	character_data	Always GENERAL (The SQL standard defines other parameter styles, which are not available in PostgreSQL.)

`is_deterministic`	`character_data`	If the function is declared immutable (called deterministic in the SQL standard), then YES, else NO. (You cannot query the other volatility levels available in PostgreSQL through the information schema.)
`sql_data_access`	`character_data`	Always MODIFIES, meaning that the function possibly modifies SQL data. This information is not useful for PostgreSQL.
`is_null_call`	`character_data`	If the function automatically returns null if any of its arguments are null, then YES, else NO.
`sql_path`	`character_data`	Applies to a feature not available in PostgreSQL
`schema_level_routine`	`character_data`	Always YES (The opposite would be a method of a user-defined type, which is a feature not available in PostgreSQL.)
`max_dynamic_result_sets`	`cardinal_number`	Applies to a feature not available in PostgreSQL
`is_user_defined_cast`	`character_data`	Applies to a feature not available in PostgreSQL
`is_implicitly_invocable`	`character_data`	Applies to a feature not available in PostgreSQL

security_type	character_data	If the function runs with the privileges of the current user, then INVOKER, if the function runs with the privileges of the user who defined it, then DEFINER.
to_sql_specific_catalog	sql_identifier	Applies to a feature not available in PostgreSQL
to_sql_specific_schema	sql_identifier	Applies to a feature not available in PostgreSQL
to_sql_specific_name	sql_identifier	Applies to a feature not available in PostgreSQL
as_locator	character_data	Applies to a feature not available in PostgreSQL
created	time_stamp	Applies to a feature not available in PostgreSQL
last_altered	time_stamp	Applies to a feature not available in PostgreSQL
new_savepoint_level	character_data	Applies to a feature not available in PostgreSQL
is_udt_dependent	character_data	Applies to a feature not available in PostgreSQL
result_cast_from_data_type	character_data	Applies to a feature not available in PostgreSQL
result_cast_as_locator	character_data	Applies to a feature not available in PostgreSQL
result_cast_char_max_length	cardinal_number	Applies to a feature not available in PostgreSQL
result_cast_char_octet_length	character_data	Applies to a feature not available in PostgreSQL
result_cast_char_set_catalog	sql_identifier	Applies to a feature not available in PostgreSQL

result_cast_char_set_schema	sql_identifier	Applies to a feature not available in PostgreSQL
result_cast_char_set_name	sql_identifier	Applies to a feature not available in PostgreSQL
result_cast_collation_catalog	sql_identifier	Applies to a feature not available in PostgreSQL
result_cast_collation_schema	sql_identifier	Applies to a feature not available in PostgreSQL
result_cast_collation_name	sql_identifier	Applies to a feature not available in PostgreSQL
result_cast_numeric_precision	cardinal_number	Applies to a feature not available in PostgreSQL
result_cast_numeric_precision_radix	cardinal_number	Applies to a feature not available in PostgreSQL
result_cast_numeric_scale	cardinal_number	Applies to a feature not available in PostgreSQL
result_cast_datetime_precision	character_data	Applies to a feature not available in PostgreSQL
result_cast_interval_type	character_data	Applies to a feature not available in PostgreSQL
result_cast_interval_precision	character_data	Applies to a feature not available in PostgreSQL
result_cast_type_udt_catalog	sql_identifier	Applies to a feature not available in PostgreSQL
result_cast_type_udt_schema	sql_identifier	Applies to a feature not available in PostgreSQL
result_cast_type_udt_name	sql_identifier	Applies to a feature not available in PostgreSQL
result_cast_scope_catalog	sql_identifier	Applies to a feature not available in PostgreSQL
result_cast_scope_schema	sql_identifier	Applies to a feature not available in PostgreSQL

`result_cast_scope_name`	`sql_identifier`	Applies to a feature not available in PostgreSQL
`result_cast_maximum_cardinality`	`cardinal_number`	Applies to a feature not available in PostgreSQL
`result_cast_dtd_identifier`	`sql_identifier`	Applies to a feature not available in PostgreSQL

Table 4.27: `routines` Columns

4.30 schemata

The view `schemata` contains all schemas in the current database that are owned by a currently enabled role.

NAME	DATA TYPE	DESCRIPTION
`catalog_name`	`sql_identifier`	Name of the database that the schema is contained in (always the current database)
`schema_name`	`sql_identifier`	Name of the schema
`schema_owner`	`sql_identifier`	Name of the owner of the schema
`default_character_set_catalog`	`sql_identifier`	Applies to a feature not available in PostgreSQL
`default_character_set_schema`	`sql_identifier`	Applies to a feature not available in PostgreSQL
`default_character_set_name`	`sql_identifier`	Applies to a feature not available in PostgreSQL
`sql_path`	`character_data`	Applies to a feature not available in PostgreSQL

Table 4.28: `schemata` Columns

4.31 sequences

The view sequences contains all sequences defined in the current database. Only those sequences are shown that the current user has access to (by way of being the owner or having some privilege).

Name	Data Type	Description
sequence_catalog	sql_identifier	Name of the database that contains the sequence (always the current database)
sequence_schema	sql_identifier	Name of the schema that contains the sequence
sequence_name	sql_identifier	Name of the sequence
data_type	character_data	The data type of the sequence. In PostgreSQL, this is currently always bigint.
numeric_precision	cardinal_number	This column contains the (declared or implicit) precision of the sequence data type (see above). The precision indicates the number of significant digits. It may be expressed in decimal (base 10) or binary (base 2) terms, as specified in the column numeric_precision_radix.
numeric_precision_radix	cardinal_number	This column indicates in which base the values in the columns numeric_precision and numeric_scale are expressed. The value is either 2 or 10.
numeric_scale	cardinal_number	This column contains the (declared or implicit) scale of the sequence data type (see above). The scale indicates the number of significant digits to the right of the decimal point. It may be expressed in decimal (base 10) or binary (base 2) terms, as specified in the column numeric_precision_radix.
maximum_value	cardinal_number	Not yet implemented
minimum_value	cardinal_number	Not yet implemented
increment	cardinal_number	Not yet implemented
cycle_option	character_data	Not yet implemented

Table 4.29: sequences Columns

4.32 sql_features

The table `sql_features` contains information about which formal features defined in the SQL standard are supported by PostgreSQL. This is the same information that is presented in Volume 1, Appendix D *SQL Conformance*. There you can also find some additional background information.

NAME	DATA TYPE	DESCRIPTION
feature_id	character_data	Identifier string of the feature
feature_name	character_data	Descriptive name of the feature
sub_feature_id	character_data	Identifier string of the subfeature, or a zero-length string if not a subfeature
sub_feature_name	character_data	Descriptive name of the subfeature, or a zero-length string if not a subfeature
is_supported	character_data	YES if the feature is fully supported by the current version of PostgreSQL, NO if not
is_verified_by	character_data	Always null, since the PostgreSQL development group does not perform formal testing of feature conformance
comments	character_data	Possibly a comment about the supported status of the feature

Table 4.30: `sql_features` Columns

4.33 sql_implementation_info

The table `sql_implementation_info` contains information about various aspects that are left implementation-defined by the SQL standard. This information is primarily intended for use in the context of the ODBC interface; users of other interfaces will probably find this information to be of little use. For this reason, the individual implementation information items are not described here; you will find them in the description of the ODBC interface.

NAME	DATA TYPE	DESCRIPTION
implementation_info_id	character_data	Identifier string of the implementation information item
implementation_info_name	character_data	Descriptive name of the implementation information item
integer_value	cardinal_number	Value of the implementation information item, or null if the value is contained in the column character_value
character_value	character_data	Value of the implementation information item, or null if the value is contained in the column integer_value
comments	character_data	Possibly a comment pertaining to the implementation information item

Table 4.31: sql_implementation_info Columns

4.34 sql_languages

The table sql_languages contains one row for each SQL language binding that is supported by PostgreSQL. PostgreSQL supports direct SQL and embedded SQL in C; that is all you will learn from this table.

NAME	DATA TYPE	DESCRIPTION
sql_language_source	character_data	The name of the source of the language definition; always ISO 9075, that is, the SQL standard
sql_language_year	character_data	The year the standard referenced in sql_language_source was approved; currently 2003
sql_language_conformance	character_data	The standard conformance level for the language binding. For ISO 9075:2003 this is always CORE.
sql_language_integrity	character_data	Always null (This value is relevant to an earlier version of the SQL standard.)
sql_language_implementation	character_data	Always null
sql_language_binding_style	character_data	The language binding style, either DIRECT or EMBEDDED
sql_language_programming_language	character_data	The programming language, if the binding style is EMBEDDED, else null. PostgreSQL only supports the language C.

Table 4.32: sql_languages Columns

4.35 sql_packages

The table sql_packages contains information about which feature packages defined in the SQL standard are supported by PostgreSQL. Refer to Volume 1, Appendix D *SQL Conformance* for background information on feature packages.

NAME	DATA TYPE	DESCRIPTION
feature_id	character_data	Identifier string of the package
feature_name	character_data	Descriptive name of the package
is_supported	character_data	YES if the package is fully supported by the current version of PostgreSQL, NO if not
is_verified_by	character_data	Always null, since the PostgreSQL development group does not perform formal testing of feature conformance
comments	character_data	Possibly a comment about the supported status of the package

Table 4.33: sql_packages Columns

4.36 sql_parts

The table sql_parts contains information about which of the several parts of the SQL standard are supported by PostgreSQL.

NAME	DATA TYPE	DESCRIPTION
feature_id	character_data	An identifier string containing the number of the part
feature_name	character_data	Descriptive name of the part
is_supported	character_data	YES if the part is fully supported by the current version of PostgreSQL, NO if not
is_verified_by	character_data	Always null, since the PostgreSQL development group does not perform formal testing of feature conformance
comments	character_data	Possibly a comment about the supported status of the part

Table 4.34: sql_parts Columns

4.37 sql_sizing

The table sql_sizing contains information about various size limits and maximum values in PostgreSQL. This information is primarily intended for use in the context of the ODBC interface; users of other interfaces will probably find this information to be of little use. For this reason, the individual sizing items are not described here; you will find them in the description of the ODBC interface.

NAME	DATA TYPE	DESCRIPTION
sizing_id	cardinal_number	Identifier of the sizing item
sizing_name	character_data	Descriptive name of the sizing item
supported_value	cardinal_number	Value of the sizing item, or 0 if the size is unlimited or cannot be determined, or null if the features for which the sizing item is applicable are not supported
comments	character_data	Possibly a comment pertaining to the sizing item

Table 4.35: sql_sizing Columns

4.38 sql_sizing_profiles

The table sql_sizing_profiles contains information about the sql_sizing values that are required by various profiles of the SQL standard. PostgreSQL does not track any SQL profiles, so this table is empty.

NAME	DATA TYPE	DESCRIPTION
sizing_id	cardinal_number	Identifier of the sizing item
sizing_name	character_data	Descriptive name of the sizing item
profile_id	character_data	Identifier string of a profile
required_value	cardinal_number	The value required by the SQL profile for the sizing item, or 0 if the profile places no limit on the sizing item, or null if the profile does not require any of the features for which the sizing item is applicable
comments	character_data	Possibly a comment pertaining to the sizing item within the profile

Table 4.36: sql_sizing_profiles Columns

4.39 table_constraints

The view `table_constraints` contains all constraints belonging to tables that
the current user owns or has some privilege on.

NAME	DATA TYPE	DESCRIPTION
constraint_catalog	sql_identifier	Name of the database that contains the constraint (always the current database)
constraint_schema	sql_identifier	Name of the schema that contains the constraint
constraint_name	sql_identifier	Name of the constraint
table_catalog	sql_identifier	Name of the database that contains the table (always the current database)
table_schema	sql_identifier	Name of the schema that contains the table
table_name	sql_identifier	Name of the table
constraint_type	character_data	Type of the constraint: CHECK, FOREIGN KEY, PRIMARY KEY, or UNIQUE
is_deferrable	character_data	YES if the constraint is deferrable, NO if not
initially_deferred	character_data	YES if the constraint is deferrable and initially deferred, NO if not

Table 4.37: `table_constraints` Columns

4.40 table_privileges

The view `table_privileges` identifies all privileges granted on tables or views
to a currently enabled role or by a currently enabled role. There is one row for
each combination of table, grantor, and grantee.

NAME	DATA TYPE	DESCRIPTION
grantor	sql_identifier	Name of the role that granted the privilege
grantee	sql_identifier	Name of the role that the privilege was granted to
table_catalog	sql_identifier	Name of the database that contains the table (always the current database)
table_schema	sql_identifier	Name of the schema that contains the table
table_name	sql_identifier	Name of the table
privilege_type	character_data	Type of the privilege: SELECT, DELETE, INSERT, UPDATE, REFERENCES, or TRIGGER
is_grantable	character_data	YES if the privilege is grantable, NO if not
with_hierarchy	character_data	Applies to a feature not available in PostgreSQL

Table 4.38: `table_privileges` Columns

4.41 tables

The view `tables` contains all tables and views defined in the current database. Only those tables and views are shown that the current user has access to (by way of being the owner or having some privilege).

NAME	DATA TYPE	DESCRIPTION
table_catalog	sql_identifier	Name of the database that contains the table (always the current database)
table_schema	sql_identifier	Name of the schema that contains the table
table_name	sql_identifier	Name of the table
table_type	character_data	Type of the table: BASE TABLE for a persistent base table (the normal table type), VIEW for a view, or LOCAL TEMPORARY for a temporary table
self_referencing_column_name	sql_identifier	Applies to a feature not available in PostgreSQL
reference_generation	character_data	Applies to a feature not available in PostgreSQL
user_defined_type_catalog	sql_identifier	Applies to a feature not available in PostgreSQL
user_defined_type_schema	sql_identifier	Applies to a feature not available in PostgreSQL
user_defined_type_name	sql_identifier	Applies to a feature not available in PostgreSQL
is_insertable_into	character_data	YES if the table is insertable into, NO if not (Base tables are always insertable into, views not necessarily.)

is_typed	character_data	Applies to a feature not available in PostgreSQL
commit_action	character_data	If the table is a temporary table, then PRESERVE, else null. (The SQL standard defines other commit actions for temporary tables, which are not supported by PostgreSQL.)

Table 4.39: tables Columns

4.42 triggers

The view triggers contains all triggers defined in the current database on tables that the current user owns or has some privilege on.

NAME	DATA TYPE	DESCRIPTION
trigger_catalog	sql_identifier	Name of the database that contains the trigger (always the current database)
trigger_schema	sql_identifier	Name of the schema that contains the trigger
trigger_name	sql_identifier	Name of the trigger
event_manipulation	character_data	Event that fires the trigger (INSERT, UPDATE, or DELETE)
event_object_catalog	sql_identifier	Name of the database that contains the table that the trigger is defined on (always the current database)
event_object_schema	sql_identifier	Name of the schema that contains the table that the trigger is defined on

event_object_table	sql_identifier	Name of the table that the trigger is defined on
action_order	cardinal_number	Not yet implemented
action_condition	character_data	Applies to a feature not available in PostgreSQL
action_statement	character_data	Statement that is executed by the trigger (currently always EXECUTE PROCEDURE function(...))
action_orientation	character_data	Identifies whether the trigger fires once for each processed row or once for each statement (ROW or STATEMENT)
condition_timing	character_data	Time at which the trigger fires (BEFORE or AFTER)
condition_reference_old_table	sql_identifier	Applies to a feature not available in PostgreSQL
condition_reference_new_table	sql_identifier	Applies to a feature not available in PostgreSQL
condition_reference_old_row	sql_identifier	Applies to a feature not available in PostgreSQL
condition_reference_new_row	sql_identifier	Applies to a feature not available in PostgreSQL
created	time_stamp	Applies to a feature not available in PostgreSQL

Table 4.40: triggers Columns

Triggers in PostgreSQL have two incompatibilities with the SQL standard that affect the representation in the information schema. First, trigger names are local to the table in PostgreSQL, rather than being independent schema objects. Therefore there may be duplicate trigger names defined in one schema,

as long as they belong to different tables. (`trigger_catalog` and `trigger_`
`schema` are really the values pertaining to the table that the trigger is defined on.) Second, triggers can be defined to fire on multiple events in PostgreSQL (e.g., `ON INSERT OR UPDATE`), whereas the SQL standard only allows
one. If a trigger is defined to fire on multiple events, it is represented as
multiple rows in the information schema, one for each type of event. As
a consequence of these two issues, the primary key of the view `triggers`
is really (`trigger_catalog, trigger_schema, trigger_name, event_object_`
`table, event_manipulation`) instead of (`trigger_catalog, trigger_schema,`
`trigger_name`), which is what the SQL standard specifies. Nonetheless, if you
define your triggers in a manner that conforms with the SQL standard (trigger
names unique in the schema and only one event type per trigger), this will not
affect you.

4.43 usage_privileges

The view `usage_privileges` is meant to identify `USAGE` privileges granted on
various kinds of objects to a currently enabled role or by a currently enabled role.
In PostgreSQL, this currently only applies to domains, and since domains do
not have real privileges in PostgreSQL, this view shows implicit `USAGE` privileges
granted to `PUBLIC` for all domains. In the future, this view may contain more
useful information.

NAME	DATA TYPE	DESCRIPTION
grantor	sql_identifier	Currently set to the name of the owner of the object
grantee	sql_identifier	Currently always PUBLIC
object_catalog	sql_identifier	Name of the database containing the object (always the current database)
object_schema	sql_identifier	Name of the schema containing the object
object_name	sql_identifier	Name of the object
object_type	character_data	Currently always DOMAIN
privilege_type	character_data	Always USAGE
is_grantable	character_data	Currently always NO

Table 4.41: usage_privileges Columns

4.44 view_column_usage

The view view_column_usage identifies all columns that are used in the query expression of a view (the SELECT statement that defines the view). A column is only included if the table that contains the column is owned by a currently enabled role.

Note: Columns of system tables are not included. This should be fixed sometime.

NAME	DATA TYPE	DESCRIPTION
view_catalog	sql_identifier	Name of the database that contains the view (always the current database)
view_schema	sql_identifier	Name of the schema that contains the view
view_name	sql_identifier	Name of the view
table_catalog	sql_identifier	Name of the database that contains the table that contains the column that is used by the view (always the current database)
table_schema	sql_identifier	Name of the schema that contains the table that contains the column that is used by the view
table_name	sql_identifier	Name of the table that contains the column that is used by the view
column_name	sql_identifier	Name of the column that is used by the view

Table 4.42: view_column_usage Columns

4.45 view_routine_usage

The view view_routine_usage identifies all routines (functions and procedures) that are used in the query expression of a view (the SELECT statement that defines the view). A routine is only included if that routine is owned by a currently enabled role.

NAME	DATA TYPE	DESCRIPTION
table_catalog	sql_identifier	Name of the database containing the view (always the current database)
table_schema	sql_identifier	Name of the schema containing the view
table_name	sql_identifier	Name of the view
specific_catalog	sql_identifier	Name of the database containing the function (always the current database)
specific_schema	sql_identifier	Name of the schema containing the function
specific_name	sql_identifier	The "specific name" of the function. See routines (page 149) for more information.

Table 4.43: view_routine_usage Columns

4.46 view_table_usage

The view view_table_usage identifies all tables that are used in the query expression of a view (the SELECT statement that defines the view). A table is only included if that table is owned by a currently enabled role.

Note: System tables are not included. This should be fixed sometime.

NAME	DATA TYPE	DESCRIPTION
view_catalog	sql_identifier	Name of the database that contains the view (always the current database)
view_schema	sql_identifier	Name of the schema that contains the view
view_name	sql_identifier	Name of the view
table_catalog	sql_identifier	Name of the database that contains the table that is used by the view (always the current database)
table_schema	sql_identifier	Name of the schema that contains the table that is used by the view
table_name	sql_identifier	Name of the table that is used by the view

Table 4.44: view_table_usage Columns

4.47 views

The view views contains all views defined in the current database. Only those views are shown that the current user has access to (by way of being the owner or having some privilege).

NAME	DATA TYPE	DESCRIPTION
table_catalog	sql_identifier	Name of the database that contains the view (always the current database)
table_schema	sql_identifier	Name of the schema that contains the view
table_name	sql_identifier	Name of the view
view_definition	character_data	Query expression defining the view (null if the view is not owned by a currently enabled role)
check_option	character_data	Applies to a feature not available in PostgreSQL
is_updatable	character_data	YES if the view is updatable (allows UPDATE and DELETE), NO if not
is_insertable_into	character_data	YES if the view is insertable into (allows INSERT), NO if not

Table 4.45: views Columns

Server Programming

This part is about extending the server functionality with user-defined functions, data types, triggers, etc. These are advanced topics which should probably be approached only after all the other user documentation about PostgreSQL has been understood. Later chapters in this part describe the server-side programming languages available in the PostgreSQL distribution as well as general issues concerning server-side programming languages. It is essential to read at least the earlier sections of Chapter 5 *Extending SQL*, page 175 (covering functions) before diving into the material about server-side programming languages.

5 Extending SQL

In the sections that follow, we will discuss how you can extend the PostgreSQL SQL query language by adding:

- functions (starting in Section 5.3 *User-Defined Functions*, page 177)
- aggregates (starting in Section 5.10 *User-Defined Aggregates*, page 216)
- data types (starting in Section 5.11 *User-Defined Types*, page 218)
- operators (starting in Section 5.12 *User-Defined Operators*, page 221)
- operator classes for indexes (starting in Section 5.14 *Interfacing Extensions To Indexes*, page 228)

5.1 How Extensibility Works

PostgreSQL is extensible because its operation is catalog-driven. If you are familiar with standard relational database systems, you know that they store information about databases, tables, columns, etc., in what are commonly known as system catalogs. (Some systems call this the data dictionary.) The catalogs appear to the user as tables like any other, but the DBMS stores its internal bookkeeping in them. One key difference between PostgreSQL and standard relational database systems is that PostgreSQL stores much more information in its catalogs: not only information about tables and columns, but also information about data types, functions, access methods, and so on. These tables can be modified by the user, and since PostgreSQL bases its operation on these tables, this means that PostgreSQL can be extended by users. By comparison, conventional database systems can only be extended by changing hardcoded procedures in the source code or by loading modules specially written by the DBMS vendor.

The PostgreSQL server can moreover incorporate user-written code into itself through dynamic loading. That is, the user can specify an object code file (e.g., a shared library) that implements a new type or function, and PostgreSQL will load it as required. Code written in SQL is even more trivial to add to the server. This ability to modify its operation "on the fly" makes PostgreSQL uniquely suited for rapid prototyping of new applications and storage structures.

5.2 The PostgreSQL Type System

PostgreSQL data types are divided into base types, composite types, domains, and pseudo-types.

5.2.1 Base Types

Base types are those, like int4, that are implemented below the level of the SQL language (typically in a low-level language such as C). They generally correspond to what are often known as abstract data types. PostgreSQL can only operate on such types through functions provided by the user and only understands the behavior of such types to the extent that the user describes them. Base types are further subdivided into scalar and array types. For each scalar type, a corresponding array type is automatically created that can hold variable-size arrays of that scalar type.

5.2.2 Composite Types

Composite types, or row types, are created whenever the user creates a table. It is also possible to use CREATE TYPE to define a "stand-alone" composite type with no associated table. A composite type is simply a list of types with associated field names. A value of a composite type is a row or record of field values. The user can access the component fields from SQL queries. Refer to Volume 1, Section 6.11 *Composite Types* for more information on composite types.

5.2.3 Domains

A domain is based on a particular base type and for many purposes is interchangeable with its base type. However, a domain may have constraints that restrict its valid values to a subset of what the underlying base type would allow.

Domains can be created using the SQL command CREATE DOMAIN. Their creation and use is not discussed in this chapter.

5.2.4 Pseudo-Types

There are a few "pseudo-types" for special purposes. Pseudo-types cannot appear as columns of tables or attributes of composite types, but they can be used to declare the argument and result types of functions. This provides a mechanism within the type system to identify special classes of functions. Table 6.20 lists the existing pseudo-types.

5.2.5 Polymorphic Types

Two pseudo-types of special interest are anyelement and anyarray, which are collectively called *polymorphic types*. Any function declared using these types is said to be a *polymorphic function*. A polymorphic function can operate on many different data types, with the specific data type(s) being determined by the data types actually passed to it in a particular call.

Polymorphic arguments and results are tied to each other and are resolved to a specific data type when a query calling a polymorphic function is parsed. Each position (either argument or return value) declared as anyelement is allowed to have any specific actual data type, but in any given call they must all be the *same* actual type. Each position declared as anyarray can have any array data type, but similarly they must all be the same type. If there are positions declared anyarray and others declared anyelement, the actual array type in the anyarray positions must be an array whose elements are the same type appearing in the anyelement positions.

Thus, when more than one argument position is declared with a polymorphic type, the net effect is that only certain combinations of actual argument types are allowed. For example, a function declared as equal(anyelement, anyelement) will take any two input values, so long as they are of the same data type.

When the return value of a function is declared as a polymorphic type, there must be at least one argument position that is also polymorphic, and the actual data type supplied as the argument determines the actual result type for that call. For example, if there were not already an array subscripting mechanism, one could define a function that implements subscripting as subscript(anyarray, integer) returns anyelement. This declaration constrains the actual first argument to be an array type, and allows the parser to infer the correct result type from the actual first argument's type.

5.3 User-Defined Functions

PostgreSQL provides four kinds of functions:

- query language functions (functions written in SQL) (Section 5.4 *Query Language (SQL) Functions*, page 178)

- procedural language functions (functions written in, for example, PL/pgSQL or PL/Tcl) (Section 5.7 *Procedural Language Functions*, page 189)

- internal functions (Section 5.8 *Internal Functions*, page 190)

- C-language functions (Section 5.9 *C-Language Functions*, page 190)

Every kind of function can take base types, composite types, or combinations of these as arguments (parameters). In addition, every kind of function can return a base type or a composite type. Functions may also be defined to return sets of base or composite values.

Many kinds of functions can take or return certain pseudo-types (such as polymorphic types), but the available facilities vary. Consult the description of each kind of function for more details.

It's easiest to define SQL functions, so we'll start by discussing those. Most of the concepts presented for SQL functions will carry over to the other types of functions.

Throughout this chapter, it can be useful to look at the reference page of the CREATE FUNCTION command to understand the examples better. Some examples from this chapter can be found in 'funcs.sql' and 'funcs.c' in the 'src/tutorial' directory in the PostgreSQL source distribution.

5.4 Query Language (SQL) Functions

SQL functions execute an arbitrary list of SQL statements, returning the result of the last query in the list. In the simple (non-set) case, the first row of the last query's result will be returned. (Bear in mind that "the first row" of a multirow result is not well-defined unless you use ORDER BY.) If the last query happens to return no rows at all, the null value will be returned.

Alternatively, an SQL function may be declared to return a set, by specifying the function's return type as SETOF *sometype*. In this case all rows of the last query's result are returned. Further details appear below.

The body of an SQL function must be a list of SQL statements separated by semicolons. A semicolon after the last statement is optional. Unless the function is declared to return void, the last statement must be a SELECT.

Any collection of commands in the SQL language can be packaged together and defined as a function. Besides SELECT queries, the commands can include data modification queries (INSERT, UPDATE, and DELETE), as well as other SQL commands. (The only exception is that you can't put BEGIN, COMMIT, ROLLBACK, or SAVEPOINT commands into a SQL function.) However, the final command must be a SELECT that returns whatever is specified as the function's return type. Alternatively, if you want to define a SQL function that performs actions but has no useful value to return, you can define it as returning void. In that case, the function body must not end with a SELECT. For example, this function removes rows with negative salaries from the emp table:

```
CREATE FUNCTION clean_emp() RETURNS void AS '
    DELETE FROM emp
        WHERE salary < 0;
' LANGUAGE SQL;

SELECT clean_emp();

 clean_emp
-----------

(1 row)
```

The syntax of the CREATE FUNCTION command requires the function body to be written as a string constant. It is usually most convenient to use dollar quoting (see Volume 1, Section 2.1.2.2 *Dollar-Quoted String Constants*) for the string constant. If you choose to use regular single-quoted string constant syntax, you must double single quote marks (') and backslashes (\) (assuming escape string syntax) in the body of the function (see Volume 1, Section 2.1.2.1 *String Constants*).

Arguments to the SQL function are referenced in the function body using the syntax $n: $1 refers to the first argument, $2 to the second, and so on. If an argument is of a composite type, then the dot notation, e.g., $1.name, may be used to access attributes of the argument. The arguments can only be used as data values, not as identifiers. Thus for example this is reasonable:

```
    INSERT INTO mytable VALUES ($1);
but this will not work:
    INSERT INTO $1 VALUES (42);
```

5.4.1 SQL Functions on Base Types

The simplest possible SQL function has no arguments and simply returns a base type, such as integer:

```
CREATE FUNCTION one() RETURNS integer AS $$
    SELECT 1 AS result;
$$ LANGUAGE SQL;

-- Alternative syntax for string literal:
CREATE FUNCTION one() RETURNS integer AS '
    SELECT 1 AS result;
' LANGUAGE SQL;

SELECT one();

  one
 -----
    1
```

Notice that we defined a column alias within the function body for the result of the function (with the name result), but this column alias is not visible outside the function. Hence, the result is labeled one instead of result.

It is almost as easy to define SQL functions that take base types as arguments. In the example below, notice how we refer to the arguments within the function as $1 and $2.

```
CREATE FUNCTION add_em(integer, integer) RETURNS integer AS $$
    SELECT $1 + $2;
$$ LANGUAGE SQL;

SELECT add_em(1, 2) AS answer;

  answer
 --------
     3
```

Here is a more useful function, which might be used to debit a bank account:

```
CREATE FUNCTION tf1 (integer, numeric) RETURNS integer AS $$
    UPDATE bank
        SET balance = balance - $2
        WHERE accountno = $1;
    SELECT 1;
$$ LANGUAGE SQL;
```

A user could execute this function to debit account 17 by $100.00 as follows:

```
SELECT tf1(17, 100.0);
```

In practice one would probably like a more useful result from the function than a constant 1, so a more likely definition is

```
CREATE FUNCTION tf1 (integer, numeric) RETURNS numeric AS $$
    UPDATE bank
        SET balance = balance - $2
        WHERE accountno = $1;
    SELECT balance FROM bank WHERE accountno = $1;
$$ LANGUAGE SQL;
```

which adjusts the balance and returns the new balance.

5.4.2 SQL Functions on Composite Types

When writing functions with arguments of composite types, we must not only specify which argument we want (as we did above with $1 and $2) but also the desired attribute (field) of that argument. For example, suppose that emp is a table containing employee data, and therefore also the name of the composite type of each row of the table. Here is a function double_salary that computes what someone's salary would be if it were doubled:

```
CREATE TABLE emp (
    name        text,
    salary      numeric,
    age         integer,
    cubicle     point
);

CREATE FUNCTION double_salary(emp) RETURNS numeric AS $$
    SELECT $1.salary * 2 AS salary;
$$ LANGUAGE SQL;

SELECT name, double_salary(emp.*) AS dream
    FROM emp
    WHERE emp.cubicle ~= point '(2,1)';

 name | dream
------+-------
 Bill |  8400
```

Notice the use of the syntax $1.salary to select one field of the argument row value. Also notice how the calling SELECT command uses * to select the entire current row of a table as a composite value. The table row can alternatively be referenced using just the table name, like this:

```
SELECT name, double_salary(emp) AS dream
    FROM emp
    WHERE emp.cubicle ~= point '(2,1)';
```

but this usage is deprecated since it's easy to get confused.

Sometimes it is handy to construct a composite argument value on-the-fly. This can be done with the ROW construct. For example, we could adjust the data being passed to the function:

```
SELECT name, double_salary(ROW(name, salary*1.1, age,
cubicle)) AS dream
    FROM emp;
```

It is also possible to build a function that returns a composite type. This is an example of a function that returns a single emp row:

```
CREATE FUNCTION new_emp() RETURNS emp AS $$
    SELECT text 'None' AS name,
        1000.0 AS salary,
        25 AS age,
        point '(2,2)' AS cubicle;
$$ LANGUAGE SQL;
```

In this example we have specified each of the attributes with a constant value, but any computation could have been substituted for these constants.

Note two important things about defining the function:

- The select list order in the query must be exactly the same as that in which the columns appear in the table associated with the composite type. (Naming the columns, as we did above, is irrelevant to the system.)

- You must typecast the expressions to match the definition of the composite type, or you will get errors like this:

  ```
  ERROR: function declared to return emp returns varchar
      instead of text at column 1
  ```

A different way to define the same function is:

```
CREATE FUNCTION new_emp() RETURNS emp AS $$
    SELECT ROW('None', 1000.0, 25, '(2,2)')::emp;
$$ LANGUAGE SQL;
```

Here we wrote a SELECT that returns just a single column of the correct composite type. This isn't really better in this situation, but it is a handy alternative in some cases—for example, if we need to compute the result by calling another function that returns the desired composite value.

We could call this function directly in either of two ways:

```
SELECT new_emp();

         new_emp
-------------------------
 (None,1000.0,25,"(2,2)")

SELECT * FROM new_emp();

 name | salary | age | cubicle
------+--------+-----+---------
 None | 1000.0 |  25 | (2,2)
```

The second way is described more fully in Section 5.4.4 *SQL Functions as Table Sources*, page 184.

When you use a function that returns a composite type, you might want only one field (attribute) from its result. You can do that with syntax like this:

```
SELECT (new_emp()).name;
```

```
 name
------
 None
```

The extra parentheses are needed to keep the parser from getting confused. If you try to do it without them, you get something like this:

```
SELECT new_emp().name;
ERROR:  syntax error at or near "." at character 17
LINE 1: SELECT new_emp().name;
                        ^
```

Another option is to use functional notation for extracting an attribute. The simple way to explain this is that we can use the notations `attribute(table)` and `table.attribute` interchangeably.

```
SELECT name(new_emp());
```

```
 name
------
 None
-- This is the same as:
-- SELECT emp.name AS youngster FROM emp WHERE emp.age < 30;
```

```
SELECT name(emp) AS youngster FROM emp WHERE age(emp) < 30;
```

```
 youngster
-----------
 Sam
 Andy
```

Tip: The equivalence between functional notation and attribute notation makes it possible to use functions on composite types to emulate "computed fields". For example, using the previous definition for `double_salary(emp)`, we can write

```
SELECT emp.name, emp.double_salary FROM emp;
```

An application using this wouldn't need to be directly aware that `double_salary` isn't a real column of the table. (You can also emulate computed fields with views.)

Another way to use a function returning a composite type is to pass the result to another function that accepts the correct row type as input:

```
CREATE FUNCTION getname(emp) RETURNS text AS $$
    SELECT $1.name;
$$ LANGUAGE SQL;

SELECT getname(new_emp());
 getname
---------
 None
(1 row)
```

Still another way to use a function that returns a composite type is to call it as a table function, as described in Section 5.4.4 *SQL Functions as Table Sources*, page 184.

5.4.3 Functions with Output Parameters

An alternative way of describing a function's results is to define it with *output parameters*, as in this example:

```
CREATE FUNCTION add_em (IN x int, IN y int, OUT sum int)
AS 'SELECT $1 + $2'
LANGUAGE SQL;

SELECT add_em(3,7);
 add_em
--------
     10
(1 row)
```

This is not essentially different from the version of add_em shown in Section 5.4.1 *SQL Functions on Base Types*, page 179. The real value of output parameters is that they provide a convenient way of defining functions that return several columns. For example,

```
CREATE FUNCTION sum_n_product (x int, y int, OUT sum int, OUT
  product int)
AS 'SELECT $1 + $2, $1 * $2'
LANGUAGE SQL;

 SELECT * FROM sum_n_product(11,42);
 sum | product
-----+---------
  53 |     462
(1 row)
```

What has essentially happened here is that we have created an anonymous composite type for the result of the function. The above example has the same end result as

```
CREATE TYPE sum_prod AS (sum int, product int);

CREATE FUNCTION sum_n_product (int, int) RETURNS sum_prod
AS 'SELECT $1 + $2, $1 * $2'
LANGUAGE SQL;
```

but not having to bother with the separate composite type definition is often handy.

Notice that output parameters are not included in the calling argument list when invoking such a function from SQL. This is because PostgreSQL considers only the input parameters to define the function's calling signature. That means also that only the input parameters matter when referencing the function for purposes such as dropping it. We could drop the above function with either of

```
DROP FUNCTION sum_n_product (x int, y int, OUT sum int, OUT
    product int);
DROP FUNCTION sum_n_product (int, int);
```

Parameters can be marked as IN (the default), OUT, or INOUT. An INOUT parameter serves as both an input parameter (part of the calling argument list) and an output parameter (part of the result record type).

5.4.4 SQL Functions as Table Sources

All SQL functions may be used in the FROM clause of a query, but it is particularly useful for functions returning composite types. If the function is defined to return a base type, the table function produces a one-column table. If the function is defined to return a composite type, the table function produces a column for each attribute of the composite type.

Here is an example:

```
CREATE TABLE foo (fooid int, foosubid int, fooname text);
INSERT INTO foo VALUES (1, 1, 'Joe');
INSERT INTO foo VALUES (1, 2, 'Ed');
INSERT INTO foo VALUES (2, 1, 'Mary');

CREATE FUNCTION getfoo(int) RETURNS foo AS $$
    SELECT * FROM foo WHERE fooid = $1;
$$ LANGUAGE SQL;

SELECT *, upper(fooname) FROM getfoo(1) AS t1;

 fooid | foosubid | fooname | upper
-------+----------+---------+-------
     1 |        1 | Joe     | JOE
(1 row)
```

As the example shows, we can work with the columns of the function's result just the same as if they were columns of a regular table.

Note that we only got one row out of the function. This is because we did not use SETOF. That is described in the next section.

5.4.5 SQL Functions Returning Sets

When an SQL function is declared as returning SETOF *sometype*, the function's final SELECT query is executed to completion, and each row it outputs is returned as an element of the result set.

This feature is normally used when calling the function in the FROM clause. In this case each row returned by the function becomes a row of the table seen by the query. For example, assume that table foo has the same contents as above, and we say:

```
CREATE FUNCTION getfoo(int) RETURNS SETOF foo AS $$
    SELECT * FROM foo WHERE fooid = $1;
$$ LANGUAGE SQL;

SELECT * FROM getfoo(1) AS t1;
```

Then we would get:

```
 fooid | foosubid | fooname
-------+----------+---------
     1 |        1 | Joe
     1 |        2 | Ed
(2 rows)
```

Currently, functions returning sets may also be called in the select list of a query. For each row that the query generates by itself, the function returning set is invoked, and an output row is generated for each element of the function's result set. Note, however, that this capability is deprecated and may be removed in future releases. The following is an example function returning a set from the select list:

```
CREATE FUNCTION listchildren(text) RETURNS SETOF text AS $$
    SELECT name FROM nodes WHERE parent = $1
$$ LANGUAGE SQL;

SELECT * FROM nodes;
    name     | parent
-----------+--------
 Top       |
 Child1    | Top
 Child2    | Top
 Child3    | Top
 SubChild1 | Child1
 SubChild2 | Child1
(6 rows)

SELECT listchildren('Top');
 listchildren
--------------
 Child1
 Child2
 Child3
(3 rows)
```

```
SELECT name, listchildren(name) FROM nodes;
   name  | listchildren
--------+--------------
 Top    | Child1
 Top    | Child2
 Top    | Child3
 Child1 | SubChild1
 Child1 | SubChild2
(5 rows)
```

In the last SELECT, notice that no output row appears for Child2, Child3, etc.
This happens because listchildren returns an empty set for those arguments,
so no result rows are generated.

5.4.6 Polymorphic SQL Functions

SQL functions may be declared to accept and return the polymorphic types
anyelement and anyarray. See Section 5.2.5 *Polymorphic Types*, page 176 for
a more detailed explanation of polymorphic functions. Here is a polymorphic
function make_array that builds up an array from two arbitrary data type
elements:

```
CREATE FUNCTION make_array(anyelement, anyelement) RETURNS
anyarray AS $$
    SELECT ARRAY[$1, $2];
$$ LANGUAGE SQL;

SELECT make_array(1, 2) AS intarray, make_array('a'::text,
'b') AS textarray;
 intarray | textarray
----------+-----------
 {1,2}    | {a,b}
(1 row)
```

Notice the use of the typecast 'a'::text to specify that the argument is
of type text. This is required if the argument is just a string literal, since
otherwise it would be treated as type unknown, and array of unknown is not a
valid type. Without the typecast, you will get errors like this:

```
ERROR:  could not determine "anyarray"/"anyelement" type
because input has type "unknown"
```

It is permitted to have polymorphic arguments with a fixed return type, but
the converse is not. For example:

```
CREATE FUNCTION is_greater(anyelement, anyelement) RETURNS
boolean AS $$
    SELECT $1 > $2;
$$ LANGUAGE SQL;

SELECT is_greater(1, 2);
 is_greater
------------
```

```
f
(1 row)
```

```
CREATE FUNCTION invalid_func() RETURNS anyelement AS $$
    SELECT 1;
$$ LANGUAGE SQL;
ERROR:   cannot determine result data type
DETAIL:  A function returning "anyarray" or "anyelement" must
    have at least one argument of either type.
```

Polymorphism can be used with functions that have output arguments. For example:

```
CREATE FUNCTION dup (f1 anyelement, OUT f2 anyelement, OUT f3
    anyarray)
AS 'select $1, array[$1,$1]' LANGUAGE sql;
```

```
SELECT * FROM dup(22);
 f2 |    f3
----+---------
 22 | {22,22}
(1 row)
```

5.5 Function Overloading

More than one function may be defined with the same SQL name, so long as the arguments they take are different. In other words, function names can be *overloaded*. When a query is executed, the server will determine which function to call from the data types and the number of the provided arguments. Overloading can also be used to simulate functions with a variable number of arguments, up to a finite maximum number.

When creating a family of overloaded functions, one should be careful not to create ambiguities. For instance, given the functions

```
CREATE FUNCTION test(int, real) RETURNS ...
CREATE FUNCTION test(smallint, double precision) RETURNS ...
```

it is not immediately clear which function would be called with some trivial input like test(1, 1.5). The currently implemented resolution rules are described in Volume 1, Chapter 8 *Type Conversion*, but it is unwise to design a system that subtly relies on this behavior.

A function that takes a single argument of a composite type should generally not have the same name as any attribute (field) of that type. Recall that attribute(table) is considered equivalent to table.attribute. In the case that there is an ambiguity between a function on a composite type and an attribute of the composite type, the attribute will always be used. It is possible to override that choice by schema-qualifying the function name (that is, schema.func(table)) but it's better to avoid the problem by not choosing conflicting names.

When overloading C-language functions, there is an additional constraint: The C name of each function in the family of overloaded functions must be different from the C names of all other functions, either internal or dynamically loaded. If this rule is violated, the behavior is not portable. You might get a run-time linker error, or one of the functions will get called (usually the internal one). The alternative form of the AS clause for the SQL CREATE FUNCTION command decouples the SQL function name from the function name in the C source code. For instance,

```
CREATE FUNCTION test(int) RETURNS int
    AS 'filename', 'test_1arg'
    LANGUAGE C;
CREATE FUNCTION test(int, int) RETURNS int
    AS 'filename', 'test_2arg'
    LANGUAGE C;
```

The names of the C functions here reflect one of many possible conventions.

5.6 Function Volatility Categories

Every function has a *volatility* classification, with the possibilities being VOLATILE, STABLE, or IMMUTABLE. VOLATILE is the default if the CREATE FUNCTION command does not specify a category. The volatility category is a promise to the optimizer about the behavior of the function:

- A VOLATILE function can do anything, including modifying the database. It can return different results on successive calls with the same arguments. The optimizer makes no assumptions about the behavior of such functions. A query using a volatile function will re-evaluate the function at every row where its value is needed.

- A STABLE function cannot modify the database and is guaranteed to return the same results given the same arguments for all rows within a single statement. This category allows the optimizer to optimize multiple calls of the function to a single call. In particular, it is safe to use an expression containing such a function in an index scan condition. (Since an index scan will evaluate the comparison value only once, not once at each row, it is not valid to use a VOLATILE function in an index scan condition.)

- An IMMUTABLE function cannot modify the database and is guaranteed to return the same results given the same arguments forever. This category allows the optimizer to pre-evaluate the function when a query calls it with constant arguments. For example, a query like SELECT ... WHERE x = 2 + 2 can be simplified on sight to SELECT ... WHERE x = 4, because the function underlying the integer addition operator is marked IMMUTABLE.

For best optimization results, you should label your functions with the strictest volatility category that is valid for them.

Any function with side-effects *must* be labeled VOLATILE, so that calls to it cannot be optimized away. Even a function with no side-effects needs to be labeled VOLATILE if its value can change within a single query; some examples are random(), currval(), timeofday().

There is relatively little difference between STABLE and IMMUTABLE categories when considering simple interactive queries that are planned and immediately executed: it doesn't matter a lot whether a function is executed once during planning or once during query execution startup. But there is a big difference if the plan is saved and reused later. Labeling a function IMMUTABLE when it really isn't may allow it to be prematurely folded to a constant during planning, resulting in a stale value being re-used during subsequent uses of the plan. This is a hazard when using prepared statements or when using function languages that cache plans (such as PL/pgSQL).

Because of the snapshotting behavior of MVCC (see Volume 1, Chapter 10 *Concurrency Control*) a function containing only SELECT commands can safely be marked STABLE, even if it selects from tables that might be undergoing modifications by concurrent queries. PostgreSQL will execute a STABLE function using the snapshot established for the calling query, and so it will see a fixed view of the database throughout that query. Also note that the current_timestamp family of functions qualify as stable, since their values do not change within a transaction.

The same snapshotting behavior is used for SELECT commands within IMMUTABLE functions. It is generally unwise to select from database tables within an IMMUTABLE function at all, since the immutability will be broken if the table contents ever change. However, PostgreSQL does not enforce that you do not do that.

A common error is to label a function IMMUTABLE when its results depend on a configuration parameter. For example, a function that manipulates timestamps might well have results that depend on the timezone setting. For safety, such functions should be labeled STABLE instead.

> Note: Before PostgreSQL release 8.0, the requirement that STABLE and IMMUTABLE functions cannot modify the database was not enforced by the system. Release 8.0 enforces it by requiring SQL functions and procedural language functions of these categories to contain no SQL commands other than SELECT. (This is not a completely bulletproof test, since such functions could still call VOLATILE functions that modify the database. If you do that, you will find that the STABLE or IMMUTABLE function does not notice the database changes applied by the called function.)

5.7 Procedural Language Functions

PostgreSQL allows user-defined functions to be written in other languages besides SQL and C. These other languages are generically called *procedural languages* (PLs). Procedural languages aren't built into the PostgreSQL server; they are offered by loadable modules. See Chapter 8 *Procedural Languages*, page 273 and following chapters for more information.

5.8 Internal Functions

Internal functions are functions written in C that have been statically linked into the PostgreSQL server. The "body" of the function definition specifies the C-language name of the function, which need not be the same as the name being declared for SQL use. (For reasons of backwards compatibility, an empty body is accepted as meaning that the C-language function name is the same as the SQL name.)

Normally, all internal functions present in the server are declared during the initialization of the database cluster (initdb), but a user could use CREATE FUNCTION to create additional alias names for an internal function. Internal functions are declared in CREATE FUNCTION with language name internal. For instance, to create an alias for the sqrt function:

```
CREATE FUNCTION square_root(double precision) RETURNS double
precision
    AS 'dsqrt'
    LANGUAGE internal
    STRICT;
```

(Most internal functions expect to be declared "strict".)

> **Note:** Not all "predefined" functions are "internal" in the above sense. Some predefined functions are written in SQL.

5.9 C-Language Functions

User-defined functions can be written in C (or a language that can be made compatible with C, such as C++). Such functions are compiled into dynamically loadable objects (also called shared libraries) and are loaded by the server on demand. The dynamic loading feature is what distinguishes "C language" functions from "internal" functions—the actual coding conventions are essentially the same for both. (Hence, the standard internal function library is a rich source of coding examples for user-defined C functions.)

Two different calling conventions are currently used for C functions. The newer "version 1" calling convention is indicated by writing a PG_FUNCTION_INFO_V1() macro call for the function, as illustrated below. Lack of such a macro indicates an old-style ("version 0") function. The language name specified in CREATE FUNCTION is C in either case. Old-style functions are now deprecated because of portability problems and lack of functionality, but they are still supported for compatibility reasons.

5.9.1 Dynamic Loading

The first time a user-defined function in a particular loadable object file is called in a session, the dynamic loader loads that object file into memory so that the function can be called. The CREATE FUNCTION for a user-defined C function must therefore specify two pieces of information for the function: the name of the loadable object file, and the C name (link symbol) of the specific function to call within that object file. If the C name is not explicitly specified then it is assumed to be the same as the SQL function name.

The following algorithm is used to locate the shared object file based on the name given in the CREATE FUNCTION command:

1. If the name is an absolute path, the given file is loaded.

2. If the name starts with the string $libdir, that part is replaced by the PostgreSQL package library directory name, which is determined at build time.

3. If the name does not contain a directory part, the file is searched for in the path specified by the configuration variable dynamic_library_path.

4. Otherwise (the file was not found in the path, or it contains a non-absolute directory part), the dynamic loader will try to take the name as given, which will most likely fail. (It is unreliable to depend on the current working directory.)

If this sequence does not work, the platform-specific shared library file name extension (often '.so') is appended to the given name and this sequence is tried again. If that fails as well, the load will fail.

It is recommended to locate shared libraries either relative to $libdir or through the dynamic library path. This simplifies version upgrades if the new installation is at a different location. The actual directory that $libdir stands for can be found out with the command pg_config --pkglibdir.

The user ID the PostgreSQL server runs as must be able to traverse the path to the file you intend to load. Making the file or a higher-level directory not readable and/or not executable by the postgres user is a common mistake.

In any case, the file name that is given in the CREATE FUNCTION command is recorded literally in the system catalogs, so if the file needs to be loaded again the same procedure is applied.

> **Note:** PostgreSQL will not compile a C function automatically. The object file must be compiled before it is referenced in a CREATE FUNCTION command. See Section 5.9.6 *Compiling and Linking Dynamically-Loaded Functions*, page 201 for additional information.

To ensure that a dynamically loaded object file is not loaded into an incompatible server, PostgreSQL checks that the file contains a "magic block" with the appropriate contents. This allows the server to detect obvious incompatibilities, such as code compiled for a different major version of PostgreSQL. A magic block is required as of PostgreSQL 8.2. To include a magic block, write this in one (and only one) of the module source files, after having included the header 'fmgr.h':

```
#ifdef PG_MODULE_MAGIC
PG_MODULE_MAGIC;
#endif
```

The #ifdef test can be omitted if the code doesn't need to compile against pre-8.2 PostgreSQL releases.

After it is used for the first time, a dynamically loaded object file is retained in memory. Future calls in the same session to the function(s) in that file will only incur the small overhead of a symbol table lookup. If you need to force a reload of an object file, for example after recompiling it, use the LOAD command or begin a fresh session.

Optionally, a dynamically loaded file can contain initialization and finalization functions. If the file includes a function named _PG_init, that function will be called immediately after loading the file. The function receives no parameters and should return void. If the file includes a function named _PG_fini, that function will be called immediately before unloading the file. Likewise, the function receives no parameters and should return void. Note that _PG_fini will only be called during an unload of the file, not during process termination. (Presently, an unload only happens in the context of re-loading the file due to an explicit LOAD command.)

5.9.2 Base Types in C-Language Functions

To know how to write C-language functions, you need to know how PostgreSQL internally represents base data types and how they can be passed to and from functions. Internally, PostgreSQL regards a base type as a "blob of memory". The user-defined functions that you define over a type in turn define the way that PostgreSQL can operate on it. That is, PostgreSQL will only store and retrieve the data from disk and use your user-defined functions to input, process, and output the data.

Base types can have one of three internal formats:

- pass by value, fixed-length
- pass by reference, fixed-length
- pass by reference, variable-length

By-value types can only be 1, 2, or 4 bytes in length (also 8 bytes, if sizeof(Datum) is 8 on your machine). You should be careful to define your types such that they will be the same size (in bytes) on all architectures. For example, the long type is dangerous because it is 4 bytes on some machines and 8 bytes on others, whereas int type is 4 bytes on most Unix machines. A reasonable implementation of the int4 type on Unix machines might be:

```
/* 4-byte integer, passed by value */
typedef int int4;
```

On the other hand, fixed-length types of any size may be passed by-reference. For example, here is a sample implementation of a PostgreSQL type:

```
/* 16-byte structure, passed by reference */
typedef struct {
  double x, y;
} Point;
```

Only pointers to such types can be used when passing them in and out of PostgreSQL functions. To return a value of such a type, allocate the right amount of memory with palloc, fill in the allocated memory, and return a pointer to it. (Also, if you just want to return the same value as one of your input arguments that's of the same data type, you can skip the extra palloc and just return the pointer to the input value.)

Finally, all variable-length types must also be passed by reference. All variable-length types must begin with a length field of exactly 4 bytes, and all data to be stored within that type must be located in the memory immediately following that length field. The length field contains the total length of the structure, that is, it includes the size of the length field itself.

> **Warning:** *Never* modify the contents of a pass-by-reference input value. If you do so you are likely to corrupt on-disk data, since the pointer you are given may well point directly into a disk buffer. The sole exception to this rule is explained in Section 5.10 *User-Defined Aggregates*, page 216.

As an example, we can define the type text as follows:

```
typedef struct {
    int4 length;
    char data[1];
} text;
```

Obviously, the data field declared here is not long enough to hold all possible strings. Since it's impossible to declare a variable-size structure in C, we rely on the knowledge that the C compiler won't range-check array subscripts. We just allocate the necessary amount of space and then access the array as if it were declared the right length. (This is a common trick, which you can read about in many textbooks about C.)

When manipulating variable-length types, we must be careful to allocate the correct amount of memory and set the length field correctly. For example, if we wanted to store 40 bytes in a text structure, we might use a code fragment like this:

```
#include "postgres.h"
...
char buffer[40]; /* our source data */
...
text *destination = (text *) palloc(VARHDRSZ + 40);
destination->length = VARHDRSZ + 40;
memcpy(destination->data, buffer, 40);
...
```

VARHDRSZ is the same as sizeof(int4), but it's considered good style to use the macro VARHDRSZ to refer to the size of the overhead for a variable-length type.

Table 5.1 specifies which C type corresponds to which SQL type when writing a C-language function that uses a built-in type of PostgreSQL. The "Defined In" column gives the header file that needs to be included to get the type definition. (The actual definition may be in a different file that is included by the listed file. It is recommended that users stick to the defined interface.) Note that you should always include 'postgres.h' first in any source file, because it declares a number of things that you will need anyway.

SQL Type	C Type	Defined In
abstime	AbsoluteTime	'utils/nabstime.h'
boolean	bool	'postgres.h' (maybe compiler built-in)
box	BOX*	'utils/geo_decls.h'
bytea	bytea*	'postgres.h'
"char"	char	(compiler built-in)
character	BpChar*	'postgres.h'
cid	CommandId	'postgres.h'
date	DateADT	'utils/date.h'
smallint (int2)	int2 or int16	'postgres.h'
int2vector	int2vector*	'postgres.h'
integer (int4)	int4 or int32	'postgres.h'
real (float4)	float4*	'postgres.h'
double precision (float8)	float8*	'postgres.h'
interval	Interval*	'utils/timestamp.h'
lseg	LSEG*	'utils/geo_decls.h'
name	Name	'postgres.h'
oid	Oid	'postgres.h'
oidvector	oidvector*	'postgres.h'
path	PATH*	'utils/geo_decls.h'
point	POINT*	'utils/geo_decls.h'
regproc	regproc	'postgres.h'
reltime	RelativeTime	'utils/nabstime.h'
text	text*	'postgres.h'
tid	ItemPointer	'storage/itemptr.h'
time	TimeADT	'utils/date.h'
time with time zone	TimeTzADT	'utils/date.h'
timestamp	Timestamp*	'utils/timestamp.h'
tinterval	TimeInterval	'utils/nabstime.h'
varchar	VarChar*	'postgres.h'
xid	TransactionId	'postgres.h'

Table 5.1: Equivalent C Types for Built-In SQL Types

Now that we've gone over all of the possible structures for base types, we can show some examples of real functions.

5.9.3 Version 0 Calling Conventions

We present the "old style" calling convention first—although this approach is now deprecated, it's easier to get a handle on initially. In the version-0 method, the arguments and result of the C function are just declared in normal C style, but being careful to use the C representation of each SQL data type as shown above.

Here are some examples:

```
#include "postgres.h"
#include <string.h>

/* by value */

int
add_one(int arg)
{
  return arg + 1;
}

/* by reference, fixed length */

float8 *
add_one_float8(float8 * arg)
{
  float8 *result = (float8 *) palloc(sizeof(float8));

  *result = *arg + 1.0;

  return result;
}

Point *
makepoint(Point * pointx, Point * pointy)
{
  Point *new_point = (Point *) palloc(sizeof(Point));

  new_point->x = pointx->x;
  new_point->y = pointy->y;

  return new_point;
}

/* by reference, variable length */

text *
copytext(text * t)
{
  /* VARSIZE is the total size of the struct in bytes. */
  text *new_t = (text *) palloc(VARSIZE(t));
  VARATT_SIZEP(new_t) = VARSIZE(t);
  /* VARDATA is a pointer to the data region of the struct. */
  memcpy((void *) VARDATA(new_t), /* destination */
         (void *) VARDATA(t), /* source */
         VARSIZE(t) - VARHDRSZ);  /* how many bytes */
  return new_t;
}
```

```
text *
concat_text(text * arg1, text * arg2)
{
  int32 new_text_size =
      VARSIZE(arg1) + VARSIZE(arg2) - VARHDRSZ;
  text *new_text = (text *) palloc(new_text_size);

  VARATT_SIZEP(new_text) = new_text_size;
  memcpy(VARDATA(new_text), VARDATA(arg1),
         VARSIZE(arg1) - VARHDRSZ);
  memcpy(VARDATA(new_text) + (VARSIZE(arg1) - VARHDRSZ),
         VARDATA(arg2), VARSIZE(arg2) - VARHDRSZ);
  return new_text;
}
```

Supposing that the above code has been prepared in file 'funcs.c' and compiled into a shared object, we could define the functions to PostgreSQL with commands like this:

```
CREATE FUNCTION add_one(integer) RETURNS integer
      AS 'DIRECTORY/funcs', 'add_one'
      LANGUAGE C STRICT;

-- note overloading of SQL function name "add_one"
CREATE FUNCTION add_one(double precision) RETURNS double
 precision
      AS 'DIRECTORY/funcs', 'add_one_float8'
      LANGUAGE C STRICT;

CREATE FUNCTION makepoint(point, point) RETURNS point
      AS 'DIRECTORY/funcs', 'makepoint'
      LANGUAGE C STRICT;

CREATE FUNCTION copytext(text) RETURNS text
      AS 'DIRECTORY/funcs', 'copytext'
      LANGUAGE C STRICT;

CREATE FUNCTION concat_text(text, text) RETURNS text
      AS 'DIRECTORY/funcs', 'concat_text'
      LANGUAGE C STRICT;
```

Here, *DIRECTORY* stands for the directory of the shared library file (for instance the PostgreSQL tutorial directory, which contains the code for the examples used in this section). (Better style would be to use just 'funcs' in the AS clause, after having added *DIRECTORY* to the search path. In any case, we may omit the system-specific extension for a shared library, commonly .so or .sl.)

Notice that we have specified the functions as "strict", meaning that the system should automatically assume a null result if any input value is null.

By doing this, we avoid having to check for null inputs in the function code. Without this, we'd have to check for null values explicitly, by checking for a null pointer for each pass-by-reference argument. (For pass-by-value arguments, we don't even have a way to check!)

Although this calling convention is simple to use, it is not very portable; on some architectures there are problems with passing data types that are smaller than int this way. Also, there is no simple way to return a null result, nor to cope with null arguments in any way other than making the function strict. The version-1 convention, presented next, overcomes these objections.

5.9.4 Version 1 Calling Conventions

The version-1 calling convention relies on macros to suppress most of the complexity of passing arguments and results. The C declaration of a version-1 function is always

```
Datum funcname(PG_FUNCTION_ARGS)
```

In addition, the macro call

```
PG_FUNCTION_INFO_V1(funcname);
```

must appear in the same source file. (Conventionally. it's written just before the function itself.) This macro call is not needed for internal-language functions, since PostgreSQL assumes that all internal functions use the version-1 convention. It is, however, required for dynamically-loaded functions.

In a version-1 function, each actual argument is fetched using a PG_GETARG_*xxx*() macro that corresponds to the argument's data type, and the result is returned using a PG_RETURN_*xxx*() macro for the return type. PG_GETARG_*xxx*() takes as its argument the number of the function argument to fetch, where the count starts at 0. PG_RETURN_*xxx*() takes as its argument the actual value to return.

Here we show the same functions as above, coded in version-1 style:

```
#include "postgres.h"
#include <string.h>
#include "fmgr.h"

/* by value */

PG_FUNCTION_INFO_V1(add_one);

Datum
add_one(PG_FUNCTION_ARGS)
{
   int32 arg = PG_GETARG_INT32(0);

   PG_RETURN_INT32(arg + 1);
}

/* by reference, fixed length */
```

```
PG_FUNCTION_INFO_V1(add_one_float8);

Datum
add_one_float8(PG_FUNCTION_ARGS)
{
  /* The macros for FLOAT8 hide its pass-by-reference
     nature. */
  float8 arg = PG_GETARG_FLOAT8(0);

  PG_RETURN_FLOAT8(arg + 1.0);
}

PG_FUNCTION_INFO_V1(makepoint);

Datum
makepoint(PG_FUNCTION_ARGS)
{
  /* Here, the pass-by-reference nature of Point is not
     hidden. */
  Point *pointx = PG_GETARG_POINT_P(0);
  Point *pointy = PG_GETARG_POINT_P(1);
  Point *new_point = (Point *) palloc(sizeof(Point));

  new_point->x = pointx->x;
  new_point->y = pointy->y;

  PG_RETURN_POINT_P(new_point);
}

/* by reference, variable length */

PG_FUNCTION_INFO_V1(copytext);

Datum
copytext(PG_FUNCTION_ARGS)
{
  text *t = PG_GETARG_TEXT_P(0);
  /* VARSIZE is the total size of the struct in bytes. */
  text *new_t = (text *) palloc(VARSIZE(t));
  VARATT_SIZEP(new_t) = VARSIZE(t);
  /* VARDATA is a pointer to the data region of the struct. */
  memcpy((void *) VARDATA(new_t), /* destination */
         (void *) VARDATA(t), /* source */
         VARSIZE(t) - VARHDRSZ); /* how many bytes */
  PG_RETURN_TEXT_P(new_t);
}

PG_FUNCTION_INFO_V1(concat_text);
```

```
Datum
concat_text(PG_FUNCTION_ARGS)
{
  text *arg1 = PG_GETARG_TEXT_P(0);
  text *arg2 = PG_GETARG_TEXT_P(1);
  int32 new_text_size =
      VARSIZE(arg1) + VARSIZE(arg2) - VARHDRSZ;
  text *new_text = (text *) palloc(new_text_size);

  VARATT_SIZEP(new_text) = new_text_size;
  memcpy(VARDATA(new_text), VARDATA(arg1),
         VARSIZE(arg1) - VARHDRSZ);
  memcpy(VARDATA(new_text) + (VARSIZE(arg1) - VARHDRSZ),
         VARDATA(arg2), VARSIZE(arg2) - VARHDRSZ);
  PG_RETURN_TEXT_P(new_text);
}
```

The CREATE FUNCTION commands are the same as for the version-0 equivalents.

At first glance, the version-1 coding conventions may appear to be just pointless obscurantism. They do, however, offer a number of improvements, because the macros can hide unnecessary detail. An example is that in coding add_one_float8, we no longer need to be aware that float8 is a pass-by-reference type. Another example is that the GETARG macros for variable-length types allow for more efficient fetching of "toasted" (compressed or out-of-line) values.

One big improvement in version-1 functions is better handling of null inputs and results. The macro PG_ARGISNULL(n) allows a function to test whether each input is null. (Of course, doing this is only necessary in functions not declared "strict".) As with the PG_GETARG_xxx() macros, the input arguments are counted beginning at zero. Note that one should refrain from executing PG_GETARG_xxx() until one has verified that the argument isn't null. To return a null result, execute PG_RETURN_NULL(); this works in both strict and nonstrict functions.

Other options provided in the new-style interface are two variants of the PG_GETARG_xxx() macros. The first of these, PG_GETARG_xxx_COPY(), guarantees to return a copy of the specified argument that is safe for writing into. (The normal macros will sometimes return a pointer to a value that is physically stored in a table, which must not be written to. Using the PG_GETARG_xxx_COPY() macros guarantees a writable result.) The second variant consists of the PG_GETARG_xxx_SLICE() macros which take three arguments. The first is the number of the function argument (as above). The second and third are the offset and length of the segment to be returned. Offsets are counted from zero, and a negative length requests that the remainder of the value be returned. These macros provide more efficient access to parts of large values in the case where they have storage type "external". (The storage type of a column can be specified using ALTER TABLE tablename ALTER COLUMN colname SET STORAGE storagetype. storagetype is one of plain, external, extended, or main.)

Finally, the version-1 function call conventions make it possible to return set results (Section 5.9.10 *Returning Sets*, page 208) and implement trigger functions (Chapter 6 *Triggers*, page 237) and procedural-language call handlers (Volume 4, Chapter 6 *Writing A Procedural Language Handler*). Version-1 code is also more portable than version-0, because it does not break restrictions on function call protocol in the C standard. For more details see 'src/backend/utils/fmgr/README' in the source distribution.

5.9.5 Writing Code

Before we turn to the more advanced topics, we should discuss some coding rules for PostgreSQL C-language functions. While it may be possible to load functions written in languages other than C into PostgreSQL, this is usually difficult (when it is possible at all) because other languages, such as C++, FOR-TRAN, or Pascal often do not follow the same calling convention as C. That is, other languages do not pass argument and return values between functions in the same way. For this reason, we will assume that your C-language functions are actually written in C.

The basic rules for writing and building C functions are as follows:

- Use pg_config --includedir-server to find out where the PostgreSQL server header files are installed on your system (or the system that your users will be running on).

- Compiling and linking your code so that it can be dynamically loaded into PostgreSQL always requires special flags. See Section 5.9.6 *Compiling and Linking Dynamically-Loaded Functions*, page 201 for a detailed explanation of how to do it for your particular operating system.

- Remember to define a "magic block" for your shared library, as described in Section 5.9.1 *Dynamic Loading*, page 190.

- When allocating memory, use the PostgreSQL functions palloc and pfree instead of the corresponding C library functions malloc and free. The memory allocated by palloc will be freed automatically at the end of each transaction, preventing memory leaks.

- Always zero the bytes of your structures using memset. Without this, it's difficult to support hash indexes or hash joins, as you must pick out only the significant bits of your data structure to compute a hash. Even if you initialize all fields of your structure, there may be alignment padding (holes in the structure) that may contain garbage values.

- Most of the internal PostgreSQL types are declared in 'postgres.h', while the function manager interfaces (PG_FUNCTION_ARGS, etc.) are in 'fmgr.h', so you will need to include at least these two files. For portability reasons it's best to include 'postgres.h' *first*, before any other system or user header files. Including 'postgres.h' will also include 'elog.h' and 'palloc.h' for you.

- Symbol names defined within object files must not conflict with each other or with symbols defined in the PostgreSQL server executable. You will have to rename your functions or variables if you get error messages to this effect.

5.9.6 Compiling and Linking Dynamically-Loaded Functions

Before you are able to use your PostgreSQL extension functions written in C, they must be compiled and linked in a special way to produce a file that can be dynamically loaded by the server. To be precise, a *shared library* needs to be created.

For information beyond what is contained in this section you should read the documentation of your operating system, in particular the manual pages for the C compiler, cc, and the link editor, ld. In addition, the PostgreSQL source code contains several working examples in the 'contrib' directory. If you rely on these examples you will make your modules dependent on the availability of the PostgreSQL source code, however.

Creating shared libraries is generally analogous to linking executables: first the source files are compiled into object files, then the object files are linked together. The object files need to be created as *position-independent code* (PIC), which conceptually means that they can be placed at an arbitrary location in memory when they are loaded by the executable. (Object files intended for executables are usually not compiled that way.) The command to link a shared library contains special flags to distinguish it from linking an executable (at least in theory—on some systems the practice is much uglier).

In the following examples we assume that your source code is in a file 'foo.c' and we will create a shared library 'foo.so'. The intermediate object file will be called 'foo.o' unless otherwise noted. A shared library can contain more than one object file, but we only use one here.

BSD/OS

> The compiler flag to create PIC is -fpic. The linker flag to create shared libraries is -shared.
>
> ```
> gcc -fpic -c foo.c
> ld -shared -o foo.so foo.o
> ```
>
> This is applicable as of version 4.0 of BSD/OS.

FreeBSD

> The compiler flag to create PIC is -fpic. To create shared libraries the compiler flag is -shared.
>
> ```
> gcc -fpic -c foo.c
> gcc -shared -o foo.so foo.o
> ```
>
> This is applicable as of version 3.0 of FreeBSD.

HP-UX

> The compiler flag of the system compiler to create PIC is +z. When using GCC it's -fpic. The linker flag for shared libraries is -b. So
>
> ```
> cc +z -c foo.c
> ```
>
> or
>
> ```
> gcc -fpic -c foo.c
> ```
>
> and then

```
ld -b -o foo.sl foo.o
```

HP-UX uses the extension '.sl' for shared libraries, unlike most other systems.

IRIX

PIC is the default, no special compiler options are necessary. The linker option to produce shared libraries is -shared.

```
cc -c foo.c
ld -shared -o foo.so foo.o
```

Linux

The compiler flag to create PIC is -fpic. On some platforms in some situations -fPIC must be used if -fpic does not work. Refer to the GCC manual for more information. The compiler flag to create a shared library is -shared. A complete example looks like this:

```
cc -fpic -c foo.c
cc -shared -o foo.so foo.o
```

MacOS X

Here is an example. It assumes the developer tools are installed.

```
cc -c foo.c
cc -bundle -flat_namespace -undefined suppress -o foo.so
  foo.o
```

NetBSD

The compiler flag to create PIC is -fpic. For ELF systems, the compiler with the flag -shared is used to link shared libraries. On the older non-ELF systems, ld -Bshareable is used.

```
gcc -fpic -c foo.c
gcc -shared -o foo.so foo.o
```

OpenBSD

The compiler flag to create PIC is -fpic. ld -Bshareable is used to link shared libraries.

```
gcc -fpic -c foo.c
ld -Bshareable -o foo.so foo.o
```

Solaris

The compiler flag to create PIC is -KPIC with the Sun compiler and -fpic with GCC. To link shared libraries, the compiler option is -G with either compiler or alternatively -shared with GCC.

```
cc -KPIC -c foo.c
cc -G -o foo.so foo.o
```

or

```
gcc -fpic -c foo.c
gcc -G -o foo.so foo.o
```

Tru64 UNIX

PIC is the default, so the compilation command is the usual one. ld with special options is used to do the linking:

```
cc -c foo.c
ld -shared -expect_unresolved '*' -o foo.so foo.o
```

The same procedure is used with GCC instead of the system compiler; no special options are required.

UnixWare

The compiler flag to create PIC is -K PIC with the SCO compiler and -fpic with GCC. To link shared libraries, the compiler option is -G with the SCO compiler and -shared with GCC.

```
cc -K PIC -c foo.c
cc -G -o foo.so foo.o
```

or

```
gcc -fpic -c foo.c
gcc -shared -o foo.so foo.o
```

Tip: If this is too complicated for you, you should consider using GNU Libtool[1], which hides the platform differences behind a uniform interface.

The resulting shared library file can then be loaded into PostgreSQL. When specifying the file name to the CREATE FUNCTION command, one must give it the name of the shared library file, not the intermediate object file. Note that the system's standard shared-library extension (usually .so or .sl) can be omitted from the CREATE FUNCTION command, and normally should be omitted for best portability.

Refer back to Section 5.9.1 *Dynamic Loading*, page 190 about where the server expects to find the shared library files.

5.9.7 Extension Building Infrastructure

If you are thinking about distributing your PostgreSQL extension modules, setting up a portable build system for them can be fairly difficult. Therefore the PostgreSQL installation provides a build infrastructure for extensions, called PGXS, so that simple extension modules can be built simply against an already installed server. Note that this infrastructure is not intended to be a universal build system framework that can be used to build all software interfacing to PostgreSQL; it simply automates common build rules for simple server extension modules. For more complicated packages, you need to write your own build system.

To use the infrastructure for your extension, you must write a simple makefile. In that makefile, you need to set some variables and finally include the global PGXS makefile. Here is an example that builds an extension module named isbn_issn consisting of a shared library, an SQL script, and a documentation text file:

---

[1] http://www.gnu.org/software/libtool/

```
MODULES = isbn_issn
DATA_built = isbn_issn.sql
DOCS = README.isbn_issn

PGXS := $(shell pg_config --pgxs)
include $(PGXS)
```

The last two lines should always be the same. Earlier in the file, you assign
variables or add custom make rules.

The following variables can be set:

MODULES

    list of shared objects to be built from source file with same stem (do not
include suffix in this list)

DATA

    random files to install into *prefix*/share/contrib

DATA_built

    random files to install into *prefix*/share/contrib, which need to be built
first

DOCS

    random files to install under *prefix*/doc/contrib

SCRIPTS

    script files (not binaries) to install into *prefix*/bin

SCRIPTS_built

    script files (not binaries) to install into *prefix*/bin, which need to be built
first

REGRESS

    list of regression test cases (without suffix), see below

or at most one of these two:

PROGRAM

    a binary program to build (list objects files in OBJS)

MODULE_big

    a shared object to build (list object files in OBJS)

The following can also be set:

EXTRA_CLEAN

    extra files to remove in make clean

PG_CPPFLAGS

    will be added to CPPFLAGS

PG_LIBS

    will be added to PROGRAM link line

SHLIB_LINK

    will be added to MODULE_big link line

Put this makefile as `Makefile` in the directory which holds your extension. Then you can do `make` to compile, and later `make install` to install your module. The extension is compiled and installed for the PostgreSQL installation that corresponds to the first `pg_config` command found in your path.

The scripts listed in the `REGRESS` variable are used for regression testing of your module, just like `make installcheck` is used for the main PostgreSQL server. For this to work you need to have a subdirectory named `sql/` in your extension's directory, within which you put one file for each group of tests you want to run. The files should have extension `.sql`, which should not be included in the `REGRESS` list in the makefile. For each test there should be a file containing the expected result in a subdirectory named `expected/`, with extension `.out`. The tests are run by executing `make installcheck`, and the resulting output will be compared to the expected files. The differences will be written to the file `regression.diffs` in `diff -c` format. Note that trying to run a test which is missing the expected file will be reported as "trouble", so make sure you have all expected files.

> **Tip:** The easiest way of creating the expected files is creating empty files, then carefully inspecting the result files after a test run (to be found in the `results/` directory), and copying them to `expected/` if they match what you want from the test.

5.9.8 Composite-Type Arguments

Composite types do not have a fixed layout like C structures. Instances of a composite type may contain null fields. In addition, composite types that are part of an inheritance hierarchy may have different fields than other members of the same inheritance hierarchy. Therefore, PostgreSQL provides a function interface for accessing fields of composite types from C.

Suppose we want to write a function to answer the query

```
SELECT name, c_overpaid(emp, 1500) AS overpaid
    FROM emp
    WHERE name = 'Bill' OR name = 'Sam';
```

Using call conventions version 0, we can define c_overpaid as:

```
#include "postgres.h"
#include "executor/executor.h"  /* for GetAttributeByName()
                                   */

bool
c_overpaid(HeapTupleHeader t, /* the current row of emp */
           int32 limit)
{
  bool isnull;
  int32 salary;

  salary =
      DatumGetInt32(GetAttributeByName
                        (t, "salary", &isnull));
  if (isnull)
```

```
      return false;
    return salary > limit;
  }
```

In version-1 coding, the above would look like this:

```
  #include "postgres.h"
  #include "executor/executor.h"   /* for GetAttributeByName()
                                      */

  PG_FUNCTION_INFO_V1(c_overpaid);

  Datum
  c_overpaid(PG_FUNCTION_ARGS)
  {
    HeapTupleHeader t = PG_GETARG_HEAPTUPLEHEADER(0);
    int32 limit = PG_GETARG_INT32(1);
    bool isnull;
    Datum salary;

    salary = GetAttributeByName(t, "salary", &isnull);
    if (isnull)
      PG_RETURN_BOOL(false);
    /* Alternatively, we might prefer to do PG_RETURN_NULL()
       for null salary. */

    PG_RETURN_BOOL(DatumGetInt32(salary) > limit);
  }
```

GetAttributeByName is the PostgreSQL system function that returns attributes out of the specified row. It has three arguments: the argument of type HeapTupleHeader passed into the function, the name of the desired attribute, and a return parameter that tells whether the attribute is null. GetAttributeByName returns a Datum value that you can convert to the proper data type by using the appropriate DatumGet*XXX*() macro. Note that the return value is meaningless if the null flag is set; always check the null flag before trying to do anything with the result.

There is also GetAttributeByNum, which selects the target attribute by column number instead of name.

The following command declares the function c_overpaid in SQL:

```
  CREATE FUNCTION c_overpaid(emp, integer) RETURNS boolean
      AS 'DIRECTORY/funcs', 'c_overpaid'
      LANGUAGE C STRICT;
```

Notice we have used STRICT so that we did not have to check whether the input arguments were NULL.

5.9.9 Returning Rows (Composite Types)

To return a row or composite-type value from a C-language function, you can use a special API that provides macros and functions to hide most of the complexity of building composite data types. To use this API, the source file must include:

```
#include "funcapi.h"
```

There are two ways you can build a composite data value (henceforth a "tuple"): you can build it from an array of Datum values, or from an array of C strings that can be passed to the input conversion functions of the tuple's column data types. In either case, you first need to obtain or construct a TupleDesc descriptor for the tuple structure. When working with Datums, you pass the TupleDesc to BlessTupleDesc, and then call heap_form_tuple for each row. When working with C strings, you pass the TupleDesc to TupleDescGetAttInMetadata, and then call BuildTupleFromCStrings for each row. In the case of a function returning a set of tuples, the setup steps can all be done once during the first call of the function.

Several helper functions are available for setting up the needed TupleDesc. The recommended way to do this in most functions returning composite values is to call

```
TypeFuncClass get_call_result_type(FunctionCallInfo fcinfo,
                                   Oid *resultTypeId,
                                   TupleDesc *resultTupleDesc)
```

passing the same fcinfo struct passed to the calling function itself. (This of course requires that you use the version-1 calling conventions.) resultTypeId can be specified as NULL or as the address of a local variable to receive the function's result type OID. resultTupleDesc should be the address of a local TupleDesc variable. Check that the result is TYPEFUNC_COMPOSITE; if so, resultTupleDesc has been filled with the needed TupleDesc. (If it is not, you can report an error along the lines of "function returning record called in context that cannot accept type record".)

> Tip: get_call_result_type can resolve the actual type of a polymorphic function result; so it is useful in functions that return scalar polymorphic results, not only functions that return composites. The resultTypeId output is primarily useful for functions returning polymorphic scalars.

> Note: get_call_result_type has a sibling get_expr_result_type, which can be used to resolve the expected output type for a function call represented by an expression tree. This can be used when trying to determine the result type from outside the function itself. There is also get_func_result_type, which can be used when only the function's OID is available. However these functions are not able to deal with functions declared to return record, and get_func_result_type cannot resolve polymorphic types, so you should preferentially use get_call_result_type.

Older, now-deprecated functions for obtaining TupleDescs are

```
TupleDesc RelationNameGetTupleDesc(const char *relname)
```
to get a `TupleDesc` for the row type of a named relation, and
```
TupleDesc TypeGetTupleDesc(Oid typeoid, List *colaliases)
```
to get a `TupleDesc` based on a type OID. This can be used to get a `TupleDesc` for a base or composite type. It will not work for a function that returns record, however, and it cannot resolve polymorphic types.

Once you have a `TupleDesc`, call
```
TupleDesc BlessTupleDesc(TupleDesc tupdesc)
```
if you plan to work with Datums, or
```
AttInMetadata *TupleDescGetAttInMetadata(TupleDesc tupdesc)
```
if you plan to work with C strings. If you are writing a function returning set, you can save the results of these functions in the `FuncCallContext` structure—use the `tuple_desc` or `attinmeta` field respectively.

When working with Datums, use
```
HeapTuple heap_form_tuple(TupleDesc tupdesc, Datum *values,
    bool *isnull)
```
to build a `HeapTuple` given user data in Datum form.

When working with C strings, use
```
HeapTuple BuildTupleFromCStrings(AttInMetadata *attinmeta,
    char **values)
```
to build a `HeapTuple` given user data in C string form. `values` is an array of C strings, one for each attribute of the return row. Each C string should be in the form expected by the input function of the attribute data type. In order to return a null value for one of the attributes, the corresponding pointer in the values array should be set to `NULL`. This function will need to be called again for each row you return.

Once you have built a tuple to return from your function, it must be converted into a Datum. Use
```
HeapTupleGetDatum(HeapTuple tuple)
```
to convert a `HeapTuple` into a valid Datum. This Datum can be returned directly if you intend to return just a single row, or it can be used as the current return value in a set-returning function.

An example appears in the next section.

5.9.10 Returning Sets

There is also a special API that provides support for returning sets (multiple rows) from a C-language function. A set-returning function must follow the version-1 calling conventions. Also, source files must include 'funcapi.h', as above.

A set-returning function (SRF) is called once for each item it returns. The SRF must therefore save enough state to remember what it was doing and return the next item on each call. The structure FuncCallContext is provided to help control this process. Within a function, `fcinfo->flinfo->fn_extra` is used to hold a pointer to FuncCallContext across calls.

```
typedef struct {
  /* Number of times we've been called before call_cntr is
     initialized to 0 for you by SRF_FIRSTCALL_INIT(), and
     incremented for you every time SRF_RETURN_NEXT() is
     called. */
  uint32 call_cntr;

  /* OPTIONAL maximum number of calls max_calls is here
     for convenience only and setting it is optional. If
     not set, you must provide alternative means to know
     when the function is done. */
  uint32 max_calls;

  /* OPTIONAL pointer to result slot This is obsolete and
     only present for backwards compatibility, viz,
     user-defined SRFs that use the deprecated
     TupleDescGetSlot(). */
  TupleTableSlot *slot;

  /* OPTIONAL pointer to miscellaneous user-provided
     context information user_fctx is for use as a pointer
     to your own data to retain arbitrary context
     information between calls of your function. */
  void *user_fctx;

  /* OPTIONAL pointer to struct containing attribute type
     input metadata attinmeta is for use when returning
     tuples (i.e., composite data types) and is not used
     when returning base data types. It is only needed if
     you intend to use BuildTupleFromCStrings() to create
     the return tuple. */
  AttInMetadata *attinmeta;

  /* memory context used for structures that must live for
     multiple calls multi_call_memory_ctx is set by
     SRF_FIRSTCALL_INIT() for you, and used by
     SRF_RETURN_DONE() for cleanup. It is the most
     appropriate memory context for any memory that is to
     be reused across multiple calls of the SRF. */
  MemoryContext multi_call_memory_ctx;

  /* OPTIONAL pointer to struct containing tuple
     description tuple_desc is for use when returning
     tuples (i.e. composite data types) and is only needed
     if you are going to build the tuples with
     heap_form_tuple() rather than with
     BuildTupleFromCStrings(). Note that the TupleDesc
     pointer stored here should usually have been run
```

```
        through BlessTupleDesc() first. */
     TupleDesc tuple_desc;

   } FuncCallContext;
```

An SRF uses several functions and macros that automatically manipulate the FuncCallContext structure (and expect to find it via `fn_extra`). Use

```
     SRF_IS_FIRSTCALL()
```

to determine if your function is being called for the first or a subsequent time. On the first call (only) use

```
     SRF_FIRSTCALL_INIT()
```

to initialize the FuncCallContext. On every function call, including the first, use

```
     SRF_PERCALL_SETUP()
```

to properly set up for using the FuncCallContext and clearing any previously returned data left over from the previous pass.

If your function has data to return, use

```
     SRF_RETURN_NEXT(funcctx, result)
```

to return it to the caller. (result must be of type Datum, either a single value or a tuple prepared as described above.) Finally, when your function is finished returning data, use

```
     SRF_RETURN_DONE(funcctx)
```

to clean up and end the SRF.

The memory context that is current when the SRF is called is a transient context that will be cleared between calls. This means that you do not need to call `pfree` on everything you allocated using `palloc`; it will go away anyway. However, if you want to allocate any data structures to live across calls, you need to put them somewhere else. The memory context referenced by `multi_call_memory_ctx` is a suitable location for any data that needs to survive until the SRF is finished running. In most cases, this means that you should switch into `multi_call_memory_ctx` while doing the first-call setup.

A complete pseudo-code example looks like the following:

```
Datum
my_set_returning_function(PG_FUNCTION_ARGS)
{
  FuncCallContext *funcctx;
  Datum result;
  MemoryContext oldcontext;
  further declarations as needed if (SRF_IS_FIRSTCALL()) {
    funcctx = SRF_FIRSTCALL_INIT();
    oldcontext =
        MemoryContextSwitchTo(funcctx->
                              multi_call_memory_ctx);
    /* One-time setup code appears here: */
    <<user code>>
    <<if returning composite>>
```

```
    <<build TupleDesc, and perhaps AttInMetadata>>
    <<endif returning composite>>
    <<user code>>
    MemoryContextSwitchTo(oldcontext);
}

/* Each-time setup code appears here: */
<<user code>>
funcctx = SRF_PERCALL_SETUP();
<<user code>>

/* this is just one way we might test whether we are
   done: */
if (funcctx->call_cntr < funcctx->max_calls) {
  /* Here we want to return another item: */
  <<user code>>
  <<obtain result Datum>>
  SRF_RETURN_NEXT(funcctx, result);
} else {
  /* Here we are done returning items and just need to
     clean up: */
  <<user code>>
  SRF_RETURN_DONE(funcctx);
}
}
```

A complete example of a simple SRF returning a composite type looks like:

```
PG_FUNCTION_INFO_V1(retcomposite);

Datum
retcomposite(PG_FUNCTION_ARGS)
{
  FuncCallContext *funcctx;
  int call_cntr;
  int max_calls;
  TupleDesc tupdesc;
  AttInMetadata *attinmeta;

  /* stuff done only on the first call of the function */
  if (SRF_IS_FIRSTCALL()) {
    MemoryContext oldcontext;

    /* create a function context for cross-call persistence
     */
    funcctx = SRF_FIRSTCALL_INIT();

    /* switch to memory context appropriate for multiple
       function calls */
    oldcontext =
```

```
        MemoryContextSwitchTo(funcctx->
                            multi_call_memory_ctx);

    /* total number of tuples to be returned */
    funcctx->max_calls = PG_GETARG_UINT32(0);

    /* Build a tuple descriptor for our result type */
    if (get_call_result_type(fcinfo, NULL, &tupdesc) !=
        TYPEFUNC_COMPOSITE)
      ereport(ERROR,
              (errcode(ERRCODE_FEATURE_NOT_SUPPORTED),
               errmsg
               ("function returning record called in context "
               "that cannot accept type record")));

    /* generate attribute metadata needed later to produce
       tuples from raw C strings */
    attinmeta = TupleDescGetAttInMetadata(tupdesc);
    funcctx->attinmeta = attinmeta;

    MemoryContextSwitchTo(oldcontext);
}

/* stuff done on every call of the function */
funcctx = SRF_PERCALL_SETUP();

call_cntr = funcctx->call_cntr;
max_calls = funcctx->max_calls;
attinmeta = funcctx->attinmeta;

if (call_cntr < max_calls) {  /* do when there is more
                                 left to send */
  char **values;
  HeapTuple tuple;
  Datum result;

  /* Prepare a values array for building the returned
     tuple. This should be an array of C strings which
     will be processed later by the type input functions. */
  values = (char **) palloc(3 * sizeof(char *));
  values[0] = (char *) palloc(16 * sizeof(char));
  values[1] = (char *) palloc(16 * sizeof(char));
  values[2] = (char *) palloc(16 * sizeof(char));

  snprintf(values[0], 16, "%d", 1 * PG_GETARG_INT32(1));
  snprintf(values[1], 16, "%d", 2 * PG_GETARG_INT32(1));
  snprintf(values[2], 16, "%d", 3 * PG_GETARG_INT32(1));
```

```
    /* build a tuple */
    tuple = BuildTupleFromCStrings(attinmeta, values);

    /* make the tuple into a datum */
    result = HeapTupleGetDatum(tuple);

    /* clean up (this is not really necessary) */
    pfree(values[0]);
    pfree(values[1]);
    pfree(values[2]);
    pfree(values);

    SRF_RETURN_NEXT(funcctx, result);
  } else {  /* do when there is no more left */

    SRF_RETURN_DONE(funcctx);
  }
}
```

One way to declare this function in SQL is:

```
CREATE TYPE __retcomposite AS (f1 integer, f2 integer, f3
  integer);

CREATE OR REPLACE FUNCTION retcomposite(integer, integer)
    RETURNS SETOF __retcomposite
    AS 'filename', 'retcomposite'
    LANGUAGE C IMMUTABLE STRICT;
```

A different way is to use OUT parameters:

```
CREATE OR REPLACE FUNCTION retcomposite(IN integer, IN integer,
    OUT f1 integer, OUT f2 integer, OUT f3 integer)
    RETURNS SETOF record
    AS 'filename', 'retcomposite'
    LANGUAGE C IMMUTABLE STRICT;
```

Notice that in this method the output type of the function is formally an anonymous record type.

The directory 'contrib/tablefunc' in the source distribution contains more examples of set-returning functions.

5.9.11 Polymorphic Arguments and Return Types

C-language functions may be declared to accept and return the polymorphic types anyelement and anyarray. See Section 5.2.5 *Polymorphic Types*, page 176 for a more detailed explanation of polymorphic functions. When function arguments or return types are defined as polymorphic types, the function author cannot know in advance what data type it will be called with, or need to return. There are two routines provided in 'fmgr.h' to allow a version-1 C function to discover the actual data types of its arguments and the type it is expected to return. The routines are called get_fn_expr_rettype(FmgrInfo *flinfo) and get_fn_expr_argtype(FmgrInfo *flinfo, int argnum). They return the result or argument type OID, or InvalidOid if the information is not available. The structure flinfo is normally accessed as fcinfo->flinfo. The parameter argnum is zero based. get_call_result_type can also be used as an alternative to get_fn_expr_rettype.

For example, suppose we want to write a function to accept a single element of any type, and return a one-dimensional array of that type:

```
PG_FUNCTION_INFO_V1(make_array);
Datum
make_array(PG_FUNCTION_ARGS)
{
  ArrayType *result;
  Oid element_type = get_fn_expr_argtype(fcinfo->flinfo, 0);
  Datum element;
  bool isnull;
  int16 typlen;
  bool typbyval;
  char typalign;
  int ndims;
  int dims[MAXDIM];
  int lbs[MAXDIM];

  if (!OidIsValid(element_type))
    elog(ERROR, "could not determine data type of input");

  /* get the provided element, being careful in case it's
     NULL */
  isnull = PG_ARGISNULL(0);
  if (isnull)
    element = (Datum) 0;
  else
    element = PG_GETARG_DATUM(0);

  /* we have one dimension */
  ndims = 1;
  /* and one element */
  dims[0] = 1;
  /* and lower bound is 1 */
  lbs[0] = 1;

  /* get required info about the element type */
  get_typlenbyvalalign(element_type, &typlen, &typbyval,
                       &typalign);

  /* now build the array */
  result =
      construct_md_array(&element, &isnull, ndims, dims,
                         lbs, element_type, typlen,
                         typbyval, typalign);
```

```
    PG_RETURN_ARRAYTYPE_P(result);
}
```

The following command declares the function `make_array` in SQL:

```
CREATE FUNCTION make_array(anyelement) RETURNS anyarray
    AS 'DIRECTORY/funcs', 'make_array'
    LANGUAGE C IMMUTABLE;
```

5.9.12 Shared Memory and LWLocks

Add-ins may reserve LWLocks (lightweight locks)[2] and an allocation of shared memory on server startup. The add-in's shared library must be preloaded by specifying it in `shared_preload_libraries` . Shared memory is reserved by calling:

```
void RequestAddinShmemSpace(int size)
```

from your _PG_init function.

LWLocks are reserved by calling:

```
void RequestAddinLWLocks(int n)
```

from _PG_init.

To avoid possible race-conditions, each backend should use the LWLock AddinShmemInitLock when connecting to and initializing its allocation of shared memory, as shown here:

```
static mystruct *ptr = NULL;

if (!ptr)
{
        bool    found;

        LWLockAcquire(AddinShmemInitLock, LW_EXCLUSIVE);
        ptr = ShmemInitStruct("my struct name", size, &found);
        if (!ptr)
                elog(ERROR, "out of shared memory");
        if (!found)
        {
                initialize contents of shmem area;
                acquire any requested LWLocks using:
                ptr->mylockid = LWLockAssign();
        }
        LWLockRelease(AddinShmemInitLock);
}
```

---

[2] Lightweight locks provide mutual exclusion of access to shared-memory data structures, see 'lwlock.c' in the PostgreSQL source.

5.10 User-Defined Aggregates

Aggregate functions in PostgreSQL are expressed in terms of *state values* and *state transition functions*. That is, an aggregate operates using a state value that is updated as each successive input row is processed. To define a new aggregate function, one selects a data type for the state value, an initial value for the state, and a state transition function. The state transition function is just an ordinary function that could also be used outside the context of the aggregate. A *final function* can also be specified, in case the desired result of the aggregate is different from the data that needs to be kept in the running state value.

Thus, in addition to the argument and result data types seen by a user of the aggregate, there is an internal state-value data type that may be different from both the argument and result types.

If we define an aggregate that does not use a final function, we have an aggregate that computes a running function of the column values from each row. sum is an example of this kind of aggregate. sum starts at zero and always adds the current row's value to its running total. For example, if we want to make a sum aggregate to work on a data type for complex numbers, we only need the addition function for that data type. The aggregate definition would be:

```
CREATE AGGREGATE sum (complex)
(
    sfunc = complex_add,
    stype = complex,
    initcond = '(0,0)'
);

SELECT sum(a) FROM test_complex;

    sum
-----------
    (34,53.9)
```

(Notice that we are relying on function overloading: there is more than one aggregate named sum, but PostgreSQL can figure out which kind of sum applies to a column of type complex.)

The above definition of sum will return zero (the initial state condition) if there are no nonnull input values. Perhaps we want to return null in that case instead—the SQL standard expects sum to behave that way. We can do this simply by omitting the initcond phrase, so that the initial state condition is null. Ordinarily this would mean that the sfunc would need to check for a null state-condition input, but for sum and some other simple aggregates like max and min, it is sufficient to insert the first nonnull input value into the state variable and then start applying the transition function at the second nonnull input value. PostgreSQL will do that automatically if the initial condition is null and the transition function is marked "strict" (i.e., not to be called for null inputs).

Another bit of default behavior for a "strict" transition function is that the previous state value is retained unchanged whenever a null input value is encountered. Thus, null values are ignored. If you need some other behavior for null inputs, do not declare your transition function as strict; instead code it to test for null inputs and do whatever is needed.

avg (average) is a more complex example of an aggregate. It requires two pieces of running state: the sum of the inputs and the count of the number of inputs. The final result is obtained by dividing these quantities. Average is typically implemented by using a two-element array as the state value. For example, the built-in implementation of avg(float8) looks like:

```
CREATE AGGREGATE avg (float8)
(
    sfunc = float8_accum,
    stype = float8[],
    finalfunc = float8_avg,
    initcond = '{0,0}'
);
```

Aggregate functions may use polymorphic state transition functions or final functions, so that the same functions can be used to implement multiple aggregates. See Section 5.2.5 *Polymorphic Types*, page 176 for an explanation of polymorphic functions. Going a step further, the aggregate function itself may be specified with polymorphic input type(s) and state type, allowing a single aggregate definition to serve for multiple input data types. Here is an example of a polymorphic aggregate:

```
CREATE AGGREGATE array_accum (anyelement)
(
    sfunc = array_append,
    stype = anyarray,
    initcond = '{}'
);
```

Here, the actual state type for any aggregate call is the array type having the actual input type as elements.

Here's the output using two different actual data types as arguments:

```
SELECT attrelid::regclass, array_accum(attname)
    FROM pg_attribute
    WHERE attnum > 0 AND attrelid = 'pg_tablespace'::regclass
    GROUP BY attrelid;


     attrelid    |              array_accum
 ---------------+-----------------------------------------
  pg_tablespace | {spcname,spcowner,spclocation,spcacl}
 (1 row)


SELECT attrelid::regclass, array_accum(atttypid)
    FROM pg_attribute
    WHERE attnum > 0 AND attrelid = 'pg_tablespace'::regclass
    GROUP BY attrelid;
```

```
    attrelid     |     array_accum
----------------+------------------
 pg_tablespace  | {19,26,25,1034}
(1 row)
```

A function written in C can detect that it is being called as an aggregate transition or final function by seeing if it was passed an AggState node as the function call "context", for example by

    if (fcinfo->context && IsA(fcinfo->context, AggState))

One reason for checking this is that when it is true, the first input must be a temporary transition value and can therefore safely be modified in-place rather than allocating a new copy. (This is the *only* case where it is safe for a function to modify a pass-by-reference input.) See int8inc() for an example.

For further details see the CREATE AGGREGATE command.

5.11 User-Defined Types

As described in Section 5.2 *The PostgreSQL Type System*, page 175, Post-greSQL can be extended to support new data types. This section describes how to define new base types, which are data types defined below the level of the SQL language. Creating a new base type requires implementing functions to operate on the type in a low-level language, usually C.

The examples in this section can be found in 'complex.sql' and 'complex.c' in the 'src/tutorial' directory of the source distribution. See the 'README' file in that directory for instructions about running the examples.

A user-defined type must always have input and output functions. These functions determine how the type appears in strings (for input by the user and output to the user) and how the type is organized in memory. The input function takes a null-terminated character string as its argument and returns the internal (in memory) representation of the type. The output function takes the internal representation of the type as argument and returns a null-terminated character string. If we want to do anything more with the type than merely store it, we must provide additional functions to implement whatever operations we'd like to have for the type.

Suppose we want to define a type complex that represents complex numbers. A natural way to represent a complex number in memory would be the following C structure:

```
typedef struct Complex {
    double    x;
    double    y;
} Complex;
```

We will need to make this a pass-by-reference type, since it's too large to fit into a single Datum value.

As the external string representation of the type, we choose a string of the form (x,y).

The input and output functions are usually not hard to write, especially the output function. But when defining the external string representation of the type, remember that you must eventually write a complete and robust parser for that representation as your input function. For instance:

```
PG_FUNCTION_INFO_V1(complex_in);

Datum
complex_in(PG_FUNCTION_ARGS)
{
    char       *str = PG_GETARG_CSTRING(0);
    double     x,
               y;
    Complex    *result;

    if (sscanf(str, " ( %lf , %lf )", &x, &y) != 2)
        ereport(ERROR,
                (errcode(ERRCODE_INVALID_TEXT_REPRESENTATION),
                 errmsg("invalid syntax for complex: \"%s\"",
                        str)));

    result = (Complex *) palloc(sizeof(Complex));
    result->x = x;
    result->y = y;
    PG_RETURN_POINTER(result);
}
```

The output function can simply be:

```
PG_FUNCTION_INFO_V1(complex_out);

Datum
complex_out(PG_FUNCTION_ARGS)
{
    Complex    *complex = (Complex *) PG_GETARG_POINTER(0);
    char       *result;

    result = (char *) palloc(100);
    snprintf(result, 100, "(%g,%g)", complex->x, complex->y);
    PG_RETURN_CSTRING(result);
}
```

You should be careful to make the input and output functions inverses of each other. If you do not, you will have severe problems when you need to dump your data into a file and then read it back in. This is a particularly common problem when floating-point numbers are involved.

Optionally, a user-defined type can provide binary input and output routines. Binary I/O is normally faster but less portable than textual I/O. As with textual I/O, it is up to you to define exactly what the external binary representation is. Most of the built-in data types try to provide a machine-independent binary representation. For complex, we will piggy-back on the binary I/O converters for type float8:

```
PG_FUNCTION_INFO_V1(complex_recv);

Datum
complex_recv(PG_FUNCTION_ARGS)
{
    StringInfo  buf = (StringInfo) PG_GETARG_POINTER(0);
    Complex     *result;

    result = (Complex *) palloc(sizeof(Complex));
    result->x = pq_getmsgfloat8(buf);
    result->y = pq_getmsgfloat8(buf);
    PG_RETURN_POINTER(result);
}


PG_FUNCTION_INFO_V1(complex_send);

Datum
complex_send(PG_FUNCTION_ARGS)
{
    Complex     *complex = (Complex *) PG_GETARG_POINTER(0);
    StringInfoData buf;

    pq_begintypsend(&buf);
    pq_sendfloat8(&buf, complex->x);
    pq_sendfloat8(&buf, complex->y);
    PG_RETURN_BYTEA_P(pq_endtypsend(&buf));
}
```

Once we have written the I/O functions and compiled them into a shared library, we can define the complex type in SQL. First we declare it as a shell type:

```
CREATE TYPE complex;
```

This serves as a placeholder that allows us to reference the type while defining its I/O functions. Now we can define the I/O functions:

```
CREATE FUNCTION complex_in(cstring)
    RETURNS complex
    AS 'filename'
    LANGUAGE C IMMUTABLE STRICT;

CREATE FUNCTION complex_out(complex)
    RETURNS cstring
    AS 'filename'
    LANGUAGE C IMMUTABLE STRICT;

CREATE FUNCTION complex_recv(internal)
    RETURNS complex
```

```
AS 'filename'
LANGUAGE C IMMUTABLE STRICT;

CREATE FUNCTION complex_send(complex)
    RETURNS bytea
    AS 'filename'
    LANGUAGE C IMMUTABLE STRICT;
```

Finally, we can provide the full definition of the data type:

```
CREATE TYPE complex (
    internallength = 16,
    input = complex_in,
    output = complex_out,
    receive = complex_recv,
    send = complex_send,
    alignment = double
);
```

When you define a new base type, PostgreSQL automatically provides support for arrays of that type. For historical reasons, the array type has the same name as the base type with the underscore character (_) prepended.

Once the data type exists, we can declare additional functions to provide useful operations on the data type. Operators can then be defined atop the functions, and if needed, operator classes can be created to support indexing of the data type. These additional layers are discussed in following sections.

If the values of your data type might exceed a few hundred bytes in size (in internal form), you should make the data type TOAST-able (see TOAST (Volume 4)). To do this, the internal representation must follow the standard layout for variable-length data: the first four bytes must be an int32 containing the total length in bytes of the datum (including itself). The C functions operating on the data type must be careful to unpack any toasted values they are handed, by using PG_DETOAST_DATUM. (This detail is customarily hidden by defining type-specific GETARG macros.) Then, when running the CREATE TYPE command, specify the internal length as variable and select the appropriate storage option.

For further details see the description of the CREATE TYPE command.

5.12 User-Defined Operators

Every operator is "syntactic sugar" for a call to an underlying function that does the real work; so you must first create the underlying function before you can create the operator. However, an operator is *not merely* syntactic sugar, because it carries additional information that helps the query planner optimize queries that use the operator. The next section will be devoted to explaining that additional information.

PostgreSQL supports left unary, right unary, and binary operators. Operators can be overloaded; that is, the same operator name can be used for different operators that have different numbers and types of operands. When a query

is executed, the system determines the operator to call from the number and
types of the provided operands.

Here is an example of creating an operator for adding two complex numbers.
We assume we've already created the definition of type complex (see Section 5.11
User-Defined Types, page 218). First we need a function that does the work,
then we can define the operator:

```
CREATE FUNCTION complex_add(complex, complex)
    RETURNS complex
    AS 'filename', 'complex_add'
    LANGUAGE C IMMUTABLE STRICT;

CREATE OPERATOR + (
    leftarg = complex,
    rightarg = complex,
    procedure = complex_add,
    commutator = +
);
```

Now we could execute a query like this:

```
SELECT (a + b) AS c FROM test_complex;

        c
------------------
(5.2,6.05)
(133.42,144.95)
```

We've shown how to create a binary operator here. To create unary operators,
just omit one of leftarg (for left unary) or rightarg (for right unary). The
procedure clause and the argument clauses are the only required items in CREATE
OPERATOR. The commutator clause shown in the example is an optional hint to
the query optimizer. Further details about commutator and other optimizer
hints appear in the next section.

5.13 Operator Optimization Information

A PostgreSQL operator definition can include several optional clauses that
tell the system useful things about how the operator behaves. These clauses
should be provided whenever appropriate, because they can make for considerable speedups in execution of queries that use the operator. But if you provide
them, you must be sure that they are right! Incorrect use of an optimization
clause can result in server process crashes, subtly wrong output, or other Bad
Things. You can always leave out an optimization clause if you are not sure
about it; the only consequence is that queries might run slower than they need
to.

Additional optimization clauses might be added in future versions of PostgreSQL. The ones described here are all the ones that release 8.2.3 understands.

5.13.1 COMMUTATOR

The COMMUTATOR clause, if provided, names an operator that is the commutator of the operator being defined. We say that operator A is the commutator of operator B if (x A y) equals (y B x) for all possible input values x, y. Notice that B is also the commutator of A. For example, operators < and > for a particular data type are usually each others' commutators, and operator + is usually commutative with itself. But operator - is usually not commutative with anything.

The left operand type of a commutable operator is the same as the right operand type of its commutator, and vice versa. So the name of the commutator operator is all that PostgreSQL needs to be given to look up the commutator, and that's all that needs to be provided in the COMMUTATOR clause.

It's critical to provide commutator information for operators that will be used in indexes and join clauses, because this allows the query optimizer to "flip around" such a clause to the forms needed for different plan types. For example, consider a query with a WHERE clause like tab1.x = tab2.y, where tab1.x and tab2.y are of a user-defined type, and suppose that tab2.y is indexed. The optimizer cannot generate an index scan unless it can determine how to flip the clause around to tab2.y = tab1.x, because the index-scan machinery expects to see the indexed column on the left of the operator it is given. PostgreSQL will *not* simply assume that this is a valid transformation—the creator of the = operator must specify that it is valid, by marking the operator with commutator information.

When you are defining a self-commutative operator, you just do it. When you are defining a pair of commutative operators, things are a little trickier: how can the first one to be defined refer to the other one, which you haven't defined yet? There are two solutions to this problem:

- One way is to omit the COMMUTATOR clause in the first operator that you define, and then provide one in the second operator's definition. Since PostgreSQL knows that commutative operators come in pairs, when it sees the second definition it will automatically go back and fill in the missing COMMUTATOR clause in the first definition.

- The other, more straightforward way is just to include COMMUTATOR clauses in both definitions. When PostgreSQL processes the first definition and realizes that COMMUTATOR refers to a nonexistent operator, the system will make a dummy entry for that operator in the system catalog. This dummy entry will have valid data only for the operator name, left and right operand types, and result type, since that's all that PostgreSQL can deduce at this point. The first operator's catalog entry will link to this dummy entry. Later, when you define the second operator, the system updates the dummy entry with the additional information from the second definition. If you try to use the dummy operator before it's been filled in, you'll just get an error message.

5.13.2 NEGATOR

The NEGATOR clause, if provided, names an operator that is the negator of the operator being defined. We say that operator A is the negator of operator B if both return Boolean results and (x A y) equals NOT (x B y) for all possible inputs x, y. Notice that B is also the negator of A. For example, < and >= are a negator pair for most data types. An operator can never validly be its own negator.

Unlike commutators, a pair of unary operators could validly be marked as each others' negators; that would mean (A x) equals NOT (B x) for all x, or the equivalent for right unary operators.

An operator's negator must have the same left and/or right operand types as the operator to be defined, so just as with COMMUTATOR, only the operator name need be given in the NEGATOR clause.

Providing a negator is very helpful to the query optimizer since it allows expressions like NOT (x = y) to be simplified into x <> y. This comes up more often than you might think, because NOT operations can be inserted as a consequence of other rearrangements.

Pairs of negator operators can be defined using the same methods explained above for commutator pairs.

5.13.3 RESTRICT

The RESTRICT clause, if provided, names a restriction selectivity estimation function for the operator. (Note that this is a function name, not an operator name.) RESTRICT clauses only make sense for binary operators that return boolean. The idea behind a restriction selectivity estimator is to guess what fraction of the rows in a table will satisfy a WHERE-clause condition of the form

    column OP constant

for the current operator and a particular constant value. This assists the optimizer by giving it some idea of how many rows will be eliminated by WHERE clauses that have this form. (What happens if the constant is on the left, you may be wondering? Well, that's one of the things that COMMUTATOR is for...)

Writing new restriction selectivity estimation functions is far beyond the scope of this chapter, but fortunately you can usually just use one of the system's standard estimators for many of your own operators. These are the standard restriction estimators:

    eqsel for =

    neqsel for <>

    scalarltsel for < or <=

    scalargtsel for > or >=

It might seem a little odd that these are the categories, but they make sense if you think about it. = will typically accept only a small fraction of the rows in a table; <> will typically reject only a small fraction. < will accept a fraction that depends on where the given constant falls in the range of values for that table column (which, it just so happens, is information collected by ANALYZE and made available to the selectivity estimator). <= will accept a slightly larger fraction than < for the same comparison constant, but they're close enough to not be worth distinguishing, especially since we're not likely to do better than a rough guess anyhow. Similar remarks apply to > and >=.

You can frequently get away with using either eqsel or neqsel for operators that have very high or very low selectivity, even if they aren't really equality or inequality. For example, the approximate-equality geometric operators use eqsel on the assumption that they'll usually only match a small fraction of the entries in a table.

You can use scalarltsel and scalargtsel for comparisons on data types that have some sensible means of being converted into numeric scalars for range comparisons. If possible, add the data type to those understood by the function convert_to_scalar() in 'src/backend/utils/adt/selfuncs.c'. (Eventually, this function should be replaced by per-data-type functions identified through a column of the pg_type system catalog; but that hasn't happened yet.) If you do not do this, things will still work, but the optimizer's estimates won't be as good as they could be.

There are additional selectivity estimation functions designed for geometric operators in 'src/backend/utils/adt/geo_selfuncs.c': areasel, positionsel, and contsel. At this writing these are just stubs, but you may want to use them (or even better, improve them) anyway.

5.13.4 JOIN

The JOIN clause, if provided, names a join selectivity estimation function for the operator. (Note that this is a function name, not an operator name.) JOIN clauses only make sense for binary operators that return boolean. The idea behind a join selectivity estimator is to guess what fraction of the rows in a pair of tables will satisfy a WHERE-clause condition of the form

    table1.column1 OP table2.column2

for the current operator. As with the RESTRICT clause, this helps the optimizer very substantially by letting it figure out which of several possible join sequences is likely to take the least work.

As before, this chapter will make no attempt to explain how to write a join selectivity estimator function, but will just suggest that you use one of the standard estimators if one is applicable:

eqjoinsel for =

neqjoinsel for <>

scalarltjoinsel for < or <=

scalargtjoinsel for > or >=

areajoinsel for 2D area-based comparisons

positionjoinsel for 2D position-based comparisons

contjoinsel for 2D containment-based comparisons

5.13.5 HASHES

The HASHES clause, if present, tells the system that it is permissible to use the hash join method for a join based on this operator. HASHES only makes sense for a binary operator that returns boolean, and in practice the operator had better be equality for some data type.

The assumption underlying hash join is that the join operator can only return true for pairs of left and right values that hash to the same hash code. If two values get put in different hash buckets, the join will never compare them at all, implicitly assuming that the result of the join operator must be false. So it never makes sense to specify HASHES for operators that do not represent equality.

To be marked HASHES, the join operator must appear in a hash index operator class. This is not enforced when you create the operator, since of course the referencing operator class couldn't exist yet. But attempts to use the operator in hash joins will fail at run time if no such operator class exists. The system needs the operator class to find the data-type-specific hash function for the operator's input data type. Of course, you must also supply a suitable hash function before you can create the operator class.

Care should be exercised when preparing a hash function, because there are machine-dependent ways in which it might fail to do the right thing. For example, if your data type is a structure in which there may be uninteresting pad bits, you can't simply pass the whole structure to hash_any. (Unless you write your other operators and functions to ensure that the unused bits are always zero, which is the recommended strategy.) Another example is that on machines that meet the IEEE floating-point standard, negative zero and positive zero are different values (different bit patterns) but they are defined to compare equal. If a float value might contain negative zero then extra steps are needed to ensure it generates the same hash value as positive zero.

> Note: The function underlying a hash-joinable operator must be marked immutable or stable. If it is volatile, the system will never attempt to use the operator for a hash join.

> Note: If a hash-joinable operator has an underlying function that is marked strict, the function must also be complete: that is, it should return true or false, never null, for any two nonnull inputs. If this rule is not followed, hash-optimization of IN operations may generate wrong results. (Specifically, IN might return false where the correct answer according to the standard would be null; or it might yield an error complaining that it wasn't prepared for a null result.)

5.13.6 MERGES (SORT1, SORT2, LTCMP, GTCMP)

The MERGES clause, if present, tells the system that it is permissible to use the merge-join method for a join based on this operator. MERGES only makes sense for a binary operator that returns boolean, and in practice the operator must represent equality for some data type or pair of data types.

Merge join is based on the idea of sorting the left- and right-hand tables into order and then scanning them in parallel. So, both data types must be capable of being fully ordered, and the join operator must be one that can only succeed for pairs of values that fall at the "same place" in the sort order. In practice this means that the join operator must behave like equality. But unlike hash join, where the left and right data types had better be the same (or at least bitwise equivalent), it is possible to merge-join two distinct data types so long as they are logically compatible. For example, the smallint-versus-integer equality operator is merge-joinable. We only need sorting operators that will bring both data types into a logically compatible sequence.

Execution of a merge join requires that the system be able to identify four operators related to the merge-join equality operator: less-than comparison for the left operand data type, less-than comparison for the right operand data type, less-than comparison between the two data types, and greater-than comparison between the two data types. (These are actually four distinct operators if the merge-joinable operator has two different operand data types; but when the operand types are the same the three less-than operators are all the same operator.) It is possible to specify these operators individually by name, as the SORT1, SORT2, LTCMP, and GTCMP options respectively. The system will fill in the default names <, <, <, > respectively if any of these are omitted when MERGES is specified. Also, MERGES will be assumed to be implied if any of these four operator options appear, so it is possible to specify just some of them and let the system fill in the rest.

The operand data types of the four comparison operators can be deduced from the operand types of the merge-joinable operator, so just as with COMMUTATOR, only the operator names need be given in these clauses. Unless you are using peculiar choices of operator names, it's sufficient to write MERGES and let the system fill in the details. (As with COMMUTATOR and NEGATOR, the system is able to make dummy operator entries if you happen to define the equality operator before the other ones.)

There are additional restrictions on operators that you mark merge-joinable. These restrictions are not currently checked by CREATE OPERATOR, but errors may occur when the operator is used if any are not true:

- A merge-joinable equality operator must have a merge-joinable commutator (itself if the two operand data types are the same, or a related equality operator if they are different).

- If there is a merge-joinable operator relating any two data types A and B, and another merge-joinable operator relating B to any third data type C, then A and C must also have a merge-joinable operator; in other words, having a merge-joinable operator must be transitive.

- Bizarre results will ensue at run time if the four comparison operators you name do not sort the data values compatibly.

Note: The function underlying a merge-joinable operator must be marked immutable or stable. If it is volatile, the system will never attempt to use the operator for a merge join.

Note: In PostgreSQL versions before 7.3, the MERGES shorthand was not available: to make a merge-joinable operator one had to write both SORT1 and SORT2 explicitly. Also, the LTCMP and GTCMP options

did not exist; the names of those operators were hardwired as < and
> respectively.

5.14 Interfacing Extensions To Indexes

The procedures described thus far let you define new types, new functions,
and new operators. However, we cannot yet define an index on a column of a
new data type. To do this, we must define an *operator class* for the new data
type. Later in this section, we will illustrate this concept in an example: a
new operator class for the B-tree index method that stores and sorts complex
numbers in ascending absolute value order.

> **Note:** Prior to PostgreSQL release 7.3, it was necessary to make
> manual additions to the system catalogs pg_amop, pg_amproc, and
> pg_opclass in order to create a user-defined operator class. That
> approach is now deprecated in favor of using CREATE OPERATOR CLASS,
> which is a much simpler and less error-prone way of creating the
> necessary catalog entries.

5.14.1 Index Methods and Operator Classes

The pg_am table contains one row for every index method (internally known
as access method). Support for regular access to tables is built into PostgreSQL,
but all index methods are described in pg_am. It is possible to add a new index
method by defining the required interface routines and then creating a row in
pg_am—but that is beyond the scope of this chapter (see Volume 4, Chapter 8
Index Access Method Interface Definition).

The routines for an index method do not directly know anything about the
data types that the index method will operate on. Instead, an *operator class*
identifies the set of operations that the index method needs to use to work with
a particular data type. Operator classes are so called because one thing they
specify is the set of WHERE-clause operators that can be used with an index (i.e.,
can be converted into an index-scan qualification). An operator class may also
specify some *support procedures* that are needed by the internal operations of
the index method, but do not directly correspond to any WHERE-clause operator
that can be used with the index.

It is possible to define multiple operator classes for the same data type and
index method. By doing this, multiple sets of indexing semantics can be defined
for a single data type. For example, a B-tree index requires a sort ordering to be
defined for each data type it works on. It might be useful for a complex-number
data type to have one B-tree operator class that sorts the data by complex
absolute value, another that sorts by real part, and so on. Typically, one of the
operator classes will be deemed most commonly useful and will be marked as
the default operator class for that data type and index method.

The same operator class name can be used for several different index methods
(for example, both B-tree and hash index methods have operator classes named
int4_ops), but each such class is an independent entity and must be defined
separately.

5.14.2 Index Method Strategies

The operators associated with an operator class are identified by "strategy numbers", which serve to identify the semantics of each operator within the context of its operator class. For example, B-trees impose a strict ordering on keys, lesser to greater, and so operators like "less than" and "greater than or equal to" are interesting with respect to a B-tree. Because PostgreSQL allows the user to define operators, PostgreSQL cannot look at the name of an operator (e.g., < or >=) and tell what kind of comparison it is. Instead, the index method defines a set of "strategies", which can be thought of as generalized operators. Each operator class specifies which actual operator corresponds to each strategy for a particular data type and interpretation of the index semantics.

The B-tree index method defines five strategies, shown in Table 5.2.

OPERATION	STRATEGY NUMBER
less than	1
less than or equal	2
equal	3
greater than or equal	4
greater than	5

Table 5.2: B-tree Strategies

Hash indexes express only bitwise equality, and so they use only one strategy, shown in Table 5.3.

OPERATION	STRATEGY NUMBER
equal	1

Table 5.3: Hash Strategies

GiST indexes are even more flexible: they do not have a fixed set of strategies at all. Instead, the "consistency" support routine of each particular GiST operator class interprets the strategy numbers however it likes. As an example, several of the built-in GiST index operator classes index two-dimensional geometric objects, providing the "R-tree" strategies shown in Table 5.4. Four of these are true two-dimensional tests (overlaps, same, contains, contained by); four of them consider only the X direction; and the other four provide the same tests in the Y direction.

OPERATION	STRATEGY NUMBER
strictly left of	1
does not extend to right of	2
overlaps	3
does not extend to left of	4
strictly right of	5
same	6
contains	7
contained by	8
does not extend above	9
strictly below	10
strictly above	11
does not extend below	12

Table 5.4: GiST Two-Dimensional "R-tree" Strategies

GIN indexes are similar to GiST indexes in flexibility: they don't have a fixed set of strategies. Instead the support routines of each operator class interpret the strategy numbers according to the operator class's definition. As an example, the strategy numbers used by the built-in operator classes for arrays are shown in Table 5.5.

OPERATION	STRATEGY NUMBER
overlap	1
contains	2
is contained by	3
equal	4

Table 5.5: GIN Array Strategies

Note that all strategy operators return Boolean values. In practice, all operators defined as index method strategies must return type boolean, since they must appear at the top level of a WHERE clause to be used with an index.

By the way, the amorderstrategy column in pg_am tells whether the index method supports ordered scans. Zero means it doesn't; if it does, amorderstrategy is the strategy number that corresponds to the ordering operator. For example, B-tree has amorderstrategy = 1, which is its "less than" strategy number.

5.14.3 Index Method Support Routines

Strategies aren't usually enough information for the system to figure out how to use an index. In practice, the index methods require additional support routines in order to work. For example, the B-tree index method must be able to compare two keys and determine whether one is greater than, equal to, or less than the other. Similarly, the hash index method must be able to compute hash codes for key values. These operations do not correspond to operators used in qualifications in SQL commands; they are administrative routines used by the index methods, internally.

Just as with strategies, the operator class identifies which specific functions should play each of these roles for a given data type and semantic interpretation.

The index method defines the set of functions it needs, and the operator class identifies the correct functions to use by assigning them to the "support function numbers".

B-trees require a single support function, shown in Table 5.6.

FUNCTION	SUPPORT NUMBER
Compare two keys and return an integer less than zero, zero, or greater than zero, indicating whether the first key is less than, equal to, or greater than the second.	1

Table 5.6: B-tree Support Functions

Hash indexes likewise require one support function, shown in Table 5.7.

FUNCTION	SUPPORT NUMBER
Compute the hash value for a key	1

Table 5.7: Hash Support Functions

GiST indexes require seven support functions, shown in Table 5.8.

FUNCTION	SUPPORT NUMBER
consistent - determine whether key satisfies the query qualifier	1
union - compute union of a set of keys	2
compress - compute a compressed representation of a key or value to be indexed	3
decompress - compute a decompressed representation of a compressed key	4
penalty - compute penalty for inserting new key into subtree with given subtree's key	5
picksplit - determine which entries of a page are to be moved to the new page and compute the union keys for resulting pages	6
equal - compare two keys and return true if they are equal	7

Table 5.8: GiST Support Functions

GIN indexes require four support functions, shown in Table 5.9.

FUNCTION	SUPPORT NUMBER
compare - compare two keys and return an integer less than zero, zero, or greater than zero, indicating whether the first key is less than, equal to, or greater than the second	1
extractValue - extract keys from a value to be indexed	2
extractQuery - extract keys from a query condition	3
consistent - determine whether value matches query condition	4

Table 5.9: GIN Support Functions

Unlike strategy operators, support functions return whichever data type the particular index method expects; for example in the case of the comparison function for B-trees, a signed integer.

5.14.4 An Example

Now that we have seen the ideas, here is the promised example of creating a new operator class. (You can find a working copy of this example in 'src/tutorial/complex.c' and 'src/tutorial/complex.sql' in the source distribution.) The operator class encapsulates operators that sort complex numbers in absolute value order, so we choose the name complex_abs_ops. First, we need a set of operators. The procedure for defining operators was discussed in Section 5.12 *User-Defined Operators*, page 221. For an operator class on B-trees, the operators we require are:

- absolute-value less-than (strategy 1)
- absolute-value less-than-or-equal (strategy 2)
- absolute-value equal (strategy 3)
- absolute-value greater-than-or-equal (strategy 4)
- absolute-value greater-than (strategy 5)

The least error-prone way to define a related set of comparison operators is to write the B-tree comparison support function first, and then write the other functions as one-line wrappers around the support function. This reduces the odds of getting inconsistent results for corner cases. Following this approach, we first write

```
#define Mag(c)   ((c)->x*(c)->x + (c)->y*(c)->y)

static int
complex_abs_cmp_internal(Complex *a, Complex *b)
{
    double      amag = Mag(a),
                bmag = Mag(b);

    if (amag < bmag)
        return -1;
    if (amag > bmag)
        return 1;
    return 0;
}
```

Now the less-than function looks like

```
PG_FUNCTION_INFO_V1(complex_abs_lt);

Datum
complex_abs_lt(PG_FUNCTION_ARGS)
{
    Complex    *a = (Complex *) PG_GETARG_POINTER(0);
    Complex    *b = (Complex *) PG_GETARG_POINTER(1);

    PG_RETURN_BOOL(complex_abs_cmp_internal(a, b) < 0);
}
```

The other four functions differ only in how they compare the internal function's result to zero.

Next we declare the functions and the operators based on the functions to SQL:

```
CREATE FUNCTION complex_abs_lt(complex, complex) RETURNS bool
    AS 'filename', 'complex_abs_lt'
    LANGUAGE C IMMUTABLE STRICT;

CREATE OPERATOR < (
   leftarg = complex, rightarg = complex, procedure =
 complex_abs_lt,
   commutator = > , negator = >= ,
   restrict = scalarltsel, join = scalarltjoinsel
);
```

It is important to specify the correct commutator and negator operators, as well as suitable restriction and join selectivity functions, otherwise the optimizer will be unable to make effective use of the index. Note that the less-than, equal, and greater-than cases should use different selectivity functions.

Other things worth noting are happening here:

- There can only be one operator named, say, = and taking type complex for both operands. In this case we don't have any other operator = for complex, but if we were building a practical data type we'd probably want = to be the ordinary equality operation for complex numbers (and not the equality of the absolute values). In that case, we'd need to use some other operator name for complex_abs_eq.

- Although PostgreSQL can cope with functions having the same SQL name as long as they have different argument data types, C can only cope with one global function having a given name. So we shouldn't name the C function something simple like 'abs_eq'. Usually it's a good practice to include the data type name in the C function name, so as not to conflict with functions for other data types.

- We could have made the SQL name of the function 'abs_eq', relying on PostgreSQL to distinguish it by argument data types from any other SQL function of the same name. To keep the example simple, we make the function have the same names at the C level and SQL level.

The next step is the registration of the support routine required by B-trees. The example C code that implements this is in the same file that contains the operator functions. This is how we declare the function:

```
CREATE FUNCTION complex_abs_cmp(complex, complex)
    RETURNS integer
    AS 'filename'
    LANGUAGE C IMMUTABLE STRICT;
```

Now that we have the required operators and support routine, we can finally create the operator class:

```
CREATE OPERATOR CLASS complex_abs_ops
    DEFAULT FOR TYPE complex USING btree AS
        OPERATOR        1          < ,
        OPERATOR        2          <= ,
        OPERATOR        3          = ,
        OPERATOR        4          >= ,
        OPERATOR        5          > ,
        FUNCTION        1          complex_abs_cmp(complex,
complex);
```

And we're done! It should now be possible to create and use B-tree indexes on complex columns.

We could have written the operator entries more verbosely, as in

```
OPERATOR        1          < (complex, complex) ,
```

but there is no need to do so when the operators take the same data type we are defining the operator class for.

The above example assumes that you want to make this new operator class the default B-tree operator class for the complex data type. If you don't, just leave out the word DEFAULT.

5.14.5 Cross-Data-Type Operator Classes

So far we have implicitly assumed that an operator class deals with only one data type. While there certainly can be only one data type in a particular index column, it is often useful to index operations that compare an indexed column to a value of a different data type. This is presently supported by the B-tree and GiST index methods.

B-trees require the left-hand operand of each operator to be the indexed data type, but the right-hand operand can be of a different type. There must be a support function having a matching signature. For example, the built-in operator class for type bigint (int8) allows cross-type comparisons to int4 and int2. It could be duplicated by this definition:

```
CREATE OPERATOR CLASS int8_ops
DEFAULT FOR TYPE int8 USING btree AS
    -- standard int8 comparisons
    OPERATOR 1 < ,
    OPERATOR 2 <= ,
    OPERATOR 3 = ,
    OPERATOR 4 >= ,
    OPERATOR 5 > ,
    FUNCTION 1 btint8cmp(int8, int8) ,

    -- cross-type comparisons to int2 (smallint)
    OPERATOR 1 < (int8, int2) ,
    OPERATOR 2 <= (int8, int2) ,
    OPERATOR 3 = (int8, int2) ,
    OPERATOR 4 >= (int8, int2) ,
    OPERATOR 5 > (int8, int2) ,
```

```
FUNCTION 1 btint82cmp(int8, int2) ,

-- cross-type comparisons to int4 (integer)
OPERATOR 1 < (int8, int4) ,
OPERATOR 2 <= (int8, int4) ,
OPERATOR 3 = (int8, int4) ,
OPERATOR 4 >= (int8, int4) ,
OPERATOR 5 > (int8, int4) ,
FUNCTION 1 btint84cmp(int8, int4) ;
```

Notice that this definition "overloads" the operator strategy and support function numbers. This is allowed (for B-tree operator classes only) so long as each instance of a particular number has a different right-hand data type. The instances that are not cross-type are the default or primary operators of the operator class.

GiST indexes do not allow overloading of strategy or support function numbers, but it is still possible to get the effect of supporting multiple right-hand data types, by assigning a distinct strategy number to each operator that needs to be supported. The consistent support function must determine what it needs to do based on the strategy number, and must be prepared to accept comparison values of the appropriate data types.

5.14.6 System Dependencies on Operator Classes

PostgreSQL uses operator classes to infer the properties of operators in more ways than just whether they can be used with indexes. Therefore, you might want to create operator classes even if you have no intention of indexing any columns of your data type.

In particular, there are SQL features such as ORDER BY and DISTINCT that require comparison and sorting of values. To implement these features on a user-defined data type, PostgreSQL looks for the default B-tree operator class for the data type. The "equals" member of this operator class defines the system's notion of equality of values for GROUP BY and DISTINCT, and the sort ordering imposed by the operator class defines the default ORDER BY ordering.

Comparison of arrays of user-defined types also relies on the semantics defined by the default B-tree operator class.

If there is no default B-tree operator class for a data type, the system will look for a default hash operator class. But since that kind of operator class only provides equality, in practice it is only enough to support array equality.

When there is no default operator class for a data type, you will get errors like "could not identify an ordering operator" if you try to use these SQL features with the data type.

Note: In PostgreSQL versions before 7.4, sorting and grouping operations would implicitly use operators named =, <, and >. The new behavior of relying on default operator classes avoids having to make any assumption about the behavior of operators with particular names.

5.14.7 Special Features of Operator Classes

There are two special features of operator classes that we have not discussed yet, mainly because they are not useful with the most commonly used index methods.

Normally, declaring an operator as a member of an operator class means that the index method can retrieve exactly the set of rows that satisfy a WHERE condition using the operator. For example,

```
SELECT * FROM table WHERE integer_column < 4;
```

can be satisfied exactly by a B-tree index on the integer column. But there are cases where an index is useful as an inexact guide to the matching rows. For example, if a GiST index stores only bounding boxes for objects, then it cannot exactly satisfy a WHERE condition that tests overlap between nonrectangular objects such as polygons. Yet we could use the index to find objects whose bounding box overlaps the bounding box of the target object, and then do the exact overlap test only on the objects found by the index. If this scenario applies, the index is said to be "lossy" for the operator, and we add RECHECK to the OPERATOR clause in the CREATE OPERATOR CLASS command. RECHECK is valid if the index is guaranteed to return all the required rows, plus perhaps some additional rows, which can be eliminated by performing the original operator invocation.

Consider again the situation where we are storing in the index only the bounding box of a complex object such as a polygon. In this case there's not much value in storing the whole polygon in the index entry—we may as well store just a simpler object of type box. This situation is expressed by the STORAGE option in CREATE OPERATOR CLASS: we'd write something like

```
CREATE OPERATOR CLASS polygon_ops
    DEFAULT FOR TYPE polygon USING gist AS
    ...
    STORAGE box;
```

At present, only the GiST and GIN index methods support a STORAGE type that's different from the column data type. The GiST compress and decompress support routines must deal with data-type conversion when STORAGE is used. In GIN, the STORAGE type identifies the type of the "key" values, which normally is different from the type of the indexed column—for example, an operator class for integer array columns might have keys that are just integers. The GIN extractValue and extractQuery support routines are responsible for extracting keys from indexed values.

6 Triggers

This chapter provides general information about writing trigger functions. Trigger functions can be written in most of the available procedural languages, including PL/pgSQL (Chapter 9 *PL/pgSQL - SQL Procedural Language*, page 277), PL/Tcl (Chapter 10 *PL/Tcl - Tcl Procedural Language*, page 327), PL/Perl (Chapter 11 *PL/Perl - Perl Procedural Language*, page 337), and PL/Python (Chapter 12 *PL/Python - Python Procedural Language*, page 349). After reading this chapter, you should consult the chapter for your favorite procedural language to find out the language-specific details of writing a trigger in it.

It is also possible to write a trigger function in C, although most people find it easier to use one of the procedural languages. It is not currently possible to write a trigger function in the plain SQL function language.

6.1 Overview of Trigger Behavior

A trigger is a specification that the database should automatically execute a particular function whenever a certain type of operation is performed. Triggers can be defined to execute either before or after any INSERT, UPDATE, or DELETE operation, either once per modified row, or once per SQL statement. If a trigger event occurs, the trigger's function is called at the appropriate time to handle the event.

The trigger function must be defined before the trigger itself can be created. The trigger function must be declared as a function taking no arguments and returning type trigger. (The trigger function receives its input through a specially-passed TriggerData structure, not in the form of ordinary function arguments.)

Once a suitable trigger function has been created, the trigger is established with CREATE TRIGGER. The same trigger function can be used for multiple triggers.

PostgreSQL offers both *per-row* triggers and *per-statement* triggers. With a per-row trigger, the trigger function is invoked once for each row that is affected by the statement that fired the trigger. In contrast, a per-statement trigger is invoked only once when an appropriate statement is executed, regardless of the number of rows affected by that statement. In particular, a statement that affects zero rows will still result in the execution of any applicable per-statement triggers. These two types of triggers are sometimes called *row-level* triggers and *statement-level* triggers, respectively.

Triggers are also classified as *before* triggers and *after* triggers. Statement-level before triggers naturally fire before the statement starts to do anything, while statement-level after triggers fire at the very end of the statement. Row-level before triggers fire immediately before a particular row is operated on, while row-level after triggers fire at the end of the statement (but before any statement-level after triggers).

Trigger functions invoked by per-statement triggers should always return NULL. Trigger functions invoked by per-row triggers can return a table row (a value of type HeapTuple) to the calling executor, if they choose. A row-level trigger fired before an operation has the following choices:

- It can return NULL to skip the operation for the current row. This instructs the executor to not perform the row-level operation that invoked the trigger (the insertion or modification of a particular table row).

- For row-level INSERT and UPDATE triggers only, the returned row becomes the row that will be inserted or will replace the row being updated. This allows the trigger function to modify the row being inserted or updated.

A row-level before trigger that does not intend to cause either of these behaviors must be careful to return as its result the same row that was passed in (that is, the NEW row for INSERT and UPDATE triggers, the OLD row for DELETE triggers).

The return value is ignored for row-level triggers fired after an operation, and so they may as well return NULL.

If more than one trigger is defined for the same event on the same relation, the triggers will be fired in alphabetical order by trigger name. In the case of before triggers, the possibly-modified row returned by each trigger becomes the input to the next trigger. If any before trigger returns NULL, the operation is abandoned for that row and subsequent triggers are not fired.

Typically, row before triggers are used for checking or modifying the data that will be inserted or updated. For example, a before trigger might be used to insert the current time into a timestamp column, or to check that two elements of the row are consistent. Row after triggers are most sensibly used to propagate the updates to other tables, or make consistency checks against other tables. The reason for this division of labor is that an after trigger can be certain it is seeing the final value of the row, while a before trigger cannot; there might be other before triggers firing after it. If you have no specific reason to make a trigger before or after, the before case is more efficient, since the information about the operation doesn't have to be saved until end of statement.

If a trigger function executes SQL commands then these commands may fire triggers again. This is known as cascading triggers. There is no direct limitation on the number of cascade levels. It is possible for cascades to cause a recursive invocation of the same trigger; for example, an INSERT trigger might execute a command that inserts an additional row into the same table, causing the INSERT trigger to be fired again. It is the trigger programmer's responsibility to avoid infinite recursion in such scenarios.

When a trigger is being defined, arguments can be specified for it. The purpose of including arguments in the trigger definition is to allow different triggers with similar requirements to call the same function. As an example, there could be a generalized trigger function that takes as its arguments two column names and puts the current user in one and the current time stamp in the other. Properly written, this trigger function would be independent of the specific table it is triggering on. So the same function could be used for INSERT events on any table with suitable columns, to automatically track creation of records in a transaction table for example. It could also be used to track last-update events if defined as an UPDATE trigger.

Each programming language that supports triggers has its own method for making the trigger input data available to the trigger function. This input data includes the type of trigger event (e.g., INSERT or UPDATE) as well as any arguments that were listed in CREATE TRIGGER. For a row-level trigger, the input data also includes the NEW row for INSERT and UPDATE triggers, and/or the OLD row for UPDATE and DELETE triggers. Statement-level triggers do not currently have any way to examine the individual row(s) modified by the statement.

6.2 Visibility of Data Changes

If you execute SQL commands in your trigger function, and these commands access the table that the trigger is for, then you need to be aware of the data visibility rules, because they determine whether these SQL commands will see the data change that the trigger is fired for. Briefly:

- Statement-level triggers follow simple visibility rules: none of the changes made by a statement are visible to statement-level triggers that are invoked before the statement, whereas all modifications are visible to statement-level after triggers.

- The data change (insertion, update, or deletion) causing the trigger to fire is naturally *not* visible to SQL commands executed in a row-level before trigger, because it hasn't happened yet.

- However, SQL commands executed in a row-level before trigger *will* see the effects of data changes for rows previously processed in the same outer command. This requires caution, since the ordering of these change events is not in general predictable; a SQL command that affects multiple rows may visit the rows in any order.

- When a row-level after trigger is fired, all data changes made by the outer command are already complete, and are visible to the invoked trigger function.

Further information about data visibility rules can be found in Section 13.4 *Visibility of Data Changes*, page 381. The example in Section 6.4 *A Complete Example*, page 242 contains a demonstration of these rules.

6.3 Writing Trigger Functions in C

This section describes the low-level details of the interface to a trigger function. This information is only needed when writing trigger functions in C. If you are using a higher-level language then these details are handled for you. In most cases you should consider using a procedural language before writing your triggers in C. The documentation of each procedural language explains how to write a trigger in that language.

Trigger functions must use the "version 1" function manager interface.

When a function is called by the trigger manager, it is not passed any normal arguments, but it is passed a "context" pointer pointing to a `TriggerData` structure. C functions can check whether they were called from the trigger manager or not by executing the macro

    CALLED_AS_TRIGGER(fcinfo)

which expands to

    ((fcinfo)->context != NULL && IsA((fcinfo)->context,
    TriggerData))

If this returns true, then it is safe to cast `fcinfo->context` to type `TriggerData *` and make use of the pointed-to `TriggerData` structure. The function must *not* alter the `TriggerData` structure or any of the data it points to.

struct `TriggerData` is defined in 'commands/trigger.h':

```
typedef struct TriggerData
{
    NodeTag         type;
    TriggerEvent    tg_event;
    Relation        tg_relation;
    HeapTuple       tg_trigtuple;
    HeapTuple       tg_newtuple;
    Trigger         *tg_trigger;
    Buffer          tg_trigtuplebuf;
    Buffer          tg_newtuplebuf;
} TriggerData;
```

where the members are defined as follows:

type

Always `T_TriggerData`.

tg_event

Describes the event for which the function is called. You may use the following macros to examine `tg_event`:

TRIGGER_FIRED_BEFORE(tg_event)

Returns true if the trigger fired before the operation.

TRIGGER_FIRED_AFTER(tg_event)

Returns true if the trigger fired after the operation.

TRIGGER_FIRED_FOR_ROW(tg_event)

Returns true if the trigger fired for a row-level event.

TRIGGER_FIRED_FOR_STATEMENT(tg_event)
> Returns true if the trigger fired for a statement-level event.

TRIGGER_FIRED_BY_INSERT(tg_event)
> Returns true if the trigger was fired by an INSERT command.

TRIGGER_FIRED_BY_UPDATE(tg_event)
> Returns true if the trigger was fired by an UPDATE command.

TRIGGER_FIRED_BY_DELETE(tg_event)
> Returns true if the trigger was fired by a DELETE command.

tg_relation
> A pointer to a structure describing the relation that the trigger fired for. Look at 'utils/rel.h' for details about this structure. The most interesting things are tg_relation->rd_att (descriptor of the relation tuples) and tg_relation->rd_rel->relname (relation name; the type is not char* but NameData; use SPI_getrelname(tg_relation) to get a char* if you need a copy of the name).

tg_trigtuple
> A pointer to the row for which the trigger was fired. This is the row being inserted, updated, or deleted. If this trigger was fired for an INSERT or DELETE then this is what you should return from the function if you don't want to replace the row with a different one (in the case of INSERT) or skip the operation.

tg_newtuple
> A pointer to the new version of the row, if the trigger was fired for an UPDATE, and NULL if it is for an INSERT or a DELETE. This is what you have to return from the function if the event is an UPDATE and you don't want to replace this row by a different one or skip the operation.

tg_trigger
> A pointer to a structure of type Trigger, defined in 'utils/rel.h':

```
typedef struct Trigger
{
    Oid         tgoid;
    char        *tgname;
    Oid         tgfoid;
    int16       tgtype;
    bool        tgenabled;
    bool        tgisconstraint;
    Oid         tgconstrrelid;
    bool        tgdeferrable;
    bool        tginitdeferred;
    int16       tgnargs;
    int16       tgnattr;
    int16       *tgattr;
    char        **tgargs;
} Trigger;
```

where tgname is the trigger's name, tgnargs is number of arguments in tgargs, and tgargs is an array of pointers to the arguments specified in the CREATE TRIGGER statement. The other members are for internal use only.

tg_trigtuplebuf

The buffer containing tg_trigtuple, or InvalidBuffer if there is no such tuple or it is not stored in a disk buffer.

tg_newtuplebuf

The buffer containing tg_newtuple, or InvalidBuffer if there is no such tuple or it is not stored in a disk buffer.

A trigger function must return either a HeapTuple pointer or a NULL pointer (*not* an SQL null value, that is, do not set isNull true). Be careful to return either tg_trigtuple or tg_newtuple, as appropriate, if you don't want to modify the row being operated on.

6.4 A Complete Example

Here is a very simple example of a trigger function written in C. (Examples of triggers written in procedural languages may be found in the documentation of the procedural languages.)

The function trigf reports the number of rows in the table ttest and skips the actual operation if the command attempts to insert a null value into the column x. (So the trigger acts as a not-null constraint but doesn't abort the transaction.)

First, the table definition:

```
CREATE TABLE ttest (
    x integer
);
```

This is the source code of the trigger function:

```
#include "postgres.h"
#include "executor/spi.h" /* this is what you need to work
                             with SPI */
#include "commands/trigger.h" /* ... and triggers */

extern Datum trigf(PG_FUNCTION_ARGS);

PG_FUNCTION_INFO_V1(trigf);

Datum
trigf(PG_FUNCTION_ARGS)
{
    TriggerData *trigdata = (TriggerData *) fcinfo->context;
    TupleDesc tupdesc;
    HeapTuple rettuple;
    char *when;
    bool checknull = false;
```

```
bool isnull;
int ret, i;

/* make sure it's called as a trigger at all */
if (!CALLED_AS_TRIGGER(fcinfo))
  elog(ERROR, "trigf: not called by trigger manager");

/* tuple to return to executor */
if (TRIGGER_FIRED_BY_UPDATE(trigdata->tg_event))
  rettuple = trigdata->tg_newtuple;
else
  rettuple = trigdata->tg_trigtuple;

/* check for null values */
if (!TRIGGER_FIRED_BY_DELETE(trigdata->tg_event)
    && TRIGGER_FIRED_BEFORE(trigdata->tg_event))
  checknull = true;

if (TRIGGER_FIRED_BEFORE(trigdata->tg_event))
  when = "before";
else
  when = "after ";

tupdesc = trigdata->tg_relation->rd_att;

/* connect to SPI manager */
if ((ret = SPI_connect()) < 0)
  elog(INFO, "trigf (fired %s): SPI_connect returned %d",
       when, ret);

/* get number of rows in table */
ret = SPI_exec("SELECT count(*) FROM ttest", 0);

if (ret < 0)
  elog(NOTICE, "trigf (fired %s): SPI_exec returned %d",
       when, ret);

/* count(*) returns int8, so be careful to convert */
i = DatumGetInt64(SPI_getbinval
                   (SPI_tuptable->vals[0],
                    SPI_tuptable->tupdesc, 1, &isnull));

elog(INFO, "trigf (fired %s): there are %d rows in ttest",
     when, i);

SPI_finish();

if (checknull) {
```

```
      SPI_getbinval(rettuple, tupdesc, 1, &isnull);
      if (isnull)
        rettuple = NULL;
   }

   return PointerGetDatum(rettuple);
 }
```

After you have compiled the source code, declare the function and the triggers:

```
 CREATE FUNCTION trigf() RETURNS trigger
     AS 'filename'
     LANGUAGE C;

 CREATE TRIGGER tbefore BEFORE INSERT OR UPDATE OR DELETE ON ttest
     FOR EACH ROW EXECUTE PROCEDURE trigf();

 CREATE TRIGGER tafter AFTER INSERT OR UPDATE OR DELETE ON ttest
     FOR EACH ROW EXECUTE PROCEDURE trigf();
```

Now you can test the operation of the trigger:

```
 => INSERT INTO ttest VALUES (NULL);
 INFO:  trigf (fired before): there are 0 rows in ttest
 INSERT 0 0

 -- Insertion skipped and AFTER trigger is not fired

 => SELECT * FROM ttest;
  x
 ---
 (0 rows)

 => INSERT INTO ttest VALUES (1);
 INFO:  trigf (fired before): there are 0 rows in ttest
 INFO:  trigf (fired after ): there are 1 rows in ttest
                            ^^^^^^^^^
          remember what we said about visibility.
 INSERT 167793 1
 vac=> SELECT * FROM ttest;
  x
 ---
  1
 (1 row)

 => INSERT INTO ttest SELECT x * 2 FROM ttest;
 INFO:  trigf (fired before): there are 1 rows in ttest
 INFO:  trigf (fired after ): there are 2 rows in ttest
                            ^^^^^^
          remember what we said about visibility.
 INSERT 167794 1
```

```
=> SELECT * FROM ttest;
 x
---
 1
 2
(2 rows)

=> UPDATE ttest SET x = NULL WHERE x = 2;
INFO:  trigf (fired before): there are 2 rows in ttest
UPDATE 0
=> UPDATE ttest SET x = 4 WHERE x = 2;
INFO:  trigf (fired before): there are 2 rows in ttest
INFO:  trigf (fired after ): there are 2 rows in ttest
UPDATE 1
vac=> SELECT * FROM ttest;
 x
---
 1
 4
(2 rows)

=> DELETE FROM ttest;
INFO:  trigf (fired before): there are 2 rows in ttest
INFO:  trigf (fired before): there are 1 rows in ttest
INFO:  trigf (fired after ): there are 0 rows in ttest
INFO:  trigf (fired after ): there are 0 rows in ttest
                                        ~~~~~~
          remember what we said about visibility.
DELETE 2
=> SELECT * FROM ttest;
 x
---
(0 rows)
```

There are more complex examples in 'src/test/regress/regress.c' and in 'contrib/spi'.

7 The Rule System

This chapter discusses the rule system in PostgreSQL. Production rule systems are conceptually simple, but there are many subtle points involved in actually using them.

Some other database systems define active database rules, which are usually stored procedures and triggers. In PostgreSQL, these can be implemented using functions and triggers as well.

The rule system (more precisely speaking, the query rewrite rule system) is totally different from stored procedures and triggers. It modifies queries to take rules into consideration, and then passes the modified query to the query planner for planning and execution. It is very powerful, and can be used for many things such as query language procedures, views, and versions. The theoretical foundations and the power of this rule system are also discussed in [Stonebraker et al, ACM, 1990] and [Ong and Goh, 1990].

7.1 The Query Tree

To understand how the rule system works it is necessary to know when it is invoked and what its input and results are.

The rule system is located between the parser and the planner. It takes the output of the parser, one query tree, and the user-defined rewrite rules, which are also query trees with some extra information, and creates zero or more query trees as result. So its input and output are always things the parser itself could have produced and thus, anything it sees is basically representable as an SQL statement.

Now what is a query tree? It is an internal representation of an SQL statement where the single parts that it is built from are stored separately. These query trees can be shown in the server log if you set the configuration parameters debug_print_parse, debug_print_rewritten, or debug_print_plan. The rule actions are also stored as query trees, in the system catalog pg_rewrite. They are not formatted like the log output, but they contain exactly the same information.

Reading a raw query tree requires some experience. But since SQL representations of query trees are sufficient to understand the rule system, this chapter will not teach how to read them.

When reading the SQL representations of the query trees in this chapter it is necessary to be able to identify the parts the statement is broken into when it is in the query tree structure. The parts of a query tree are

the command type
> This is a simple value telling which command (SELECT, INSERT, UPDATE, DELETE) produced the query tree.

the range table

> The range table is a list of relations that are used in the query. In a SELECT statement these are the relations given after the FROM key word.
>
> Every range table entry identifies a table or view and tells by which name it is called in the other parts of the query. In the query tree, the range table entries are referenced by number rather than by name, so here it doesn't matter if there are duplicate names as it would in an SQL statement. This can happen after the range tables of rules have been merged in. The examples in this chapter will not have this situation.

the result relation

> This is an index into the range table that identifies the relation where the results of the query go.
>
> SELECT queries normally don't have a result relation. The special case of a SELECT INTO is mostly identical to a CREATE TABLE followed by a INSERT ... SELECT and is not discussed separately here.
>
> For INSERT, UPDATE, and DELETE commands, the result relation is the table (or view!) where the changes are to take effect.

the target list

> The target list is a list of expressions that define the result of the query. In the case of a SELECT, these expressions are the ones that build the final output of the query. They correspond to the expressions between the key words SELECT and FROM. (* is just an abbreviation for all the column names of a relation. It is expanded by the parser into the individual columns, so the rule system never sees it.)
>
> DELETE commands don't need a target list because they don't produce any result. In fact, the planner will add a special CTID entry to the empty target list, but this is after the rule system and will be discussed later; for the rule system, the target list is empty.
>
> For INSERT commands, the target list describes the new rows that should go into the result relation. It consists of the expressions in the VALUES clause or the ones from the SELECT clause in INSERT ... SELECT. The first step of the rewrite process adds target list entries for any columns that were not assigned to by the original command but have defaults. Any remaining columns (with neither a given value nor a default) will be filled in by the planner with a constant null expression.
>
> For UPDATE commands, the target list describes the new rows that should replace the old ones. In the rule system, it contains just the expressions from the SET column = expression part of the command. The planner will handle missing columns by inserting expressions that copy the values from the old row into the new one. And it will add the special CTID entry just as for DELETE, too.
>
> Every entry in the target list contains an expression that can be a constant value, a variable pointing to a column of one of the relations in the range table, a parameter, or an expression tree made of function calls, constants, variables, operators, etc.

the qualification
>The query's qualification is an expression much like one of those contained
>in the target list entries. The result value of this expression is a Boolean
>that tells whether the operation (INSERT, UPDATE, DELETE, or SELECT) for
>the final result row should be executed or not. It corresponds to the WHERE
>clause of an SQL statement.

the join tree
>The query's join tree shows the structure of the FROM clause. For a simple
>query like SELECT ... FROM a, b, c, the join tree is just a list of the FROM
>items, because we are allowed to join them in any order. But when JOIN
>expressions, particularly outer joins, are used, we have to join in the order
>shown by the joins. In that case, the join tree shows the structure of the
>JOIN expressions. The restrictions associated with particular JOIN clauses
>(from ON or USING expressions) are stored as qualification expressions at-
>tached to those join-tree nodes. It turns out to be convenient to store the
>top-level WHERE expression as a qualification attached to the top-level join-
>tree item, too. So really the join tree represents both the FROM and WHERE
>clauses of a SELECT.

the others
>The other parts of the query tree like the ORDER BY clause aren't of interest
>here. The rule system substitutes some entries there while applying rules,
>but that doesn't have much to do with the fundamentals of the rule system.

7.2 Views and the Rule System

Views in PostgreSQL are implemented using the rule system. In fact, there
is essentially no difference between

```
CREATE VIEW myview AS SELECT * FROM mytab;
```

compared against the two commands

```
CREATE TABLE myview (same column list as mytab);
CREATE RULE "_RETURN" AS ON SELECT TO myview DO INSTEAD
    SELECT * FROM mytab;
```

because this is exactly what the CREATE VIEW command does internally. This
has some side effects. One of them is that the information about a view in the
PostgreSQL system catalogs is exactly the same as it is for a table. So for the
parser, there is absolutely no difference between a table and a view. They are
the same thing: relations.

7.2.1 How SELECT Rules Work

Rules ON SELECT are applied to all queries as the last step, even if the command given is an INSERT, UPDATE or DELETE. And they have different semantics from rules on the other command types in that they modify the query tree in place instead of creating a new one. So SELECT rules are described first.

Currently, there can be only one action in an ON SELECT rule, and it must be an unconditional SELECT action that is INSTEAD. This restriction was required to make rules safe enough to open them for ordinary users, and it restricts ON SELECT rules to act like views.

The examples for this chapter are two join views that do some calculations and some more views using them in turn. One of the two first views is customized later by adding rules for INSERT, UPDATE, and DELETE operations so that the final result will be a view that behaves like a real table with some magic functionality. This is not such a simple example to start from and this makes things harder to get into. But it's better to have one example that covers all the points discussed step by step rather than having many different ones that might mix up in mind.

For the example, we need a little min function that returns the lower of 2 integer values. We create that as

```
CREATE FUNCTION min(integer, integer) RETURNS integer AS $$
    SELECT CASE WHEN $1 < $2 THEN $1 ELSE $2 END
$$ LANGUAGE SQL STRICT;
```

The real tables we need in the first two rule system descriptions are these:

```
CREATE TABLE shoe_data (
    shoename    text,        -- primary key
    sh_avail    integer,     -- available number of pairs
    slcolor     text,        -- preferred shoelace color
    slminlen    real,        -- minimum shoelace length
    slmaxlen    real,        -- maximum shoelace length
    slunit      text         -- length unit
);

CREATE TABLE shoelace_data (
    sl_name     text,        -- primary key
    sl_avail    integer,     -- available number of pairs
    sl_color    text,        -- shoelace color
    sl_len      real,        -- shoelace length
    sl_unit     text         -- length unit
);

CREATE TABLE unit (
    un_name     text,        -- primary key
    un_fact     real         -- factor to transform to cm
);
```

As you can see, they represent shoe-store data.

The views are created as

```
CREATE VIEW shoe AS
    SELECT sh.shoename,
           sh.sh_avail,
           sh.slcolor,
           sh.slminlen,
           sh.slminlen * un.un_fact AS slminlen_cm,
           sh.slmaxlen,
           sh.slmaxlen * un.un_fact AS slmaxlen_cm,
           sh.slunit
      FROM shoe_data sh, unit un
     WHERE sh.slunit = un.un_name;

CREATE VIEW shoelace AS
    SELECT s.sl_name,
           s.sl_avail,
           s.sl_color,
           s.sl_len,
           s.sl_unit,
           s.sl_len * u.un_fact AS sl_len_cm
      FROM shoelace_data s, unit u
     WHERE s.sl_unit = u.un_name;

CREATE VIEW shoe_ready AS
    SELECT rsh.shoename,
           rsh.sh_avail,
           rsl.sl_name,
           rsl.sl_avail,
           min(rsh.sh_avail, rsl.sl_avail) AS total_avail
      FROM shoe rsh, shoelace rsl
     WHERE rsl.sl_color = rsh.slcolor
       AND rsl.sl_len_cm >= rsh.slminlen_cm
       AND rsl.sl_len_cm <= rsh.slmaxlen_cm;
```

The CREATE VIEW command for the shoelace view (which is the simplest one we have) will create a relation shoelace and an entry in pg_rewrite that tells that there is a rewrite rule that must be applied whenever the relation shoelace is referenced in a query's range table. The rule has no rule qualification (discussed later, with the non-SELECT rules, since SELECT rules currently cannot have them) and it is INSTEAD. Note that rule qualifications are not the same as query qualifications. The action of our rule has a query qualification. The action of the rule is one query tree that is a copy of the SELECT statement in the view creation command.

Note: The two extra range table entries for NEW and OLD (named *NEW* and *OLD* for historical reasons in the printed query tree) you can see in the pg_rewrite entry aren't of interest for SELECT rules.

Now we populate unit, shoe_data and shoelace_data and run a simple query on a view:

```
INSERT INTO unit VALUES ('cm', 1.0);
INSERT INTO unit VALUES ('m', 100.0);
INSERT INTO unit VALUES ('inch', 2.54);

INSERT INTO shoe_data VALUES ('sh1', 2, 'black', 70.0, 90.0,
   'cm');
INSERT INTO shoe_data VALUES ('sh2', 0, 'black', 30.0, 40.0,
   'inch');
INSERT INTO shoe_data VALUES ('sh3', 4, 'brown', 50.0, 65.0,
   'cm');
INSERT INTO shoe_data VALUES ('sh4', 3, 'brown', 40.0, 50.0,
   'inch');

INSERT INTO shoelace_data VALUES ('sl1', 5, 'black', 80.0, 'cm');
INSERT INTO shoelace_data VALUES ('sl2', 6, 'black', 100.0,
   'cm');
INSERT INTO shoelace_data VALUES ('sl3', 0, 'black', 35.0 ,
   'inch');
INSERT INTO shoelace_data VALUES ('sl4', 8, 'black', 40.0 ,
   'inch');
INSERT INTO shoelace_data VALUES ('sl5', 4, 'brown', 1.0 , 'm');
INSERT INTO shoelace_data VALUES ('sl6', 0, 'brown', 0.9 , 'm');
INSERT INTO shoelace_data VALUES ('sl7', 7, 'brown', 60 , 'cm');
INSERT INTO shoelace_data VALUES ('sl8', 1, 'brown', 40 ,
   'inch');

SELECT * FROM shoelace;
```

sl_name	sl_avail	sl_color	sl_len	sl_unit	sl_len_cm
sl1	5	black	80	cm	80
sl2	6	black	100	cm	100
sl7	7	brown	60	cm	60
sl3	0	black	35	inch	88.9
sl4	8	black	40	inch	101.6
sl8	1	brown	40	inch	101.6
sl5	4	brown	1	m	100
sl6	0	brown	0.9	m	90

(8 rows)

This is the simplest SELECT you can do on our views, so we take this opportunity to explain the basics of view rules. The SELECT * FROM shoelace was interpreted by the parser and produced the query tree

```
SELECT shoelace.sl_name, shoelace.sl_avail,
       shoelace.sl_color, shoelace.sl_len,
       shoelace.sl_unit, shoelace.sl_len_cm
   FROM shoelace shoelace;
```

and this is given to the rule system. The rule system walks through the range table and checks if there are rules for any relation. When processing the range table entry for shoelace (the only one up to now) it finds the _RETURN rule with the query tree

```
SELECT s.sl_name, s.sl_avail,
       s.sl_color, s.sl_len, s.sl_unit,
       s.sl_len * u.un_fact AS sl_len_cm
  FROM shoelace *OLD*, shoelace *NEW*,
       shoelace_data s, unit u
 WHERE s.sl_unit = u.un_name;
```

To expand the view, the rewriter simply creates a subquery range-table entry containing the rule's action query tree, and substitutes this range table entry for the original one that referenced the view. The resulting rewritten query tree is almost the same as if you had typed

```
SELECT shoelace.sl_name, shoelace.sl_avail,
       shoelace.sl_color, shoelace.sl_len,
       shoelace.sl_unit, shoelace.sl_len_cm
  FROM (SELECT s.sl_name,
               s.sl_avail,
               s.sl_color,
               s.sl_len,
               s.sl_unit,
               s.sl_len * u.un_fact AS sl_len_cm
          FROM shoelace_data s, unit u
         WHERE s.sl_unit = u.un_name) shoelace;
```

There is one difference however: the subquery's range table has two extra entries shoelace *OLD* and shoelace *NEW*. These entries don't participate directly in the query, since they aren't referenced by the subquery's join tree or target list. The rewriter uses them to store the access privilege check information that was originally present in the range-table entry that referenced the view. In this way, the executor will still check that the user has proper privileges to access the view, even though there's no direct use of the view in the rewritten query.

That was the first rule applied. The rule system will continue checking the remaining range-table entries in the top query (in this example there are no more), and it will recursively check the range-table entries in the added subquery to see if any of them reference views. (But it won't expand *OLD* or *NEW*— otherwise we'd have infinite recursion!) In this example, there are no rewrite rules for shoelace_data or unit, so rewriting is complete and the above is the final result given to the planner.

Now we want to write a query that finds out for which shoes currently in the store we have the matching shoelaces (color and length) and where the total number of exactly matching pairs is greater or equal to two.

```
SELECT * FROM shoe_ready WHERE total_avail >= 2;
```

shoename	sh_avail	sl_name	sl_avail	total_avail
sh1	2	sl1	5	2
sh3	4	sl7	7	4

(2 rows)

The output of the parser this time is the query tree

```
SELECT shoe_ready.shoename, shoe_ready.sh_avail,
       shoe_ready.sl_name, shoe_ready.sl_avail,
       shoe_ready.total_avail
  FROM shoe_ready shoe_ready
 WHERE shoe_ready.total_avail >= 2;
```

The first rule applied will be the one for the shoe_ready view and it results in
the query tree

```
SELECT shoe_ready.shoename, shoe_ready.sh_avail,
       shoe_ready.sl_name, shoe_ready.sl_avail,
       shoe_ready.total_avail
  FROM (SELECT rsh.shoename,
               rsh.sh_avail,
               rsl.sl_name,
               rsl.sl_avail,
               min(rsh.sh_avail, rsl.sl_avail) AS total_avail
          FROM shoe rsh, shoelace rsl
         WHERE rsl.sl_color = rsh.slcolor
           AND rsl.sl_len_cm >= rsh.slminlen_cm
           AND rsl.sl_len_cm <= rsh.slmaxlen_cm) shoe_ready
 WHERE shoe_ready.total_avail >= 2;
```

Similarly, the rules for shoe and shoelace are substituted into the range table
of the subquery, leading to a three-level final query tree:

```
SELECT shoe_ready.shoename, shoe_ready.sh_avail,
       shoe_ready.sl_name, shoe_ready.sl_avail,
       shoe_ready.total_avail
  FROM (SELECT rsh.shoename,
               rsh.sh_avail,
               rsl.sl_name,
               rsl.sl_avail,
               min(rsh.sh_avail, rsl.sl_avail) AS total_avail
          FROM (SELECT sh.shoename,
                       sh.sh_avail,
                       sh.slcolor,
                       sh.slminlen,
                       sh.slminlen * un.un_fact AS slminlen_cm,
                       sh.slmaxlen,
                       sh.slmaxlen * un.un_fact AS slmaxlen_cm,
                       sh.slunit
                  FROM shoe_data sh, unit un
                 WHERE sh.slunit = un.un_name) rsh,
               (SELECT s.sl_name,
                       s.sl_avail,
                       s.sl_color,
                       s.sl_len,
                       s.sl_unit,
                       s.sl_len * u.un_fact AS sl_len_cm
```

```
                          FROM shoelace_data s, unit u
                          WHERE s.sl_unit = u.un_name) rsl
                    WHERE rsl.sl_color = rsh.slcolor
                      AND rsl.sl_len_cm >= rsh.slminlen_cm
                      AND rsl.sl_len_cm <= rsh.slmaxlen_cm) shoe_ready
                WHERE shoe_ready.total_avail > 2;
```

It turns out that the planner will collapse this tree into a two-level query tree: the bottommost SELECT commands will be "pulled up" into the middle SELECT since there's no need to process them separately. But the middle SELECT will remain separate from the top, because it contains aggregate functions. If we pulled those up it would change the behavior of the topmost SELECT, which we don't want. However, collapsing the query tree is an optimization that the rewrite system doesn't have to concern itself with.

7.2.2 View Rules in Non-SELECT Statements

Two details of the query tree aren't touched in the description of view rules above. These are the command type and the result relation. In fact, view rules don't need this information.

There are only a few differences between a query tree for a SELECT and one for any other command. Obviously, they have a different command type and for a command other than a SELECT, the result relation points to the range-table entry where the result should go. Everything else is absolutely the same. So having two tables t1 and t2 with columns a and b, the query trees for the two statements

```
SELECT t2.b FROM t1, t2 WHERE t1.a = t2.a;

UPDATE t1 SET b = t2.b FROM t2 WHERE t1.a = t2.a;
```

are nearly identical. In particular:

- The range tables contain entries for the tables t1 and t2.

- The target lists contain one variable that points to column b of the range table entry for table t2.

- The qualification expressions compare the columns a of both range-table entries for equality.

- The join trees show a simple join between t1 and t2.

The consequence is, that both query trees result in similar execution plans: They are both joins over the two tables. For the UPDATE the missing columns from t1 are added to the target list by the planner and the final query tree will read as

```
UPDATE t1 SET a = t1.a, b = t2.b FROM t2 WHERE t1.a = t2.a;
```

and thus the executor run over the join will produce exactly the same result set as a

```
SELECT t1.a, t2.b FROM t1, t2 WHERE t1.a = t2.a;
```

will do. But there is a little problem in UPDATE: The executor does not care
what the results from the join it is doing are meant for. It just produces a result
set of rows. The difference that one is a SELECT command and the other is an
UPDATE is handled in the caller of the executor. The caller still knows (looking
at the query tree) that this is an UPDATE, and it knows that this result should
go into table t1. But which of the rows that are there has to be replaced by
the new row?

To resolve this problem, another entry is added to the target list in UPDATE
(and also in DELETE) statements: the current tuple ID (CTID). This is a system
column containing the file block number and position in the block for the row.
Knowing the table, the CTID can be used to retrieve the original row of t1 to
be updated. After adding the CTID to the target list, the query actually looks
like

```
SELECT t1.a, t2.b, t1.ctid FROM t1, t2 WHERE t1.a = t2.a;
```

Now another detail of PostgreSQL enters the stage. Old table rows aren't
overwritten, and this is why ROLLBACK is fast. In an UPDATE, the new result row
is inserted into the table (after stripping the CTID) and in the row header of
the old row, which the CTID pointed to, the cmax and xmax entries are set to
the current command counter and current transaction ID. Thus the old row is
hidden, and after the transaction commits the vacuum cleaner can really remove
it.

Knowing all that, we can simply apply view rules in absolutely the same way
to any command. There is no difference.

7.2.3 The Power of Views in PostgreSQL

The above demonstrates how the rule system incorporates view definitions
into the original query tree. In the second example, a simple SELECT from one
view created a final query tree that is a join of 4 tables (unit was used twice
with different names).

The benefit of implementing views with the rule system is, that the planner
has all the information about which tables have to be scanned plus the rela-
tionships between these tables plus the restrictive qualifications from the views
plus the qualifications from the original query in one single query tree. And
this is still the situation when the original query is already a join over views.
The planner has to decide which is the best path to execute the query, and
the more information the planner has, the better this decision can be. And the
rule system as implemented in PostgreSQL ensures, that this is all information
available about the query up to that point.

7.2.4 Updating a View

What happens if a view is named as the target relation for an INSERT, UPDATE, or DELETE? After doing the substitutions described above, we will have a query tree in which the result relation points at a subquery range-table entry. This will not work, so the rewriter throws an error if it sees it has produced such a thing.

To change this, we can define rules that modify the behavior of these kinds of commands. This is the topic of the next section.

7.3 Rules on INSERT, UPDATE, and DELETE

Rules that are defined on INSERT, UPDATE, and DELETE are significantly different from the view rules described in the previous section. First, their CREATE RULE command allows more:

- They are allowed to have no action.
- They can have multiple actions.
- They can be INSTEAD or ALSO (the default).
- The pseudorelations NEW and OLD become useful.
- They can have rule qualifications.

Second, they don't modify the query tree in place. Instead they create zero or more new query trees and can throw away the original one.

7.3.1 How Update Rules Work

Keep the syntax

```
CREATE [ OR REPLACE ] RULE name AS ON event
    TO table [ WHERE condition ]
    DO [ ALSO | INSTEAD ] { NOTHING | command | ( command ;
command ... ) }
```

in mind. In the following, *update rules* means rules that are defined on INSERT, UPDATE, or DELETE.

Update rules get applied by the rule system when the result relation and the command type of a query tree are equal to the object and event given in the CREATE RULE command. For update rules, the rule system creates a list of query trees. Initially the query-tree list is empty. There can be zero (NOTHING key word), one, or multiple actions. To simplify, we will look at a rule with one action. This rule can have a qualification or not and it can be INSTEAD or ALSO (the default).

What is a rule qualification? It is a restriction that tells when the actions of the rule should be done and when not. This qualification can only reference the pseudorelations NEW and/or OLD, which basically represent the relation that was given as object (but with a special meaning).

So we have three cases that produce the following query trees for a one-action rule.

No qualification, with either ALSO or INSTEAD
> the query tree from the rule action with the original query tree's qualification added

Qualification given and ALSO
> the query tree from the rule action with the rule qualification and the original query tree's qualification added

Qualification given and INSTEAD
> the query tree from the rule action with the rule qualification and the original query tree's qualification; and the original query tree with the negated rule qualification added

Finally, if the rule is ALSO, the unchanged original query tree is added to the list. Since only qualified INSTEAD rules already add the original query tree, we end up with either one or two output query trees for a rule with one action.

For ON INSERT rules, the original query (if not suppressed by INSTEAD) is done before any actions added by rules. This allows the actions to see the inserted row(s). But for ON UPDATE and ON DELETE rules, the original query is done after the actions added by rules. This ensures that the actions can see the to-be-updated or to-be-deleted rows; otherwise, the actions might do nothing because they find no rows matching their qualifications.

The query trees generated from rule actions are thrown into the rewrite system again, and maybe more rules get applied resulting in more or less query trees. So a rule's actions must have either a different command type or a different result relation than the rule itself is on, otherwise this recursive process will end up in an infinite loop. (Recursive expansion of a rule will be detected and reported as an error.)

The query trees found in the actions of the pg_rewrite system catalog are only templates. Since they can reference the range-table entries for NEW and OLD, some substitutions have to be made before they can be used. For any reference to NEW, the target list of the original query is searched for a corresponding entry. If found, that entry's expression replaces the reference. Otherwise, NEW means the same as OLD (for an UPDATE) or is replaced by a null value (for an INSERT). Any reference to OLD is replaced by a reference to the range-table entry that is the result relation.

After the system is done applying update rules, it applies view rules to the produced query tree(s). Views cannot insert new update actions so there is no need to apply update rules to the output of view rewriting.

7.3.1.1 A First Rule Step by Step

Say we want to trace changes to the sl_avail column in the shoelace_data
relation. So we set up a log table and a rule that conditionally writes a log
entry when an UPDATE is performed on shoelace_data.

```
CREATE TABLE shoelace_log (
    sl_name     text,           -- shoelace changed
    sl_avail    integer,        -- new available value
    log_who     text,           -- who did it
    log_when    timestamp       -- when
);


CREATE RULE log_shoelace AS ON UPDATE TO shoelace_data
    WHERE NEW.sl_avail <> OLD.sl_avail
    DO INSERT INTO shoelace_log VALUES (
                            NEW.sl_name, NEW.sl_avail,
                            current_user,
                            current_timestamp
                    );
```

Now someone does:

```
UPDATE shoelace_data SET sl_avail = 6 WHERE sl_name = 'sl7';
```

and we look at the log table:

```
SELECT * FROM shoelace_log;

 sl_name | sl_avail | log_who |
---------+----------+---------+
 sl7     |        6 | Al      |
 log_when
---------------------------------
 Tue Oct 20 16:14:45 1998 MET DST
(1 row)
```

That's what we expected. What happened in the background is the following.
The parser created the query tree

```
UPDATE shoelace_data SET sl_avail = 6
  FROM shoelace_data shoelace_data
  WHERE shoelace_data.sl_name = 'sl7';
```

There is a rule log_shoelace that is ON UPDATE with the rule qualification expression

```
NEW.sl_avail <> OLD.sl_avail
```

and the action

```
INSERT INTO shoelace_log VALUES (
        *NEW*.sl_name, *NEW*.sl_avail,
        current_user, current_timestamp )
    FROM shoelace_data *NEW*, shoelace_data *OLD*;
```

(This looks a little strange since you can't normally write INSERT ... VALUES
... FROM. The FROM clause here is just to indicate that there are range-table

entries in the query tree for *NEW* and *OLD*. These are needed so that they
can be referenced by variables in the INSERT command's query tree.)

The rule is a qualified ALSO rule, so the rule system has to return two query
trees: the modified rule action and the original query tree. In step 1, the range
table of the original query is incorporated into the rule's action query tree. This
results in:

```
INSERT INTO shoelace_log VALUES (
        *NEW*.sl_name, *NEW*.sl_avail,
        current_user, current_timestamp )
    FROM shoelace_data *NEW*, shoelace_data *OLD*,
        shoelace_data shoelace_data;
```

In step 2, the rule qualification is added to it, so the result set is restricted to
rows where sl_avail changes:

```
INSERT INTO shoelace_log VALUES (
        *NEW*.sl_name, *NEW*.sl_avail,
        current_user, current_timestamp )
    FROM shoelace_data *NEW*, shoelace_data *OLD*,
        shoelace_data shoelace_data
  WHERE *NEW*.sl_avail <> *OLD*.sl_avail;
```

(This looks even stranger, since INSERT ... VALUES doesn't have a WHERE clause
either, but the planner and executor will have no difficulty with it. They need
to support this same functionality anyway for INSERT ... SELECT.)

In step 3, the original query tree's qualification is added, restricting the result
set further to only the rows that would have been touched by the original query:

```
INSERT INTO shoelace_log VALUES (
        *NEW*.sl_name, *NEW*.sl_avail,
        current_user, current_timestamp )
    FROM shoelace_data *NEW*, shoelace_data *OLD*,
        shoelace_data shoelace_data
  WHERE *NEW*.sl_avail <> *OLD*.sl_avail
    AND shoelace_data.sl_name = 'sl7';
```

Step 4 replaces references to NEW by the target list entries from the original
query tree or by the matching variable references from the result relation:

```
INSERT INTO shoelace_log VALUES (
        shoelace_data.sl_name, 6,
        current_user, current_timestamp )
    FROM shoelace_data *NEW*, shoelace_data *OLD*,
        shoelace_data shoelace_data
  WHERE 6 <> *OLD*.sl_avail
    AND shoelace_data.sl_name = 'sl7';
```

Step 5 changes OLD references into result relation references:

```
INSERT INTO shoelace_log VALUES (
        shoelace_data.sl_name, 6,
        current_user, current_timestamp )
    FROM shoelace_data *NEW*, shoelace_data *OLD*,
        shoelace_data shoelace_data
```

```
    WHERE 6 <> shoelace_data.sl_avail
      AND shoelace_data.sl_name = 'sl7';
```

That's it. Since the rule is ALSO, we also output the original query tree. In short, the output from the rule system is a list of two query trees that correspond to these statements:

```
INSERT INTO shoelace_log VALUES (
        shoelace_data.sl_name, 6,
        current_user, current_timestamp )
  FROM shoelace_data
 WHERE 6 <> shoelace_data.sl_avail
   AND shoelace_data.sl_name = 'sl7';

UPDATE shoelace_data SET sl_avail = 6
 WHERE sl_name = 'sl7';
```

These are executed in this order, and that is exactly what the rule was meant to do.

The substitutions and the added qualifications ensure that, if the original query would be, say,

```
UPDATE shoelace_data SET sl_color = 'green'
 WHERE sl_name = 'sl7';
```

no log entry would get written. In that case, the original query tree does not contain a target list entry for sl_avail, so NEW.sl_avail will get replaced by shoelace_data.sl_avail. Thus, the extra command generated by the rule is

```
INSERT INTO shoelace_log VALUES (
        shoelace_data.sl_name, shoelace_data.sl_avail,
        current_user, current_timestamp )
  FROM shoelace_data
 WHERE shoelace_data.sl_avail <> shoelace_data.sl_avail
   AND shoelace_data.sl_name = 'sl7';
```

and that qualification will never be true.

It will also work if the original query modifies multiple rows. So if someone issued the command

```
UPDATE shoelace_data SET sl_avail = 0
 WHERE sl_color = 'black';
```

four rows in fact get updated (sl1, sl2, sl3, and sl4). But sl3 already has sl_avail = 0. In this case, the original query trees qualification is different and that results in the extra query tree

```
INSERT INTO shoelace_log
SELECT shoelace_data.sl_name, 0,
        current_user, current_timestamp
  FROM shoelace_data
 WHERE 0 <> shoelace_data.sl_avail
   AND shoelace_data.sl_color = 'black';
```

being generated by the rule. This query tree will surely insert three new log entries. And that's absolutely correct.

Here we can see why it is important that the original query tree is executed last. If the UPDATE had been executed first, all the rows would have already been set to zero, so the logging INSERT would not find any row where 0 <> shoelace_data.sl_avail.

7.3.2 Cooperation with Views

A simple way to protect view relations from the mentioned possibility that someone can try to run INSERT, UPDATE, or DELETE on them is to let those query trees get thrown away. So we could create the rules

```
CREATE RULE shoe_ins_protect AS ON INSERT TO shoe
    DO INSTEAD NOTHING;
CREATE RULE shoe_upd_protect AS ON UPDATE TO shoe
    DO INSTEAD NOTHING;
CREATE RULE shoe_del_protect AS ON DELETE TO shoe
    DO INSTEAD NOTHING;
```

If someone now tries to do any of these operations on the view relation shoe, the rule system will apply these rules. Since the rules have no actions and are INSTEAD, the resulting list of query trees will be empty and the whole query will become nothing because there is nothing left to be optimized or executed after the rule system is done with it.

A more sophisticated way to use the rule system is to create rules that rewrite the query tree into one that does the right operation on the real tables. To do that on the shoelace view, we create the following rules:

```
CREATE RULE shoelace_ins AS ON INSERT TO shoelace
    DO INSTEAD
    INSERT INTO shoelace_data VALUES (
            NEW.sl_name, NEW.sl_avail, NEW.sl_color,
    NEW.sl_len, NEW.sl_unit
    );

CREATE RULE shoelace_upd AS ON UPDATE TO shoelace
    DO INSTEAD
    UPDATE shoelace_data
        SET sl_name = NEW.sl_name,
            sl_avail = NEW.sl_avail,
            sl_color = NEW.sl_color,
            sl_len = NEW.sl_len,
            sl_unit = NEW.sl_unit
      WHERE sl_name = OLD.sl_name;

CREATE RULE shoelace_del AS ON DELETE TO shoelace
    DO INSTEAD
    DELETE FROM shoelace_data
        WHERE sl_name = OLD.sl_name;
```

If you want to support RETURNING queries on the view, you need to make the rules include RETURNING clauses that compute the view rows. This is usually pretty trivial for views on a single table, but it's a bit tedious for join views such as shoelace. An example for the insert case is

```
CREATE RULE shoelace_ins AS ON INSERT TO shoelace
    DO INSTEAD
    INSERT INTO shoelace_data VALUES (
            NEW.sl_name, NEW.sl_avail, NEW.sl_color,
    NEW.sl_len, NEW.sl_unit
    )
    RETURNING
            shoelace_data.*,
            (SELECT shoelace_data.sl_len * u.un_fact
             FROM unit u WHERE shoelace_data.sl_unit = u.un_name);
```

Note that this one rule supports both INSERT and INSERT RETURNING queries on the view—the RETURNING clause is simply ignored for INSERT.

Now assume that once in a while, a pack of shoelaces arrives at the shop and a big parts list along with it. But you don't want to manually update the shoelace view every time. Instead we setup two little tables: one where you can insert the items from the part list, and one with a special trick. The creation commands for these are:

```
CREATE TABLE shoelace_arrive (
    arr_name    text,
    arr_quant   integer
);

CREATE TABLE shoelace_ok (
    ok_name     text,
    ok_quant    integer
);

CREATE RULE shoelace_ok_ins AS ON INSERT TO shoelace_ok
    DO INSTEAD
    UPDATE shoelace
       SET sl_avail = sl_avail + NEW.ok_quant
     WHERE sl_name = NEW.ok_name;
```

Now you can fill the table shoelace_arrive with the data from the parts list:

```
SELECT * FROM shoelace_arrive;

 arr_name | arr_quant
----------+-----------
 sl3      |        10
 sl6      |        20
 sl8      |        20
(3 rows)
```

Take a quick look at the current data:

```
SELECT * FROM shoelace;
```

sl_name	sl_avail	sl_color	sl_len	sl_unit	sl_len_cm
sl1	5	black	80	cm	80
sl2	6	black	100	cm	100
sl7	6	brown	60	cm	60
sl3	0	black	35	inch	88.9
sl4	8	black	40	inch	101.6
sl8	1	brown	40	inch	101.6
sl5	4	brown	1	m	100
sl6	0	brown	0.9	m	90

(8 rows)

Now move the arrived shoelaces in:

```
INSERT INTO shoelace_ok SELECT * FROM shoelace_arrive;
```

and check the results:

```
SELECT * FROM shoelace ORDER BY sl_name;
```

sl_name	sl_avail	sl_color	sl_len	sl_unit	sl_len_cm
sl1	5	black	80	cm	80
sl2	6	black	100	cm	100
sl7	6	brown	60	cm	60
sl4	8	black	40	inch	101.6
sl3	10	black	35	inch	88.9
sl8	21	brown	40	inch	101.6
sl5	4	brown	1	m	100
sl6	20	brown	0.9	m	90

(8 rows)

```
SELECT * FROM shoelace_log;
```

sl_name	sl_avail	log_who	log_when
sl7	6	Al	Tue Oct 20 19:14:45 1998 MET DST
sl3	10	Al	Tue Oct 20 19:25:16 1998 MET DST
sl6	20	Al	Tue Oct 20 19:25:16 1998 MET DST
sl8	21	Al	Tue Oct 20 19:25:16 1998 MET DST

(4 rows)

It's a long way from the one INSERT ... SELECT to these results. And the description of the query-tree transformation will be the last in this chapter. First, there is the parser's output

```
INSERT INTO shoelace_ok
SELECT shoelace_arrive.arr_name, shoelace_arrive.arr_quant
    FROM shoelace_arrive shoelace_arrive, shoelace_ok shoelace_ok;
```

Now the first rule shoelace_ok_ins is applied and turns this into

```
UPDATE shoelace
   SET sl_avail = shoelace.sl_avail + shoelace_arrive.arr_quant
  FROM shoelace_arrive shoelace_arrive, shoelace_ok shoelace_ok,
       shoelace_ok *OLD*, shoelace_ok *NEW*,
       shoelace shoelace
 WHERE shoelace.sl_name = shoelace_arrive.arr_name;
```

and throws away the original INSERT on shoelace_ok. This rewritten query
is passed to the rule system again, and the second applied rule shoelace_upd
produces

```
UPDATE shoelace_data
   SET sl_name = shoelace.sl_name,
       sl_avail = shoelace.sl_avail + shoelace_arrive.arr_quant,
       sl_color = shoelace.sl_color,
       sl_len = shoelace.sl_len,
       sl_unit = shoelace.sl_unit
  FROM shoelace_arrive shoelace_arrive, shoelace_ok shoelace_ok,
       shoelace_ok *OLD*, shoelace_ok *NEW*,
       shoelace shoelace, shoelace *OLD*,
       shoelace *NEW*, shoelace_data shoelace_data
 WHERE shoelace.sl_name = shoelace_arrive.arr_name
   AND shoelace_data.sl_name = shoelace.sl_name;
```

Again it's an INSTEAD rule and the previous query tree is trashed. Note that
this query still uses the view shoelace. But the rule system isn't finished with
this step, so it continues and applies the _RETURN rule on it, and we get

```
UPDATE shoelace_data
   SET sl_name = s.sl_name,
       sl_avail = s.sl_avail + shoelace_arrive.arr_quant,
       sl_color = s.sl_color,
       sl_len = s.sl_len,
       sl_unit = s.sl_unit
  FROM shoelace_arrive shoelace_arrive, shoelace_ok shoelace_ok,
       shoelace_ok *OLD*, shoelace_ok *NEW*,
       shoelace shoelace, shoelace *OLD*,
       shoelace *NEW*, shoelace_data shoelace_data,
       shoelace *OLD*, shoelace *NEW*,
       shoelace_data s, unit u
 WHERE s.sl_name = shoelace_arrive.arr_name
   AND shoelace_data.sl_name = s.sl_name;
```

Finally, the rule log_shoelace gets applied, producing the extra query tree

```
INSERT INTO shoelace_log
SELECT s.sl_name,
       s.sl_avail + shoelace_arrive.arr_quant,
       current_user,
       current_timestamp
  FROM shoelace_arrive shoelace_arrive, shoelace_ok shoelace_ok,
       shoelace_ok *OLD*, shoelace_ok *NEW*,
       shoelace shoelace, shoelace *OLD*,
```

```
            shoelace *NEW*, shoelace_data shoelace_data,
            shoelace *OLD*, shoelace *NEW*,
            shoelace_data s, unit u,
            shoelace_data *OLD*, shoelace_data *NEW*
            shoelace_log shoelace_log
    WHERE s.sl_name = shoelace_arrive.arr_name
      AND shoelace_data.sl_name = s.sl_name
      AND (s.sl_avail + shoelace_arrive.arr_quant) <> s.sl_avail;
```

After that the rule system runs out of rules and returns the generated query
trees.

So we end up with two final query trees that are equivalent to the SQL
statements

```
    INSERT INTO shoelace_log
    SELECT s.sl_name,
           s.sl_avail + shoelace_arrive.arr_quant,
           current_user,
           current_timestamp
      FROM shoelace_arrive shoelace_arrive, shoelace_data
    shoelace_data,
           shoelace_data s
     WHERE s.sl_name = shoelace_arrive.arr_name
       AND shoelace_data.sl_name = s.sl_name
       AND s.sl_avail + shoelace_arrive.arr_quant <> s.sl_avail;

    UPDATE shoelace_data
       SET sl_avail = shoelace_data.sl_avail +
    shoelace_arrive.arr_quant
      FROM shoelace_arrive shoelace_arrive,
           shoelace_data shoelace_data,
           shoelace_data s
     WHERE s.sl_name = shoelace_arrive.sl_name
       AND shoelace_data.sl_name = s.sl_name;
```

The result is that data coming from one relation inserted into another, changed
into updates on a third, changed into updating a fourth plus logging that final
update in a fifth gets reduced into two queries.

There is a little detail that's a bit ugly. Looking at the two queries, it turns
out that the shoelace_data relation appears twice in the range table where it
could definitely be reduced to one. The planner does not handle it and so the
execution plan for the rule systems output of the INSERT will be

```
    Nested Loop
      -> Merge Join
            -> Seq Scan
                  -> Sort
                        -> Seq Scan on s
            -> Seq Scan
                  -> Sort
                        -> Seq Scan on shoelace_arrive
```

```
    -> Seq Scan on shoelace_data
```
while omitting the extra range table entry would result in a
```
Merge Join
    -> Seq Scan
        -> Sort
            -> Seq Scan on s
    -> Seq Scan
        -> Sort
            -> Seq Scan on shoelace_arrive
```
which produces exactly the same entries in the log table. Thus, the rule system caused one extra scan on the table shoelace_data that is absolutely not necessary. And the same redundant scan is done once more in the UPDATE. But it was a really hard job to make that all possible at all.

Now we make a final demonstration of the PostgreSQL rule system and its power. Say you add some shoelaces with extraordinary colors to your database:
```
INSERT INTO shoelace VALUES ('sl9', 0, 'pink', 35.0, 'inch',
    0.0);
INSERT INTO shoelace VALUES ('sl10', 1000, 'magenta', 40.0,
    'inch', 0.0);
```
We would like to make a view to check which shoelace entries do not fit any shoe in color. The view for this is
```
CREATE VIEW shoelace_mismatch AS
    SELECT * FROM shoelace WHERE NOT EXISTS
        (SELECT shoename FROM shoe WHERE slcolor = sl_color);
```
Its output is
```
SELECT * FROM shoelace_mismatch;
```

sl_name	sl_avail	sl_color	sl_len	sl_unit	sl_len_cm
sl9	0	pink	35	inch	88.9
sl10	1000	magenta	40	inch	101.6

Now we want to set it up so that mismatching shoelaces that are not in stock are deleted from the database. To make it a little harder for PostgreSQL, we don't delete it directly. Instead we create one more view
```
CREATE VIEW shoelace_can_delete AS
    SELECT * FROM shoelace_mismatch WHERE sl_avail = 0;
```
and do it this way:
```
DELETE FROM shoelace WHERE EXISTS
    (SELECT * FROM shoelace_can_delete
            WHERE sl_name = shoelace.sl_name);
```
Voilà:

```
SELECT * FROM shoelace;
```

sl_name	sl_avail	sl_color	sl_len	sl_unit	sl_len_cm
sl1	5	black	80	cm	80
sl2	6	black	100	cm	100
sl7	6	brown	60	cm	60
sl4	8	black	40	inch	101.6
sl3	10	black	35	inch	88.9
sl8	21	brown	40	inch	101.6
sl110	1000	magenta	40	inch	101.6
sl5	4	brown	1	m	100
sl6	20	brown	0.9	m	90

(9 rows)

A DELETE on a view, with a subquery qualification that in total uses 4 nesting/joined views, where one of them itself has a subquery qualification containing a view and where calculated view columns are used, gets rewritten into one single query tree that deletes the requested data from a real table.

There are probably only a few situations out in the real world where such a construct is necessary. But it makes you feel comfortable that it works.

7.4 Rules and Privileges

Due to rewriting of queries by the PostgreSQL rule system, other tables/views than those used in the original query get accessed. When update rules are used, this can include write access to tables.

Rewrite rules don't have a separate owner. The owner of a relation (table or view) is automatically the owner of the rewrite rules that are defined for it. The PostgreSQL rule system changes the behavior of the default access control system. Relations that are used due to rules get checked against the privileges of the rule owner, not the user invoking the rule. This means that a user only needs the required privileges for the tables/views named explicitly in their queries.

For example: A user has a list of phone numbers where some of them are private, the others are of interest for the secretary of the office. He can construct the following:

```
CREATE TABLE phone_data (person text, phone text, private
    boolean);
CREATE VIEW phone_number AS
    SELECT person, phone FROM phone_data WHERE NOT private;
GRANT SELECT ON phone_number TO secretary;
```

Nobody except him (and the database superusers) can access the phone_data table. But because of the GRANT, the secretary can run a SELECT on the phone_number view. The rule system will rewrite the SELECT from phone_number into a SELECT from phone_data and add the qualification that only entries where private is false are wanted. Since the user is the owner of phone_number and therefore the owner of the rule, the read access to phone_data is now checked against his privileges and the query is permitted. The check for accessing phone_number is also performed, but this is done against the invoking user, so nobody but the user and the secretary can use it.

The privileges are checked rule by rule. So the secretary is for now the only one who can see the public phone numbers. But the secretary can setup another view and grant access to that to the public. Then, anyone can see the phone_number data through the secretary's view. What the secretary cannot do is to create a view that directly accesses phone_data. (Actually this is possible, but it will not work since every access will be denied during the permission checks.) And as soon as the user will notice, that the secretary opened his phone_number view, he can revoke his access. Immediately, any access to the secretary's view would fail.

One might think that this rule-by-rule checking is a security hole, but in fact it isn't. But if it did not work this way, the secretary could set up a table with the same columns as phone_number and copy the data to there once per day. Then it's his own data and he can grant access to everyone he wants. A GRANT command means, "I trust you". If someone you trust does the thing above, it's time to think it over and then use REVOKE.

This mechanism also works for update rules. In the examples of the previous section, the owner of the tables in the example database could grant the privileges SELECT, INSERT, UPDATE, and DELETE on the shoelace view to someone else, but only SELECT on shoelace_log. The rule action to write log entries will still be executed successfully, and that other user could see the log entries. But he cannot create fake entries, nor could he manipulate or remove existing ones.

7.5 Rules and Command Status

The PostgreSQL server returns a command status string, such as INSERT 149592 1, for each command it receives. This is simple enough when there are no rules involved, but what happens when the query is rewritten by rules?

Rules affect the command status as follows:

- If there is no unconditional INSTEAD rule for the query, then the originally given query will be executed, and its command status will be returned as usual. (But note that if there were any conditional INSTEAD rules, the negation of their qualifications will have been added to the original query. This may reduce the number of rows it processes, and if so the reported status will be affected.)

- If there is any unconditional INSTEAD rule for the query, then the original query will not be executed at all. In this case, the server will return the command status for the last query that was inserted by an INSTEAD rule (conditional or unconditional) and is of the same command type (INSERT, UPDATE, or DELETE) as the original query. If no query meeting those requirements is added by any rule, then the returned command status shows the original query type and zeroes for the row-count and OID fields.

(This system was established in PostgreSQL 7.3. In versions before that, the command status might show different results when rules exist.)

The programmer can ensure that any desired INSTEAD rule is the one that sets the command status in the second case, by giving it the alphabetically last rule name among the active rules, so that it gets applied last.

7.6 Rules versus Triggers

Many things that can be done using triggers can also be implemented using the PostgreSQL rule system. One of the things that cannot be implemented by rules are some kinds of constraints, especially foreign keys. It is possible to place a qualified rule that rewrites a command to NOTHING if the value of a column does not appear in another table. But then the data is silently thrown away and that's not a good idea. If checks for valid values are required, and in the case of an invalid value an error message should be generated, it must be done by a trigger.

On the other hand, a trigger that is fired on INSERT on a view can do the same as a rule: put the data somewhere else and suppress the insert in the view. But it cannot do the same thing on UPDATE or DELETE, because there is no real data in the view relation that could be scanned, and thus the trigger would never get called. Only a rule will help.

For the things that can be implemented by both, which is best depends on the usage of the database. A trigger is fired for any affected row once. A rule manipulates the query or generates an additional query. So if many rows are affected in one statement, a rule issuing one extra command is likely to be faster than a trigger that is called for every single row and must execute its operations many times. However, the trigger approach is conceptually far simpler than the rule approach, and is easier for novices to get right.

Here we show an example of how the choice of rules versus triggers plays out in one situation. There are two tables:

```
CREATE TABLE computer (
    hostname        text,      -- indexed
    manufacturer    text       -- indexed
);
```

```
CREATE TABLE software (
    software        text,      -- indexed
    hostname        text       -- indexed
);
```

Both tables have many thousands of rows and the indexes on hostname are unique. The rule or trigger should implement a constraint that deletes rows from software that reference a deleted computer. The trigger would use this command:

```
DELETE FROM software WHERE hostname = $1;
```

Since the trigger is called for each individual row deleted from computer, it can prepare and save the plan for this command and pass the hostname value in the parameter. The rule would be written as

```
CREATE RULE computer_del AS ON DELETE TO computer
    DO DELETE FROM software WHERE hostname = OLD.hostname;
```

Now we look at different types of deletes. In the case of a

```
DELETE FROM computer WHERE hostname = 'mypc.local.net';
```

the table computer is scanned by index (fast), and the command issued by the trigger would also use an index scan (also fast). The extra command from the rule would be

```
DELETE FROM software WHERE computer.hostname = 'mypc.local.net'
                        AND software.hostname = computer.hostname;
```

Since there are appropriate indexes setup, the planner will create a plan of

```
Nestloop
  -> Index Scan using comp_hostidx on computer
  -> Index Scan using soft_hostidx on software
```

So there would be not that much difference in speed between the trigger and the rule implementation.

With the next delete we want to get rid of all the 2000 computers where the hostname starts with old. There are two possible commands to do that. One is

```
DELETE FROM computer WHERE hostname >= 'old'
                       AND hostname <  'ole'
```

The command added by the rule will be

```
DELETE FROM software WHERE computer.hostname >= 'old' AND
    computer.hostname < 'ole'
                        AND software.hostname = computer.hostname;
```

with the plan

```
Hash Join
  -> Seq Scan on software
  -> Hash
    -> Index Scan using comp_hostidx on computer
```

The other possible command is

```
DELETE FROM computer WHERE hostname ~ '^old';
```

which results in the following executing plan for the command added by the rule:

```
Nestloop
  -> Index Scan using comp_hostidx on computer
  -> Index Scan using soft_hostidx on software
```

This shows, that the planner does not realize that the qualification for hostname in computer could also be used for an index scan on software when there are multiple qualification expressions combined with AND, which is what it does in the regular-expression version of the command. The trigger will get invoked once for each of the 2000 old computers that have to be deleted, and that will result in one index scan over computer and 2000 index scans over software. The rule implementation will do it with two commands that use indexes. And it depends on the overall size of the table software whether the rule will still be faster in the sequential scan situation. 2000 command executions from the trigger over the SPI manager take some time, even if all the index blocks will soon be in the cache.

The last command we look at is

```
DELETE FROM computer WHERE manufacturer = 'bim';
```

Again this could result in many rows to be deleted from computer. So the trigger will again run many commands through the executor. The command generated by the rule will be

```
DELETE FROM software WHERE computer.manufacturer = 'bim'
                      AND software.hostname = computer.hostname;
```

The plan for that command will again be the nested loop over two index scans, only using a different index on computer:

```
Nestloop
    -> Index Scan using comp_manufidx on computer
    -> Index Scan using soft_hostidx on software
```

In any of these cases, the extra commands from the rule system will be more or less independent from the number of affected rows in a command.

The summary is, rules will only be significantly slower than triggers if their actions result in large and badly qualified joins, a situation where the planner fails.

8 Procedural Languages

PostgreSQL allows user-defined functions to be written in other languages besides SQL and C. These other languages are generically called *procedural languages* (PLs). For a function written in a procedural language, the database server has no built-in knowledge about how to interpret the function's source text. Instead, the task is passed to a special handler that knows the details of the language. The handler could either do all the work of parsing, syntax analysis, execution, etc. itself, or it could serve as "glue" between PostgreSQL and an existing implementation of a programming language. The handler itself is a C language function compiled into a shared object and loaded on demand, just like any other C function.

There are currently four procedural languages available in the standard PostgreSQL distribution: PL/pgSQL (Chapter 9 *PL/pgSQL - SQL Procedural Language*, page 277), PL/Tcl (Chapter 10 *PL/Tcl - Tcl Procedural Language*, page 327), PL/Perl (Chapter 11 *PL/Perl - Perl Procedural Language*, page 337), and PL/Python (Chapter 12 *PL/Python - Python Procedural Language*, page 349). There are additional procedural languages available that are not included in the core distribution. In addition other languages can be defined by users; the basics of developing a new procedural language are covered in Volume 4, Chapter 6 *Writing A Procedural Language Handler*.

8.1 Installing Procedural Languages

A procedural language must be "installed" into each database where it is to be used. But procedural languages installed in the database `template1` are automatically available in all subsequently created databases, since their entries in `template1` will be copied by `CREATE DATABASE`. So the database administrator can decide which languages are available in which databases and can make some languages available by default if desired.

For the languages supplied with the standard distribution, it is only necessary to execute `CREATE LANGUAGE` *language_name* to install the language into the current database. Alternatively, the program `createlang` may be used to do this from the shell command line. For example, to install the language PL/pgSQL into the database `template1`, use

```
createlang plpgsql template1
```

The manual procedure described below is only recommended for installing custom languages that `CREATE LANGUAGE` does not know about.

Manual Procedural Language Installation :

A procedural language is installed in a database in four steps, which must be carried out by a database superuser. (For languages known to `CREATE LANGUAGE`, the second and third steps can be omitted, because they will be carried out automatically if needed.)

1. The shared object for the language handler must be compiled and installed
   into an appropriate library directory. This works in the same way as
   building and installing modules with regular user-defined C functions does;
   see Section 5.9.6 *Compiling and Linking Dynamically-Loaded Functions*,
   page 201. Often, the language handler will depend on an external library
   that provides the actual programming language engine; if so, that must
   be installed as well.

2. The handler must be declared with the command

   ```
   CREATE FUNCTION handler_function_name ()
       RETURNS language_handler
       AS 'path-to-shared-object'
       LANGUAGE C;
   ```

   The special return type of `language_handler` tells the database system
   that this function does not return one of the defined SQL data types and
   is not directly usable in SQL statements.

3. Optionally, the language handler may provide a "validator" function that
   checks a function definition for correctness without actually executing it.
   The validator function is called by CREATE FUNCTION if it exists. If a validator function is provided by the handler, declare it with a command
   like

   ```
   CREATE FUNCTION validator_function_name (oid)
       RETURNS void
       AS 'path-to-shared-object'
       LANGUAGE C;
   ```

4. The PL must be declared with the command

   ```
   CREATE [TRUSTED] [PROCEDURAL] LANGUAGE language-name
       HANDLER handler_function_name
       [VALIDATOR validator_function_name] ;
   ```

   The optional key word TRUSTED specifies that ordinary database users that
   have no superuser privileges should be allowed to use this language to create functions and trigger procedures. Since PL functions are executed
   inside the database server, the TRUSTED flag should only be given for languages that do not allow access to database server internals or the file
   system. The languages PL/pgSQL, PL/Tcl, and PL/Perl are considered trusted; the languages PL/TclU, PL/PerlU, and PL/PythonU are
   designed to provide unlimited functionality and should *not* be marked
   trusted.

Manual Installation of PL/pgSQL shows how the manual installation procedure would work with the language PL/pgSQL.

Manual Installation of PL/pgSQL:

The following command tells the database server where to find the shared
object for the PL/pgSQL language's call handler function.

```
CREATE FUNCTION plpgsql_call_handler() RETURNS
  language_handler AS
    '$libdir/plpgsql' LANGUAGE C;
```

PL/pgSQL has a validator function, so we declare that too:

```
CREATE FUNCTION plpgsql_validator(oid) RETURNS void AS
    '$libdir/plpgsql' LANGUAGE C;
```

The command

```
CREATE TRUSTED PROCEDURAL LANGUAGE plpgsql
    HANDLER plpgsql_call_handler
    VALIDATOR plpgsql_validator;
```

then defines that the previously declared functions should be invoked for functions and trigger procedures where the language attribute is plpgsql.

In a default PostgreSQL installation, the handler for the PL/pgSQL language is built and installed into the "library" directory. If Tcl support is configured in, the handlers for PL/Tcl and PL/TclU are also built and installed in the same location. Likewise, the PL/Perl and PL/PerlU handlers are built and installed if Perl support is configured, and the PL/PythonU handler is installed if Python support is configured.

9 PL/pgSQL - SQL Procedural Language

PL/pgSQL is a loadable procedural language for the PostgreSQL database system. The design goals of PL/pgSQL were to create a loadable procedural language that

- can be used to create functions and trigger procedures,
- adds control structures to the SQL language,
- can perform complex computations,
- inherits all user-defined types, functions, and operators,
- can be defined to be trusted by the server,
- is easy to use.

Except for input/output conversion and calculation functions for user-defined types, anything that can be defined in C language functions can also be done with PL/pgSQL. For example, it is possible to create complex conditional computation functions and later use them to define operators or use them in index expressions.

9.1 Overview

The PL/pgSQL call handler parses the function's source text and produces an internal binary instruction tree the first time the function is called (within each session). The instruction tree fully translates the PL/pgSQL statement structure, but individual SQL expressions and SQL commands used in the function are not translated immediately.

As each expression and SQL command is first used in the function, the PL/pgSQL interpreter creates a prepared execution plan (using the SPI manager's SPI_prepare and SPI_saveplan functions). Subsequent visits to that expression or command reuse the prepared plan. Thus, a function with conditional code that contains many statements for which execution plans might be required will only prepare and save those plans that are really used during the lifetime of the database connection. This can substantially reduce the total amount of time required to parse and generate execution plans for the statements in a PL/pgSQL function. A disadvantage is that errors in a specific expression or command may not be detected until that part of the function is reached in execution.

Once PL/pgSQL has made an execution plan for a particular command in a function, it will reuse that plan for the life of the database connection. This is usually a win for performance, but it can cause some problems if you dynamically alter your database schema. For example:

```
CREATE FUNCTION populate() RETURNS integer AS $$
DECLARE
    -- declarations
BEGIN
    PERFORM my_function();
```

```
END;
$$ LANGUAGE plpgsql;
```

If you execute the above function, it will reference the OID for `my_function()` in the execution plan produced for the `PERFORM` statement. Later, if you drop and recreate `my_function()`, then `populate()` will not be able to find `my_function()` anymore. You would then have to recreate `populate()`, or at least start a new database session so that it will be compiled afresh. Another way to avoid this problem is to use `CREATE OR REPLACE FUNCTION` when updating the definition of `my_function` (when a function is "replaced", its OID is not changed).

Because PL/pgSQL saves execution plans in this way, SQL commands that appear directly in a PL/pgSQL function must refer to the same tables and columns on every execution; that is, you cannot use a parameter as the name of a table or column in an SQL command. To get around this restriction, you can construct dynamic commands using the PL/pgSQL `EXECUTE` statement—at the price of constructing a new execution plan on every execution.

> **Note:** The PL/pgSQL `EXECUTE` statement is not related to the Volume 1, Section 12.78 *EXECUTE* SQL statement supported by the PostgreSQL server. The server's `EXECUTE` statement cannot be used within PL/pgSQL functions (and is not needed).

9.1.1 Advantages of Using PL/pgSQL

SQL is the language PostgreSQL and most other relational databases use as their query language. It's portable and easy to learn. But every SQL statement must be executed individually by the database server.

That means that your client application must send each query to the database server, wait for it to be processed, receive and process the results, do some computation, then send further queries to the server. All this incurs interprocess communication and will also incur network overhead if your client is on a different machine than the database server.

With PL/pgSQL you can group a block of computation and a series of queries *inside* the database server, thus having the power of a procedural language and the ease of use of SQL, but with considerable savings because you don't have the whole client/server communication overhead.

- Elimination of additional round trips between client and server
- Intermediate results that the client does not need do not need to be marshaled or transferred between server and client
- There is no need for additional rounds of query parsing

This can allow for a considerable performance increase as compared to an application that does not use stored functions.

Also, with PL/pgSQL you can use all the data types, operators and functions of SQL.

9.1.2 Supported Argument and Result Data Types

Functions written in PL/pgSQL can accept as arguments any scalar or array data type supported by the server, and they can return a result of any of these types. They can also accept or return any composite type (row type) specified by name. It is also possible to declare a PL/pgSQL function as returning record, which means that the result is a row type whose columns are determined by specification in the calling query, as discussed in Volume 1, Section 5.2.1.4 *Table Functions*.

PL/pgSQL functions may also be declared to accept and return the poly-morphic types anyelement and anyarray. The actual data types handled by a polymorphic function can vary from call to call, as discussed in Section 5.2.5 *Polymorphic Types*, page 176. An example is shown in Section 9.4.1 *Aliases for Function Parameters*, page 284.

PL/pgSQL functions can also be declared to return a "set", or table, of any data type they can return a single instance of. Such a function generates its output by executing RETURN NEXT for each desired element of the result set.

Finally, a PL/pgSQL function may be declared to return void if it has no useful return value.

PL/pgSQL functions can also be declared with output parameters in place of an explicit specification of the return type. This does not add any fundamental capability to the language, but it is often convenient, especially for returning multiple values.

Specific examples appear in Section 9.4.1 *Aliases for Function Parameters*, page 284 and Section 9.7.1 *Returning From a Function*, page 294.

9.2 Tips for Developing in PL/pgSQL

One good way to develop in PL/pgSQL is to use the text editor of your choice to create your functions, and in another window, use psql to load and test those functions. If you are doing it this way, it is a good idea to write the function using CREATE OR REPLACE FUNCTION. That way you can just reload the file to update the function definition. For example:

```
CREATE OR REPLACE FUNCTION testfunc(integer) RETURNS integer
AS $$
        ....
$$ LANGUAGE plpgsql;
```

While running psql, you can load or reload such a function definition file with

```
\i filename.sql
```

and then immediately issue SQL commands to test the function.

Another good way to develop in PL/pgSQL is with a GUI database access tool that facilitates development in a procedural language. One example of such as a tool is PgAccess, although others exist. These tools often provide convenient features such as escaping single quotes and making it easier to recreate and debug functions.

9.2.1　Handling of Quotation Marks

The code of a PL/pgSQL function is specified in CREATE FUNCTION as a string literal. If you write the string literal in the ordinary way with surrounding single quotes, then any single quotes inside the function body must be doubled; likewise any backslashes must be doubled (assuming escape string syntax is used). Doubling quotes is at best tedious, and in more complicated cases the code can become downright incomprehensible, because you can easily find yourself needing half a dozen or more adjacent quote marks. It's recommended that you instead write the function body as a "dollar-quoted" string literal (see Volume 1, Section 2.1.2.2 *Dollar-Quoted String Constants*). In the dollar-quoting approach, you never double any quote marks, but instead take care to choose a different dollar-quoting delimiter for each level of nesting you need. For example, you might write the CREATE FUNCTION command as

```
CREATE OR REPLACE FUNCTION testfunc(integer) RETURNS integer
AS $PROC$
    ....
$PROC$ LANGUAGE plpgsql;
```

Within this, you might use quote marks for simple literal strings in SQL commands and $$ to delimit fragments of SQL commands that you are assembling as strings. If you need to quote text that includes $$, you could use Q, and so on.

The following chart shows what you have to do when writing quote marks without dollar quoting. It may be useful when translating pre-dollar quoting code into something more comprehensible.

1 quotation mark

To begin and end the function body, for example:

```
CREATE FUNCTION foo() RETURNS integer AS '
    ....
' LANGUAGE plpgsql;
```

Anywhere within a single-quoted function body, quote marks *must* appear in pairs.

2 quotation marks

For string literals inside the function body, for example:

```
a_output := ''Blah'';
SELECT * FROM users WHERE f_name=''foobar'';
```

In the dollar-quoting approach, you'd just write

```
a_output := 'Blah';
SELECT * FROM users WHERE f_name='foobar';
```

which is exactly what the PL/pgSQL parser would see in either case.

4 quotation marks

When you need a single quotation mark in a string constant inside the function body, for example:

```
    a_output := a_output || '' AND name LIKE ''''foobar''''
    AND xyz''
```

The value actually appended to a_output would be: AND name LIKE
'foobar' AND xyz.

In the dollar-quoting approach, you'd write

```
    a_output := a_output || $$ AND name LIKE 'foobar' AND xyz$$
```

being careful that any dollar-quote delimiters around this are not just $$.

6 quotation marks

When a single quotation mark in a string inside the function body is ad-
jacent to the end of that string constant, for example:

```
    a_output := a_output || '' AND name LIKE ''''foobar''''''
```

The value appended to a_output would then be: AND name LIKE
'foobar'.

In the dollar-quoting approach, this becomes

```
    a_output := a_output || $$ AND name LIKE 'foobar'$$
```

10 quotation marks

When you want two single quotation marks in a string constant (which
accounts for 8 quotation marks) and this is adjacent to the end of that
string constant (2 more). You will probably only need that if you are
writing a function that generates other functions, as in *Porting a Function
that Creates Another Function from PL/SQL to PL/pgSQL*, page 316. For
example:

```
    a_output := a_output || '' if v_'' ||
       referrer_keys.kind || '' like '''''''''
       || referrer_keys.key_string || '''''''''
       then return ''''''  || referrer_keys.referrer_type
       || ''''''; end if;'';
```

The value of a_output would then be:

```
    if v_... like ''...'' then return ''...''; end if;
```

In the dollar-quoting approach, this becomes

```
    a_output := a_output || $$ if v_$$ || referrer_keys.kind
    || $$ like '$$
       || referrer_keys.key_string || $$'
       then return '$$ || referrer_keys.referrer_type
       || $$'; end if;$$;
```

where we assume we only need to put single quote marks into a_output,
because it will be re-quoted before use.

9.3 Structure of PL/pgSQL

PL/pgSQL is a block-structured language. The complete text of a function definition must be a *block*. A block is defined as:

```
[ <<label>> ]
[ DECLARE
    declarations ]
BEGIN
    statements
END [ label ];
```

Each declaration and each statement within a block is terminated by a semi-colon. A block that appears within another block must have a semicolon after END, as shown above; however the final END that concludes a function body does not require a semicolon.

All key words and identifiers can be written in mixed upper and lower case. Identifiers are implicitly converted to lowercase unless double-quoted.

There are two types of comments in PL/pgSQL. A double dash (--) starts a comment that extends to the end of the line. A /* starts a block comment that extends to the next occurrence of */. Block comments cannot be nested, but double dash comments can be enclosed into a block comment and a double dash can hide the block comment delimiters /* and */.

Any statement in the statement section of a block can be a *subblock*. Sub-blocks can be used for logical grouping or to localize variables to a small group of statements.

The variables declared in the declarations section preceding a block are initialized to their default values every time the block is entered, not only once per function call. For example:

```
CREATE FUNCTION somefunc() RETURNS integer AS $$
DECLARE
    quantity integer := 30;
BEGIN
    RAISE NOTICE 'Quantity here is %', quantity;   -- Quantity
here is 30
    quantity := 50;
    --
    -- Create a subblock
    --
    DECLARE
        quantity integer := 80;
    BEGIN
        RAISE NOTICE 'Quantity here is %', quantity;   --
Quantity here is 80
    END;

    RAISE NOTICE 'Quantity here is %', quantity;   -- Quantity
here is 50
```

```
    RETURN quantity;
END;
$$ LANGUAGE plpgsql;
```

It is important not to confuse the use of BEGIN/END for grouping statements in PL/pgSQL with the database commands for transaction control. PL/pgSQL's BEGIN/END are only for grouping; they do not start or end a transaction. Functions and trigger procedures are always executed within a transaction established by an outer query—they cannot start or commit that transaction, since there would be no context for them to execute in. However, a block containing an EXCEPTION clause effectively forms a subtransaction that can be rolled back without affecting the outer transaction. For more about that see Section 9.7.5 *Trapping Errors*, page 302.

9.4 Declarations

All variables used in a block must be declared in the declarations section of the block. (The only exception is that the loop variable of a FOR loop iterating over a range of integer values is automatically declared as an integer variable.)

PL/pgSQL variables can have any SQL data type, such as integer, varchar, and char.

Here are some examples of variable declarations:

```
user_id integer;
quantity numeric(5);
url varchar;
myrow tablename%ROWTYPE;
myfield tablename.columnname%TYPE;
arow RECORD;
```

The general syntax of a variable declaration is:

```
name [ CONSTANT ] type [ NOT NULL ] [ { DEFAULT | := }
    expression ];
```

The DEFAULT clause, if given, specifies the initial value assigned to the variable when the block is entered. If the DEFAULT clause is not given then the variable is initialized to the SQL null value. The CONSTANT option prevents the variable from being assigned to, so that its value remains constant for the duration of the block. If NOT NULL is specified, an assignment of a null value results in a run-time error. All variables declared as NOT NULL must have a nonnull default value specified.

The default value is evaluated every time the block is entered. So, for example, assigning now() to a variable of type timestamp causes the variable to have the time of the current function call, not the time when the function was precompiled.

Examples:

```
quantity integer DEFAULT 32;
url varchar := 'http://mysite.com';
user_id CONSTANT integer := 10;
```

9.4.1 Aliases for Function Parameters

Parameters passed to functions are named with the identifiers $1, $2, etc.
Optionally, aliases can be declared for $n parameter names for increased read-
ability. Either the alias or the numeric identifier can then be used to refer to
the parameter value.

There are two ways to create an alias. The preferred way is to give a name
to the parameter in the CREATE FUNCTION command, for example:

```
CREATE FUNCTION sales_tax(subtotal real) RETURNS real AS $$
BEGIN
    RETURN subtotal * 0.06;
END;
$$ LANGUAGE plpgsql;
```

The other way, which was the only way available before PostgreSQL 8.0, is to
explicitly declare an alias, using the declaration syntax

    name ALIAS FOR $n;

The same example in this style looks like

```
CREATE FUNCTION sales_tax(real) RETURNS real AS $$
DECLARE
    subtotal ALIAS FOR $1;
BEGIN
    RETURN subtotal * 0.06;
END;
$$ LANGUAGE plpgsql;
```

Some more examples:

```
CREATE FUNCTION instr(varchar, integer) RETURNS integer AS $$
DECLARE
    v_string ALIAS FOR $1;
    index ALIAS FOR $2;
BEGIN
    -- some computations using v_string and index here
END;
$$ LANGUAGE plpgsql;


CREATE FUNCTION concat_selected_fields(in_t sometablename)
 RETURNS text AS $$
BEGIN
    RETURN in_t.f1 || in_t.f3 || in_t.f5 || in_t.f7;
END;
$$ LANGUAGE plpgsql;
```

When a PL/pgSQL function is declared with output parameters, the output
parameters are given $n names and optional aliases in just the same way as the
normal input parameters. An output parameter is effectively a variable that
starts out NULL; it should be assigned to during the execution of the function.
The final value of the parameter is what is returned. For instance, the sales-tax
example could also be done this way:

```
CREATE FUNCTION sales_tax(subtotal real, OUT tax real) AS $$
BEGIN
    tax := subtotal * 0.06;
END;
$$ LANGUAGE plpgsql;
```

Notice that we omitted RETURNS real—we could have included it, but it would be redundant.

Output parameters are most useful when returning multiple values. A trivial example is:

```
CREATE FUNCTION sum_n_product(x int, y int, OUT sum int, OUT
  prod int) AS $$
BEGIN
    sum := x + y;
    prod := x * y;
END;
$$ LANGUAGE plpgsql;
```

As discussed in Section 5.4.3 *Functions with Output Parameters*, page 183, this effectively creates an anonymous record type for the function's results. If a RETURNS clause is given, it must say RETURNS record.

When the return type of a PL/pgSQL function is declared as a polymorphic type (anyelement or anyarray), a special parameter $0 is created. Its data type is the actual return type of the function, as deduced from the actual input types (see Section 5.2.5 *Polymorphic Types*, page 176). This allows the function to access its actual return type as shown in Section 9.4.2 *Copying Types*, page 286. $0 is initialized to null and can be modified by the function, so it can be used to hold the return value if desired, though that is not required. $0 can also be given an alias. For example, this function works on any data type that has a + operator:

```
CREATE FUNCTION add_three_values(v1 anyelement, v2
  anyelement, v3 anyelement)
RETURNS anyelement AS $$
DECLARE
    result ALIAS FOR $0;
BEGIN
    result := v1 + v2 + v3;
    RETURN result;
END;
$$ LANGUAGE plpgsql;
```

The same effect can be had by declaring one or more output parameters as anyelement or anyarray. In this case the special $0 parameter is not used; the output parameters themselves serve the same purpose. For example:

```
CREATE FUNCTION add_three_values(v1 anyelement, v2
  anyelement, v3 anyelement,
                            OUT sum anyelement)
AS $$
BEGIN
    sum := v1 + v2 + v3;
```

```
END;
$$ LANGUAGE plpgsql;
```

9.4.2 Copying Types

> `variable%TYPE`

%TYPE provides the data type of a variable or table column. You can use this to declare variables that will hold database values. For example, let's say you have a column named user_id in your users table. To declare a variable with the same data type as users.user_id you write:

> `user_id users.user_id%TYPE;`

By using %TYPE you don't need to know the data type of the structure you are referencing, and most importantly, if the data type of the referenced item changes in the future (for instance: you change the type of user_id from integer to real), you may not need to change your function definition.

%TYPE is particularly valuable in polymorphic functions, since the data types needed for internal variables may change from one call to the next. Appropriate variables can be created by applying %TYPE to the function's arguments or result placeholders.

9.4.3 Row Types

> `name  table_name%ROWTYPE;`
> `name  composite_type_name;`

A variable of a composite type is called a *row* variable (or *row-type* variable). Such a variable can hold a whole row of a SELECT or FOR query result, so long as that query's column set matches the declared type of the variable. The individual fields of the row value are accessed using the usual dot notation, for example rowvar.field.

A row variable can be declared to have the same type as the rows of an existing table or view, by using the *table_name*%ROWTYPE notation; or it can be declared by giving a composite type's name. (Since every table has an associated composite type of the same name, it actually does not matter in PostgreSQL whether you write %ROWTYPE or not. But the form with %ROWTYPE is more portable.)

Parameters to a function can be composite types (complete table rows). In that case, the corresponding identifier $n will be a row variable, and fields can be selected from it, for example $1.user_id.

Only the user-defined columns of a table row are accessible in a row-type variable, not the OID or other system columns (because the row could be from a view). The fields of the row type inherit the table's field size or precision for data types such as char(n).

Here is an example of using composite types. table1 and table2 are existing tables having at least the mentioned fields:

```
CREATE FUNCTION merge_fields(t_row table1) RETURNS text AS $$
DECLARE
    t2_row table2%ROWTYPE;
BEGIN
    SELECT * INTO t2_row FROM table2 WHERE ... ;
    RETURN t_row.f1 || t2_row.f3 || t_row.f5 || t2_row.f7;
END;
$$ LANGUAGE plpgsql;

SELECT merge_fields(t.*) FROM table1 t WHERE ... ;
```

9.4.4 Record Types

```
name RECORD;
```

Record variables are similar to row-type variables, but they have no predefined structure. They take on the actual row structure of the row they are assigned during a SELECT or FOR command. The substructure of a record variable can change each time it is assigned to. A consequence of this is that until a record variable is first assigned to, it has no substructure, and any attempt to access a field in it will draw a run-time error.

Note that RECORD is not a true data type, only a placeholder. One should also realize that when a PL/pgSQL function is declared to return type record, this is not quite the same concept as a record variable, even though such a function may well use a record variable to hold its result. In both cases the actual row structure is unknown when the function is written, but for a function returning record the actual structure is determined when the calling query is parsed, whereas a record variable can change its row structure on-the-fly.

9.4.5 RENAME

```
RENAME oldname TO newname;
```

Using the RENAME declaration you can change the name of a variable, record or row. This is primarily useful if NEW or OLD should be referenced by another name inside a trigger procedure. See also ALIAS.

Examples:

```
RENAME id TO user_id;
RENAME this_var TO that_var;
```

Note: RENAME appears to be broken as of PostgreSQL 7.3. Fixing this is of low priority, since ALIAS covers most of the practical uses of RENAME.

9.5 Expressions

All expressions used in PL/pgSQL statements are processed using the server's regular SQL executor. In effect, a query like

```
SELECT expression
```

is executed using the SPI manager. Before evaluation, occurrences of PL/pgSQL variable identifiers are replaced by parameters, and the actual values from the variables are passed to the executor in the parameter array. This allows the query plan for the SELECT to be prepared just once and then reused for subsequent evaluations.

The evaluation done by the PostgreSQL main parser has some side effects on the interpretation of constant values. In detail there is a difference between what these two functions do:

```
CREATE FUNCTION logfunc1(logtxt text) RETURNS timestamp AS $$
    BEGIN
        INSERT INTO logtable VALUES (logtxt, 'now');
        RETURN 'now';
    END;
$$ LANGUAGE plpgsql;
```

and

```
CREATE FUNCTION logfunc2(logtxt text) RETURNS timestamp AS $$
    DECLARE
        curtime timestamp;
    BEGIN
        curtime := 'now';
        INSERT INTO logtable VALUES (logtxt, curtime);
        RETURN curtime;
    END;
$$ LANGUAGE plpgsql;
```

In the case of logfunc1, the PostgreSQL main parser knows when preparing the plan for the INSERT that the string 'now' should be interpreted as timestamp because the target column of logtable is of that type. Thus, 'now' will be converted to a constant when the INSERT is planned, and then used in all invocations of logfunc1 during the lifetime of the session. Needless to say, this isn't what the programmer wanted.

In the case of logfunc2, the PostgreSQL main parser does not know what type 'now' should become and therefore it returns a data value of type text containing the string now. During the ensuing assignment to the local variable curtime, the PL/pgSQL interpreter casts this string to the timestamp type by calling the text_out and timestamp_in functions for the conversion. So, the computed time stamp is updated on each execution as the programmer expects.

The mutable nature of record variables presents a problem in this connection. When fields of a record variable are used in expressions or statements, the data types of the fields must not change between calls of one and the same expression, since the expression will be planned using the data type that is present when the expression is first reached. Keep this in mind when writing trigger procedures that handle events for more than one table. (EXECUTE can be used to get around this problem when necessary.)

9.6 Basic Statements

In this section and the following ones, we describe all the statement types that are explicitly understood by PL/pgSQL. Anything not recognized as one of these statement types is presumed to be an SQL command and is sent to the main database engine to execute, as described in Section 9.6.2 *Executing a Query With No Result* and Section 9.6.3 *Executing a Query with a Single-Row Result*, page 290.

9.6.1 Assignment

An assignment of a value to a PL/pgSQL variable or row/record field is written as:

```
identifier := expression;
```

As explained above, the expression in such a statement is evaluated by means of an SQL SELECT command sent to the main database engine. The expression must yield a single value.

If the expression's result data type doesn't match the variable's data type, or the variable has a specific size/precision (like char(20)), the result value will be implicitly converted by the PL/pgSQL interpreter using the result type's output-function and the variable type's input-function. Note that this could potentially result in run-time errors generated by the input function, if the string form of the result value is not acceptable to the input function.

Examples:

```
user_id := 20;
tax := subtotal * 0.06;
```

9.6.2 Executing a Query With No Result

For any SQL query that does not return rows, for example INSERT without a RETURNING clause, you can execute the query within a PL/pgSQL function just by writing the query.

Any PL/pgSQL variable name appearing in the query text is replaced by a parameter symbol, and then the current value of the variable is provided as the parameter value at run time. This allows the same textual query to do different things in different calls of the function.

Note: This two-step process allows PL/pgSQL to plan the query just once and re-use the plan on subsequent executions. As an example, if you write

```
DECLARE
    key TEXT;
    delta INTEGER;
BEGIN
    ...
    UPDATE mytab SET val = val + delta WHERE id = key;
```

the query text seen by the main SQL engine will look like

```
UPDATE mytab SET val = val + $1 WHERE id = $2;
```

Although you don't normally have to think about this, it's helpful to know it when you need to make sense of syntax-error messages.

Caution: PL/pgSQL will substitute for any identifier matching one of the function's declared variables; it is not bright enough to know whether that's what you meant! Thus, it is a bad idea to use a variable name that is the same as any table or column name that you need to reference in queries within the function. Sometimes you can work around this by using qualified names in the query: PL/pgSQL will not substitute in a qualified name *foo.bar*, even if *foo* or *bar* is a declared variable name.

Sometimes it is useful to evaluate an expression or SELECT query but discard the result, for example when calling a function that has side-effects but no useful result value. To do this in PL/pgSQL, use the PERFORM statement:

```
PERFORM query;
```

This executes *query* and discards the result. Write the *query* the same way you would write an SQL SELECT command, but replace the initial keyword SELECT with PERFORM. PL/pgSQL variables will be substituted into the query as usual. Also, the special variable FOUND is set to true if the query produced at least one row, or false if it produced no rows.

Note: One might expect that writing SELECT directly would accomplish this result, but at present the only accepted way to do it is PERFORM. A SQL command that can return rows, such as SELECT, will be rejected as an error unless it has an INTO clause as discussed in the next section.

An example:

```
PERFORM create_mv('cs_session_page_requests_mv', my_query);
```

9.6.3 Executing a Query with a Single-Row Result

The result of a SQL command yielding a single row (possibly of multiple columns) can be assigned to a record variable, row-type variable, or list of scalar variables. This is done by writing the base SQL command and adding an INTO clause. For example,

```
SELECT select_expressions INTO [STRICT] target FROM ...;
INSERT ... RETURNING expressions INTO [STRICT] target;
UPDATE ... RETURNING expressions INTO [STRICT] target;
DELETE ... RETURNING expressions INTO [STRICT] target;
```

where *target* can be a record variable, a row variable, or a comma-separated list of simple variables and record/row fields. PL/pgSQL variables will be substituted into the rest of the query as usual. This works for SELECT, INSERT/UPDATE/DELETE with RETURNING, and utility commands that return rowset results (such as EXPLAIN). Except for the INTO clause, the SQL command is the same as it would be written outside PL/pgSQL.

Tip: Note that this interpretation of SELECT with INTO is quite different from PostgreSQL's regular SELECT INTO command, wherein the INTO target is a newly created table. If you want to create a table from a SELECT result inside a PL/pgSQL function, use the syntax CREATE TABLE ... AS SELECT.

If a row or a variable list is used as target, the query's result columns must exactly match the structure of the target as to number and data types, or a run-time error occurs. When a record variable is the target, it automatically configures itself to the row type of the query result columns.

The INTO clause can appear almost anywhere in the SQL command. Customarily it is written either just before or just after the list of *select_expressions* in a SELECT command, or at the end of the command for other command types. It is recommended that you follow this convention in case the PL/pgSQL parser becomes stricter in future versions.

If STRICT is not specified, then *target* will be set to the first row returned by the query, or to nulls if the query returned no rows. (Note that "the first row" is not well-defined unless you've used ORDER BY.) Any result rows after the first row are discarded. You can check the special FOUND variable (see Section 9.6.6 *Obtaining the Result Status*, page 294) to determine whether a row was returned:

```
SELECT * INTO myrec FROM emp WHERE empname = myname;
IF NOT FOUND THEN
    RAISE EXCEPTION 'employee % not found', myname;
END IF;
```

If the STRICT option is specified, the query must return exactly one row or a run-time error will be reported, either NO_DATA_FOUND (no rows) or TOO_MANY_ROWS (more than one row). You can use an exception block if you wish to catch the error, for example:

```
BEGIN;
    SELECT * INTO STRICT myrec FROM emp WHERE empname = myname;
    EXCEPTION
        WHEN NO_DATA_FOUND THEN
            RAISE EXCEPTION 'employee % not found', myname;
        WHEN TOO_MANY_ROWS THEN
            RAISE EXCEPTION 'employee % not unique', myname;
END;
```

Successful execution of a command with STRICT always sets FOUND to true.

For INSERT/UPDATE/DELETE with RETURNING, PL/pgSQL reports an error for more than one returned row, even when STRICT is not specified. This is because there is no option such as ORDER BY with which to determine which affected row would be returned.

Note: The STRICT option matches the behavior of Oracle PL/SQL's SELECT INTO and related statements.

To handle cases where you need to process multiple result rows from a SQL query, see Section 9.7.4 *Looping Through Query Results*, page 300.

9.6.4 Doing Nothing At All

Sometimes a placeholder statement that does nothing is useful. For example, it can indicate that one arm of an if/then/else chain is deliberately empty. For this purpose, use the NULL statement:

```
NULL;
```

For example, the following two fragments of code are equivalent:

```
BEGIN
    y := x / 0;
EXCEPTION
    WHEN division_by_zero THEN
        NULL;  -- ignore the error
END;
BEGIN
    y := x / 0;
EXCEPTION
    WHEN division_by_zero THEN  -- ignore the error
END;
```

Which is preferable is a matter of taste.

> **Note:** In Oracle's PL/SQL, empty statement lists are not allowed, and so NULL statements are *required* for situations such as this. PL/pgSQL allows you to just write nothing, instead.

9.6.5 Executing Dynamic Commands

Oftentimes you will want to generate dynamic commands inside your PL/pgSQL functions, that is, commands that will involve different tables or different data types each time they are executed. PL/pgSQL's normal attempts to cache plans for commands will not work in such scenarios. To handle this sort of problem, the EXECUTE statement is provided:

```
EXECUTE command-string [ INTO [STRICT] target ];
```

where *command-string* is an expression yielding a string (of type text) containing the command to be executed and *target* is a record variable, row variable, or a comma-separated list of simple variables and record/row fields.

Note in particular that no substitution of PL/pgSQL variables is done on the computed command string. The values of variables must be inserted in the command string as it is constructed.

Unlike all other commands in PL/pgSQL, a command run by an EXECUTE statement is not prepared and saved just once during the life of the session. Instead, the command is prepared each time the statement is run. The command string can be dynamically created within the function to perform actions on different tables and columns.

The INTO clause specifies where the results of a SQL command returning rows should be assigned. If a row or variable list is provided, it must exactly match the structure of the query's results (when a record variable is used, it will configure itself to match the result structure automatically). If multiple rows are returned, only the first will be assigned to the INTO variable. If no rows are returned, NULL is assigned to the INTO variable. If no INTO clause is specified, the query results are discarded.

If the STRICT option is given, an error is reported unless the query produces exactly one row.

SELECT INTO is not currently supported within EXECUTE.

When working with dynamic commands you will often have to handle escaping of single quotes. The recommended method for quoting fixed text in your function body is dollar quoting. (If you have legacy code that does not use dollar quoting, please refer to the overview in Section 9.2.1 *Handling of Quotation Marks*, page 280, which can save you some effort when translating said code to a more reasonable scheme.)

Dynamic values that are to be inserted into the constructed query require special handling since they might themselves contain quote characters. An example (this assumes that you are using dollar quoting for the function as a whole, so the quote marks need not be doubled):

```
EXECUTE 'UPDATE tbl SET '
        || quote_ident(colname)
        || ' = '
        || quote_literal(newvalue)
        || ' WHERE key = '
        || quote_literal(keyvalue);
```

This example demonstrates the use of the quote_ident and quote_literal functions. For safety, expressions containing column and table identifiers should be passed to quote_ident. Expressions containing values that should be literal strings in the constructed command should be passed to quote_literal. Both take the appropriate steps to return the input text enclosed in double or single quotes respectively, with any embedded special characters properly escaped.

Note that dollar quoting is only useful for quoting fixed text. It would be a very bad idea to try to do the above example as

```
EXECUTE 'UPDATE tbl SET '
        || quote_ident(colname)
        || ' = $$'
        || newvalue
        || '$$ WHERE key = '
        || quote_literal(keyvalue);
```

because it would break if the contents of newvalue happened to contain $$. The same objection would apply to any other dollar-quoting delimiter you might pick. So, to safely quote text that is not known in advance, you *must* use quote_literal.

A much larger example of a dynamic command and EXECUTE can be seen in *Porting a Function that Creates Another Function from PL/SQL to PL/pgSQL*, page 316, which builds and executes a CREATE FUNCTION command to define a new function.

9.6.6 Obtaining the Result Status

There are several ways to determine the effect of a command. The first method is to use the GET DIAGNOSTICS command, which has the form:

```
GET DIAGNOSTICS variable = item [ , ... ];
```

This command allows retrieval of system status indicators. Each *item* is a key word identifying a state value to be assigned to the specified variable (which should be of the right data type to receive it). The currently available status items are ROW_COUNT, the number of rows processed by the last SQL command sent down to the SQL engine, and RESULT_OID, the OID of the last row inserted by the most recent SQL command. Note that RESULT_OID is only useful after an INSERT command into a table containing OIDs.

An example:

```
GET DIAGNOSTICS integer_var = ROW_COUNT;
```

The second method to determine the effects of a command is to check the special variable named FOUND, which is of type boolean. FOUND starts out false within each PL/pgSQL function call. It is set by each of the following types of statements:

- A SELECT INTO statement sets FOUND true if a row is assigned, false if no row is returned.

- A PERFORM statement sets FOUND true if it produces (and discards) a row, false if no row is produced.

- UPDATE, INSERT, and DELETE statements set FOUND true if at least one row is affected, false if no row is affected.

- A FETCH statement sets FOUND true if it returns a row, false if no row is returned.

- A FOR statement sets FOUND true if it iterates one or more times, else false. This applies to all three variants of the FOR statement (integer FOR loops, record-set FOR loops, and dynamic record-set FOR loops). FOUND is set this way when the FOR loop exits; inside the execution of the loop, FOUND is not modified by the FOR statement, although it may be changed by the execution of other statements within the loop body.

FOUND is a local variable within each PL/pgSQL function; any changes to it affect only the current function.

9.7 Control Structures

Control structures are probably the most useful (and important) part of PL/pgSQL. With PL/pgSQL's control structures, you can manipulate PostgreSQL data in a very flexible and powerful way.

9.7.1 Returning From a Function

There are two commands available that allow you to return data from a function: RETURN and RETURN NEXT.

9.7.1.1 RETURN

```
RETURN expression;
```

RETURN with an expression terminates the function and returns the value of *expression* to the caller. This form is to be used for PL/pgSQL functions that do not return a set.

When returning a scalar type, any expression can be used. The expression's result will be automatically cast into the function's return type as described for assignments. To return a composite (row) value, you must write a record or row variable as the *expression*.

If you declared the function with output parameters, write just RETURN with no expression. The current values of the output parameter variables will be returned.

If you declared the function to return void, a RETURN statement can be used to exit the function early; but do not write an expression following RETURN.

The return value of a function cannot be left undefined. If control reaches the end of the top-level block of the function without hitting a RETURN statement, a run-time error will occur. This restriction does not apply to functions with output parameters and functions returning void, however. In those cases a RETURN statement is automatically executed if the top-level block finishes.

9.7.1.2 RETURN NEXT

```
RETURN NEXT expression;
```

When a PL/pgSQL function is declared to return SETOF *sometype*, the procedure to follow is slightly different. In that case, the individual items to return are specified in RETURN NEXT commands, and then a final RETURN command with no argument is used to indicate that the function has finished executing. RETURN NEXT can be used with both scalar and composite data types; with a composite result type, an entire "table" of results will be returned.

RETURN NEXT does not actually return from the function—it simply saves away the value of the expression. Execution then continues with the next statement in the PL/pgSQL function. As successive RETURN NEXT commands are executed, the result set is built up. A final RETURN, which should have no argument, causes control to exit the function (or you can just let control reach the end of the function).

If you declared the function with output parameters, write just RETURN NEXT with no expression. The current values of the output parameter variable(s) will be saved for eventual return. Note that you must declare the function as returning SETOF record when there are multiple output parameters, or SETOF *sometype* when there is just one output parameter of type *sometype*, in order to create a set-returning function with output parameters.

Functions that use RETURN NEXT should be called in the following fashion:

```
SELECT * FROM some_func();
```

That is, the function must be used as a table source in a FROM clause.

Note: The current implementation of RETURN NEXT for PL/pgSQL
stores the entire result set before returning from the function, as discussed above. That means that if a PL/pgSQL function produces a
very large result set, performance may be poor: data will be written
to disk to avoid memory exhaustion, but the function itself will not
return until the entire result set has been generated. A future version
of PL/pgSQL may allow users to define set-returning functions that
do not have this limitation. Currently, the point at which data begins being written to disk is controlled by the work_mem configuration
variable. Administrators who have sufficient memory to store larger
result sets in memory should consider increasing this parameter.

9.7.2 Conditionals

IF statements let you execute commands based on certain conditions.
PL/pgSQL has five forms of IF:

- IF ... THEN
- IF ... THEN ... ELSE
- IF ... THEN ... ELSE IF
- IF ... THEN ... ELSIF ... THEN ... ELSE
- IF ... THEN ... ELSEIF ... THEN ... ELSE

9.7.2.1 IF-THEN

```
IF boolean-expression THEN
    statements
END IF;
```

IF-THEN statements are the simplest form of IF. The statements between
THEN and END IF will be executed if the condition is true. Otherwise, they are
skipped.

Example:

```
IF v_user_id <> 0 THEN
    UPDATE users SET email = v_email WHERE user_id = v_user_id;
END IF;
```

9.7.2.2 IF-THEN-ELSE

```
IF boolean-expression THEN
    statements
ELSE
    statements
END IF;
```

IF-THEN-ELSE statements add to IF-THEN by letting you specify an alternative
set of statements that should be executed if the condition evaluates to false.

Examples:

```
IF parentid IS NULL OR parentid = ''
THEN
    RETURN fullname;
ELSE
    RETURN hp_true_filename(parentid) || '/' || fullname;
END IF;
IF v_count > 0 THEN
    INSERT INTO users_count (count) VALUES (v_count);
    RETURN 't';
ELSE
    RETURN 'f';
END IF;
```

9.7.2.3 IF-THEN-ELSE IF

IF statements can be nested, as in the following example:

```
IF demo_row.sex = 'm' THEN
    pretty_sex := 'man';
ELSE
    IF demo_row.sex = 'f' THEN
        pretty_sex := 'woman';
    END IF;
END IF;
```

When you use this form, you are actually nesting an IF statement inside the ELSE part of an outer IF statement. Thus you need one END IF statement for each nested IF and one for the parent IF-ELSE. This is workable but grows tedious when there are many alternatives to be checked. Hence the next form.

9.7.2.4 IF-THEN-ELSIF-ELSE

```
IF boolean-expression THEN
    statements
[ ELSIF boolean-expression THEN
    statements
[ ELSIF boolean-expression THEN
    statements
    ...]]
[ ELSE
    statements ]
END IF;
```

IF-THEN-ELSIF-ELSE provides a more convenient method of checking many alternatives in one statement. Formally it is equivalent to nested IF-THEN-ELSE-IF-THEN commands, but only one END IF is needed.

Here is an example:

```
IF number = 0 THEN
    result := 'zero';
ELSIF number > 0 THEN
    result := 'positive';
```

```
ELSIF number < 0 THEN
    result := 'negative';
ELSE
    -- hmm, the only other possibility is that number is null
    result := 'NULL';
END IF;
```

9.7.2.5 IF-THEN-ELSEIF-ELSE

ELSEIF is an alias for ELSIF.

9.7.3 Simple Loops

With the LOOP, EXIT, CONTINUE, WHILE, and FOR statements, you can arrange for your PL/pgSQL function to repeat a series of commands.

9.7.3.1 LOOP

```
[ <<label>> ]
LOOP
    statements
END LOOP [ label ];
```

LOOP defines an unconditional loop that is repeated indefinitely until terminated by an EXIT or RETURN statement. The optional *label* can be used by EXIT and CONTINUE statements in nested loops to specify which loop the statement should be applied to.

9.7.3.2 EXIT

```
EXIT [ label ] [ WHEN expression ];
```

If no *label* is given, the innermost loop is terminated and the statement following END LOOP is executed next. If *label* is given, it must be the label of the current or some outer level of nested loop or block. Then the named loop or block is terminated and control continues with the statement after the loop's/block's corresponding END.

If WHEN is specified, the loop exit occurs only if *expression* is true. Otherwise, control passes to the statement after EXIT.

EXIT can be used with all types of loops; it is not limited to use with unconditional loops. When used with a BEGIN block, EXIT passes control to the next statement after the end of the block.

Examples:

```
LOOP
    -- some computations
    IF count > 0 THEN
        EXIT;  -- exit loop
    END IF;
END LOOP;

LOOP
```

```
    -- some computations
    EXIT WHEN count > 0;  -- same result as previous example
END LOOP;

BEGIN
    -- some computations
    IF stocks > 100000 THEN
        EXIT;  -- causes exit from the BEGIN block
    END IF;
END;
```

9.7.3.3 CONTINUE

```
CONTINUE [ label ] [ WHEN expression ];
```

If no *label* is given, the next iteration of the innermost loop is begun. That is, control is passed back to the loop control expression (if any), and the body of the loop is re-evaluated. If *label* is present, it specifies the label of the loop whose execution will be continued.

If WHEN is specified, the next iteration of the loop is begun only if *expression* is true. Otherwise, control passes to the statement after CONTINUE.

CONTINUE can be used with all types of loops; it is not limited to use with unconditional loops.

Examples:

```
LOOP
    -- some computations
    EXIT WHEN count > 100;
    CONTINUE WHEN count < 50;
    -- some computations for count IN [50 .. 100]
END LOOP;
```

9.7.3.4 WHILE

```
[ <<label>> ]
WHILE expression LOOP
    statements
END LOOP [ label ];
```

The WHILE statement repeats a sequence of statements so long as the condition expression evaluates to true. The condition is checked just before each entry to the loop body.

For example:

```
WHILE amount_owed > 0 AND gift_certificate_balance > 0 LOOP
    -- some computations here
END LOOP;

WHILE NOT boolean_expression LOOP
    -- some computations here
END LOOP;
```

9.7.3.5 FOR (integer variant)

```
[ <<label>> ]
FOR name IN [ REVERSE ] expression .. expression [ BY
  expression ] LOOP
    statements
END LOOP [ label ];
```

This form of FOR creates a loop that iterates over a range of integer values. The variable *name* is automatically defined as type integer and exists only inside the loop (any existing definition of the variable name is ignored within the loop). The two expressions giving the lower and upper bound of the range are evaluated once when entering the loop. If the BY clause isn't specified the iteration step is 1 otherwise it's the value specified in the BY clause. If REVERSE is specified then the step value is considered negative.

Some examples of integer FOR loops:

```
FOR i IN 1..10 LOOP
    -- some computations here
    RAISE NOTICE 'i is %', i;
END LOOP;

FOR i IN REVERSE 10..1 LOOP
    -- some computations here
END LOOP;

FOR i IN REVERSE 10..1 BY 2 LOOP
    -- some computations here
    RAISE NOTICE 'i is %', i;
END LOOP;
```

If the lower bound is greater than the upper bound (or less than, in the REVERSE case), the loop body is not executed at all. No error is raised.

9.7.4 Looping Through Query Results

Using a different type of FOR loop, you can iterate through the results of a query and manipulate that data accordingly. The syntax is:

```
[ <<label>> ]
FOR target IN query LOOP
    statements
END LOOP [ label ];
```

The *target* is a record variable, row variable, or comma-separated list of scalar variables. The *target* is successively assigned each row resulting from the *query* and the loop body is executed for each row. Here is an example:

```
CREATE FUNCTION cs_refresh_mviews() RETURNS integer AS $$
DECLARE
    mviews RECORD;
BEGIN
    PERFORM cs_log('Refreshing materialized views...');
```

```
        FOR mviews IN SELECT * FROM cs_materialized_views ORDER
    BY sort_key LOOP

            -- Now "mviews" has one record from cs_materialized_views

            PERFORM cs_log('Refreshing materialized view ' ||
    quote_ident(mviews.mv_name) || ' ...');
                EXECUTE 'TRUNCATE TABLE ' || quote_ident(mviews.mv_name);
                EXECUTE 'INSERT INTO ' || quote_ident(mviews.mv_name)
    || ' ' || mviews.mv_query;
        END LOOP;

        PERFORM cs_log('Done refreshing materialized views.');
        RETURN 1;
    END;
    $$ LANGUAGE plpgsql;
```

If the loop is terminated by an EXIT statement, the last assigned row value is still accessible after the loop.

The *query* used in this type of FOR statement can be any SQL command that returns rows to the caller: SELECT is the most common case, but you can also use INSERT, UPDATE, or DELETE with a RETURNING clause. Some utility commands such as EXPLAIN will work too.

The FOR-IN-EXECUTE statement is another way to iterate over rows:

```
[ <<label>> ]
FOR target IN EXECUTE text_expression LOOP
    statements
END LOOP [ label ];
```

This is like the previous form, except that the source query is specified as a string expression, which is evaluated and replanned on each entry to the FOR loop. This allows the programmer to choose the speed of a preplanned query or the flexibility of a dynamic query, just as with a plain EXECUTE statement.

Note: The PL/pgSQL parser presently distinguishes the two kinds of FOR loops (integer or query result) by checking whether .. appears outside any parentheses between IN and LOOP. If .. is not seen then the loop is presumed to be a loop over rows. Mistyping the .. is thus likely to lead to a complaint along the lines of "loop variable of loop over rows must be a record or row variable or list of scalar variables", rather than the simple syntax error one might expect to get.

9.7.5 Trapping Errors

By default, any error occurring in a PL/pgSQL function aborts execution of the function, and indeed of the surrounding transaction as well. You can trap errors and recover from them by using a BEGIN block with an EXCEPTION clause. The syntax is an extension of the normal syntax for a BEGIN block:

```
[ <<label>> ]
[ DECLARE
    declarations ]
BEGIN
    statements
EXCEPTION
    WHEN condition [ OR condition ... ] THEN
        handler_statements
    [ WHEN condition [ OR condition ... ] THEN
        handler_statements
      ... ]
END;
```

If no error occurs, this form of block simply executes all the *statements*, and then control passes to the next statement after END. But if an error occurs within the *statements*, further processing of the *statements* is abandoned, and control passes to the EXCEPTION list. The list is searched for the first *condition* matching the error that occurred. If a match is found, the corresponding *handler_statements* are executed, and then control passes to the next statement after END. If no match is found, the error propagates out as though the EXCEPTION clause were not there at all: the error can be caught by an enclosing block with EXCEPTION, or if there is none it aborts processing of the function.

The *condition* names can be any of those shown in Volume 1, Appendix A *PostgreSQL Error Codes*. A category name matches any error within its category. The special condition name OTHERS matches every error type except QUERY_CANCELED. (It is possible, but often unwise, to trap QUERY_CANCELED by name.) Condition names are not case-sensitive.

If a new error occurs within the selected *handler_statements*, it cannot be caught by this EXCEPTION clause, but is propagated out. A surrounding EXCEPTION clause could catch it.

When an error is caught by an EXCEPTION clause, the local variables of the PL/pgSQL function remain as they were when the error occurred, but all changes to persistent database state within the block are rolled back. As an example, consider this fragment:

```
INSERT INTO mytab(firstname, lastname) VALUES('Tom', 'Jones');
BEGIN
    UPDATE mytab SET firstname = 'Joe' WHERE lastname = 'Jones';
    x := x + 1;
    y := x / 0;
EXCEPTION
    WHEN division_by_zero THEN
        RAISE NOTICE 'caught division_by_zero';
        RETURN x;
```

```
END;
```

When control reaches the assignment to y, it will fail with a division_by_zero error. This will be caught by the EXCEPTION clause. The value returned in the RETURN statement will be the incremented value of x, but the effects of the UPDATE command will have been rolled back. The INSERT command preceding the block is not rolled back, however, so the end result is that the database contains Tom Jones not Joe Jones.

Tip: A block containing an EXCEPTION clause is significantly more expensive to enter and exit than a block without one. Therefore, don't use EXCEPTION without need.

Within an exception handler, the SQLSTATE variable contains the error code that corresponds to the exception that was raised (refer to Table A.1 for a list of possible error codes). The SQLERRM variable contains the error message associated with the exception. These variables are undefined outside exception handlers.

Exceptions with UPDATE/INSERT:

This example uses exception handling to perform either UPDATE or INSERT, as appropriate.

```
CREATE TABLE db (a INT PRIMARY KEY, b TEXT);

CREATE FUNCTION merge_db(key INT, data TEXT) RETURNS VOID AS
$$
BEGIN
    LOOP
        UPDATE db SET b = data WHERE a = key;
        IF found THEN
            RETURN;
        END IF;

        BEGIN
            INSERT INTO db(a,b) VALUES (key, data);
            RETURN;
        EXCEPTION WHEN unique_violation THEN
            -- do nothing
        END;
    END LOOP;
END;
$$
LANGUAGE plpgsql;

SELECT merge_db(1, 'david');
SELECT merge_db(1, 'dennis');
```

9.8 Cursors

Rather than executing a whole query at once, it is possible to set up a *cursor* that encapsulates the query, and then read the query result a few rows at a time. One reason for doing this is to avoid memory overrun when the result contains a large number of rows. (However, PL/pgSQL users do not normally need to worry about that, since FOR loops automatically use a cursor internally to avoid memory problems.) A more interesting usage is to return a reference to a cursor that a function has created, allowing the caller to read the rows. This provides an efficient way to return large row sets from functions.

9.8.1 Declaring Cursor Variables

All access to cursors in PL/pgSQL goes through cursor variables, which are always of the special data type refcursor. One way to create a cursor variable is just to declare it as a variable of type refcursor. Another way is to use the cursor declaration syntax, which in general is:

    name CURSOR [(arguments)] FOR query;

(FOR may be replaced by IS for Oracle compatibility.) *arguments*, if specified, is a comma-separated list of pairs *name datatype* that define names to be replaced by parameter values in the given query. The actual values to substitute for these names will be specified later, when the cursor is opened.

Some examples:

```
DECLARE
    curs1 refcursor;
    curs2 CURSOR FOR SELECT * FROM tenk1;
    curs3 CURSOR (key integer) IS SELECT * FROM tenk1 WHERE
unique1 = key;
```

All three of these variables have the data type refcursor, but the first may be used with any query, while the second has a fully specified query already *bound* to it, and the last has a parameterized query bound to it. (key will be replaced by an integer parameter value when the cursor is opened.) The variable curs1 is said to be *unbound* since it is not bound to any particular query.

9.8.2 Opening Cursors

Before a cursor can be used to retrieve rows, it must be *opened*. (This is the equivalent action to the SQL command DECLARE CURSOR.) PL/pgSQL has three forms of the OPEN statement, two of which use unbound cursor variables while the third uses a bound cursor variable.

9.8.2.1 OPEN FOR query

```
OPEN unbound_cursor FOR query;
```

The cursor variable is opened and given the specified query to execute. The cursor cannot be open already, and it must have been declared as an unbound cursor (that is, as a simple refcursor variable). The query must be a SELECT, or something else that returns rows (such as EXPLAIN). The query is treated in the same way as other SQL commands in PL/pgSQL: PL/pgSQL variable names are substituted, and the query plan is cached for possible reuse.

An example:

```
OPEN curs1 FOR SELECT * FROM foo WHERE key = mykey;
```

9.8.2.2 OPEN FOR EXECUTE

```
OPEN unbound_cursor FOR EXECUTE query_string;
```

The cursor variable is opened and given the specified query to execute. The cursor cannot be open already, and it must have been declared as an unbound cursor (that is, as a simple refcursor variable). The query is specified as a string expression, in the same way as in the EXECUTE command. As usual, this gives flexibility so the query can vary from one run to the next.

An example:

```
OPEN curs1 FOR EXECUTE 'SELECT * FROM ' || quote_ident($1);
```

9.8.2.3 Opening a Bound Cursor

```
OPEN bound_cursor [ ( argument_values ) ];
```

This form of OPEN is used to open a cursor variable whose query was bound to it when it was declared. The cursor cannot be open already. A list of actual argument value expressions must appear if and only if the cursor was declared to take arguments. These values will be substituted in the query. The query plan for a bound cursor is always considered cacheable; there is no equivalent of EXECUTE in this case.

Examples:

```
OPEN curs2;
OPEN curs3(42);
```

9.8.3 Using Cursors

Once a cursor has been opened, it can be manipulated with the statements described here.

These manipulations need not occur in the same function that opened the cursor to begin with. You can return a refcursor value out of a function and let the caller operate on the cursor. (Internally, a refcursor value is simply the string name of a so-called portal containing the active query for the cursor. This name can be passed around, assigned to other refcursor variables, and so on, without disturbing the portal.)

All portals are implicitly closed at transaction end. Therefore a refcursor value is usable to reference an open cursor only until the end of the transaction.

9.8.3.1 FETCH

```
FETCH cursor INTO target ;
```

FETCH retrieves the next row from the cursor into a target, which may be a row variable, a record variable, or a comma-separated list of simple variables, just like SELECT INTO. As with SELECT INTO, the special variable FOUND may be checked to see whether a row was obtained or not.

An example:

```
FETCH curs1 INTO rowvar;
FETCH curs2 INTO foo, bar, baz;
```

9.8.3.2 CLOSE

```
CLOSE cursor ;
```

CLOSE closes the portal underlying an open cursor. This can be used to release resources earlier than end of transaction, or to free up the cursor variable to be opened again.

An example:

```
CLOSE curs1;
```

9.8.3.3 Returning Cursors

PL/pgSQL functions can return cursors to the caller. This is useful to return multiple rows or columns, especially with very large result sets. To do this, the function opens the cursor and returns the cursor name to the caller (or simply opens the cursor using a portal name specified by or otherwise known to the caller). The caller can then fetch rows from the cursor. The cursor can be closed by the caller, or it will be closed automatically when the transaction closes.

The portal name used for a cursor can be specified by the programmer or automatically generated. To specify a portal name, simply assign a string to the refcursor variable before opening it. The string value of the refcursor variable will be used by OPEN as the name of the underlying portal. However, if the refcursor variable is null, OPEN automatically generates a name that does not conflict with any existing portal, and assigns it to the refcursor variable.

> Note: A bound cursor variable is initialized to the string value representing its name, so that the portal name is the same as the cursor variable name, unless the programmer overrides it by assignment before opening the cursor. But an unbound cursor variable defaults to the null value initially, so it will receive an automatically-generated unique name, unless overridden.

The following example shows one way a cursor name can be supplied by the caller:

```
CREATE TABLE test (col text);
INSERT INTO test VALUES ('123');

CREATE FUNCTION reffunc(refcursor) RETURNS refcursor AS '
BEGIN
    OPEN $1 FOR SELECT col FROM test;
```

```
      RETURN $1;
  END;
  ' LANGUAGE plpgsql;

  BEGIN;
  SELECT reffunc('funccursor');
  FETCH ALL IN funccursor;
  COMMIT;
```

The following example uses automatic cursor name generation:

```
  CREATE FUNCTION reffunc2() RETURNS refcursor AS '
  DECLARE
      ref refcursor;
  BEGIN
      OPEN ref FOR SELECT col FROM test;
      RETURN ref;
  END;
  ' LANGUAGE plpgsql;

  BEGIN;
  SELECT reffunc2();

      reffunc2
  -------------------
   <unnamed cursor 1>
  (1 row)

  FETCH ALL IN "<unnamed cursor 1>";
  COMMIT;
```

The following example shows one way to return multiple cursors from a single function:

```
  CREATE FUNCTION myfunc(refcursor, refcursor) RETURNS SETOF
   refcursor AS $$
  BEGIN
      OPEN $1 FOR SELECT * FROM table_1;
      RETURN NEXT $1;
      OPEN $2 FOR SELECT * FROM table_2;
      RETURN NEXT $2;
  END;
  $$ LANGUAGE plpgsql;

  -- need to be in a transaction to use cursors.
  BEGIN;

  SELECT * FROM myfunc('a', 'b');

  FETCH ALL FROM a;
  FETCH ALL FROM b;
```

```
COMMIT;
```

9.9 Errors and Messages

Use the RAISE statement to report messages and raise errors.

```
RAISE level 'format' [, expression [, ...]];
```

Possible levels are DEBUG, LOG, INFO, NOTICE, WARNING, and EXCEPTION. EXCEPTION raises an error (which normally aborts the current transaction); the other levels only generate messages of different priority levels. Whether messages of a particular priority are reported to the client, written to the server log, or both is controlled by the log_min_messages and client_min_messages configuration variables. See Volume 3, Chapter 4 *Server Configuration* for more information.

Inside the format string, % is replaced by the next optional argument's string representation. Write %% to emit a literal %. Arguments can be simple variables or expressions, and the format must be a simple string literal.

In this example, the value of v_job_id will replace the % in the string:

```
RAISE NOTICE 'Calling cs_create_job(%)', v_job_id;
```

This example will abort the transaction with the given error message:

```
RAISE EXCEPTION 'Nonexistent ID --> %', user_id;
```

RAISE EXCEPTION presently always generates the same SQLSTATE code, P0001, no matter what message it is invoked with. It is possible to trap this exception with EXCEPTION ... WHEN RAISE_EXCEPTION THEN ... but there is no way to tell one RAISE from another.

9.10 Trigger Procedures

PL/pgSQL can be used to define trigger procedures. A trigger procedure is created with the CREATE FUNCTION command, declaring it as a function with no arguments and a return type of trigger. Note that the function must be declared with no arguments even if it expects to receive arguments specified in CREATE TRIGGER—trigger arguments are passed via TG_ARGV, as described below.

When a PL/pgSQL function is called as a trigger, several special variables are created automatically in the top-level block. They are:

NEW

> Data type RECORD; variable holding the new database row for INSERT/UPDATE operations in row-level triggers. This variable is NULL in statement-level triggers.

OLD

> Data type RECORD; variable holding the old database row for UPDATE/DELETE operations in row-level triggers. This variable is NULL in statement-level triggers.

TG_NAME

> Data type name; variable that contains the name of the trigger actually fired.

TG_WHEN
> Data type text; a string of either BEFORE or AFTER depending on the trigger's definition.

TG_LEVEL
> Data type text; a string of either ROW or STATEMENT depending on the trigger's definition.

TG_OP
> Data type text; a string of INSERT, UPDATE, or DELETE telling for which operation the trigger was fired.

TG_RELID
> Data type oid; the object ID of the table that caused the trigger invocation.

TG_RELNAME
> Data type name; the name of the table that caused the trigger invocation. This is now deprecated, and could disappear in a future release. Use TG_TABLE_NAME instead.

TG_TABLE_NAME
> Data type name; the name of the table that caused the trigger invocation.

TG_TABLE_SCHEMA
> Data type name; the name of the schema of the table that caused the trigger invocation.

TG_NARGS
> Data type integer; the number of arguments given to the trigger procedure in the CREATE TRIGGER statement.

TG_ARGV[]
> Data type array of text; the arguments from the CREATE TRIGGER statement. The index counts from 0. Invalid indices (less than 0 or greater than or equal to tg_nargs) result in a null value.

A trigger function must return either NULL or a record/row value having exactly the structure of the table the trigger was fired for.

Row-level triggers fired BEFORE may return null to signal the trigger manager to skip the rest of the operation for this row (i.e., subsequent triggers are not fired, and the INSERT/UPDATE/DELETE does not occur for this row). If a nonnull value is returned then the operation proceeds with that row value. Returning a row value different from the original value of NEW alters the row that will be inserted or updated (but has no direct effect in the DELETE case). To alter the row to be stored, it is possible to replace single values directly in NEW and return the modified NEW, or to build a complete new record/row to return.

The return value of a BEFORE or AFTER statement-level trigger or an AFTER row-level trigger is always ignored; it may as well be null. However, any of these types of triggers can still abort the entire operation by raising an error.

A PL/pgSQL Trigger Procedure shows an example of a trigger procedure in PL/pgSQL.

A PL/pgSQL Trigger Procedure:

This example trigger ensures that any time a row is inserted or updated in the table, the current user name and time are stamped into the row. And it checks that an employee's name is given and that the salary is a positive value.

```
CREATE TABLE emp (
    empname text,
    salary integer,
    last_date timestamp,
    last_user text
);


CREATE FUNCTION emp_stamp() RETURNS trigger AS $emp_stamp$
    BEGIN
        -- Check that empname and salary are given
        IF NEW.empname IS NULL THEN
            RAISE EXCEPTION 'empname cannot be null';
        END IF;
        IF NEW.salary IS NULL THEN
            RAISE EXCEPTION '% cannot have null salary',
NEW.empname;
        END IF;

        -- Who works for us when she must pay for it?
        IF NEW.salary < 0 THEN
            RAISE EXCEPTION '% cannot have a negative
salary', NEW.empname;
        END IF;

        -- Remember who changed the payroll when
        NEW.last_date := current_timestamp;
        NEW.last_user := current_user;
        RETURN NEW;
    END;
$emp_stamp$ LANGUAGE plpgsql;


CREATE TRIGGER emp_stamp BEFORE INSERT OR UPDATE ON emp
    FOR EACH ROW EXECUTE PROCEDURE emp_stamp();
```

Another way to log changes to a table involves creating a new table that holds a row for each insert, update, or delete that occurs. This approach can be thought of as auditing changes to a table. *A PL/pgSQL Trigger Procedure For Auditing* shows an example of an audit trigger procedure in PL/pgSQL.

A PL/pgSQL Trigger Procedure For Auditing:

This example trigger ensures that any insert, update or delete of a row in the emp table is recorded (i.e., audited) in the emp_audit table. The current time and user name are stamped into the row, together with the type of operation performed on it.

```
CREATE TABLE emp (
    empname             text NOT NULL,
    salary              integer
);

CREATE TABLE emp_audit(
    operation           char(1)   NOT NULL,
    stamp               timestamp NOT NULL,
    userid              text      NOT NULL,
    empname             text      NOT NULL,
    salary integer
);

CREATE OR REPLACE FUNCTION process_emp_audit() RETURNS
 TRIGGER AS $emp_audit$
    BEGIN
        --
        -- Create a row in emp_audit to reflect the
        -- operation performed on emp, make use of the
        -- special variable TG_OP to work out the
        -- operation.
        --
        IF (TG_OP = 'DELETE') THEN
            INSERT INTO emp_audit SELECT 'D', now(), user, OLD.*;
            RETURN OLD;
        ELSIF (TG_OP = 'UPDATE') THEN
            INSERT INTO emp_audit SELECT 'U', now(), user, NEW.*;
            RETURN NEW;
        ELSIF (TG_OP = 'INSERT') THEN
            INSERT INTO emp_audit SELECT 'I', now(), user, NEW.*;
            RETURN NEW;
        END IF;
        RETURN NULL; -- result is ignored since this is an
  AFTER trigger
    END;
$emp_audit$ LANGUAGE plpgsql;

CREATE TRIGGER emp_audit
AFTER INSERT OR UPDATE OR DELETE ON emp
    FOR EACH ROW EXECUTE PROCEDURE process_emp_audit();
```

One use of triggers is to maintain a summary table of another table. The resulting summary can be used in place of the original table for certain queries—often with vastly reduced run times. This technique is commonly used in Data Warehousing, where the tables of measured or observed data (called fact tables) can be extremely large. *A PL/pgSQL Trigger Procedure For Maintaining A Summary Table* shows an example of a trigger procedure in PL/pgSQL that maintains a summary table for a fact table in a data warehouse.

A PL/pgSQL Trigger Procedure For Maintaining A Summary Table:

The schema detailed here is partly based on the *Grocery Store* example from
The Data Warehouse Toolkit by Ralph Kimball.

```
--
-- Main tables - time dimension and sales fact.
--
CREATE TABLE time_dimension (
    time_key                integer NOT NULL,
    day_of_week             integer NOT NULL,
    day_of_month            integer NOT NULL,
    month                   integer NOT NULL,
    quarter                 integer NOT NULL,
    year                    integer NOT NULL
);
CREATE UNIQUE INDEX time_dimension_key ON
 time_dimension(time_key);

CREATE TABLE sales_fact (
    time_key                integer NOT NULL,
    product_key             integer NOT NULL,
    store_key               integer NOT NULL,
    amount_sold             numeric(12,2) NOT NULL,
    units_sold              integer NOT NULL,
    amount_cost             numeric(12,2) NOT NULL
);
CREATE INDEX sales_fact_time ON sales_fact(time_key);


--
-- Summary table - sales by time.
--
CREATE TABLE sales_summary_bytime (
    time_key                integer NOT NULL,
    amount_sold             numeric(15,2) NOT NULL,
    units_sold              numeric(12) NOT NULL,
    amount_cost             numeric(15,2) NOT NULL
);
CREATE UNIQUE INDEX sales_summary_bytime_key ON
 sales_summary_bytime(time_key);


--
-- Function and trigger to amend summarized column(s) on
 UPDATE, INSERT, DELETE.
--
CREATE OR REPLACE FUNCTION maint_sales_summary_bytime()
 RETURNS TRIGGER AS $maint_sales_summary_bytime$
    DECLARE
        delta_time_key          integer;
        delta_amount_sold       numeric(15,2);
        delta_units_sold        numeric(12);
```

```
                delta_amount_cost          numeric(15,2);
    BEGIN

        -- Work out the increment/decrement amount(s).
        IF (TG_OP = 'DELETE') THEN

            delta_time_key = OLD.time_key;
            delta_amount_sold = -1 * OLD.amount_sold;
            delta_units_sold = -1 * OLD.units_sold;
            delta_amount_cost = -1 * OLD.amount_cost;

        ELSIF (TG_OP = 'UPDATE') THEN

            -- forbid updates that change the time_key -
            -- (probably not too onerous, as DELETE + INSERT
is how most
            -- changes will be made).
            IF ( OLD.time_key != NEW.time_key) THEN
                RAISE EXCEPTION 'Update of time_key : % -> %
not allowed', OLD.time_key, NEW.time_key;
            END IF;

            delta_time_key = OLD.time_key;
            delta_amount_sold = NEW.amount_sold -
OLD.amount_sold;
            delta_units_sold = NEW.units_sold - OLD.units_sold;
            delta_amount_cost = NEW.amount_cost -
OLD.amount_cost;

        ELSIF (TG_OP = 'INSERT') THEN

            delta_time_key = NEW.time_key;
            delta_amount_sold = NEW.amount_sold;
            delta_units_sold = NEW.units_sold;
            delta_amount_cost = NEW.amount_cost;

        END IF;


        -- Insert or update the summary row with the new values.
        <<insert_update>>
        LOOP
            UPDATE sales_summary_bytime
                SET amount_sold = amount_sold +
delta_amount_sold,
                    units_sold = units_sold + delta_units_sold,
                    amount_cost = amount_cost + delta_amount_cost
                WHERE time_key = delta_time_key;
```

```
            EXIT insert_update WHEN found;

            BEGIN
                INSERT INTO sales_summary_bytime (
                        time_key,
                        amount_sold,
                        units_sold,
                        amount_cost)
                    VALUES (
                        delta_time_key,
                        delta_amount_sold,
                        delta_units_sold,
                        delta_amount_cost
                        );

                EXIT insert_update;

            EXCEPTION
                WHEN UNIQUE_VIOLATION THEN
                    -- do nothing
            END;
        END LOOP insert_update;

        RETURN NULL;

    END;
$maint_sales_summary_bytime$ LANGUAGE plpgsql;

CREATE TRIGGER maint_sales_summary_bytime
AFTER INSERT OR UPDATE OR DELETE ON sales_fact
    FOR EACH ROW EXECUTE PROCEDURE maint_sales_summary_bytime();

INSERT INTO sales_fact VALUES(1,1,1,10,3,15);
INSERT INTO sales_fact VALUES(1,2,1,20,5,35);
INSERT INTO sales_fact VALUES(2,2,1,40,15,135);
INSERT INTO sales_fact VALUES(2,3,1,10,1,13);
SELECT * FROM sales_summary_bytime;
DELETE FROM sales_fact WHERE product_key = 1;
SELECT * FROM sales_summary_bytime;
UPDATE sales_fact SET units_sold = units_sold * 2;
SELECT * FROM sales_summary_bytime;
```

9.11 Porting from Oracle PL/SQL

This section explains differences between PostgreSQL's PL/pgSQL language and Oracle's PL/SQL language, to help developers who port applications from Oracle(TM) to PostgreSQL.

PL/pgSQL is similar to PL/SQL in many aspects. It is a block-structured, imperative language, and all variables have to be declared. Assignments, loops, conditionals are similar. The main differences you should keep in mind when porting from PL/SQL to PL/pgSQL are:

* There are no default values for parameters in PostgreSQL.

* You can overload function names in PostgreSQL. This is often used to work around the lack of default parameters.

* You cannot use parameter names that are the same as columns that are referenced in the function. Oracle allows you to do this if you qualify the parameter name using function_name.parameter_name. In PL/pgSQL, you can instead avoid a conflict by qualifying the column or table name.

* No need for cursors in PL/pgSQL, just put the query in the FOR statement. (See *Porting a Function that Creates Another Function from PL/SQL to PL/pgSQL*, page 316.)

* In PostgreSQL the function body must be written as a string literal. Therefore you need to use dollar quoting or escape single quotes in the function body. See Section 9.2.1 *Handling of Quotation Marks*, page 280.

* Instead of packages, use schemas to organize your functions into groups.

* Since there are no packages, there are no package-level variables either. This is somewhat annoying. You can keep per-session state in temporary tables instead.

9.11.1 Porting Examples

Porting a Simple Function from PL/SQL to PL/pgSQL shows how to port a simple function from PL/SQL to PL/pgSQL.

Porting a Simple Function from PL/SQL to PL/pgSQL:

Here is an Oracle PL/SQL function:

```
CREATE OR REPLACE FUNCTION cs_fmt_browser_version(v_name
 varchar, v_version varchar)
RETURN varchar IS
BEGIN
    IF v_version IS NULL THEN
        RETURN v_name;
    END IF;
    RETURN v_name || '/' || v_version;
END;
/
show errors;
```

Let's go through this function and see the differences compared to PL/pgSQL:

- The RETURN key word in the function prototype (not the function body) becomes RETURNS in PostgreSQL. Also, IS becomes AS, and you need to add a LANGUAGE clause because PL/pgSQL is not the only possible function language.

- In PostgreSQL, the function body is considered to be a string literal, so you need to use quote marks or dollar quotes around it. This substitutes for the terminating / in the Oracle approach.

- The show errors command does not exist in PostgreSQL, and is not needed since errors are reported automatically.

This is how this function would look when ported to PostgreSQL:

```
CREATE OR REPLACE FUNCTION cs_fmt_browser_version(v_name
varchar, v_version varchar)
RETURNS varchar AS $$
BEGIN
    IF v_version IS NULL THEN
        RETURN v_name;
    END IF;
    RETURN v_name || '/' || v_version;
END;
$$ LANGUAGE plpgsql;
```

Porting a Function that Creates Another Function from PL/SQL to PL/pgSQL shows how to port a function that creates another function and how to handle the ensuing quoting problems.

Porting a Function that Creates Another Function from PL/SQL to PL/pgSQL:

The following procedure grabs rows from a SELECT statement and builds a large function with the results in IF statements, for the sake of efficiency. Notice particularly the differences in the cursor and the FOR loop.

This is the Oracle version:

```
CREATE OR REPLACE PROCEDURE cs_update_referrer_type_proc IS
    CURSOR referrer_keys IS
        SELECT * FROM cs_referrer_keys
        ORDER BY try_order;

    func_cmd VARCHAR(4000);
BEGIN
    func_cmd := 'CREATE OR REPLACE FUNCTION
cs_find_referrer_type(v_host IN VARCHAR, v_domain IN
VARCHAR, v_url IN VARCHAR) RETURN VARCHAR IS BEGIN';

    FOR referrer_key IN referrer_keys LOOP
        func_cmd := func_cmd ||
          ' IF v_' || referrer_key.kind
          || ' LIKE ''' || referrer_key.key_string
          || ''' THEN RETURN ''' || referrer_key.referrer_type
          || '''; END IF;';
```

```
        END LOOP;

        func_cmd := func_cmd || ' RETURN NULL; END;';

        EXECUTE IMMEDIATE func_cmd;
    END;
    /
    show errors;
```

Here is how this function would end up in PostgreSQL:

```
    CREATE OR REPLACE FUNCTION cs_update_referrer_type_proc()
     RETURNS void AS $func$
    DECLARE
        referrer_key RECORD;   -- declare a generic record to be
    used in a FOR
        func_body text;
        func_cmd text;
    BEGIN
        func_body := 'BEGIN';

        -- Notice how we scan through the results of a
        -- query in a FOR loop using the FOR <record>
        -- construct.

        FOR referrer_key IN SELECT * FROM cs_referrer_keys ORDER
    BY try_order LOOP
            func_body := func_body ||
                ' IF v_' || referrer_key.kind
                || ' LIKE ' || quote_literal(referrer_key.key_string)
                || ' THEN RETURN '
                || quote_literal(referrer_key.referrer_type)
                || '; END IF;' ;
        END LOOP;

        func_body := func_body || ' RETURN NULL; END;';

        func_cmd :=
            'CREATE OR REPLACE FUNCTION cs_find_referrer_type(v_host
    varchar, v_domain varchar, v_url varchar)
            RETURNS varchar AS '
         || quote_literal(func_body)
         || ' LANGUAGE plpgsql;' ;

        EXECUTE func_cmd;
    END;
    $func$ LANGUAGE plpgsql;
```

Notice how the body of the function is built separately and passed through quote_literal to double any quote marks in it. This technique is needed because we cannot safely use dollar quoting for defining the new function: we

do not know for sure what strings will be interpolated from the `referrer_`
`key.key_string` field. (We are assuming here that `referrer_key.kind` can
be trusted to always be host, domain, or url, but `referrer_key.key_string`
might be anything, in particular it might contain dollar signs.) This function
is actually an improvement on the Oracle original, because it will not generate
broken code when `referrer_key.key_string` or `referrer_key.referrer_type`
contain quote marks.

*Porting a Procedure With String Manipulation and OUT Parameters from
PL/SQL to PL/pgSQL* shows how to port a function with OUT parameters and
string manipulation. PostgreSQL does not have a built-in `instr` function, but
you can create one using a combination of other functions. In Section 9.11.3
Appendix, page 323 there is a PL/pgSQL implementation of `instr` that you
can use to make your porting easier.

Porting a Procedure With String Manipulation and OUT Parameters from PL/SQL to PL/pgSQL:

The following Oracle PL/SQL procedure is used to parse a URL and return
several elements (host, path, and query).

This is the Oracle version:

```
CREATE OR REPLACE PROCEDURE cs_parse_url(
    v_url IN VARCHAR,
    v_host OUT VARCHAR,   -- This will be passed back
    v_path OUT VARCHAR,   -- This one too
    v_query OUT VARCHAR) -- And this one
IS
    a_pos1 INTEGER;
    a_pos2 INTEGER;
BEGIN
    v_host := NULL;
    v_path := NULL;
    v_query := NULL;
    a_pos1 := instr(v_url, '//');

    IF a_pos1 = 0 THEN
        RETURN;
    END IF;
    a_pos2 := instr(v_url, '/', a_pos1 + 2);
    IF a_pos2 = 0 THEN
        v_host := substr(v_url, a_pos1 + 2);
        v_path := '/';
        RETURN;
    END IF;

    v_host := substr(v_url, a_pos1 + 2, a_pos2 - a_pos1 - 2);
    a_pos1 := instr(v_url, '?', a_pos2 + 1);

    IF a_pos1 = 0 THEN
        v_path := substr(v_url, a_pos2);
```

```
            RETURN;
        END IF;

        v_path := substr(v_url, a_pos2, a_pos1 - a_pos2);
        v_query := substr(v_url, a_pos1 + 1);
    END;
    /
    show errors;
```

Here is a possible translation into PL/pgSQL:

```
    CREATE OR REPLACE FUNCTION cs_parse_url(
        v_url IN VARCHAR,
        v_host OUT VARCHAR,  -- This will be passed back
        v_path OUT VARCHAR,  -- This one too
        v_query OUT VARCHAR) -- And this one
    AS $$
    DECLARE
        a_pos1 INTEGER;
        a_pos2 INTEGER;
    BEGIN
        v_host := NULL;
        v_path := NULL;
        v_query := NULL;
        a_pos1 := instr(v_url, '//');

        IF a_pos1 = 0 THEN
            RETURN;
        END IF;
        a_pos2 := instr(v_url, '/', a_pos1 + 2);
        IF a_pos2 = 0 THEN
            v_host := substr(v_url, a_pos1 + 2);
            v_path := '/';
            RETURN;
        END IF;

        v_host := substr(v_url, a_pos1 + 2, a_pos2 - a_pos1 - 2);
        a_pos1 := instr(v_url, '?', a_pos2 + 1);

        IF a_pos1 = 0 THEN
            v_path := substr(v_url, a_pos2);
            RETURN;
        END IF;

        v_path := substr(v_url, a_pos2, a_pos1 - a_pos2);
        v_query := substr(v_url, a_pos1 + 1);
    END;
    $$ LANGUAGE plpgsql;
```

This function could be used like this:

```
    SELECT * FROM cs_parse_url('http://foobar.com/query.cgi?baz');
```

Porting a Procedure from PL/SQL to PL/pgSQL shows how to port a procedure that uses numerous features that are specific to Oracle.

Porting a Procedure from PL/SQL to PL/pgSQL:

The Oracle version:

```
    CREATE OR REPLACE PROCEDURE cs_create_job(v_job_id IN INTEGER) IS
        a_running_job_count INTEGER;
        PRAGMA AUTONOMOUS_TRANSACTION; (note 1)
    BEGIN
        LOCK TABLE cs_jobs IN EXCLUSIVE MODE; (note 2)

        SELECT count(*) INTO a_running_job_count FROM cs_jobs
    WHERE end_stamp IS NULL;

        IF a_running_job_count > 0 THEN
            COMMIT; -- free lock (note 3)
            raise_application_error(-20000, 'Unable to create a
    new job: a job is currently running.');
        END IF;

        DELETE FROM cs_active_job;
        INSERT INTO cs_active_job(job_id) VALUES (v_job_id);

        BEGIN
            INSERT INTO cs_jobs (job_id, start_stamp) VALUES
    (v_job_id, sysdate);
        EXCEPTION
            WHEN dup_val_on_index THEN NULL; -- don't worry if it
    already exists
        END;
        COMMIT;
    END;
    /
    show errors
```

Procedures like this can easily be converted into PostgreSQL functions returning void. This procedure in particular is interesting because it can teach us some things:

Note 1:

There is no `PRAGMA` statement in PostgreSQL.

Note 2:

If you do a `LOCK TABLE` in PL/pgSQL, the lock will not be released until the calling transaction is finished.

Note 3:

> You cannot issue COMMIT in a PL/pgSQL function. The function is running within some outer transaction and so COMMIT would imply terminating the function's execution. However, in this particular case it is not necessary anyway, because the lock obtained by the LOCK TABLE will be released when we raise an error.

This is how we could port this procedure to PL/pgSQL:

```
CREATE OR REPLACE FUNCTION cs_create_job(v_job_id integer)
 RETURNS void AS $$
DECLARE
    a_running_job_count integer;
BEGIN
    LOCK TABLE cs_jobs IN EXCLUSIVE MODE;

    SELECT count(*) INTO a_running_job_count FROM cs_jobs
WHERE end_stamp IS NULL;

    IF a_running_job_count > 0 THEN
        RAISE EXCEPTION 'Unable to create a new job: a job is
currently running'; (note 1)
    END IF;

    DELETE FROM cs_active_job;
    INSERT INTO cs_active_job(job_id) VALUES (v_job_id);

    BEGIN
        INSERT INTO cs_jobs (job_id, start_stamp) VALUES
(v_job_id, now());
    EXCEPTION
        WHEN unique_violation THEN  (note 2)
            -- don't worry if it already exists
    END;
END;
$$ LANGUAGE plpgsql;
```

Note 1:

> The syntax of RAISE is considerably different from Oracle's similar statement.

Note 2:

> The exception names supported by PL/pgSQL are different from Oracle's. The set of built-in exception names is much larger (see Volume 1, Appendix A *PostgreSQL Error Codes*). There is not currently a way to declare user-defined exception names.

The main functional difference between this procedure and the Oracle equivalent is that the exclusive lock on the cs_jobs table will be held until the calling transaction completes. Also, if the caller later aborts (for example due to an error), the effects of this procedure will be rolled back.

9.11.2 Other Things to Watch For

This section explains a few other things to watch for when porting Oracle PL/SQL functions to PostgreSQL.

9.11.2.1 Implicit Rollback after Exceptions

In PL/pgSQL, when an exception is caught by an EXCEPTION clause, all database changes since the block's BEGIN are automatically rolled back. That is, the behavior is equivalent to what you'd get in Oracle with

```
BEGIN
    SAVEPOINT s1;
    ... code here ...
EXCEPTION
    WHEN ... THEN
        ROLLBACK TO s1;
        ... code here ...
    WHEN ... THEN
        ROLLBACK TO s1;
        ... code here ...
END;
```

If you are translating an Oracle procedure that uses SAVEPOINT and ROLLBACK TO in this style, your task is easy: just omit the SAVEPOINT and ROLLBACK TO. If you have a procedure that uses SAVEPOINT and ROLLBACK TO in a different way then some actual thought will be required.

9.11.2.2 EXECUTE

The PL/pgSQL version of EXECUTE works similarly to the PL/SQL version, but you have to remember to use quote_literal and quote_ident as described in Section 9.6.5 *Executing Dynamic Commands*, page 292. Constructs of the type EXECUTE 'SELECT * FROM $1'; will not work reliably unless you use these functions.

9.11.2.3 Optimizing PL/pgSQL Functions

PostgreSQL gives you two function creation modifiers to optimize execution: "volatility" (whether the function always returns the same result when given the same arguments) and "strictness" (whether the function returns null if any argument is null). Consult the CREATE FUNCTION reference page for details.

When making use of these optimization attributes, your CREATE FUNCTION statement might look something like this:

```
CREATE FUNCTION foo(...) RETURNS integer AS $$
...
$$ LANGUAGE plpgsql STRICT IMMUTABLE;
```

9.11.3 Appendix

This section contains the code for a set of Oracle-compatible instr functions that you can use to simplify your porting efforts.

```
--
-- instr functions that mimic Oracle's counterpart
-- Syntax: instr(string1, string2, [n], [m]) where []
-- denotes optional parameters.
--
-- Searches string1 beginning at the nth character for
-- the mth occurrence of string2. If n is negative,
-- search backwards. If m is not passed, assume 1
-- (search starts at first character).
--


CREATE FUNCTION instr(varchar, varchar) RETURNS integer AS $$
DECLARE
    pos integer;
BEGIN
    pos:= instr($1, $2, 1);
    RETURN pos;
END;
$$ LANGUAGE plpgsql STRICT IMMUTABLE;


CREATE FUNCTION instr(string varchar, string_to_search
 varchar, beg_index integer)
RETURNS integer AS $$
DECLARE
    pos integer NOT NULL DEFAULT 0;
    temp_str varchar;
    beg integer;
    length integer;
    ss_length integer;
BEGIN
    IF beg_index > 0 THEN
        temp_str := substring(string FROM beg_index);
        pos := position(string_to_search IN temp_str);

        IF pos = 0 THEN
            RETURN 0;
        ELSE
            RETURN pos + beg_index - 1;
        END IF;
    ELSE
        ss_length := char_length(string_to_search);
        length := char_length(string);
        beg := length + beg_index - ss_length + 2;
```

```
        WHILE beg > 0 LOOP
            temp_str := substring(string FROM beg FOR ss_length);
            pos := position(string_to_search IN temp_str);

            IF pos > 0 THEN
                RETURN beg;
            END IF;

            beg := beg - 1;
        END LOOP;

        RETURN 0;
    END IF;
END;
$$ LANGUAGE plpgsql STRICT IMMUTABLE;


CREATE FUNCTION instr(string varchar, string_to_search varchar,
                      beg_index integer, occur_index integer)
RETURNS integer AS $$
DECLARE
    pos integer NOT NULL DEFAULT 0;
    occur_number integer NOT NULL DEFAULT 0;
    temp_str varchar;
    beg integer;
    i integer;
    length integer;
    ss_length integer;
BEGIN
    IF beg_index > 0 THEN
        beg := beg_index;
        temp_str := substring(string FROM beg_index);

        FOR i IN 1..occur_index LOOP
            pos := position(string_to_search IN temp_str);

            IF i = 1 THEN
                beg := beg + pos - 1;
            ELSE
                beg := beg + pos;
            END IF;

            temp_str := substring(string FROM beg + 1);
        END LOOP;

        IF pos = 0 THEN
            RETURN 0;
        ELSE
```

```
                    RETURN beg;
                END IF;
        ELSE
            ss_length := char_length(string_to_search);
            length := char_length(string);
            beg := length + beg_index - ss_length + 2;

            WHILE beg > 0 LOOP
                temp_str := substring(string FROM beg FOR ss_length);
                pos := position(string_to_search IN temp_str);

                IF pos > 0 THEN
                    occur_number := occur_number + 1;

                    IF occur_number = occur_index THEN
                        RETURN beg;
                    END IF;
                END IF;

                beg := beg - 1;
            END LOOP;

            RETURN 0;
        END IF;
END;
$$ LANGUAGE plpgsql STRICT IMMUTABLE;
```

10 PL/Tcl - Tcl Procedural Language

PL/Tcl is a loadable procedural language for the PostgreSQL database system that enables the Tcl language[1] to be used to write functions and trigger procedures.

10.1 Overview

PL/Tcl offers most of the capabilities a function writer has in the C language, with a few restrictions, and with the addition of the powerful string processing libraries that are available for Tcl.

One compelling *good* restriction is that everything is executed from within the safety of the context of a Tcl interpreter. In addition to the limited command set of safe Tcl, only a few commands are available to access the database via SPI and to raise messages via elog(). PL/Tcl provides no way to access internals of the database server or to gain OS-level access under the permissions of the PostgreSQL server process, as a C function can do. Thus, unprivileged database users may be trusted to use this language; it does not give them unlimited authority.

The other notable implementation restriction is that Tcl functions may not be used to create input/output functions for new data types.

Sometimes it is desirable to write Tcl functions that are not restricted to safe Tcl. For example, one might want a Tcl function that sends email. To handle these cases, there is a variant of PL/Tcl called PL/TclU (for untrusted Tcl). This is the exact same language except that a full Tcl interpreter is used. *If PL/TclU is used, it must be installed as an untrusted procedural language* so that only database superusers can create functions in it. The writer of a PL/TclU function must take care that the function cannot be used to do anything unwanted, since it will be able to do anything that could be done by a user logged in as the database administrator.

The shared object code for the PL/Tcl and PL/TclU call handlers is automatically built and installed in the PostgreSQL library directory if Tcl support is specified in the configuration step of the installation procedure. To install PL/Tcl and/or PL/TclU in a particular database, use the createlang program, for example createlang pltcl *dbname* or createlang pltclu *dbname*.

---

[1] http://www.tcl.tk/

10.2 PL/Tcl Functions and Arguments

To create a function in the PL/Tcl language, use the standard CREATE
FUNCTION syntax:

```
CREATE FUNCTION funcname (argument-types) RETURNS return-type
AS $$
    # PL/Tcl function body
$$ LANGUAGE pltcl;
```

PL/TclU is the same, except that the language has to be specified as pltclu.

The body of the function is simply a piece of Tcl script. When the function
is called, the argument values are passed as variables $1 ... $n to the Tcl
script. The result is returned from the Tcl code in the usual way, with a return
statement.

For example, a function returning the greater of two integer values could be
defined as:

```
CREATE FUNCTION tcl_max(integer, integer) RETURNS integer AS $$
    if {$1 > $2} {return $1}
    return $2
$$ LANGUAGE pltcl STRICT;
```

Note the clause STRICT, which saves us from having to think about null input
values: if a null value is passed, the function will not be called at all, but will
just return a null result automatically.

In a nonstrict function, if the actual value of an argument is null, the corresponding $n variable will be set to an empty string. To detect whether a
particular argument is null, use the function argisnull. For example, suppose
that we wanted tcl_max with one null and one nonnull argument to return the
nonnull argument, rather than null:

```
CREATE FUNCTION tcl_max(integer, integer) RETURNS integer AS $$
    if {[argisnull 1]} {
        if {[argisnull 2]} { return_null }
        return $2
    }
    if {[argisnull 2]} { return $1 }
    if {$1 > $2} {return $1}
    return $2
$$ LANGUAGE pltcl;
```

As shown above, to return a null value from a PL/Tcl function, execute
return_null. This can be done whether the function is strict or not.

Composite-type arguments are passed to the function as Tcl arrays. The
element names of the array are the attribute names of the composite type. If
an attribute in the passed row has the null value, it will not appear in the array.
Here is an example:

```
CREATE TABLE employee (
    name text,
    salary integer,
    age integer
);
```

```
CREATE FUNCTION overpaid(employee) RETURNS boolean AS $$
    if {200000.0 < $1(salary)} {
        return "t"
    }
    if {$1(age) < 30 && 100000.0 < $1(salary)} {
        return "t"
    }
    return "f"
$$ LANGUAGE pltcl;
```

There is currently no support for returning a composite-type result value, nor for returning sets.

PL/Tcl does not currently have full support for domain types: it treats a domain the same as the underlying scalar type. This means that constraints associated with the domain will not be enforced. This is not an issue for function arguments, but it is a hazard if you declare a PL/Tcl function as returning a domain type.

10.3 Data Values in PL/Tcl

The argument values supplied to a PL/Tcl function's code are simply the input arguments converted to text form (just as if they had been displayed by a SELECT statement). Conversely, the return command will accept any string that is an acceptable input format for the function's declared return type. So, within the PL/Tcl function, all values are just text strings.

10.4 Global Data in PL/Tcl

Sometimes it is useful to have some global data that is held between two calls to a function or is shared between different functions. This is easily done since all PL/Tcl functions executed in one session share the same safe Tcl interpreter. So, any global Tcl variable is accessible to all PL/Tcl function calls and will persist for the duration of the SQL session. (Note that PL/TclU functions likewise share global data, but they are in a different Tcl interpreter and cannot communicate with PL/Tcl functions.)

To help protect PL/Tcl functions from unintentionally interfering with each other, a global array is made available to each function via the upvar command. The global name of this variable is the function's internal name, and the local name is GD. It is recommended that GD be used for persistent private data of a function. Use regular Tcl global variables only for values that you specifically intend to be shared among multiple functions.

An example of using GD appears in the spi_execp example below.

10.5 Database Access from PL/Tcl

The following commands are available to access the database from the body of a PL/Tcl function:

spi_exec [-count n] [-array name] command [loop-body]

   Executes an SQL command given as a string. An error in the command causes an error to be raised. Otherwise, the return value of spi_exec is the number of rows processed (selected, inserted, updated, or deleted) by the command, or zero if the command is a utility statement. In addition, if the command is a SELECT statement, the values of the selected columns are placed in Tcl variables as described below.

   The optional -count value tells spi_exec the maximum number of rows to process in the command. The effect of this is comparable to setting up a query as a cursor and then saying FETCH n.

   If the command is a SELECT statement, the values of the result columns are placed into Tcl variables named after the columns. If the -array option is given, the column values are instead stored into the named associative array, with the column names used as array indexes.

   If the command is a SELECT statement and no *loop-body* script is given, then only the first row of results are stored into Tcl variables; remaining rows, if any, are ignored. No storing occurs if the query returns no rows. (This case can be detected by checking the result of spi_exec.) For example,

        spi_exec "SELECT count(*) AS cnt FROM pg_proc"

   will set the Tcl variable $cnt to the number of rows in the pg_proc system catalog.

   If the optional *loop-body* argument is given, it is a piece of Tcl script that is executed once for each row in the query result. (*loop-body* is ignored if the given command is not a SELECT.) The values of the current row's columns are stored into Tcl variables before each iteration. For example,

        spi_exec -array C "SELECT * FROM pg_class" {
            elog DEBUG "have table $C(relname)"
        }

   will print a log message for every row of pg_class. This feature works similarly to other Tcl looping constructs; in particular continue and break work in the usual way inside the loop body.

   If a column of a query result is null, the target variable for it is "unset" rather than being set.

spi_prepare *query typelist*

   Prepares and saves a query plan for later execution. The saved plan will be retained for the life of the current session.

   The query may use parameters, that is, placeholders for values to be supplied whenever the plan is actually executed. In the query string, refer to parameters by the symbols $1 ... $n. If the query uses parameters, the names of the parameter types must be given as a Tcl list. (Write an empty list for *typelist* if no parameters are used.) Presently, the parameter types must be identified by the internal type names shown in the system table pg_type; for example int4 not integer.

The return value from spi_prepare is a query ID to be used in subsequent calls to spi_execp. See spi_execp for an example.

spi_execp [-count *n*] [-array *name*] [-nulls *string*] *queryid*
[*value-list*] [*loop-body*]

Executes a query previously prepared with spi_prepare. *queryid* is the ID returned by spi_prepare. If the query references parameters, a *value-list* must be supplied. This is a Tcl list of actual values for the parameters. The list must be the same length as the parameter type list previously given to spi_prepare. Omit *value-list* if the query has no parameters.

The optional value for -nulls is a string of spaces and 'n' characters telling spi_execp which of the parameters are null values. If given, it must have exactly the same length as the *value-list*. If it is not given, all the parameter values are nonnull.

Except for the way in which the query and its parameters are specified, spi_execp works just like spi_exec. The -count, -array, and *loop-body* options are the same, and so is the result value.

Here's an example of a PL/Tcl function using a prepared plan:

```
CREATE FUNCTION t1_count(integer, integer) RETURNS
  integer AS $$
    if {![ info exists GD(plan) ]} {
        # prepare the saved plan on the first call
        set GD(plan) [ spi_prepare \
                "SELECT count(*) AS cnt FROM t1 WHERE num
>= \$1 AND num <= \$2" \
                [ list int4 int4 ] ]
    }
    spi_execp -count 1 $GD(plan) [ list $1 $2 ]
    return $cnt
$$ LANGUAGE pltcl;
```

We need backslashes inside the query string given to spi_prepare to ensure that the $*n* markers will be passed through to spi_prepare as-is, and not replaced by Tcl variable substitution.

spi_lastoid

Returns the OID of the row inserted by the last spi_exec or spi_execp, if the command was a single-row INSERT and the modified table contained OIDs. (If not, you get zero.)

quote *string*

Doubles all occurrences of single quote and backslash characters in the given string. This may be used to safely quote strings that are to be inserted into SQL commands given to spi_exec or spi_prepare. For example, think about an SQL command string like

```
"SELECT '$val' AS ret"
```

where the Tcl variable val actually contains doesn't. This would result in the final command string

```
SELECT 'doesn't' AS ret
```

which would cause a parse error during spi_exec or spi_prepare. To work properly, the submitted command should contain

```
SELECT 'doesn''t' AS ret
```

which can be formed in PL/Tcl using

```
"SELECT '[ quote $val ]' AS ret"
```

One advantage of spi_execp is that you don't have to quote parameter values like this, since the parameters are never parsed as part of an SQL command string.

elog *level msg*

Emits a log or error message. Possible levels are DEBUG, LOG, INFO, NOTICE, WARNING, ERROR, and FATAL. ERROR raises an error condition; if this is not trapped by the surrounding Tcl code, the error propagates out to the calling query, causing the current transaction or subtransaction to be aborted. This is effectively the same as the Tcl error command. FATAL aborts the transaction and causes the current session to shut down. (There is probably no good reason to use this error level in PL/Tcl functions, but it's provided for completeness.) The other levels only generate messages of different priority levels. Whether messages of a particular priority are reported to the client, written to the server log, or both is controlled by the log_min_messages and client_min_messages configuration variables. See Volume 3, Chapter 4 *Server Configuration* for more information.

10.6 Trigger Procedures in PL/Tcl

Trigger procedures can be written in PL/Tcl. PostgreSQL requires that a procedure that is to be called as a trigger must be declared as a function with no arguments and a return type of trigger.

The information from the trigger manager is passed to the procedure body in the following variables:

$TG_name

The name of the trigger from the CREATE TRIGGER statement.

$TG_relid

The object ID of the table that caused the trigger procedure to be invoked.

$TG_table_name

The name of the table that caused the trigger procedure to be invoked.

$TG_table_schema

The schema of the table that caused the trigger procedure to be invoked.

$TG_relatts
: A Tcl list of the table column names, prefixed with an empty list element. So looking up a column name in the list with Tcl's lsearch command returns the element's number starting with 1 for the first column, the same way the columns are customarily numbered in PostgreSQL. (Empty list elements also appear in the positions of columns that have been dropped, so that the attribute numbering is correct for columns to their right.)

$TG_when
: The string BEFORE or AFTER depending on the type of trigger call.

$TG_level
: The string ROW or STATEMENT depending on the type of trigger call.

$TG_op
: The string INSERT, UPDATE, or DELETE depending on the type of trigger call.

$NEW
: An associative array containing the values of the new table row for INSERT or UPDATE actions, or empty for DELETE. The array is indexed by column name. Columns that are null will not appear in the array.

$OLD
: An associative array containing the values of the old table row for UPDATE or DELETE actions, or empty for INSERT. The array is indexed by column name. Columns that are null will not appear in the array.

$args
: A Tcl list of the arguments to the procedure as given in the CREATE TRIGGER statement. These arguments are also accessible as $1 ... $n in the procedure body.

The return value from a trigger procedure can be one of the strings OK or SKIP, or a list as returned by the array get Tcl command. If the return value is OK, the operation (INSERT/UPDATE/DELETE) that fired the trigger will proceed normally. SKIP tells the trigger manager to silently suppress the operation for this row. If a list is returned, it tells PL/Tcl to return a modified row to the trigger manager that will be inserted instead of the one given in $NEW. (This works for INSERT and UPDATE only.) Needless to say that all this is only meaningful when the trigger is BEFORE and FOR EACH ROW; otherwise the return value is ignored.

Here's a little example trigger procedure that forces an integer value in a table to keep track of the number of updates that are performed on the row. For new rows inserted, the value is initialized to 0 and then incremented on every update operation.

```
CREATE FUNCTION trigfunc_modcount() RETURNS trigger AS $$
    switch $TG_op {
        INSERT {
            set NEW($1) 0
        }
```

```
            UPDATE {
                set NEW($1) $OLD($1)
                incr NEW($1)
            }
            default {
                return OK
            }
        }
        return [array get NEW]
    $$ LANGUAGE pltcl;

    CREATE TABLE mytab (num integer, description text, modcnt
      integer);

    CREATE TRIGGER trig_mytab_modcount BEFORE INSERT OR UPDATE ON
      mytab
          FOR EACH ROW EXECUTE PROCEDURE trigfunc_modcount('modcnt');
```

Notice that the trigger procedure itself does not know the column name; that's supplied from the trigger arguments. This lets the trigger procedure be reused with different tables.

10.7 Modules and the unknown command

PL/Tcl has support for autoloading Tcl code when used. It recognizes a special table, pltcl_modules, which is presumed to contain modules of Tcl code. If this table exists, the module unknown is fetched from the table and loaded into the Tcl interpreter immediately after creating the interpreter.

While the unknown module could actually contain any initialization script you need, it normally defines a Tcl unknown procedure that is invoked whenever Tcl does not recognize an invoked procedure name. PL/Tcl's standard version of this procedure tries to find a module in pltcl_modules that will define the required procedure. If one is found, it is loaded into the interpreter, and then execution is allowed to proceed with the originally attempted procedure call. A secondary table pltcl_modfuncs provides an index of which functions are defined by which modules, so that the lookup is reasonably quick.

The PostgreSQL distribution includes support scripts to maintain these tables: pltcl_loadmod, pltcl_listmod, pltcl_delmod, as well as source for the standard unknown module in 'share/unknown.pltcl'. This module must be loaded into each database initially to support the autoloading mechanism.

The tables pltcl_modules and pltcl_modfuncs must be readable by all, but it is wise to make them owned and writable only by the database administrator.

10.8 Tcl Procedure Names

In PostgreSQL, one and the same function name can be used for different functions as long as the number of arguments or their types differ. Tcl, however, requires all procedure names to be distinct. PL/Tcl deals with this by making the internal Tcl procedure names contain the object ID of the function from the system table pg_proc as part of their name. Thus, PostgreSQL functions with the same name and different argument types will be different Tcl procedures, too. This is not normally a concern for a PL/Tcl programmer, but it might be visible when debugging.

11 PL/Perl - Perl Procedural Language

PL/Perl is a loadable procedural language that enables you to write Post-greSQL functions in the Perl programming language[1].

The usual advantage to using PL/Perl is that this allows use, within stored functions, of the manyfold "string munging" operators and functions available for Perl. Parsing complex strings may be easier using Perl than it is with the string functions and control structures provided in PL/pgSQL.

To install PL/Perl in a particular database, use `createlang plperl` *dbname*.

> **Tip:** If a language is installed into `template1`, all subsequently created databases will have the language installed automatically.

> **Note:** Users of source packages must specially enable the build of PL/Perl during the installation process. (Refer to Volume 3, Section 1.1 *Short Version* for more information.) Users of binary packages might find PL/Perl in a separate subpackage.

11.1 PL/Perl Functions and Arguments

To create a function in the PL/Perl language, use the standard `CREATE FUNCTION` syntax:

```
CREATE FUNCTION funcname (argument-types) RETURNS return-type
AS $$
    # PL/Perl function body
$$ LANGUAGE plperl;
```

The body of the function is ordinary Perl code. In fact, the PL/Perl glue code wraps it inside a Perl subroutine. A PL/Perl function must always return a scalar value. You can return more complex structures (arrays, records, and sets) by returning a reference, as discussed below. Never return a list.

> **Note:** The use of named nested subroutines is dangerous in Perl, especially if they refer to lexical variables in the enclosing scope. Because a PL/Perl function is wrapped in a subroutine, any named subroutine you create will be nested. In general, it is far safer to create anonymous subroutines which you call via a coderef. See the `perldiag` man page for more details.

The syntax of the `CREATE FUNCTION` command requires the function body to be written as a string constant. It is usually most convenient to use dollar quoting (see Volume 1, Section 2.1.2.2 *Dollar-Quoted String Constants*) for the string constant. If you choose to use escape string syntax E' ', you must double the single quote marks (') and backslashes (\) used in the body of the function (see Volume 1, Section 2.1.2.1 *String Constants*).

Arguments and results are handled as in any other Perl subroutine: arguments are passed in @_, and a result value is returned with `return` or as the last expression evaluated in the function.

---

[1] http://www.perl.com

For example, a function returning the greater of two integer values could be defined as:

```
CREATE FUNCTION perl_max (integer, integer) RETURNS integer AS $$
    if ($_[0] > $_[1]) { return $_[0]; }
    return $_[1];
$$ LANGUAGE plperl;
```

If an SQL null value is passed to a function, the argument value will appear as "undefined" in Perl. The above function definition will not behave very nicely with null inputs (in fact, it will act as though they are zeroes). We could add STRICT to the function definition to make PostgreSQL do something more reasonable: if a null value is passed, the function will not be called at all, but will just return a null result automatically. Alternatively, we could check for undefined inputs in the function body. For example, suppose that we wanted perl_max with one null and one nonnull argument to return the nonnull argument, rather than a null value:

```
CREATE FUNCTION perl_max (integer, integer) RETURNS integer AS $$
    my ($x,$y) = @_;
    if (! defined $x) {
        if (! defined $y) { return undef; }
        return $y;
    }
    if (! defined $y) { return $x; }
    if ($x > $y) { return $x; }
    return $y;
$$ LANGUAGE plperl;
```

As shown above, to return an SQL null value from a PL/Perl function, return an undefined value. This can be done whether the function is strict or not.

Perl can return PostgreSQL arrays as references to Perl arrays. Here is an example:

```
CREATE OR REPLACE function returns_array()
RETURNS text[][] AS $$
    return [['a"b','c,d'],['e\\f','g']];
$$ LANGUAGE plperl;

select returns_array();
```

Composite-type arguments are passed to the function as references to hashes. The keys of the hash are the attribute names of the composite type. Here is an example:

```
CREATE TABLE employee (
    name text,
    basesalary integer,
    bonus integer
);

CREATE FUNCTION empcomp(employee) RETURNS integer AS $$
    my ($emp) = @_;
    return $emp->{basesalary} + $emp->{bonus};
```

```
$$ LANGUAGE plperl;
```

```
SELECT name, empcomp(employee.*) FROM employee;
```
A PL/Perl function can return a composite-type result using the same approach: return a reference to a hash that has the required attributes. For example,

```
CREATE TYPE testrowperl AS (f1 integer, f2 text, f3 text);
```

```
CREATE OR REPLACE FUNCTION perl_row() RETURNS testrowperl AS $$
    return {f2 => 'hello', f1 => 1, f3 => 'world'};
$$ LANGUAGE plperl;
```

```
SELECT * FROM perl_row();
```
Any columns in the declared result data type that are not present in the hash will be returned as null values.

PL/Perl functions can also return sets of either scalar or composite types. Usually you'll want to return rows one at a time, both to speed up startup time and to keep from queueing up the entire result set in memory. You can do this with return_next as illustrated below. Note that after the last return_next, you must put either return or (better) return undef.

```
CREATE OR REPLACE FUNCTION perl_set_int(int)
RETURNS SETOF INTEGER AS $$
    foreach (0..$_[0]) {
        return_next($_);
    }
    return undef;
$$ LANGUAGE plperl;
```

```
SELECT * FROM perl_set_int(5);
```

```
CREATE OR REPLACE FUNCTION perl_set()
RETURNS SETOF testrowperl AS $$
    return_next({ f1 => 1, f2 => 'Hello', f3 => 'World' });
    return_next({ f1 => 2, f2 => 'Hello', f3 => 'PostgreSQL' });
    return_next({ f1 => 3, f2 => 'Hello', f3 => 'PL/Perl' });
    return undef;
$$ LANGUAGE plperl;
```
For small result sets, you can return a reference to an array that contains either scalars, references to arrays, or references to hashes for simple types, array types, and composite types, respectively. Here are some simple examples of returning the entire result set as an array reference:

```
CREATE OR REPLACE FUNCTION perl_set_int(int) RETURNS SETOF
  INTEGER AS $$
    return [0..$_[0]];
$$ LANGUAGE plperl;
```

```
SELECT * FROM perl_set_int(5);
```

```
CREATE OR REPLACE FUNCTION perl_set() RETURNS SETOF
testrowperl AS $$
    return [
        { f1 => 1, f2 => 'Hello', f3 => 'World' },
        { f1 => 2, f2 => 'Hello', f3 => 'PostgreSQL' },
        { f1 => 3, f2 => 'Hello', f3 => 'PL/Perl' }
    ];
$$ LANGUAGE plperl;
```

```
SELECT * FROM perl_set();
```

If you wish to use the strict pragma with your code, the easiest way to do so is to SET plperl.use_strict to true. This parameter affects subsequent compilations of PL/Perl functions, but not functions already compiled in the current session. To set the parameter before PL/Perl has been loaded, it is necessary to have added "plperl" to the custom_variable_classes list in 'postgresql.conf'.

Another way to use the strict pragma is to put

```
use strict;
```

in the function body. But this only works in PL/PerlU functions, since use is not a trusted operation. In PL/Perl functions you can instead do

```
BEGIN { strict->import(); }
```

11.2 Database Access from PL/Perl

Access to the database itself from your Perl function can be done via the function spi_exec_query described below, or via an experimental module DBD::PgSPI[2] (also available at CPAN mirror sites[3]). This module makes available a DBI-compliant database-handle named $pg_dbh that can be used to perform queries with normal DBI syntax.

PL/Perl provides additional Perl commands:

```
spi_exec_query(query [, max-rows])
spi_query(command)
spi_fetchrow(cursor)
spi_prepare(command, argument types)
spi_exec_prepared(plan)
spi_query_prepared(plan [, attributes], arguments)
spi_cursor_close(cursor)
spi_freeplan(plan)
```

spi_exec_query executes an SQL command and returns the entire row set as a reference to an array of hash references. *You should only use this command when you know that the result set will be relatively small.* Here is an example of a query (SELECT command) with the optional maximum number of rows:

---

[2] http://www.cpan.org/modules/by-module/DBD/APILOS/

[3] http://www.cpan.org/SITES.html

```
$rv = spi_exec_query('SELECT * FROM my_table', 5);
```

This returns up to 5 rows from the table my_table. If my_table has a
column my_column, you can get that value from row $i of the result like
this:

```
$foo = $rv->{rows}[$i]->{my_column};
```

The total number of rows returned from a SELECT query can be accessed
like this:

```
$nrows = $rv->{processed}
```

Here is an example using a different command type:

```
$query = "INSERT INTO my_table VALUES (1, 'test')";
$rv = spi_exec_query($query);
```

You can then access the command status (e.g., SPI_OK_INSERT) like this:

```
$res = $rv->{status};
```

To get the number of rows affected, do:

```
$nrows = $rv->{processed};
```

Here is a complete example:

```
CREATE TABLE test (
    i int,
    v varchar
);

INSERT INTO test (i, v) VALUES (1, 'first line');
INSERT INTO test (i, v) VALUES (2, 'second line');
INSERT INTO test (i, v) VALUES (3, 'third line');
INSERT INTO test (i, v) VALUES (4, 'immortal');

CREATE OR REPLACE FUNCTION test_munge() RETURNS SETOF
  test AS $$
    my $rv = spi_exec_query('select i, v from test;');
    my $status = $rv->{status};
    my $nrows = $rv->{processed};
    foreach my $rn (0 .. $nrows - 1) {
        my $row = $rv->{rows}[$rn];
        $row->{i} += 200 if defined($row->{i});
        $row->{v} =~ tr/A-Za-z/a-zA-Z/ if
  (defined($row->{v}));
        return_next($row);
    }
    return undef;
$$ LANGUAGE plperl;

SELECT * FROM test_munge();
```

spi_query and spi_fetchrow work together as a pair for row sets which
may be large, or for cases where you wish to return rows as they arrive.

spi_fetchrow works *only* with spi_query. The following example illustrates how you use them together:

```
CREATE TYPE foo_type AS (the_num INTEGER, the_text TEXT);

CREATE OR REPLACE FUNCTION lotsa_md5 (INTEGER) RETURNS
 SETOF foo_type AS $$
    use Digest::MD5 qw(md5_hex);
    my $file = '/usr/share/dict/words';
    my $t = localtime;
    elog(NOTICE, "opening file $file at $t" );
    open my $fh, '<', $file # ooh, it's a file access!
        or elog(ERROR, "can't open $file for reading: $!");
    my @words = <$fh>;
    close $fh;
    $t = localtime;
    elog(NOTICE, "closed file $file at $t");
    chomp(@words);
    my $row;
    my $sth = spi_query("SELECT * FROM generate_series(1,
$_[0]) AS b(a)");
    while (defined ($row = spi_fetchrow($sth))) {
        return_next({
            the_num => $row->{a},
            the_text => md5_hex($words[rand @words])
        });
    }
    return;
$$ LANGUAGE plperlu;

SELECT * from lotsa_md5(500);
```

spi_prepare, spi_query_prepared, spi_exec_prepared, and spi_freeplan implement the same functionality but for prepared queries. Once a query plan is prepared by a call to spi_prepare, the plan can be used instead of the string query, either in spi_exec_prepared, where the result is the same as returned by spi_exec_query, or in spi_query_prepared which returns a cursor exactly as spi_query does, which can be later passed to spi_fetchrow.

The advantage of prepared queries is that is it possible to use one prepared plan for more than one query execution. After the plan is not needed anymore, it may be freed with spi_freeplan:

```
CREATE OR REPLACE FUNCTION init() RETURNS INTEGER AS $$
        $_SHARED{my_plan} = spi_prepare( 'SELECT (now() +
    $1)::date AS now', 'INTERVAL');
$$ LANGUAGE plperl;

CREATE OR REPLACE FUNCTION add_time( INTERVAL ) RETURNS
 TEXT AS $$
```

```
            return spi_exec_prepared(
                $_SHARED{my_plan},
                $_[0],
            )->{rows}->[0]->{now};
    $$ LANGUAGE plperl;

    CREATE OR REPLACE FUNCTION done() RETURNS INTEGER AS $$
            spi_freeplan( $_SHARED{my_plan});
            undef $_SHARED{my_plan};
    $$ LANGUAGE plperl;

    SELECT init();
    SELECT add_time('1 day'), add_time('2 days'), add_time('3
     days');
    SELECT done();

        add_time  |  add_time  |  add_time
    ------------+------------+------------
     2005-12-10 | 2005-12-11 | 2005-12-12
```

Note that the parameter subscript in spi_prepare is defined via $1, $2, $3, etc, so avoid declaring query strings in double quotes that might easily lead to hard-to-catch bugs.

Normally, spi_fetchrow should be repeated until it returns undef, indicating that there are no more rows to read. The cursor is automatically freed when spi_fetchrow returns undef. If you do not wish to read all the rows, instead call spi_cursor_close to free the cursor. Failure to do so will result in memory leaks.

elog(*level*, *msg*)

Emit a log or error message. Possible levels are DEBUG, LOG, INFO, NOTICE, WARNING, and ERROR. ERROR raises an error condition; if this is not trapped by the surrounding Perl code, the error propagates out to the calling query, causing the current transaction or subtransaction to be aborted. This is effectively the same as the Perl die command. The other levels only generate messages of different priority levels. Whether messages of a particular priority are reported to the client, written to the server log, or both is controlled by the log_min_messages and client_min_messages configuration variables. See Volume 3, Chapter 4 *Server Configuration* for more information.

11.3 Data Values in PL/Perl

The argument values supplied to a PL/Perl function's code are simply the input arguments converted to text form (just as if they had been displayed by a SELECT statement). Conversely, the return command will accept any string that is an acceptable input format for the function's declared return type. So, within the PL/Perl function, all values are just text strings.

11.4 Global Values in PL/Perl

You can use the global hash %_SHARED to store data, including code references, between function calls for the lifetime of the current session.

Here is a simple example for shared data:

```
CREATE OR REPLACE FUNCTION set_var(name text, val text)
RETURNS text AS $$
    if ($_SHARED{$_[0]} = $_[1]) {
        return 'ok';
    } else {
        return "can't set shared variable $_[0] to $_[1]";
    }
$$ LANGUAGE plperl;

CREATE OR REPLACE FUNCTION get_var(name text) RETURNS text AS $$
    return $_SHARED{$_[0]};
$$ LANGUAGE plperl;

SELECT set_var('sample', 'Hello, PL/Perl!  How's tricks?');
SELECT get_var('sample');
```

Here is a slightly more complicated example using a code reference:

```
CREATE OR REPLACE FUNCTION myfuncs() RETURNS void AS $$
    $_SHARED{myquote} = sub {
        my $arg = shift;
        $arg =~ s/(['\\])/\\$1/g;
        return "'$arg'";
    };
$$ LANGUAGE plperl;

SELECT myfuncs(); /* initializes the function */

/* Set up a function that uses the quote function */

CREATE OR REPLACE FUNCTION use_quote(TEXT) RETURNS text AS $$
    my $text_to_quote = shift;
    my $qfunc = $_SHARED{myquote};
    return &$qfunc($text_to_quote);
$$ LANGUAGE plperl;
```

(You could have replaced the above with the one-liner return $_SHARED{myquote}->($_[0]); at the expense of readability.)

11.5 Trusted and Untrusted PL/Perl

Normally, PL/Perl is installed as a "trusted" programming language named `plperl`. In this setup, certain Perl operations are disabled to preserve security. In general, the operations that are restricted are those that interact with the environment. This includes file handle operations, `require`, and use (for external modules). There is no way to access internals of the database server process or to gain OS-level access with the permissions of the server process, as a C function can do. Thus, any unprivileged database user may be permitted to use this language.

Here is an example of a function that will not work because file system operations are not allowed for security reasons:

```
CREATE FUNCTION badfunc() RETURNS integer AS $$
    my $tmpfile = "/tmp/badfile";
    open my $fh, '>', $tmpfile
        or elog(ERROR, qq{could not open the file "$tmpfile":
$!});
    print $fh "Testing writing to a file\n";
    close $fh or elog(ERROR, qq{could not close the file
"$tmpfile": $!});
    return 1;
$$ LANGUAGE plperl;
```

The creation of this function will fail as its use of a forbidden operation will be caught by the validator.

Sometimes it is desirable to write Perl functions that are not restricted. For example, one might want a Perl function that sends mail. To handle these cases, PL/Perl can also be installed as an "untrusted" language (usually called PL/PerlU). In this case the full Perl language is available. If the `createlang` program is used to install the language, the language name `plperlu` will select the untrusted PL/Perl variant.

The writer of a PL/PerlU function must take care that the function cannot be used to do anything unwanted, since it will be able to do anything that could be done by a user logged in as the database administrator. Note that the database system allows only database superusers to create functions in untrusted languages.

If the above function was created by a superuser using the language `plperlu`, execution would succeed.

Note: For security reasons, to stop a leak of privileged operations from PL/PerlU to PL/Perl, these two languages have to run in separate instances of the Perl interpreter. If your Perl installation has been appropriately compiled, this is not a problem. However, not all installations are compiled with the requisite flags. If PostgreSQL detects that this is the case then it will not start a second interpreter, but instead create an error. In consequence, in such an installation, you cannot use both PL/PerlU and PL/Perl in the same backend process. The remedy for this is to obtain a Perl installation created with the appropriate flags, namely either usemultiplicity or both usethreads and useithreads. For more details, see the perlembed manual page.

11.6 PL/Perl Triggers

PL/Perl can be used to write trigger functions. In a trigger function, the hash reference $_TD contains information about the current trigger event. $_TD is a global variable, which gets a separate local value for each invocation of the trigger. The fields of the $_TD hash reference are:

$_TD->{new}{foo}
    NEW value of column foo

$_TD->{old}{foo}
    OLD value of column foo

$_TD->{name}
    Name of the trigger being called

$_TD->{event}
    Trigger event: INSERT, UPDATE, DELETE, or UNKNOWN

$_TD->{when}
    When the trigger was called: BEFORE, AFTER, or UNKNOWN

$_TD->{level}
    The trigger level: ROW, STATEMENT, or UNKNOWN

$_TD->{relid}
    OID of the table on which the trigger fired

$_TD->{table_name}
    Name of the table on which the trigger fired

$_TD->{relname}
    Name of the table on which the trigger fired. This has been deprecated, and could be removed in a future release. Please use $_TD->{table_name} instead.

$_TD->{table_schema}
    Name of the schema in which the table on which the trigger fired, is

$_TD->{argc}
    Number of arguments of the trigger function

@{$_TD->{args}}
    Arguments of the trigger function. Does not exist if $_TD->{argc} is 0.

Triggers can return one of the following:

return;
    Execute the statement

"SKIP"
    Don't execute the statement

"MODIFY"
>Indicates that the NEW row was modified by the trigger function

Here is an example of a trigger function, illustrating some of the above:

```
CREATE TABLE test (
    i int,
    v varchar
);

CREATE OR REPLACE FUNCTION valid_id() RETURNS trigger AS $$
    if (($_TD->{new}{i} >= 100) || ($_TD->{new}{i} <= 0)) {
        return "SKIP";    # skip INSERT/UPDATE command
    } elsif ($_TD->{new}{v} ne "immortal") {
        $_TD->{new}{v} .= "(modified by trigger)";
        return "MODIFY";  # modify row and execute
  INSERT/UPDATE command
    } else {
        return;           # execute INSERT/UPDATE command
    }
$$ LANGUAGE plperl;

CREATE TRIGGER test_valid_id_trig
    BEFORE INSERT OR UPDATE ON test
    FOR EACH ROW EXECUTE PROCEDURE valid_id();
```

11.7 Limitations and Missing Features

The following features are currently missing from PL/Perl, but they would make welcome contributions.

- PL/Perl functions cannot call each other directly (because they are anonymous subroutines inside Perl).
- SPI is not yet fully implemented.
- If you are fetching very large data sets using spi_exec_query, you should be aware that these will all go into memory. You can avoid this by using spi_query/spi_fetchrow as illustrated earlier.

   A similar problem occurs if a set-returning function passes a large set of rows back to PostgreSQL via return. You can avoid this problem too by instead using return_next for each row returned, as shown previously.

12 PL/Python - Python Procedural Language

The PL/Python procedural language allows PostgreSQL functions to be written in the Python language[1].

To install PL/Python in a particular database, use `createlang plpythonu dbname`.

> **Tip:** If a language is installed into `template1`, all subsequently created databases will have the language installed automatically.

As of PostgreSQL 7.4, PL/Python is only available as an "untrusted" language (meaning it does not offer any way of restricting what users can do in it). It has therefore been renamed to plpythonu. The trusted variant plpython may become available again in future, if a new secure execution mechanism is developed in Python.

> **Note:** Users of source packages must specially enable the build of PL/Python during the installation process. (Refer to the installation instructions for more information.) Users of binary packages might find PL/Python in a separate subpackage.

12.1 PL/Python Functions

Functions in PL/Python are declared via the standard `CREATE FUNCTION` syntax:

```
CREATE FUNCTION funcname (argument-list)
  RETURNS return-type
AS $$
  # PL/Python function body
$$ LANGUAGE plpythonu;
```

The body of a function is simply a Python script. When the function is called, its arguments are passed as elements of the array `args[]`; named arguments are also passed as ordinary variables to the Python script. The result is returned from the Python code in the usual way, with `return` or `yield` (in case of a result-set statement).

For example, a function to return the greater of two integers can be defined as:

```
CREATE FUNCTION pymax (a integer, b integer)
  RETURNS integer
AS $$
  if a > b:
    return a
  return b
$$ LANGUAGE plpythonu;
```

---

[1] http://www.python.org

The Python code that is given as the body of the function definition is transformed into a Python function. For example, the above results in

```
def __plpython_procedure_pymax_23456():
  if a > b:
    return a
  return b
```

assuming that 23456 is the OID assigned to the function by PostgreSQL.

The PostgreSQL function parameters are available in the global args list. In the pymax example, args[0] contains whatever was passed in as the first argument and args[1] contains the second argument's value. Alternatively, one can use named parameters as shown in the example above. Use of named parameters is usually more readable.

If an SQL null value is passed to a function, the argument value will appear as None in Python. The above function definition will return the wrong answer for null inputs. We could add STRICT to the function definition to make PostgreSQL do something more reasonable: if a null value is passed, the function will not be called at all, but will just return a null result automatically. Alternatively, we could check for null inputs in the function body:

```
CREATE FUNCTION pymax (a integer, b integer)
  RETURNS integer
AS $$
  if (a is None) or (b is None):
    return None
  if a > b:
    return a
  return b
$$ LANGUAGE plpythonu;
```

As shown above, to return an SQL null value from a PL/Python function, return the value None. This can be done whether the function is strict or not.

Composite-type arguments are passed to the function as Python mappings. The element names of the mapping are the attribute names of the composite type. If an attribute in the passed row has the null value, it has the value None in the mapping. Here is an example:

```
CREATE TABLE employee (
  name text,
  salary integer,
  age integer
);

CREATE FUNCTION overpaid (e employee)
  RETURNS boolean
AS $$
  if e["salary"] > 200000:
    return True
  if (e["age"] < 30) and (e["salary"] > 100000):
    return True
  return False
```

```
$$ LANGUAGE plpythonu;
```

There are multiple ways to return row or composite types from a Python function. The following examples assume we have:

```
CREATE TYPE named_value AS (
    name    text,
    value   integer
);
```

A composite result can be returned as a:

Sequence type (a tuple or list, but not a set because it is not indexable)

Returned sequence objects must have the same number of items as the composite result type has fields. The item with index 0 is assigned to the first field of the composite type, 1 to the second and so on. For example:

```
CREATE FUNCTION make_pair (name text, value integer)
  RETURNS named_value
AS $$
  return [ name, value ]
  # or alternatively, as tuple: return ( name, value )
$$ LANGUAGE plpythonu;
```

To return a SQL null for any column, insert None at the corresponding position.

Mapping (dictionary)

The value for each result type column is retrieved from the mapping with the column name as key. Example:

```
CREATE FUNCTION make_pair (name text, value integer)
  RETURNS named_value
AS $$
  return { "name": name, "value": value }
$$ LANGUAGE plpythonu;
```

Any extra dictionary key/value pairs are ignored. Missing keys are treated as errors. To return a SQL null value for any column, insert None with the corresponding column name as the key.

Object (any object providing method __getattr__)

This works the same as a mapping. Example:

```
CREATE FUNCTION make_pair (name text, value integer)
  RETURNS named_value
AS $$
  class named_value:
    def __init__ (self, n, v):
      self.name = n
      self.value = v
  return named_value(name, value)

  # or simply
  class nv: pass
  nv.name = name
```

```
          nv.value = value
          return nv
       $$ LANGUAGE plpythonu;
```

If you do not provide a return value, Python returns the default None.
PL/Python translates Python's None into the SQL null value.

A PL/Python function can also return sets of scalar or composite types.
There are several ways to achieve this because the returned object is internally
turned into an iterator. The following examples assume we have composite type:

```
    CREATE TYPE greeting AS (
       how text,
       who text
    );
```

A set result can be returned from a:

Sequence type (tuple, list, set)

```
          CREATE FUNCTION greet (how text)
          RETURNS SETOF greeting
       AS $$
          # return tuple containing lists as composite types
          # all other combinations work also
          return ( [ how, "World" ], [ how, "PostgreSQL" ], [
          how, "PL/Python" ] )
       $$ LANGUAGE plpythonu;
```

Iterator (any object providing __iter__ and next methods)

```
          CREATE FUNCTION greet (how text)
          RETURNS SETOF greeting
       AS $$
          class producer:
            def __init__ (self, how, who):
              self.how = how
              self.who = who
              self.ndx = -1

            def __iter__ (self):
            return self

            def next (self):
              self.ndx += 1
              if self.ndx == len(self.who):
                raise StopIteration
              return ( self.how, self.who[self.ndx] )

          return producer(how, [ "World", "PostgreSQL",
          "PL/Python" ])
       $$ LANGUAGE plpythonu;
```

Generator (yield)

```
CREATE FUNCTION greet (how text)
  RETURNS SETOF greeting
AS $$
  for who in [ "World", "PostgreSQL", "PL/Python" ]:
    yield ( how, who )
$$ LANGUAGE plpythonu;
```

Warning: Currently, due to Python bug #1483133[2], some debug versions of Python 2.4 (configured and compiled with option --with-pydebug) are known to crash the PostgreSQL server when using an iterator to return a set result. Unpatched versions of Fedora 4 contain this bug. It does not happen in production versions of Python or on patched versions of Fedora 4.

The global dictionary SD is available to store data between function calls. This variable is private static data. The global dictionary GD is public data, available to all Python functions within a session. Use with care.

Each function gets its own execution environment in the Python interpreter, so that global data and function arguments from myfunc are not available to myfunc2. The exception is the data in the GD dictionary, as mentioned above.

12.2 Trigger Functions

When a function is used as a trigger, the dictionary TD contains trigger-related values. The trigger rows are in TD["new"] and/or TD["old"] depending on the trigger event. TD["event"] contains the event as a string (INSERT, UPDATE, DELETE, or UNKNOWN). TD["when"] contains one of BEFORE, AFTER, and UNKNOWN. TD["level"] contains one of ROW, STATEMENT, and UNKNOWN. TD["name"] contains the trigger name, TD["table_name"] contains the name of the table on which the trigger occurred, TD["table_schema"] contains the schema of the table on which the trigger occurred, TD["name"] contains the trigger name, and TD["relid"] contains the OID of the table on which the trigger occurred. If the CREATE TRIGGER command included arguments, they are available in TD["args"][0] to TD["args"][(n-1)].

If TD["when"] is BEFORE, you may return None or "OK" from the Python function to indicate the row is unmodified, "SKIP" to abort the event, or "MODIFY" to indicate you've modified the row.

---

[2] http://sourceforge.net/tracker/index.php?func=detail&aid=1483133&group_id=5470&atid=105470

12.3 Database Access

The PL/Python language module automatically imports a Python module called plpy. The functions and constants in this module are available to you in the Python code as plpy.*foo*. At present plpy implements the functions plpy.debug(*msg*), plpy.log(*msg*), plpy.info(*msg*), plpy.notice(*msg*), plpy.warning(*msg*), plpy.error(*msg*), and plpy.fatal(*msg*). plpy.error and plpy.fatal actually raise a Python exception which, if uncaught, propagates out to the calling query, causing the current transaction or subtransaction to be aborted. raise plpy.ERROR(*msg*) and raise plpy.FATAL(*msg*) are equivalent to calling plpy.error and plpy.fatal, respectively. The other functions only generate messages of different priority levels. Whether messages of a particular priority are reported to the client, written to the server log, or both is controlled by the log_min_messages and client_min_messages configuration variables. See Volume 3, Chapter 4 *Server Configuration* for more information.

Additionally, the plpy module provides two functions called execute and prepare. Calling plpy.execute with a query string and an optional limit argument causes that query to be run and the result to be returned in a result object. The result object emulates a list or dictionary object. The result object can be accessed by row number and column name. It has these additional methods: nrows which returns the number of rows returned by the query, and status which is the SPI_execute() return value. The result object can be modified.

For example,

```
rv = plpy.execute("SELECT * FROM my_table", 5)
```

returns up to 5 rows from my_table. If my_table has a column my_column, it would be accessed as

```
foo = rv[i]["my_column"]
```

The second function, plpy.prepare, prepares the execution plan for a query. It is called with a query string and a list of parameter types, if you have parameter references in the query. For example:

```
plan = plpy.prepare("SELECT last_name FROM my_users WHERE
    first_name = $1", [ "text" ])
```

text is the type of the variable you will be passing for $1. After preparing a statement, you use the function plpy.execute to run it:

```
rv = plpy.execute(plan, [ "name" ], 5)
```

The third argument is the limit and is optional.

When you prepare a plan using the PL/Python module it is automatically saved. Read the SPI documentation (Chapter 13 *Server Programming Interface*, page 357) for a description of what this means. In order to make effective use of this across function calls one needs to use one of the persistent storage dictionaries SD or GD (see Section 12.1 *PL/Python Functions*, page 349). For example:

```
CREATE FUNCTION usesavedplan() RETURNS trigger AS $$
    if SD.has_key("plan"):
        plan = SD["plan"]
    else:
        plan = plpy.prepare("SELECT 1")
        SD["plan"] = plan
    # rest of function
$$ LANGUAGE plpythonu;
```

13   Server Programming Interface

The *Server Programming Interface* (SPI) gives writers of user-defined C functions the ability to run SQL commands inside their functions. SPI is a set of interface functions to simplify access to the parser, planner, optimizer, and executor. SPI also does some memory management.

> Note: The available procedural languages provide various means to execute SQL commands from procedures. Most of these facilities are based on SPI, so this documentation might be of use for users of those languages as well.

To avoid misunderstanding we'll use the term "function" when we speak of SPI interface functions and "procedure" for a user-defined C-function that is using SPI.

Note that if a command invoked via SPI fails, then control will not be returned to your procedure. Rather, the transaction or subtransaction in which your procedure executes will be rolled back. (This may seem surprising given that the SPI functions mostly have documented error-return conventions. Those conventions only apply for errors detected within the SPI functions themselves, however.) It is possible to recover control after an error by establishing your own subtransaction surrounding SPI calls that might fail. This is not currently documented because the mechanisms required are still in flux.

SPI functions return a nonnegative result on success (either via a returned integer value or in the global variable SPI_result, as described below). On error, a negative result or NULL will be returned.

Source code files that use SPI must include the header file 'executor/spi.h'.

13.1   Interface Functions

13.1.1   SPI_connect

Name

SPI_connect — connect a procedure to the SPI manager

Synopsis

```
int SPI_connect(void)
```

Description

SPI_connect opens a connection from a procedure invocation to the SPI manager. You must call this function if you want to execute commands through SPI. Some utility SPI functions may be called from unconnected procedures.

If your procedure is already connected, SPI_connect will return the error code SPI_ERROR_CONNECT. This could happen if a procedure that has called SPI_connect directly calls another procedure that calls SPI_connect. While recursive calls to the SPI manager are permitted when an SQL command called through SPI invokes another function that uses SPI, directly nested calls to SPI_connect and SPI_finish are forbidden. (But see SPI_push and SPI_pop.)

Return Value

SPI_OK_CONNECT
    on success

SPI_ERROR_CONNECT
    on error

13.1.2 SPI_finish

Name

SPI_finish — disconnect a procedure from the SPI manager

Synopsis

```
int SPI_finish(void)
```

Description

SPI_finish closes an existing connection to the SPI manager. You must call this function after completing the SPI operations needed during your procedure's current invocation. You do not need to worry about making this happen, however, if you abort the transaction via elog(ERROR). In that case SPI will clean itself up automatically.

If SPI_finish is called without having a valid connection, it will return SPI_ERROR_UNCONNECTED. There is no fundamental problem with this; it means that the SPI manager has nothing to do.

Return Value

SPI_OK_FINISH
    if properly disconnected

SPI_ERROR_UNCONNECTED
    if called from an unconnected procedure

13.1.3 SPI_push

Name

SPI_push — push SPI stack to allow recursive SPI usage

Synopsis

```
void SPI_push(void)
```

Description

SPI_push should be called before executing another procedure that might itself wish to use SPI. After SPI_push, SPI is no longer in a "connected" state, and SPI function calls will be rejected unless a fresh SPI_connect is done. This ensures a clean separation between your procedure's SPI state and that of another procedure you call. After the other procedure returns, call SPI_pop to restore access to your own SPI state.

Note that SPI_execute and related functions automatically do the equivalent of SPI_push before passing control back to the SQL execution engine, so it is not necessary for you to worry about this when using those functions. Only when you are directly calling arbitrary code that might contain SPI_connect calls do you need to issue SPI_push and SPI_pop.

13.1.4 SPI_pop

Name

SPI_pop — pop SPI stack to return from recursive SPI usage

Synopsis

```
void SPI_pop(void)
```

Description

SPI_pop pops the previous environment from the SPI call stack. See SPI_push.

13.1.5 SPI_execute

Name

SPI_execute — execute a command

Synopsis

```
int SPI_execute(const char * command, bool read_only, long count)
```

Description

SPI_execute executes the specified SQL command for count rows. If read_only is true, the command must be read-only, and execution overhead is somewhat reduced.

This function may only be called from a connected procedure.

If count is zero then the command is executed for all rows that it applies to. If count is greater than 0, then the number of rows for which the command will be executed is restricted (much like a LIMIT clause). For example,

    SPI_execute("INSERT INTO foo SELECT * FROM bar", false, 5);

will allow at most 5 rows to be inserted into the table.

You may pass multiple commands in one string. SPI_execute returns the result for the command executed last. The count limit applies to each command separately, but it is not applied to hidden commands generated by rules.

When read_only is false, SPI_execute increments the command counter and computes a new *snapshot* before executing each command in the string. The snapshot does not actually change if the current transaction isolation level is SERIALIZABLE, but in READ COMMITTED mode the snapshot update allows each command to see the results of newly committed transactions from other sessions. This is essential for consistent behavior when the commands are modifying the database.

When read_only is true, SPI_execute does not update either the snapshot or the command counter, and it allows only plain SELECT commands to appear in the command string. The commands are executed using the snapshot previously established for the surrounding query. This execution mode is somewhat faster than the read/write mode due to eliminating per-command overhead. It also allows genuinely *stable* functions to be built: since successive executions will all use the same snapshot, there will be no change in the results.

It is generally unwise to mix read-only and read-write commands within a single function using SPI; that could result in very confusing behavior, since the read-only queries would not see the results of any database updates done by the read-write queries.

The actual number of rows for which the (last) command was executed is returned in the global variable SPI_processed. If the return value of the function is SPI_OK_SELECT, SPI_OK_INSERT_RETURNING, SPI_OK_DELETE_RETURNING, or SPI_OK_UPDATE_RETURNING, then you may use the global pointer SPITupleTable *SPI_tuptable to access the result rows. Some utility commands (such as EXPLAIN) also return row sets, and SPI_tuptable will contain the result in these cases too.

The structure SPITupleTable is defined thus:

```
typedef struct {
  MemoryContext tuptabcxt;  /* memory context of result
                               table */
  uint32 alloced;           /* number of alloced vals */
  uint32 free;              /* number of free vals */
  TupleDesc tupdesc;        /* row descriptor */
  HeapTuple *vals;          /* rows */
```

} SPITupleTable;

vals is an array of pointers to rows. (The number of valid entries is given by SPI_processed.) tupdesc is a row descriptor which you may pass to SPI functions dealing with rows. tuptabcxt, alloced, and free are internal fields not intended for use by SPI callers.

SPI_finish frees all SPITupleTables allocated during the current procedure. You can free a particular result table earlier, if you are done with it, by calling SPI_freetuptable.

Arguments

const char * command
    string containing command to execute

bool read_only
    true for read-only execution

long count
    maximum number of rows to process or return

Return Value

If the execution of the command was successful then one of the following (nonnegative) values will be returned:

SPI_OK_SELECT
    if a SELECT (but not SELECT INTO) was executed

SPI_OK_SELINTO
    if a SELECT INTO was executed

SPI_OK_INSERT
    if an INSERT was executed

SPI_OK_DELETE
    if a DELETE was executed

SPI_OK_UPDATE
    if an UPDATE was executed

SPI_OK_INSERT_RETURNING
    if an INSERT RETURNING was executed

SPI_OK_DELETE_RETURNING
    if a DELETE RETURNING was executed

SPI_OK_UPDATE_RETURNING
    if an UPDATE RETURNING was executed

SPI_OK_UTILITY
    if a utility command (e.g., CREATE TABLE) was executed

On error, one of the following negative values is returned:

SPI_ERROR_ARGUMENT
:   if command is NULL or count is less than 0

SPI_ERROR_COPY
:   if COPY TO stdout or COPY FROM stdin was attempted

SPI_ERROR_CURSOR
:   if DECLARE, CLOSE, or FETCH was attempted

SPI_ERROR_TRANSACTION
:   if any command involving transaction manipulation was attempted (BEGIN, COMMIT, ROLLBACK, SAVEPOINT, PREPARE TRANSACTION, COMMIT PREPARED, ROLLBACK PREPARED, or any variant thereof)

SPI_ERROR_OPUNKNOWN
:   if the command type is unknown (shouldn't happen)

SPI_ERROR_UNCONNECTED
:   if called from an unconnected procedure

Notes

The functions SPI_execute, SPI_exec, SPI_execute_plan, and SPI_execp change both SPI_processed and SPI_tuptable (just the pointer, not the contents of the structure). Save these two global variables into local procedure variables if you need to access the result table of SPI_execute or a related function across later calls.

13.1.6 SPI_exec

Name

SPI_exec — execute a read/write command

Synopsis

```
int SPI_exec(const char * command, long count)
```

Description

SPI_exec is the same as SPI_execute, with the latter's read_only parameter always taken as false.

Arguments

const char * command
:   string containing command to execute

long count
:   maximum number of rows to process or return

Return Value

See SPI_execute.

13.1.7 SPI_prepare

Name

SPI_prepare — prepare a plan for a command, without executing it yet

Synopsis

```
void * SPI_prepare(const char * command, int nargs, Oid *
argtypes)
```

Description

SPI_prepare creates and returns an execution plan for the specified command but doesn't execute the command. This function should only be called from a connected procedure.

When the same or a similar command is to be executed repeatedly, it may be advantageous to perform the planning only once. SPI_prepare converts a command string into an execution plan that can be executed repeatedly using SPI_execute_plan.

A prepared command can be generalized by writing parameters ($1, $2, etc.) in place of what would be constants in a normal command. The actual values of the parameters are then specified when SPI_execute_plan is called. This allows the prepared command to be used over a wider range of situations than would be possible without parameters.

The plan returned by SPI_prepare can be used only in the current invocation of the procedure, since SPI_finish frees memory allocated for a plan. But a plan can be saved for longer using the function SPI_saveplan.

Arguments

const char * command
    command string

int nargs
    number of input parameters ($1, $2, etc.)

Oid * argtypes
    pointer to an array containing the OIDs of the data types of the parameters

Return Value

SPI_prepare returns a non-null pointer to an execution plan. On error, NULL will be returned, and SPI_result will be set to one of the same error codes used by SPI_execute, except that it is set to SPI_ERROR_ARGUMENT if command is NULL, or if nargs is less than 0, or if nargs is greater than 0 and argtypes is NULL.

Notes

There is a disadvantage to using parameters: since the planner does not know the values that will be supplied for the parameters, it may make worse planning choices than it would make for a normal command with all constants visible.

13.1.8 SPI_getargcount

Name

SPI_getargcount — return the number of arguments needed by a plan prepared by SPI_prepare

Synopsis

```
int SPI_getargcount(void * plan)
```

Description

SPI_getargcount returns the number of arguments needed to execute a plan prepared by SPI_prepare.

Arguments

void * plan
    execution plan (returned by SPI_prepare)

Return Value

The expected argument count for the plan, or SPI_ERROR_ARGUMENT if the plan is NULL

13.1.9 SPI_getargtypeid

Name

SPI_getargtypeid — return the data type OID for an argument of a plan prepared by SPI_prepare

Synopsis

```
Oid SPI_getargtypeid(void * plan, int argIndex)
```

Description

SPI_getargtypeid returns the OID representing the type id for the argIndex'th argument of a plan prepared by SPI_prepare. First argument is at index zero.

Arguments

void * plan
    execution plan (returned by SPI_prepare)

int argIndex
    zero based index of the argument

Return Value

The type id of the argument at the given index, or SPI_ERROR_ARGUMENT if the plan is NULL or argIndex is less than 0 or not less than the number of arguments declared for the plan

13.1.10 SPI_is_cursor_plan

Name

SPI_is_cursor_plan — return true if a plan prepared by SPI_prepare can be used with SPI_cursor_open

Synopsis

```
bool SPI_is_cursor_plan(void * plan)
```

Description

SPI_is_cursor_plan returns true if a plan prepared by SPI_prepare can be passed as an argument to SPI_cursor_open, or false if that is not the case. The criteria are that the plan represents one single command and that this command returns tuples to the caller; for example, SELECT is allowed unless it contains an INTO clause, and UPDATE is allowed only if it contains a RETURNING clause.

Arguments

void * plan
    execution plan (returned by SPI_prepare)

Return Value

true or false to indicate if the plan can produce a cursor or not, or SPI_ERROR_ARGUMENT if the plan is NULL

13.1.11 SPI_execute_plan

Name

SPI_execute_plan — execute a plan prepared by SPI_prepare

Synopsis

```
int SPI_execute_plan(void * plan, Datum * values, const char
* nulls, bool read_only, long count)
```

Description

SPI_execute_plan executes a plan prepared by SPI_prepare. read_only and count have the same interpretation as in SPI_execute.

Arguments

void * plan
> execution plan (returned by SPI_prepare)

Datum * values
> An array of actual parameter values. Must have same length as the plan's number of arguments.

const char * nulls
> An array describing which parameters are null. Must have same length as the plan's number of arguments. n indicates a null value (entry in values will be ignored); a space indicates a nonnull value (entry in values is valid).

> If nulls is NULL then SPI_execute_plan assumes that no parameters are null.

bool read_only
> true for read-only execution

long count
> maximum number of rows to process or return

Return Value

The return value is the same as for SPI_execute, with the following additional possible error (negative) results:

SPI_ERROR_ARGUMENT
> if plan is NULL or count is less than 0

SPI_ERROR_PARAM
> if values is NULL and plan was prepared with some parameters

> SPI_processed and SPI_tuptable are set as in SPI_execute if successful.

Notes

If one of the objects (a table, function, etc.) referenced by the prepared plan is dropped during the session then the result of SPI_execute_plan for this plan will be unpredictable.

13.1.12 SPI_execp

Name

SPI_execp — execute a plan in read/write mode

Synopsis

```
int SPI_execp(void * plan, Datum * values, const char *
nulls, long count)
```

Description

SPI_execp is the same as SPI_execute_plan, with the latter's read_only parameter always taken as false.

Arguments

void * plan
    execution plan (returned by SPI_prepare)

Datum * values
    An array of actual parameter values. Must have same length as the plan's number of arguments.

const char * nulls
    An array describing which parameters are null. Must have same length as the plan's number of arguments. n indicates a null value (entry in values will be ignored); a space indicates a nonnull value (entry in values is valid).

    If nulls is NULL then SPI_execp assumes that no parameters are null.

long count
    maximum number of rows to process or return

Return Value

See SPI_execute_plan.

SPI_processed and SPI_tuptable are set as in SPI_execute if successful.

13.1.13 SPI_cursor_open

Name

SPI_cursor_open — set up a cursor using a plan created with SPI_prepare

Synopsis

```
Portal SPI_cursor_open(const char * name, void * plan,
                       Datum * values, const char * nulls,
                       bool read_only)
```

Description

SPI_cursor_open sets up a cursor (internally, a portal) that will execute a plan prepared by SPI_prepare. The parameters have the same meanings as the corresponding parameters to SPI_execute_plan.

Using a cursor instead of executing the plan directly has two benefits. First, the result rows can be retrieved a few at a time, avoiding memory overrun for queries that return many rows. Second, a portal can outlive the current procedure (it can, in fact, live to the end of the current transaction). Returning the portal name to the procedure's caller provides a way of returning a row set as result.

Arguments

const char * name
> name for portal, or NULL to let the system select a name

void * plan
> execution plan (returned by SPI_prepare)

Datum * values
> An array of actual parameter values. Must have same length as the plan's number of arguments.

const char * nulls
> An array describing which parameters are null. Must have same length as the plan's number of arguments. n indicates a null value (entry in values will be ignored); a space indicates a nonnull value (entry in values is valid).
>
> If nulls is NULL then SPI_cursor_open assumes that no parameters are null.

bool read_only
> true for read-only execution

Return Value

pointer to portal containing the cursor, or NULL on error

13.1.14 SPI_cursor_find

Name

SPI_cursor_find — find an existing cursor by name

Synopsis

```
Portal SPI_cursor_find(const char * name)
```

Description

SPI_cursor_find finds an existing portal by name. This is primarily useful to resolve a cursor name returned as text by some other function.

Arguments

const char * name
> name of the portal

Return Value

> pointer to the portal with the specified name, or NULL if none was found

13.1.15 SPI_cursor_fetch

Name

> SPI_cursor_fetch — fetch some rows from a cursor

Synopsis

> void SPI_cursor_fetch(Portal portal, bool forward, long count)

Description

SPI_cursor_fetch fetches some rows from a cursor. This is equivalent to the SQL command FETCH.

Arguments

Portal portal
> portal containing the cursor

bool forward
> true for fetch forward, false for fetch backward

long count
> maximum number of rows to fetch

Return Value

> SPI_processed and SPI_tuptable are set as in SPI_execute if successful.

13.1.16 SPI_cursor_move

Name

> SPI_cursor_move — move a cursor

Synopsis

> void SPI_cursor_move(Portal portal, bool forward, long count)

Description

SPI_cursor_move skips over some number of rows in a cursor. This is equivalent to the SQL command MOVE.

Arguments

`Portal portal`
> portal containing the cursor

`bool forward`
> true for move forward, false for move backward

`long count`
> maximum number of rows to move

13.1.17 SPI_cursor_close

Name

SPI_cursor_close — close a cursor

Synopsis

```
void SPI_cursor_close(Portal portal)
```

Description

SPI_cursor_close closes a previously created cursor and releases its portal storage.

All open cursors are closed automatically at the end of a transaction. SPI_cursor_close need only be invoked if it is desirable to release resources sooner.

Arguments

`Portal portal`
> portal containing the cursor

13.1.18 SPI_saveplan

Name

SPI_saveplan — save a plan

Synopsis

```
void * SPI_saveplan(void * plan)
```

Description

SPI_saveplan saves a passed plan (prepared by SPI_prepare) in memory protected from freeing by SPI_finish and by the transaction manager and returns a pointer to the saved plan. This gives you the ability to reuse prepared plans in the subsequent invocations of your procedure in the current session.

Arguments

void * plan
> the plan to be saved

Return Value

Pointer to the saved plan; NULL if unsuccessful. On error, SPI_result is set thus:

SPI_ERROR_ARGUMENT
> if plan is NULL

SPI_ERROR_UNCONNECTED
> if called from an unconnected procedure

Notes

If one of the objects (a table, function, etc.) referenced by the prepared plan is dropped during the session then the results of SPI_execute_plan for this plan will be unpredictable.

13.2 Interface Support Functions

The functions described here provide an interface for extracting information from result sets returned by SPI_execute and other SPI functions.

All functions described in this section may be used by both connected and unconnected procedures.

13.2.1 SPI_fname

Name

SPI_fname — determine the column name for the specified column number

Synopsis

```
char * SPI_fname(TupleDesc rowdesc, int colnumber)
```

Description

SPI_fname returns a copy of the column name of the specified column. (You can use pfree to release the copy of the name when you don't need it anymore.)

Arguments

TupleDesc rowdesc
> input row description

int colnumber
> column number (count starts at 1)

Return Value

The column name; NULL if colnumber is out of range. SPI_result set to
SPI_ERROR_NOATTRIBUTE on error.

13.2.2 SPI_fnumber

Name

SPI_fnumber — determine the column number for the specified column name

Synopsis

```
int SPI_fnumber(TupleDesc rowdesc, const char * colname)
```

Description

SPI_fnumber returns the column number for the column with the specified
name.

If colname refers to a system column (e.g., oid) then the appropriate negative
column number will be returned. The caller should be careful to test the return
value for exact equality to SPI_ERROR_NOATTRIBUTE to detect an error; testing
the result for less than or equal to 0 is not correct unless system columns should
be rejected.

Arguments

TupleDesc rowdesc
    input row description

const char * colname
    column name

Return Value

Column number (count starts at 1), or SPI_ERROR_NOATTRIBUTE if the named
column was not found.

13.2.3 SPI_getvalue

Name

SPI_getvalue — return the string value of the specified column

Synopsis

```
char * SPI_getvalue(HeapTuple row, TupleDesc rowdesc, int
colnumber)
```

Description

SPI_getvalue returns the string representation of the value of the specified column.

The result is returned in memory allocated using palloc. (You can use pfree to release the memory when you don't need it anymore.)

Arguments

HeapTuple row
>   input row to be examined

TupleDesc rowdesc
>   input row description

int colnumber
>   column number (count starts at 1)

Return Value

Column value, or NULL if the column is null, colnumber is out of range (SPI_result is set to SPI_ERROR_NOATTRIBUTE), or no output function is available (SPI_result is set to SPI_ERROR_NOOUTFUNC).

13.2.4 SPI_getbinval

Name

SPI_getbinval — return the binary value of the specified column

Synopsis

```
Datum SPI_getbinval(HeapTuple row, TupleDesc rowdesc, int
colnumber, bool * isnull)
```

Description

SPI_getbinval returns the value of the specified column in the internal form (as type Datum).

This function does not allocate new space for the datum. In the case of a pass-by-reference data type, the return value will be a pointer into the passed row.

Arguments

HeapTuple row
>   input row to be examined

TupleDesc rowdesc
>   input row description

int colnumber
>   column number (count starts at 1)

```
bool * isnull
```
   flag for a null value in the column

Return Value

The binary value of the column is returned. The variable pointed to by
isnull is set to true if the column is null, else to false.

SPI_result is set to SPI_ERROR_NOATTRIBUTE on error.

13.2.5 SPI_gettype

Name

SPI_gettype — return the data type name of the specified column

Synopsis

```
char * SPI_gettype(TupleDesc rowdesc, int colnumber)
```

Description

SPI_gettype returns a copy of the data type name of the specified column.
(You can use pfree to release the copy of the name when you don't need it
anymore.)

Arguments

```
TupleDesc rowdesc
```
   input row description

```
int colnumber
```
   column number (count starts at 1)

Return Value

The data type name of the specified column, or NULL on error. SPI_result
is set to SPI_ERROR_NOATTRIBUTE on error.

13.2.6 SPI_gettypeid

Name

SPI_gettypeid — return the data type OID of the specified column

Synopsis

```
Oid SPI_gettypeid(TupleDesc rowdesc, int colnumber)
```

Description

SPI_gettypeid returns the OID of the data type of the specified column.

Arguments

```
TupleDesc rowdesc
```
input row description

```
int colnumber
```
column number (count starts at 1)

Return Value

The OID of the data type of the specified column or InvalidOid on error. On error, SPI_result is set to SPI_ERROR_NOATTRIBUTE.

13.2.7 SPI_getrelname

Name

SPI_getrelname — return the name of the specified relation

Synopsis

```
char * SPI_getrelname(Relation rel)
```

Description

SPI_getrelname returns a copy of the name of the specified relation. (You can use pfree to release the copy of the name when you don't need it anymore.)

Arguments

```
Relation rel
```
input relation

Return Value

The name of the specified relation.

13.2.8 SPI_getnspname

Name

SPI_getnspname — return the namespace of the specified relation

Synopsis

```
char * SPI_getnspname(Relation rel)
```

Description

SPI_getnspname returns a copy of the name of the namespace that the specified Relation belongs to. This is equivalent to the relation's schema. You should pfree the return value of this function when you are finished with it.

Arguments

Relation rel
    input relation

Return Value

The name of the specified relation's namespace.

13.3 Memory Management

PostgreSQL allocates memory within *memory contexts* , which provide a convenient method of managing allocations made in many different places that need to live for differing amounts of time. Destroying a context releases all the memory that was allocated in it. Thus, it is not necessary to keep track of individual objects to avoid memory leaks; instead only a relatively small number of contexts have to be managed. palloc and related functions allocate memory from the "current" context.

SPI_connect creates a new memory context and makes it current. SPI_finish restores the previous current memory context and destroys the context created by SPI_connect. These actions ensure that transient memory allocations made inside your procedure are reclaimed at procedure exit, avoiding memory leakage.

However, if your procedure needs to return an object in allocated memory (such as a value of a pass-by-reference data type), you cannot allocate that memory using palloc, at least not while you are connected to SPI. If you try, the object will be deallocated by SPI_finish, and your procedure will not work reliably. To solve this problem, use SPI_palloc to allocate memory for your return object. SPI_palloc allocates memory in the "upper executor context", that is, the memory context that was current when SPI_connect was called, which is precisely the right context for a value returned from your procedure.

If SPI_palloc is called while the procedure is not connected to SPI, then it acts the same as a normal palloc. Before a procedure connects to the SPI manager, the current memory context is the upper executor context, so all allocations made by the procedure via palloc or by SPI utility functions are made in this context.

When SPI_connect is called, the private context of the procedure, which is created by SPI_connect, is made the current context. All allocations made by palloc, repalloc, or SPI utility functions (except for SPI_copytuple, SPI_returntuple, SPI_modifytuple, and SPI_palloc) are made in this context. When a procedure disconnects from the SPI manager (via SPI_finish) the current context is restored to the upper executor context, and all allocations made in the procedure memory context are freed and cannot be used any more.

All functions described in this section may be used by both connected and unconnected procedures. In an unconnected procedure, they act the same as the underlying ordinary server functions (palloc, etc.).

13.3.1 SPI_palloc

Name

SPI_palloc — allocate memory in the upper executor context

Synopsis

```
void * SPI_palloc(Size size)
```

Description

SPI_palloc allocates memory in the upper executor context.

Arguments

`Size size`
    size in bytes of storage to allocate

Return Value

pointer to new storage space of the specified size

13.3.2 SPI_repalloc

Name

SPI_repalloc — reallocate memory in the upper executor context

Synopsis

```
void * SPI_repalloc(void * pointer, Size size)
```

Description

SPI_repalloc changes the size of a memory segment previously allocated using SPI_palloc.

This function is no longer different from plain repalloc. It's kept just for backward compatibility of existing code.

Arguments

`void * pointer`
    pointer to existing storage to change

`Size size`
    size in bytes of storage to allocate

Return Value

pointer to new storage space of specified size with the contents copied from the existing area

13.3.3 SPI_pfree

Name

SPI_pfree — free memory in the upper executor context

Synopsis

```
void SPI_pfree(void * pointer)
```

Description

SPI_pfree frees memory previously allocated using SPI_palloc or SPI_repalloc.

This function is no longer different from plain pfree. It's kept just for backward compatibility of existing code.

Arguments

void * pointer
  pointer to existing storage to free

13.3.4 SPI_copytuple

Name

SPI_copytuple — make a copy of a row in the upper executor context

Synopsis

```
HeapTuple SPI_copytuple(HeapTuple row)
```

Description

SPI_copytuple makes a copy of a row in the upper executor context. This is normally used to return a modified row from a trigger. In a function declared to return a composite type, use SPI_returntuple instead.

Arguments

HeapTuple row
  row to be copied

Return Value

the copied row; NULL only if tuple is NULL

13.3.5 SPI_returntuple

Name

SPI_returntuple — prepare to return a tuple as a Datum

Synopsis

```
HeapTupleHeader SPI_returntuple(HeapTuple row, TupleDesc rowdesc)
```

Description

SPI_returntuple makes a copy of a row in the upper executor context, returning it in the form of a row type Datum. The returned pointer need only be converted to Datum via PointerGetDatum before returning.

Note that this should be used for functions that are declared to return composite types. It is not used for triggers; use SPI_copytuple for returning a modified row in a trigger.

Arguments

HeapTuple row
   row to be copied

TupleDesc rowdesc
   descriptor for row (pass the same descriptor each time for most effective caching)

Return Value

HeapTupleHeader pointing to copied row; NULL only if row or rowdesc is NULL

13.3.6 SPI_modifytuple

Name

SPI_modifytuple — create a row by replacing selected fields of a given row

Synopsis

```
HeapTuple SPI_modifytuple(Relation rel, HeapTuple row, ncols,
    colnum, Datum * values, const char * nulls)
```

Description

SPI_modifytuple creates a new row by substituting new values for selected columns, copying the original row's columns at other positions. The input row is not modified.

Arguments

Relation rel
   Used only as the source of the row descriptor for the row. (Passing a relation rather than a row descriptor is a misfeature.)

HeapTuple row
   row to be modified

int ncols
   number of column numbers in the array colnum

int * colnum
   array of the numbers of the columns that are to be changed (column numbers start at 1)

```
Datum * values
```
new values for the specified columns

```
const char * Nulls
```
which new values are null, if any (see SPI_execute_plan for the format)

Return Value

new row with modifications, allocated in the upper executor context; NULL only if row is NULL

On error, SPI_result is set as follows:

SPI_ERROR_ARGUMENT
if rel is NULL, or if row is NULL, or if ncols is less than or equal to 0, or if colnum is NULL, or if values is NULL.

SPI_ERROR_NOATTRIBUTE
if colnum contains an invalid column number (less than or equal to 0 or greater than the number of column in row)

13.3.7 SPI_freetuple

Name

SPI_freetuple — free a row allocated in the upper executor context

Synopsis

```
void SPI_freetuple(HeapTuple row)
```

Description

SPI_freetuple frees a row previously allocated in the upper executor context.

This function is no longer different from plain heap_freetuple. It's kept just for backward compatibility of existing code.

Arguments

```
HeapTuple row
```
row to free

13.3.8 SPI_freetuptable

Name

SPI_freetuptable — free a row set created by SPI_execute or a similar function

Synopsis

```
void SPI_freetuptable(SPITupleTable * tuptable)
```

Description

SPI_freetuptable frees a row set created by a prior SPI command execution function, such as SPI_execute. Therefore, this function is usually called with the global variable SPI_tupletable as argument.

This function is useful if a SPI procedure needs to execute multiple commands and does not want to keep the results of earlier commands around until it ends. Note that any unfreed row sets will be freed anyway at SPI_finish.

Arguments

SPITupleTable * tuptable
    pointer to row set to free

13.3.9 SPI_freeplan

Name

SPI_freeplan — free a previously saved plan

Synopsis

```
int SPI_freeplan(void *plan)
```

Description

SPI_freeplan releases a command execution plan previously returned by SPI_prepare or saved by SPI_saveplan.

Arguments

void * plan
    pointer to plan to free

Return Value

SPI_ERROR_ARGUMENT if plan is NULL.

13.4 Visibility of Data Changes

The following rules govern the visibility of data changes in functions that use SPI (or any other C function):

- During the execution of an SQL command, any data changes made by the command are invisible to the command itself. For example, in

      INSERT INTO a SELECT * FROM a;

  the inserted rows are invisible to the SELECT part.

- Changes made by a command C are visible to all commands that are started after C, no matter whether they are started inside C (during the execution of C) or after C is done.

- Commands executed via SPI inside a function called by an SQL command (either an ordinary function or a trigger) follow one or the other of the above rules depending on the read/write flag passed to SPI. Commands executed in read-only mode follow the first rule: they can't see changes of the calling command. Commands executed in read-write mode follow the second rule: they can see all changes made so far.

- All standard procedural languages set the SPI read-write mode depending on the volatility attribute of the function. Commands of STABLE and IMMUTABLE functions are done in read-only mode, while commands of VOLATILE functions are done in read-write mode. While authors of C functions are able to violate this convention, it's unlikely to be a good idea to do so.

The next section contains an example that illustrates the application of these rules.

13.5 Examples

This section contains a very simple example of SPI usage. The procedure execq takes an SQL command as its first argument and a row count as its second, executes the command using SPI_exec and returns the number of rows that were processed by the command. You can find more complex examples for SPI in the source tree in 'src/test/regress/regress.c' and in 'contrib/spi'.

```
#include "executor/spi.h"

int execq(text * sql, int cnt);

int
execq(text * sql, int cnt)
{
  char *command;
  int ret;
  int proc;

  /* Convert given text object to a C string */
  command =
      DatumGetCString(DirectFunctionCall1
                      (textout, PointerGetDatum(sql)));

  SPI_connect();

  ret = SPI_exec(command, cnt);

  proc = SPI_processed;
  /* If some rows were fetched, print them via elog(INFO). */
  if (ret > 0 && SPI_tuptable != NULL) {
    TupleDesc tupdesc = SPI_tuptable->tupdesc;
    SPITupleTable *tuptable = SPI_tuptable;
```

```
        char buf[8192];
        int i, j;

        for (j = 0; j < proc; j++) {
          HeapTuple tuple = tuptable->vals[j];

          for (i = 1, buf[0] = 0; i <= tupdesc->natts; i++)
            snprintf(buf + strlen(buf),
                     sizeof(buf) - strlen(buf), " %s%s",
                     SPI_getvalue(tuple, tupdesc, i),
                     (i == tupdesc->natts) ? " " : " |");
          elog(INFO, "EXECQ: %s", buf);
        }
      }

      SPI_finish();
      pfree(command);

      return (proc);
    }
```

(This function uses call convention version 0, to make the example easier to understand. In real applications you should use the new version 1 interface.)

This is how you declare the function after having compiled it into a shared library:

```
    CREATE FUNCTION execq(text, integer) RETURNS integer
        AS 'filename'
        LANGUAGE C;
```

Here is a sample session:

```
    => SELECT execq('CREATE TABLE a (x integer)', 0);
     execq
    -------
         0
    (1 row)

    => INSERT INTO a VALUES (execq('INSERT INTO a VALUES (0)', 0));
    INSERT 0 1
    => SELECT execq('SELECT * FROM a', 0);
    INFO:  EXECQ:  0    -- inserted by execq
    INFO:  EXECQ:  1    -- returned by execq and inserted by
     upper INSERT

     execq
    -------
         2
    (1 row)

    => SELECT execq('INSERT INTO a SELECT x + 2 FROM a', 1);
```

```
  execq
-------
     1
(1 row)

=> SELECT execq('SELECT * FROM a', 10);
INFO:  EXECQ:  0
INFO:  EXECQ:  1
INFO:  EXECQ:  2    -- 0 + 2, only one row inserted -
                    -- as specified

  execq
-------
     3                -- 10 is the max value only, 3 is the
 real number of rows
(1 row)

=> DELETE FROM a;
DELETE 3
=> INSERT INTO a VALUES (execq('SELECT * FROM a', 0) + 1);
INSERT 0 1
=> SELECT * FROM a;
 x
---
 1                    -- no rows in a (0) + 1
(1 row)

=> INSERT INTO a VALUES (execq('SELECT * FROM a', 0) + 1);
INFO:  EXECQ:  1
INSERT 0 1
=> SELECT * FROM a;
 x
---
 1
 2                    -- there was one row in a + 1
(2 rows)

-- This demonstrates the data changes visibility rule:

=> INSERT INTO a SELECT execq('SELECT * FROM a', 0) * x FROM a;
INFO:  EXECQ:  1
INFO:  EXECQ:  2
INFO:  EXECQ:  1
INFO:  EXECQ:  2
INFO:  EXECQ:  2
INSERT 0 2
=> SELECT * FROM a;
 x
```

```
 ---
  1
  2
  2          -- 2 rows * 1 (x in first row)
  6          -- 3 rows (2 + 1 just inserted) * 2 (x in second row)
(4 rows)     ^^^^^^
             rows visible to execq() in different invocations
```

Books from the publisher

Network Theory publishes books about free software under free documentation licenses. Our current catalogue includes the following titles:

- **PostgreSQL Reference Manual: Volume 1** (ISBN 0-9546120-2-7) $49.95 (£32.00)

  This manual documents the SQL language and commands of PostgreSQL. For each copy of this manual sold, $1 is donated to the PostgreSQL project.

- **PostgreSQL Reference Manual: Volume 2** (ISBN 0-9546120-3-5) $34.95 (£19.95)

  This manual documents the client and server programming interfaces of PostgreSQL. For each copy of this manual sold, $1 is donated to the PostgreSQL project.

- **PostgreSQL Reference Manual: Volume 3** (ISBN 0-9546120-4-3) $24.95 (£13.95)

  This manual is a guide to the configuration and maintenance of PostgreSQL database servers. For each copy of this manual sold, $1 is donated to the PostgreSQL project.

- **GNU Bash Reference Manual** by Chet Ramey and Brian Fox (ISBN 0-9541617-7-7) $29.95 (£19.95)

  This manual is the definitive reference for GNU Bash, the standard GNU command-line interpreter. GNU Bash is a complete implementation of the POSIX.2 Bourne shell specification, with additional features from the C-shell and Korn shell. For each copy of this manual sold, $1 is donated to the Free Software Foundation.

- **Version Management with CVS** by Per Cederqvist et al. (ISBN 0-9541617-1-8) $29.95 (£19.95)

  This manual describes how to use CVS, the concurrent versioning system—one of the most widely-used source-code management systems available today. The manual provides tutorial examples for new users of CVS, as well as the definitive reference documentation for every CVS command and configuration option.

- **Comparing and Merging Files with GNU diff and patch** by David MacKenzie, Paul Eggert, and Richard Stallman (ISBN 0-9541617-5-0) $19.95 (£12.95)

  This manual describes how to compare and merge files using GNU diff and patch. It includes an extensive tutorial that guides the reader through all the options of the diff and patch commands. For each copy of this manual sold, $1 is donated to the Free Software Foundation.

- **An Introduction to GCC** by Brian J. Gough, foreword by Richard M. Stallman. (ISBN 0-9541617-9-3) $19.95 (£12.95)

  This manual provides a tutorial introduction to the GNU C and C++ compilers, gcc and g++. Many books teach the C and C++ languages, but this book explains how to use the compiler itself. Based on years of observation of questions posted on mailing lists, it guides the reader straight to the important options of GCC.

- **An Introduction to Python** by Guido van Rossum and Fred L. Drake, Jr. (ISBN 0-9541617-6-9) $19.95 (£12.95)

  This tutorial provides an introduction to Python, an easy to learn object oriented programming language. For each copy of this manual sold, $1 is donated to the Python Software Foundation.

- **Python Language Reference Manual** by Guido van Rossum and Fred L. Drake, Jr. (ISBN 0-9541617-8-5) $19.95 (£12.95)

  This manual is the official reference for the Python language itself. It describes the syntax of Python and its built-in datatypes in depth, This manual is suitable for readers who need to be familiar with the details and rules of the Python language and its object system. For each copy of this manual sold, $1 is donated to the Python Software Foundation.

- **GNU Octave Manual** by John W. Eaton (ISBN 0-9541617-2-6) $29.99 (£19.99)

  This manual is the definitive guide to GNU Octave, an interactive environment for numerical computation with matrices and vectors. For each copy sold $1 is donated to the GNU Octave Development Fund.

- **GNU Scientific Library Reference Manual—Revised Second Edition** by M. Galassi, et al (ISBN 0-9541617-3-4) $39.99 (£24.99)

  This reference manual is the definitive guide to the GNU Scientific Library (GSL), a numerical library for C and C++ programmers. The manual documents over 1,000 mathematical routines needed for solving problems in science and engineering. All the money raised from the sale of this book supports the development of the GNU Scientific Library.

- **An Introduction to R** by W.N. Venables, D.M. Smith and the R Development Core Team (ISBN 0-9541617-4-2) $19.95 (£12.95)

  This tutorial manual provides a comprehensive introduction to GNU R, a free software package for statistical computing and graphics.

- **The R Reference Manual—Base Package (Volumes 1 & 2)** by the R Development Core Team (ISBN 0-9546120-0-0 and 0-9546120-1-9) $69.95 each (£39.95 each)

These volumes are the complete reference manual for the base package of GNU R, a free software environment for statistical computing and graphics. The main commands of the base package of R are described in volume one, while the other functions (such as graphics) are described in volume two. For each set of manuals sold, $10 is donated to the R Foundation.

All titles are available for order from bookstores worldwide.

Sales of the manuals fund the development of more free software and documentation.

For details, visit the website http://www.network-theory.co.uk/

Index

#

#define, with ECPG 114
#ifdef, with ECPG 115
#undef, with ECPG 114

$

$libdir 191

.

.pgpass........................... 47

_

_PG_fini 192
_PG_init 192

A

administrable_role_authorizations
.... 120
aggregate function, user-defined 216
aliases, in PL/pgSQL 284
applicable role..................... 120
applicable_roles.................. 120
argument types, in PL/pgSQL..... 279
arguments, composite type 205
array, of user-defined type 221
assignment, in PL/pgSQL 289
asynchronous commands, libpq 31
asynchronous notification............ 37
attributes, in information schema
.... 121

B

base type 175
base types, in C functions 192
binary large objects 63
BLOB............................. 63
BSD/OS, shared library 201
bytea, in libpq..................... 29

C

C................................. 5, 73
C preprocessor, with ECPG 114
C, user-defined functions 190
callbacks, with ECPG 108
calling conventions 194
canceling, SQL command 35
check_constraint_routine_usage, in
information schema 124
check_constraints, in information
schema 124
client library, C..................... 5
column_domain_usage, in information
schema 125
column_privileges, in information
schema 125
column_udt_usage, in information
schema 126
columns, in information schema..... 127
command execution, libpq 15
command status, with rules......... 269
COMMUTATOR....................... 223
compatibility mode, Informix 95
compiling, libpq applications......... 50
composite type..................... 175
composite type, arguments 205
computed field 182
conditionals, in PL/pgSQL 296
connection service file 48
connection, with ECPG 74
connection, with libpq 5
constants, with ECPG 95
constraint_column_usage, in
information schema........... 131
constraint_table_usage, in information
schema 132
CONTINUE, in PL/pgSQL......... 299
control functions, libpq............. 43
control structures, in PL/pgSQL.... 294
COPY, with libpq................... 38
copying types, in PL/pgSQL........ 286
cross-data-type operator classes..... 234
CTID 256
cursor, in PL/pgSQL 304

D

data type, base...................... 175
data type, composite............... 175
data type, internal organization..... 192
data type, user-defined............. 218
data types, in information schema.. 119
data types, in PL/pgSQL........... 279
data values, in PL/Perl............. 343
data values, in PL/Tcl............. 329
data_type_privileges, in information
    schema....................... 132
date type, with ECPG.............. 85
DBI.............................. 340
decimal type, with ECPG........... 94
declarations, in PL/pgSQL......... 283
declare sections, with ECPG........ 77
descriptor areas................... 107
Digital UNIX..................... 202
domain_constraints, in information
    schema....................... 133
domain_udt_usage, in information
    schema....................... 134
domains.......................... 176
domains, in information schema..... 134
dynamic commands, in PL/pgSQL.. 292
dynamic loading.............. 190, 201
dynamic SQL...................... 81
dynamic_library_path.............. 191

E

ECPG............................. 73
element_types, in information schema
    137
elog, in PL/Perl................... 343
elog, in PL/Python................. 354
elog, in PL/Tcl................... 332
embedded SQL, in C............... 73
enabled role...................... 140
enabled_roles, in information schema
    140
encryption, passwords.............. 44
environment variable.............. 45
errno, with ECPG.................. 94
error codes, libpq................. 21
error handling, with ECPG........ 108
error message..................... 14
errors, in PL/PgSQL......... 302, 308
escaping strings, in libpq........... 28

escaping, in PL/pgSQL............. 280
exceptions, in PL/PgSQL.......... 302
execution, in PL/pgSQL........... 289
EXIT, in PL/pgSQL............... 298
expressions, in PL/pgSQL......... 288
extending SQL.................... 175

F

fast path......................... 36
FETCH INTO, with ECPG......... 79
field, computed................... 182
FreeBSD, shared library........... 201
function parameters, aliases........ 284
function, internal................. 190
function, output parameter........ 183
function, polymorphic............. 176
function, user-defined............. 177
function, user-defined, in C........ 190
function, user-defined, in SQL...... 178
functions, in PL/Perl............. 337
functions, in PL/Python........... 349
functions, in PL/Tcl.............. 328

G

global data, in PL/Perl............. 344
global data, in PL/Python......... 353
global data, in PL/Tcl............. 329
GTCMP........................... 226

H

HASHES........................... 226
host name......................... 6
host variables, with ECPG......... 77
HP-UX, shared library............. 201

I

IMMUTABLE...................... 188
include files, with ECPG.......... 114
Index............................ 391
index methods..................... 228
index, for user-defined data type.... 228
indicators......................... 80
information schema................ 119
information_schema_catalog_name
    120

Informix, compatibility mode 95
input function 218
input function, of a data type 218
installing procedural languages 273
instr 318
internal functions 190
internals, ECPG 117
interval type, with ECPG 93
IRIX, shared library 202

J

JOIN 225

K

key_column_usage, in information
   schema 141

L

languages, procedural 273
large object 63
large objects, client interface 63
large objects, server functions 66
LDAP connection parameter lookup
   48
libpq 5
libpq-fe.h 5, 12
libpq-int.h 12
library finalization function 192
library function, with ECPG 116
library initialization function 192
Linux, shared library 202
lo_close 66
lo_creat 64, 66
lo_create 64, 66
lo_export 64, 66
lo_import 64, 66
lo_lseek 66
lo_open 65
lo_read 65
lo_tell 66
lo_unlink 66
lo_write 65
loop, in PL/pgSQL 298
LTCMP 226
LWlocks 215

M

MacOS X, shared library 202
magic block 191
memory context, in SPI 376
MERGES 226
modules, in PL/Tcl 334
multithreaded programs, with libpq .. 49

N

NEGATOR 224
NetBSD, shared library 202
nonblocking connection 8, 31
notice processing, in libpq 44
notice processor 44
notice receiver 44
NOTIFY, in libpq 37
null value, in libpq 25
null value, in PL/Perl 338
null value, PL/Python 350
numeric type, with ECPG 82

O

OID, in libpq 27
OpenBSD, shared library 202
operator class 228
operator, user-defined 221
optimization, of operators 222
Oracle, porting from PL/SQL to
   PL/pgSQL 315
ordering operator 235
output function 218
output function, of a data type 218
overloading, functions 187
overloading, operators 221

P

palloc 200
parameters, in information schema
   142
password encryption, libpq 44
password file 47
Perl 337
pfree 200
pg_config, with libpq 50
pg_config, with user-defined C functions
   200

pg_service.conf 48
PGcancel 35
PGCLIENTENCODING 47
PGconn 5
PGCONNECT_TIMEOUT 46
PGDATABASE 46
PGDATESTYLE 47
PGGEQO 47
PGHOST 45
PGHOSTADDR 45
PGKRBSRVNAME 46
PGLOCALEDIR 47
PGOPTIONS 46
PGPASSFILE 46
PGPASSWORD 46
PGPORT 46
PGREALM 46
PGREQUIRESSL 46
PGresult 19
PGSERVICE 46
PGSSLMODE 46
PGSYSCONFDIR 47
pgtypes 82
PGTZ 47
PGUSER 46
pgxs 203
PIC 201
PID, determining PID of server process,
    in libpq 15
PL/Perl 337
PL/PerlU 345
PL/pgSQL 277
PL/Python 349
PL/SQL (Oracle), porting to PL/pgSQL
    315
PL/Tcl 327
polymorphic arguments 213
polymorphic function 176, 186
polymorphic type 176
port 6
PQbackendPID 15
PQbinaryTuples 25
PQbinaryTuples, with COPY 38
PQcancel 35
PQclear 22
PQcmdStatus 27
PQcmdTuples 27
PQconndefaults 10
PQconnectdb 5

PQconnectPoll 8
PQconnectStart 8
PQconsumeInput 33
PQdb 12
PQdescribePortal 19
PQdescribePrepared 18
PQencryptPassword 44
PQendcopy 42
PQerrorMessage 14
PQescapeBytea 29
PQescapeByteaConn 29
PQescapeString 28
PQescapeStringConn 28
PQexec 15
PQexecParams 15
PQexecPrepared 18
PQfformat 24
PQfformat, with COPY 39
PQfinish 11
PQflush 35
PQfmod 24
PQfn 36
PQfname 23
PQfnumber 23
PQfreeCancel 35
PQfreemem 30
PQfsize 25
PQftable 23
PQftablecol 24
PQftype 24
PQgetCancel 35
PQgetCopyData 40
PQgetisnull 25
PQgetlength 26
PQgetline 40
PQgetlineAsync 41
PQgetResult 33
PQgetssl 15
PQgetvalue 25
PQhost 12
PQisBusy 34
PQisnonblocking 34
PQisthreadsafe 49
PQmakeEmptyPGresult 22
PQnfields 23
PQnfields, with COPY 38
PQnotifies 37
PQnparams 26
PQntuples 23

PQoidStatus 27
PQoidValue 27
PQoptions 12
PQparameterStatus 13
PQparamtype 26
PQpass 12
PQport 12
PQprepare 17
PQprint 26
PQprotocolVersion 14
PQputCopyData 39
PQputCopyEnd 39
PQputline 41
PQputnbytes 42
PQrequestCancel 36
PQreset 11
PQresetPoll 11
PQresetStart 11
PQresStatus 20
PQresultErrorField 20
PQresultErrorMessage 20
PQresultStatus 19
PQsendDescribePortal 32
PQsendDescribePrepared 32
PQsendPrepare 32
PQsendQuery 31
PQsendQueryParams 31
PQsendQueryPrepared 32
PQserverVersion 14
PQsetdb 8
PQsetdbLogin 7
PQsetErrorVerbosity 43
PQsetnonblocking 34
PQsetNoticeProcessor 44
PQsetNoticeReceiver 44
PQsocket 14
PQstatus 12
PQtrace 43
PQtransactionStatus 13
PQtty 12
PQunescapeBytea 30
PQuntrace 43
PQuser 12
preparing a query, in PL/pgSQL 277
preparing a query, in PL/Python . . . 354
preparing a query, in PL/Tcl 330
preprocessor, with ECPG 114
privilege, with rules 268
privilege, with views 268

procedural language 273
procedural language functions 189
procedure names, in PL/Tcl 335
pseudo-types 176
Python 349

Q

queries, in PL/Perl 340
queries, in PL/pgSQL 289
queries, in PL/Python 354
queries, in PL/Tcl 330
query tree 247
quote_ident, use in PL/PgSQL 293
quote_literal, use in PL/PgSQL 293
quotes, in PL/pgSQL 280

R

RAISE 308
range table 248
receiving COPY data 40
record types, in PL/pgSQL 287
referential_constraints, in
        information schema 145
RENAME, in PL/pgSQL 287
reporting errors, in PL/PgSQL 308
RESTRICT 224
result status, in PL/pgSQL 294
result types, in PL/pgSQL 279
retrieving results, libpq 23
RETURNING INTO, in PL/pgSQL
        290
returning, from function in PL/pgSQL
        294
role, applicable 120
role, enabled 140
role_column_grants, in information
        schema 146
role_routine_grants, in information
        schema 147
role_table_grants, in information
        schema 147
role_usage_grants, in information
        schema 148
routine_privileges, in information
        schema 149
routines, in information schema 149
row types, in PL/pgSQL 286

rows, returning.................... 207
rule............................... 247
rule, and views.................... 249
rule, compared with triggers....... 270
rule, for DELETE.................. 257
rule, for INSERT.................. 257
rule, for SELECT.................. 250
rule, for UPDATE.................. 257

S

schemata, in information schema.... 157
SELECT INTO, in PL/pgSQL 290
SELECT INTO, with ECPG 79
sending COPY data................. 39
sequences, in information schema .. 158
server programming interface (SPI)
.... 357
SETOF 178
sets............................... 185
sets, returning.................... 208
shared library 190, 201
shared memory.................... 215
shared-preload-libraries............. 215
Solaris, shared library.............. 202
SORT1, SORT2 226
SPI............................... 357
SPI_connect....................... 357
SPI_copytuple..................... 378
SPI_cursor_close................... 370
SPI_cursor_fetch 369
SPI_cursor_find 368
SPI_cursor_move 369
SPI_cursor_open................... 367
SPI_exec......................... 362
spi_exec_query, in PL/Perl......... 340
SPI_execp......................... 367
SPI_execute....................... 359
SPI_execute_plan.................. 365
SPI_finish......................... 358
SPI_fname......................... 371
SPI_fnumber 372
SPI_freeplan 381
SPI_freetuple..................... 380
SPI_freetuptable 380
SPI_getargcount................... 364
SPI_getargtypeid.................. 364
SPI_getbinval 373
SPI_getnspname................... 375

SPI_getrelname 375
SPI_gettype....................... 374
SPI_gettypeid 374
SPI_getvalue...................... 372
SPI_is_cursor_plan 365
spi_lastoid........................ 331
SPI_modifytuple 379
SPI_palloc 377
SPI_pfree 378
SPI_pop........................... 359
SPI_prepare....................... 363
SPI_push.......................... 359
SPI_repalloc....................... 377
SPI_returntuple 378
SPI_saveplan...................... 370
SQL Procedural Language, PL/pgSQL
.... 277
sql_features, in information schema
.... 159
sql_implementation_info, in
    information schema........... 159
sql_languages, in information schema
.... 160
sql_packages, in information schema
.... 161
sql_parts, in information schema .. 162
sql_sizing, in information schema
.... 162
sql_sizing_profiles, in information
    schema....................... 163
sqlca............................. 110
SQLCODE........................ 111
SQLSTATE 111
SSL............................... 49
SSL, in libpq 15
SSL, with libpq.................... 7
STABLE........................... 188
statements, in PL/pgSQL 289
status, in PL/pgSQL 294
status, libpq...................... 27
status, of connection.............. 12
status, with rules................. 269
strategies, index methods.......... 229
support routines, index methods.... 230

T

table sources 184

table_constraints, in information
    schema 164
table_privileges, in information
    schema 164
tables, in information schema 165
target list 248
Tcl 327
threads, with libpq 49
timestamp type, with ECPG 89
TOAST, and user-defined types 221
TOAST, versus large objects 63
tracing, libpq 43
trigger 237
trigger, arguments for trigger functions
    238
trigger, compared with rules 270
trigger, in C 240
trigger, in PL/Perl 346
trigger, in PL/pgSQL 308
trigger, in PL/Python 353
trigger, in PL/Tcl 332
triggers, in information schema 167
Tru64 UNIX, shared library 202
trusted, PL/Perl 345
type system 175
type, polymorphic 176

U

Unix domain socket 6
UnixWare, shared library 203
update rules, explanation 257

usage_privileges, in information
    schema 169
user-defined aggregates 216
user-defined functions 177
user-defined operators 221
user-defined types 218

V

verbosity, libpq 43
version 0, calling convention 194
version 1, calling convention 197
view rules in Non-SELECT Statements
    255
view, implementation through rules
    249
view, updating 257, 262
view_column_usage, in information
    schema 170
view_routine_usage, in information
    schema 170
view_table_usage, in information
    schema 171
views, in information schema 172
visibility, in server programming
    interface 381
visibility, in triggers 239
VOLATILE 188
volatility, functions 188

W

WHILE, in PL/pgSQL 299

Printed in the United Kingdom
by Lightning Source UK Ltd.
135380UK00001B/208/A